FARMER JOHN'S COOKBOOK

Temp 1

Our Cook

Today I went to the tomatoes. There are six rows of tomatoes, maybe one-ninth of a mile long, and I spotted the reddest one halfway down the row. My harvest bucket grew heavier as, on my way, I noticed three or four more I would have regretted not basketing. At the end of the row I realized I was near those calming, hydrating, cooling cucumbers. I was soon shoeless in the vines and slightly radiant in the sun, searching out the plumpest cucumbers. I felt lured toward the fennel, their strong, lingering licorice scent contrasting with their delicate and feathery leaves. They soon made perfect shade in the bucket for my tomatoes. I harvested mizuna greens and a head of garlic. I began to visualize tearing leaves of basil, tarragon, and parsley when I caught my breath. Here to my left, down below my knees, was a pepper—a beautiful purple pepper. I had not been expecting peppers to have arrived so fully without my observance. I knelt and reached, watching the sun reflect from different angles as I turned the pepper over and pulled it from the plant. I looked left and right. I was surrounded not only by bright purple peppers, but also by small green jalapeño chili plants. I sang about Peter Piper and his peck of pickled peppers on my way back to the kitchen. I paused along the rows of drying alliums to swing an onion into my colorful and bountiful harvest bucket. Later I chopped all the vegetables, along with small chunks of mozzarella, and layered them in a serving dish with the herbs and greens. I gave it a splash of extra virgin olive oil, a sprinkling of balsamic vinegar, dustings of sea salt and pepper, and I shared it with my friends here at the farm.

A Shareholder

One Wednesday night I had worked late, then had a terrible commute and walked into the house hot and tired after picking up my vegetable box. I opened it and saw one of your watermelons staring me in the face. Something about the melon spoke to me. I put the other vegetables away and cut open the melon. As I stood over the sink sinking my teeth into the succulent flesh, my mind's eye held the memory of our last farm visit when my wife was pregnant with our son. I remember looking over the melon patch with my wife and thinking that this would be a great place to bring our child so he would know where food comes from. As the sweet melon juices quenched my thirst and nourished my body, knowing where it came from–and a flood of memories from our last trip–nourished my soul. I finished the entire melon in one sitting and went to bed refreshed and revived.

FARMER JOHN'S COOKBOOK

THE REAL DIRT

ON VEGETABLES

FARMER JOHN PETERSON
AND ANGELIC ORGANICS

with Lesley Littlefield Freeman

Gibbs Smith, Publisher
Salt Lake City

First Edition

10 09 08 07 06   10 9 8 7 6 5 4 3 2 1

Text © 2006 John Peterson and Angelic Organics
Photos © 2006 John Peterson and Angelic Organics except:
    pages 121, 237, and 269 © 2006 Taggart Siegel
    pages 63 and 142 courtesy Johnny's Selected Seeds

Published by
Gibbs Smith, Publisher
P.O. Box 667
Layton, Utah 84041

www.gibbs-smith.com
Orders: 1.800.7458.5439

Cover design: Bob's Your Uncle
Interior production: Kurt Wahlner
Printed and bound in Canada

Library of Congress Control Number: 2006920206

ISBN 1-4236-0014-2

Downloadable recipe samples from this cookbook are available to CSA farmers and market gardeners at www.AngelicOrganics.com

This book is dedicated to the farmers who work with the earth lovingly, and to those who support these farmers and the earth itself through their choices.

"**A**nd now we come to what I always say. People come and ask: Is it better not to drink alcohol or to drink alcohol? Is it better to be a vegetarian or to eat meat? I never tell anyone whether he should give up alcohol or drink it, whether he should eat plants or meat. I say to people: alcohol does so and so. I simply explain its effect, and then they may decide whether to drink or not. I do the same with regard to vegetarian or meat diet: meat does this and plants do that. And the result is that they can decide for themselves.

That is what one must have above all in science—respect for human freedom. One should never have the feeling that anyone is ordered or forbidden to do something; instead one tells him the facts. . . . What is right to do he then finds out of himself. In this way we will get somewhere. In this way free men will be able to direct themselves. This must be our aim. This is the way to real social reform."

—LECTURE BY RUDOLF STEINER, *Nutrition and Stimulants*

Overheard

The highlight of my fifth decade is rediscovering hot dogs. I don't have the ups and downs with hot dogs that I do with sugar. I still feel good several hours after I eat one.

Several hours later . . .

After eating that hot dog, I don't feel so good. But maybe it's the Somebunny Loves Me ice cream I ate. I didn't really trust the colored marshmallows.

Contents

*Material presented in *Farmer John's Cookbook* is from a wide variety of sources on an impressive range of subjects. Some excerpts appearing in this book have been given new titles that more accurately reflect the content of the quoted text. These descriptive titles are enclosed in quotation marks and will hopefully assist the reader in navigating the essays.

"I don't know if it was the lime or the Biodynamic herbal sprays we used extensively last season or the subsoiling—but the soil has turned into something wonderfully different from last year's cement. The ground is spongy, almost bouncy as you step on it—even after a rain, and even after it has been worked with the tractor. I'm so glad to know that the roots of all the vegetables get to play around in that paradise. On some level it's got to make the plants happy. And maybe on some level, while you're eating them, your vegetables will do the same for you."

—FARMER JOHN, HARVEST WEEK 1, 1994, NEWSLETTER

Preface
A Life of Farming

Farming from a Young Age

I've been farming for over forty years on the same farm. I started in 1956 when I was seven, taking care of the chickens. By age nine I was milking seventeen cows twice a day.

By the mid-sixties, many of the homey little farms that dotted the countryside were either going through expansion in order to survive or were closing their barn doors. The Peterson farm went the expansion route, until financial calamity arrived in the early 1980s and almost closed the farm down for good.

However, enough of my land survived the shakeout to build anew. In the late eighties, I began to imagine a natural system by which to farm, a system in which results were derived from the integrity of the soil, not the shenanigans of crop chemicals and petroleum-based fertilizers. I envisioned a system that married me to the land, not divorced me from it. By this time, I had seen too many people on drugs—their personalities hardly recognizable, their voices slurred, their eyes glazed. I resented drugs. Drugs concealed who people were. I didn't want drugs concealing what my crops were.

And what are farm chemicals but drugs by a different name? Consider that anhydrous ammonia, the most common petroleum-based nitrogen fertilizer, is routinely stolen in the countryside and used to make methamphetamine, a brutal form of speed. (Other uses of anhydrous ammonia? It was used extensively during World War II for the task of turning soil into rock-hard landing strips. It also was an essential ingredient in making explosives.) I sought more benign inputs for my new farming operation.

> ### Farmer John Writes
> The farm chemical industry has phased out the term *crop chemicals* in favor of the more beneficent term *crop protectors*. Crop protector does have a nicer ring. Of course, today the term domestic violence is preferred to wife or husband beating.

Angelic Organics was reborn out of my great losses of the 1980s, reborn with an eye to the well-being of the earth we live on and the food we eat. The farm slowly got its footing in the challenging new world of organic vegetable production. Why slowly? The organic approach required looking at underlying causes of plant health—not just shotgunning chemicals at the crops to fix problems. It required looking at fertility from the standpoint of natural processes, learning how to work with green manures, compost, and fallow land. It necessitated a comprehensive and complex system of weed, blight, and insect control, and raising more than fifty different types of vegetables and herbs meant accommodating numerous rhythms within one farming operation: learning the needs of each vegetable, how to seed it, tend it, harvest it, clean it, and store it. This was a far cry from the simple days of raising corn and beans and hay, of tending cattle and hogs with straightforward, widely available technology. Raising vegetables organically required much more hand labor, a whole different set of technology, a revamping of facilities, and a vastly different farming mind-set. This transition required many one-hundred-hour workweeks from me in the first several years of vegetable farming. I had to learn on the fly how to integrate all of the newness into the farm in a way that would make it survive in the marketplace.

Seeking a truly comprehensive approach to farming, one that went even beyond organics, I began learning about Biodynamics, a practice and a philosophy that conceives of the farm as a living organism. (To learn more about Biodynamics, see Andrew Lorand's essay "Biodynamics Between Myth and Reality," page 34.)

Farmer John Writes

Biodynamics goes way beyond . . . homeopathy. It takes into account the sky, the earth, the flowers, the birds, the orchard. Worms. Vegetables. Livestock. The manure from the livestock—totally important for building compost that's sort of a celestial beacon. Biodynamics covers everything a healthy farm can be, and it puts the whole thing together in a harmonious way.

—FROM JOHN'S BOOK *FARMER JOHN ON GLITTER & GREASE*

The Farm Today: Community Supported Agriculture

My way of farming is not just about growing vegetables. It is also about building relationships between the farm and the people who receive our vegetables. For my whole adult life, I have been fascinated with farming, with farms, and I have always loved to bring non-farm people into the mysterious, dynamic sphere of agriculture through farm tours, writing and telling stories, and raising food. And what better way to include people in farming than Community Supported Agriculture (CSA)? It is a new socioeconomic form in which the farmer and consumer enter into a sort of partnership, an alliance to take care of each other's needs. This results in an annual contract in which the farmer agrees to provide a season's worth of vegetables to the consumer (usually known as a shareholder). The shareholder gets a taste of farm life through his or her relationship with the farm—through the vegetables, our newsletter, farm-based events, and perhaps occasionally volunteering to work on the farm. Reciprocally, the farmer gets an ongoing relationship with his or her shareholders via the long-term arrangement for providing their vegetables.

Although many shareholders visit our farm each year to participate in open houses and to volunteer, few are able to enjoy sustained, personal contact with our soil and with our farm team. It's true that eating food from the farm each week builds a very tangible connection, but unlike crew members who work on the farm, shareholders are unable to witness the growth of all the seedlings, the ripening of all the eggplants, the harvest of all the melons.

> CSA is a new socioeconomic form in which the farmer and consumer enter into a sort of partnership, an alliance to take care of each other's needs.

One tool we've used to bridge the gap between our fields and our shareholders' kitchens is our weekly newsletter. Over the years, the essays and farm updates in those newsletters have brought Angelic Organics home to our members, helping them get to know the farmers and staff who grow their food; giving them tours of our fields in rain, sun, wind, and snow; and welcoming them as virtual guests at farm social gatherings. Shareholders read about the groups that visit Angelic Organics through the CSA Learning Center, a not-for-profit educational organization based on the farm (see www.CSALearningCenter.org), and they learn about issues and current events in the world of food and agriculture that are important to them and their farmers.

Another highlight of each newsletter is a cooking page written by our farm cook. "Vegetable of the Week" gives shareholders tips and recipes for using that week's featured vegetable. Many longtime shareholders say they archived their newsletters, keeping them for reference for the next time the vegetable showed up in their box.

The Genesis of *Farmer John's Cookbook*

We recognized that, while many shareholders seem to treasure their dog-eared collections of cooking pages, the information we were able to supply in a newsletter format often provided inadequate support for cooking with vegetables and herbs from the farm. For one thing, first-season shareholders don't have a backlog of recipe pages to refer to, and these new shareholders are the ones who need the most information about identifying, storing, handling, and cooking the vegetables. Also, a "Vegetable of the Week" column does not reflect the pattern in which shareholders actually receive vegetables and need information. Shareholders get more than just one vegetable in a week, and often they need recipes and information on vegetables that don't make a cameo in that week's newsletter.

As we reflected on the shortcomings of the newsletter's cooking pages, an idea for a farm cookbook unfolded. Our cookbook drafts began including excerpts from newsletters that integrated the experiences of shareholders and the experiences of the farm team. As we began compiling recipes and information on storing and cooking the vegetables, as well as the reflections of our farm cooks, field managers, and shareholders, we realized that the book was emerging not as a conventional cookbook, but as an image of a farm in motion. The seasonal arrangement of the vegetable chapters and the harmony of voices found in newsletter excerpts and sidebars wove a tapestry, providing readers the experience of a dynamic farm, one that continues to evolve over the years and with the seasons.

Along the way we also realized that our recipes have a broader audience than ourselves, our farm team, and our shareholders. With the exploding national interest in organic produce, community supported farms, and simply in eating and living more healthfully, people are hungry for new ways to cook and serve fresh, locally grown foods.

As shareholders have expressed a ripening interest in the concept of the farm as an organism that is capable of growing, changing, and maturing, our interest in educating people about Biodynamics and anthroposophical nutrition has also ripened. As a natural extension of our use of Biodynamic farming practices, we have come to see our vegetables and herbs not only as ingredients to be washed and chopped and tossed into stir-fries but also as plants with life forces that can enhance health on many levels. (See essays and lectures on anthroposophical nutrition and Biodynamics throughout this book.)

The farm is a source of life; a stage on which dramas of optimism, fear, abundance, and joy continually unfold; an opportunity for expression; and a way to be in touch with the tempestuousness, the lavishness, the mystery of nature. It is a place of inner training, of learning when to let go and when to hang on, when to wait and when to act. It is a place of outer training, of learning weather, soil, plants, insects, weeds, machinery. The farm is a place of people growing, struggling, achieving. It is the place where the great and mysterious story of food originates.

> We have come to see our vegetables and herbs not only as ingredients to be washed and chopped and tossed into stir-fries but also as plants with life forces that can enhance health on many levels.

Hoisin Sauce

O hoisin, O hoisin
Where've you been hangin?!
A millennia I've spent
Out of breath and bent
Over a stir fry without thee.
O blessings to thee,
  Hoisin Sauce,
And to thy sweet and
  silly jar.

—**LESLEY LITTLEFIELD**

A Shareholder

I was moved to tears reading this week's newsletter and just want to let you know what an honor you give us shareholders by nurturing our lovely vegetables and fruits. I truly *do* feel the love you send us when I open my box each week, as I prepare my family's food, and as I share this wonderful earth's goodness with family and friends. Often I make a lunch for myself, a slow preparation, enjoying the whole process. And when I sit down to eat, this glorious food calls me to go slow, breathe, and be thankful. I look out my window, see the *blue* sky, feel the warmth of the *yellow* sun, and I am centered, at peace, by the grace of this bounty you provide.

Acknowledgments

Farmer John's Cookbook was a vast collaborative effort.

Farm staff were involved in this book project: Growing Manager Meagan Cocke, General Manager and farm photographer Bob Bower, and Administrative Assistant Shannon Fountain. Later, Growing Manager Kirsten Maue and Office Assistant Shelly Anderson were involved.

Shannon Fountain spent considerable time working on the vegetable descriptions after she left the farm.

Jennelle Thimmesch, who interned at the farm in 1999, served for one and a half years as assistant editor.

Andy Blair worked steadily and conscientiously for a year on recipe revisions from Mexico.

Lora Krogman cataloged, selected, and shot photos. She also tested and submitted numerous recipes.

Former intern and cook Hannah Bennett provided her vegetable illustrations.

Shareholder Tanja Hamilton supervised and coordinated the initial shareholder recipe-testing and did the initial formatting of many of the recipes.

Our cooks Ari Divine, Judy Berkshire, Kristen Speegle, Vicki Ramos, and Hannah Bennett devised and submitted recipes, tested them in our farm kitchen, evaluated others' recipe suggestions, wrote great observations about harvesting lunches from our fields, and were ongoingly involved in writing our newsletter recipe pages, from which so much of *Farmer John's Cookbook* originated.

Lesley Littlefield Freeman, songwriter, assistant editor and project coordinator, spent three years diligently helping bring the cookbook to completion. (Lesley and I, Farmer John, made two of Lesley's farmy songs into insane music videos. See www.Angelic-Organics.com).

Former intern and master of the grill Matt Hohmann tested, modified, and rewrote a flurry of recipes as this project neared its conclusion. He also shot many photos in 2000, the season he interned at the farm.

Joe Gallagher, farm intern in 2003, shot essential vegetable photos as the 2003 season ended.

Isa Jacoby, farm cook in 1978 and present-day California caterer, submitted several recipes in her legendary culinary style.

Slava Doval chose the photographs from a catalog of thousands of farm photos. She also shot many of the photographs herself.

Jennifer Case, farmer/caterer from central Indiana, offered her culinary talents as a recipe consultant.

Jenny Meyer, former farm intern and administrative assistant, brought a discerning eye to the book as assistant project manager.

Richard Taylor, Anahi Astudillo, Jonathan Sword, and Tom Spaulding shot vegetable photos.

Bob Scheffler adjusted and laid out the color photos (and shot one).

Special thanks to Bob Bower, General Manager, who was involved in the project from the beginning as technical consultant and assistant editor and who managed myriad details at the farm for several winters, enabling the author to be in Mexico working on the project.

Rudolf Steiner brought an illuminating perspective to the book from the standpoint of nutrition and farming. He also brought a certain liveliness to the project due to his inspiration to think in a living way.

Andrew Lorand, Thomas Cowan, M.D., and Louise Frazier added dimension to the cookbook with their essays on Biodynamics and nutrition from an anthroposophical standpoint. See their bios on page 355.

Many shareholders were involved in testing recipes, and hundreds of shareholders have sent us recipes over the years, many of which we used in the cookbook. Thanks to all of the farm shareholders and friends who submitted and tested recipes.

Editorial Consultant Kate Thompson edited the manuscript.

Thank you to all mentioned above, and to all others who helped create this book.

—**Farmer John**

"**H**ow can it happen that the spiritual impulse, and especially the inner schooling for which you are constantly providing stimulus and guidance, bear so little fruit? Why do the people concerned give so little evidence of spiritual experience, in spite of all their efforts? Why, worst of all, is the will for action, for the carrying out of these spiritual impulses, so weak?

And then came Rudolf Steiner's surprising and thought-provoking answer: 'This is a problem of nutrition. Nutrition as it is today does not supply the strength necessary for manifesting the spirit in physical life. A bridge can no longer be built from thinking to will and action. Food plants no longer contain the forces people need for this.'"

—**EHRENFRIED PFEIFFER, EARLY BIODYNAMIC PIONEER**

Farmer John Writes

Just cleaning my house back then was the biggest struggle, just sweeping the floor. "This is a broom," I'd think to myself. "A broom sweeps the floor, but in order to sweep the floor, I'll have to take hold of the broom with both hands. How will I accomplish this huge task of taking the broom with two hands and then pushing it about on the floor?"

—**FROM JOHN'S BOOK *FARMER JOHN***
ON GLITTER & GREASE

Farmer John Writes

HARVEST WEEK 2, 2000, NEWSLETTER

When the crop has to be planted, a problem becomes a most surreal event, an impossibility occurring in a world where there is only one possibility: the possibility of getting the crop in. A planting problem has the capacity to make the impossible happen: delay the planting. So a breakdown, such as a broken tractor tie-rod, has a very bizarre aspect to it—it cannot happen. And yet it does happen. A thing that cannot happen that does happen results in two conflicting realities occurring simultaneously, sort of a reality breakdown. Problems happen. We don't let them happen. They happen.

So when the tie-rod was dangling from the front end of the tractor just as the fields were finally drying up from oceans of rain, we yanked part after part out of our shop, flung about ideas, and stared imploringly at the welder. In a certain way, we willed the tie-rod back into place. We got the crops in. Then it rained.

—**FROM JOHN'S BOOK *FARMER JOHN ON GLITTER AND GREASE***

Introduction

Food Then and Now

Thousands of years ago, men and women learned to cultivate the soil and domesticate plants and animals. Over time they learned to make use of an astounding array of edible plant species and breeds of livestock. With few exceptions, this bounty of grains, vegetables, fruits, and animal goods remained close to their land of origin, nourishing the people who raised them, as well as others who lived nearby. For centuries people relied on local ecosystems, neighbors, and on their own hands to raise food. However, this last century has witnessed a shift from small family farms to a complicated system that packs food on semis and planes destined for distant states or even countries.

Recently, many consumers have begun to sense that something is lacking in their experience of food. Perhaps they miss the flavor and freshness in their produce or the celebration that comes with a harvest; maybe they long to touch and smell the soil or to see the familiar face of a farmer. Whatever their individual

reasons, these people are embracing a movement that recognizes food in relationship to a specific piece of land and to a particular group of people. This worldwide movement, called Community Supported Agriculture (CSA), honors a commitment between growers and consumers in which consumers pay a grower upfront for a weekly share of the harvest. Bypassing distributors and supermarkets gives farmers financial support, which in many cases enables them to continue farming. In turn, the consumers, often known as shareholders, receive regular boxes or baskets of fresh, local, and often organically raised produce, from a source they know and trust.

Most CSA members say that what they bring home with their weekly harvest shares is much more than just food. Shareholders experience many rewards that emanate from their connection to a farm. There's the magic of opening a box of food that brims with color, freshness, and vitality, and there's the understanding that their produce was raised using sustainable farming practices. There's also the knowledge that our food choices positively impact the environment, the local economy, and our health.

A Shareholder

Please know that we truly appreciate your labor of love. I am (hopefully) a cancer survivor, and I try my best to avoid chemicals, antibiotics, etc. My Wednesday box is a wonderful, positive thing in my life. Farmer John and Company, I love you!

There's the magic of opening a box of food that brims with color, freshness, and vitality.

Neanderthal man came into a store. He wanted to buy something. He wasn't hunting. He should have been hunting. He has no instincts, now that he doesn't hunt. He wouldn't even know how to hunt. What has happened to Neanderthal man? It was a big grocery store, massive. He had no gathering instincts, but here he was gathering food, without his instincts.

Overheard

I have taken a full time job at Whole Foods, in their produce department. I create these pyramids of fruits and veggies that some old woman always picks from the bottom, and of course the beautiful structure of living food tumbles, and I smile and begin all over again.

Even though you can sense from the above that we at Angelic Organics are excited about Community Supported Agriculture, we know that a CSA might not be your source of vegetables. Perhaps there's no CSA in your community, or perhaps you want more—or less—variety than a CSA farm can offer, or maybe you want more control over the quantity of your vegetables.

If you are not a CSA member, maybe you support your local farms by purchasing vegetables at a farmers market or from a stand at a local farm. These are also great ways to get to know your farmers, to support your local economy, and to develop a more intimate relationship with weather and with your bioregion in general.

Or maybe you have your own garden, and you raise most of your own vegetables. (Then you can know your farmer by knowing yourself.)

Or, you may find that you do most of your vegetable acquisitions in the produce section of your favorite grocery store.

However you obtain your produce, this book is a great guide for cooking with vegetables and for connecting you to the source of your food. *Farmer John's Cookbook* is for people who love vegetables and the earth that provides them.

The Challenges of CSA

As a CSA shareholder, you might find your enthusiasm dampened when challenges and questions crop up while you're cooking with produce straight off the farm. Like most of us, you probably weren't raised eating a variety of fresh, whole foods, so your decision to join a CSA might mean you must build an entirely new relationship to the food you eat, even if you've been buying at farmers markets or health food stores for years.

The biggest change for most people who have signed up for a vegetable share is that they no longer go shopping for many veggies, so they don't personally choose which types of food to bring home in a given week.

Even though you've chosen to consume high-quality, local vegetables, your food selection is now dependent on new factors, like the farmer's field plans, the farm's climate, and the effects of weather on crops. It's not surprising that when you open your weekly box, there are some hits but also some misses; you'll find many of your time-honored favorites as well as some things that might take getting used to.

Perhaps, for example, you groan when you get a big bunch of beets: you hate beets. Or maybe you were thrilled last week when you got basil, but this week you got even more basil—and there's still some left over from before! Or suppose you've just encountered this strange specimen you're pretty sure must be kohlrabi. Now you ask yourself, "Is this something that's supposed to be cooked?"

This book will help answer the many "kitchen questions" that may arise as you embark on your farm journey and will support all cooks—both veterans and novices, CSA members and non–CSA members—who are looking for new and time-honored ways to use vegetables and herbs.

A Shareholder

HARVEST WEEK 18, 1999, NEWSLETTER

What is all this talk about complaints this year? Count me out of that camp. I am here to sing praises. I have been a shareholder for five years and, yes, it does seem the boxes are less full than in past years. I didn't sign on to get a steal on veggies. I signed on to get good quality food and to give the farm a fairer break in the market. Rain, shine, drought or whatever, I know I've gotten the best of the deal. I know the source of my food. I know how much work it takes to get it to me. And, I know how good the food is. I can taste all the care that goes into it. It nourishes me on many levels. When the season ends, I'll miss your weekly gifts. To all you Angelic creators, thank you.

How to Use This Book

Farmer John's Cookbook **is:**

Practical. It informs you about vegetables and how to work with them.

Poetic. It offers you myriad insights into the dance of farming at Angelic Organics.

Illuminating. It suggests hidden possibilities about the forces that lie within your food.

Vegetable Identification

For many first- and second-season CSA shareholders, the first challenge of using farm vegetables and herbs lies in the early moments of unpacking the box. Contentedly, maybe even delightedly, you lift out carrots, onions, and lettuce . . . but what is this?! You suspect it might be a turnip. But what if it's really a rutabaga?

Or what if your spouse brings a squash home from the market, and you don't recognize it, and she or he doesn't remember its name?

If you don't know what your vegetable is, the quickest and easiest solution is to turn to the Illustrated Vegetable Identification Guide, page 336. In this handy guide you'll find illustrations of most of the vegetables and herbs distributed by Angelic Organics. These drawings will help you differentiate between chard and choi, celery and celeriac. If, after looking at the Identification Guide, you're only able to narrow it down to two or three vegetables, consult each of those chapters individually in the main text of the book and look for other identifying details in the introductory material. You might want to taste or smell the vegetable to determine if it fits the descriptions given there.

> If you don't know what your vegetable is, the quickest and easiest solution is to turn to the Illustrated Vegetable Identification Guide, page 336.

We have chosen not to identify the varieties of vegetables we raise at Angelic Organics because we often try new varieties and abandon old ones. In some chapters, however, we do elaborate on the varieties we raise, showcasing the diversity of select vegetable families.

Storage (and Preservation)

Storing your vegetables promptly and correctly will help them retain their freshness and vitality. Many vegetables require a bit of pre-storage nipping and tucking. Some store best when you separate the stalks or greens from the roots; others will need to be trimmed and placed with their stems upright in water. You can consult each chapter individually for storage information, or you can refer to the

Vegetable Storage Guide in the Appendix, page 339, where you'll find a compilation of storage instructions.

We address some long-term storage methods in the vegetable introductions. For more comprehensive information on long-term vegetable and herb storage and preservation (such as freezing, drying, canning, and lactic acid fermentation) consult the Web.

Preparation

As you prepare to cook with vegetables and herbs, you'll find helpful notes in each chapter under the heading "Handling." (Of course, you'll always want to thoroughly wash all of your vegetables just before eating or cooking them.) Learning how to handle ingredients properly can prevent you from tossing out delicious but often overlooked vegetable trimmings like broccoli stalks and turnip greens. It can also save you lots of mishaps in later stages of cooking. The way you cut kale, for example, or whether you peel a rutabaga can determine whether you'll love or dislike a particular dish.

Culinary Uses

In each chapter "Culinary Uses" will introduce you to a few of the many dishes you can prepare using a certain vegetable. In some instances this section will also give simple instructions for cooking the vegetable.

> Learning how to handle ingredients properly can prevent you from tossing out delicious but often overlooked vegetable trimmings like broccoli stalks and turnip greens.

Partners for . . .

Improvisers in the kitchen can consult the "Partners for . . ." lists that are located toward the beginning of each chapter. Here we've noted some of the best herbs, spices, nuts, oils, fruits, vegetables, and other foods to combine with each vegetable. These ingredients not only enhance the vegetable's flavor, but in some cases improve its digestibility as well.

In addition, Louise Frazier, a farm friend and the author of the anthroposophical cookbook *Louise's Leaves,* has generously let us reproduce her anthroposophically inspired Complementary Herbs & Spices chart. You will find it in the Appendix, page 344, along with her Simple & Good Wholegrain Cookery chart, page 346.

Recipes

The recipes in *Farmer John's Cookbook* feature the beautiful, bountiful vegetables raised at Angelic Organics and delivered weekly to shareholders (customers who subscribe to a season of vegetables).

My three-year-old daughter and I have been delighted with the weekly box of food. Our meals center around that box. Each week, we head over to the delivery site, return home with the little red wagon loaded with food, and excitedly go through the box on the kitchen table. We discuss what everything is and begin planning our meals. We look through cookbooks, come up with our recipes, hunt down any additional ingredients, and begin cooking. We schedule what gets eaten right away, what can be stored to the end of the week, and what gets cooked and frozen to provide dinner for the Friday meal.

Overheard

I read recipes the same way I read science fiction. I get to the end and I think, "Well, that's not going to happen."

Recipes are grouped by vegetable and are located in the second part of each vegetable chapter. Each recipe begins with a short, descriptive introductory note providing cooking tips, serving suggestions, and evocative descriptions of the dishes. Each recipe also includes the number of servings it yields. Many recipes are quite basic and will familiarize readers with new foods. Others show readers ways to use up a surplus of basil or cabbage or lettuce. Still others are intended to stretch readers' culinary imagination—imagine cooked cucumbers and beet cake!—and will help them avoid any mid-season cooking doldrums. All the recipes are easy to prepare and can be made with basic kitchen equipment. The recipes are written in straightforward language, demystifying more complicated vegetable cooking techniques.

Most of the recipes in *Farmer John's Cookbook* were submitted by Angelic Organics farm cooks or shareholders and have appeared in the cooking section of our weekly newsletter. All have been tested and approved by shareholders who were enlisted in our recipe-testing initiative. And many have the Angelic Organics "farm worker seal of approval" from the famished farm crew (who nurture the vegetables by day and in turn are sustained by them at mealtime). Sources for submissions fall at the end of the recipe headnotes.

In addition to recipes submitted by our cooks and shareholders, several came from other sources—relatives of shareholders, friends of the farm, guest cooks—which created a chaos of writing styles. In many instances, it was difficult to determine the original sources of these recipes: how were we to trace the origin of a family hand-me-down recipe? In addition, recipe submitters often made modifications to the original recipes to improve them, and recipe testers often enhanced submitted recipes with their own input. To remedy the chaotic recipe styles and confusing recipe origins, we undertook to modify all recipes in three significant ways, thereby unifying them into a single voice and transforming them into our own creations. In doing so, we streamed in tantalizing recipe introductions and achieved a clearer, more enjoyable book. However, when we are aware that a recipe originated in a publication, we acknowledge the source with an attribution. (Since we feel it is important to give credit to the original inspiration for these recipes, we have done considerable sleuthing to determine and acknowledge the sources of these recipes.)

Vegan? Vegetarian? Carnivore? and our Recipes

Angelic Organics doesn't endorse any particular food regimen, and we encourage individuals to make their own informed decisions about whether to adopt a diet that includes meat, one that is totally vegan, or one that falls elsewhere on the spectrum. The recipes and food advice in this book represent a "middle way." (Please see the essay "Thoughts on Nutrition" by Thomas Cowan, M.D., page 155, for his anthroposophical perspective on the middle way.) Vegans can substitute a quality vegetable oil, such as olive oil, for butter, and they can replace dairy products or eggs with commercial or homemade vegan alternatives. Likewise, meat eaters can simmer rice and legumes in meat stock. Many recipes included here are conducive to additions of meat, tofu, or tempeh, and many dishes can be served as sides to meat or vegan entrées. We encourage anyone who chooses to consume animal products to seek out sources of dairy, eggs, and meat from organically grown, pasture-fed, hormone-free livestock, ideally from a local farmer whose farming methods and personal style you can come to know.

Farmer John Writes

Since I could see the hogs from my bedroom window, I planned to turn on the fountain and lights from my bed and watch the pigs romp in the colored water. The lights were going to be purple, yellow, and magenta. Even though I knew that a hog fountain needed four lights, I never determined the color of the fourth light.

—**FROM JOHN'S BOOK** *FARMER JOHN ON GLITTER & GREASE*

Seasonal Organization

Another important aspect of this cookbook is that the vegetables are arranged seasonally, according to whether they are harvested and distributed predominantly in the early, mid-, or late parts of the season at Angelic Organics. However, don't be surprised to find a few early season crops in the Late Season and some late season crops in the Early Season, since many of them thrive at other times of the year as well. There are many variables in a CSA farm's harvest equation that impact when we actually distribute a particular vegetable. The most significant of these variables is weather, which changes from year to year and impacts the development and maturity of our crops. When in doubt about whether a vegetable is an early, mid-, or late season crop, turn to the table of contents for the exact page number.

The Crop

HARVEST WEEK 2, 1997, NEWSLETTER

Long before the first luscious red tomato ripens, you may be twitching with tomato anticipation. Or perhaps you are one of those sweet corn anticipation kinds of people. Rest assured that we have row after row of vigorous young tomato plants reaching toward the sky and thousands of corn spears pointing toward the heavens. In the spirit of eating seasonally, however, your first few weeks of the harvest are dominated by greens. Then the zucchini, cucumbers, and onions nudge their way in. Then come the heavy hitters: melons, corn, and tomatoes.

Rudolf Steiner on Food and Agriculture

This book introduces the anthroposophical perspective on food and nutrition; it goes beyond the materialist, reductionist attitude towards food that is so prevalent today. Food is more than a collection of vitamins and minerals; food is a potential carrier for forces that build up our thinking, feeling, and willing. Anthroposophy maintains that

We encourage anyone who chooses to consume animal products to seek out sources of dairy, eggs, and meat from organically grown, pasture-fed, hormone-free livestock, ideally from a local farmer whose farming methods and personal style you can come to know.

food imbued with these forces (which are especially enhanced by Biodynamic practices) can contribute immensely to the task of bringing healthy social impulses to humanity.

Note: You may notice the absence of a section highlighting familiar nutritional components of vegetables, such as vitamins and minerals. Because there is such variability in growing conditions on farms, we think claims about nutrient levels in vegetables are unreliable. In addition, we have also chosen not to include traditional medicinal uses of vegetables, as this is a vast subject that seems fraught with conflicting information. While we believe that vegetables probably are curative in specific ways, this is a realm beyond the scope of this cookbook.

Anthroposophical Nutrition

Farmer John's Cookbook includes several essays that address food and nutrition from an anthroposophical and Biodynamic perspective. (Anthroposophy is a vast field of knowledge, action, and inquiry inspired by Rudolf Steiner. Biodynamics is the agricultural branch of Anthroposophy. An overview of Steiner, Anthroposophy, and Biodynamics by Andrew Lorand, M.D., can be found in "Biodynamics Between Myth and Reality," page 34.)

Forces in Food

Rudolf Steiner made insightful references to a few of the vegetables we raise. Steiner's observations on food, diet, and digestion sometimes expand on popular convention, and sometimes refute it. We are including some of his vegetable comments in the hopes of broadening (and challenging) the contemporary understanding of food.

Farmer John

As a lifelong resident on the farm with over forty-five years of farming experience, John Peterson brings farming (and more) into your kitchen via several essays in this cookbook.

Sidebars

Farmer John occasionally brings his humor and sense of the absurd into this book via his selection and placement of sidebars. These are titled Overheard, Farmer John Writes, A Shareholder, The Crop, The Crew, and Our Cook, among others. "Think of these as word spices for the main text," Farmer John says. "We don't want to get too lofty with our message now, do we?" To further explore John's concept of literary seasoning, see the essay "The Pig Completes the Bunny," in the Appendix, page 348. For more stories by Farmer John and information on his books and other creative farm projects, visit www.AngelicOrganics.com.

Years of Newsletters

Farmer John's Cookbook contains excerpts from over ten years of Angelic Organics newsletters. Sometimes the week and year are noted in the excerpt so you don't get our distant history confused with our present.

Food is more than a collection of vitamins and minerals; food is a potential carrier for forces that build up our thinking, feeling, and willing.

Forces in Food

"There is more in food than just matter. If the factor of . . . cosmic influence is at the minimum, we may get big yields, but the vital energies carried into the food will be low. Increasing nervous disorders, even the inability to make decisions, or to adjust to the faster pace of life, may result."

—Ehrenfried Pfeiffer, early Biodynamic pioneer

Farmer John Writes

There were great civilizations before there were farm chemicals. Those people ate.

—From John's essay "We're Not an Eco-Novelty," page 45.

Peruse, Peruse . . .

Finally, when you find yourself in the kitchen passively sautéing onions or waiting for water to boil, read a sidebar or two—they will bring the flavor and spirit of our farm into your own kitchen. Study photos of our farm crew in action. Peruse weather variations from year to year in the beginning of each season's section. Read shareholders' comments on our vegetables. Study the legacy of our crops and our farm over the years via newsletter excerpts. Enter the farming world of Angelic Organics while you prepare culinary delights, perhaps even from your own weekly box of vegetables.

SLOW FOOD

A nod to the contrast with fast food values, Slow Food is a reference to living an unhurried life, beginning at the table. We at Angelic Organics proudly feel that our farm and this cookbook embody the ideals of Slow Food. From their Web site (www.Slowfood.com): "Slow Food is an international association that promotes food and wine culture while defending food and agricultural biodiversity worldwide. Through its understanding of gastronomy with relation to politics, agriculture, and the environment, Slow Food has become an active player in agriculture and ecology. Slow Food links pleasure and food with awareness and responsibility. The association's activities seek to defend biodiversity in our food supply, spread the education of taste, and link producers of excellent foods to consumers through events and initiatives." (Even though our vegetables make *us* hurry in the fields, we hope they help *you* slow down in your home.)

The leader of Slow Food in America is Alice Waters, founder of Chez Panisse, a restaurant over three decades old that adheres to the ethic that the best-tasting food is organically grown and harvested in ways that are ecologically sound by people who are taking care of the land for future generations.

To quote Alice: "There is a profound disconnection between the kind of human experience that our society values, and the way we actually live our lives. Most people submit unthinkingly to dehumanizing experiences of food-in-workplace cafeterias, food courts, and fast food chains. How can one marvel at the world and then feed oneself in a completely unmarvelous way? I think it's because we don't learn the vital relationship of food to agriculture and of food to culture, and how food affects the quality of our everyday lives. There is nothing else as universal. When you understand where your food comes from, you look at the world in an entirely different way."

A Farmer's Dream

Does Farmer John Have the Right to Make This Cookbook? Does Jack Nicholson?

by John Peterson

One Sunday night I dreamt that a group of shareholders were disgruntled because I was making certain claims about their vegetables that couldn't be substantiated. I would claim in the newsletter, for instance, that a head of cabbage was large, or the lettuce leaves were somewhat tattered. The shareholders felt that I did not have the authority to make these pronouncements about size or quality. Then it occurred to the group that I also did not have the right to call the vegetables by name. To call a vegetable a "broccoli" or a "tomato" was a fantastically presumptuous and arrogant act.

The outraged shareholders contacted the FDA, which initiated an investigation into the adjectives that I used to describe the vegetable quantities and quality. The FDA concluded that I was completely out of bounds, not only in my use of adjectives but in presuming the authority to give the vegetables names. Out of the FDA committee's work, it was discovered that I was not the head farmer at Angelic Organics. This was a great relief to the concerned shareholders, because they felt it was fine for anybody to name the vegetables and assign them characteristics as long as it was not the head farmer.

Through the FDA investigation, it emerged that the head farmer of Angelic Organics was Jack Nicholson. The shareholders were thrilled, not because Jack Nicholson was a movie star, but because he had not been naming the vegetables. Many of the committee members showed up at a public swimming pool to swim after Jack Nicholson and thank him for not naming the vegetables. All the committee members were women. As they began swimming towards Jack, it dawned

---

> To call a vegetable a "broccoli" or a "tomato" was a fantastically presumptuous and arrogant act.

---

on them that Jack had actually been naming the vegetables too. They became furious at his transgression. They swam harder, hoping to reach him and hurt him for what he had done.

—FOR MORE STORIES BY FARMER JOHN, VISIT WWW.ANGELICORGANICS.COM

Farmer John Writes

The closest I can describe my bond to farming is a shudder I get, an irrepressible vibration when it's time to work the fields. I can be eating, sleeping, or having a great conversation, and when the time is right to plow or plant my body registers some mysterious sensation, an irresistible beckoning. My legs take me to the work, put me on the tractor; I am all surrender. And the joy of pushing dirt around, the ecstasy of spraying potentized silica, the thrill of organizing little dots of green into straight lines on bare soil—these invoke in me a subtle delirium.

—FROM JOHN'S BOOK

Farmer John on Glitter & Grease

Angelic Organics Mission and Guiding Principles

Our Mission

Angelic Organics is dedicated to creating and forwarding an economically viable, organic, Biodynamic farm that nurtures its soil, plants, animals, and community of workers and enlivens the connection between people and the source of their food. We are committed to providing the freshest, most vibrant food possible to our customers.

Our Guiding Principles

We strive to:

- Build a sustainable farm system that includes the soil, plants, animals, and humans.
- Provide our customers with the highest quality products and best service possible.
- Build community amongst our members.
- Build and maintain optimal soil fertility.
- Provide a safe environment.
- Conduct business in a financially responsible manner.
- Monitor performance against standards.
- Conduct all work in a timely manner.
- Conduct all work efficiently.
- Share our knowledge and resources with the larger community.
- Provide employees with opportunities for growth, a balanced life, and adequate financial compensation.
- Provide an orderly succession of management.
- Foster research and development.
- Provide the best possible life for farm animals.
- Create and maintain infrastructure that supports the sustainability of the farm.
- Maintain a commitment to aesthetics and beauty.

Seeking Volunteers

HARVEST WEEK 13, 1997, NEWSLETTER

It's fun to spend a day working here. You eat well. You mingle. You walk the fields. You have a sensuous experience. No one is mean to you. No one makes fun of you.

Angelic Organics Publications

In keeping with our mission of *enlivening the connection between people and the source of their food,* we have undertaken this publication, which supports the guiding principles above of *sharing our knowledge and resources with the larger community* and *building community amongst our members.*

Other publications by, or produced in cooperation with, Angelic Organics with a similar goal of connecting people to their food are now or soon will be available. These include books, music, and film.

Books:

* ❖ *Angelic Organics: A Farm Reborn*
* ❖ *Farmer John on Glitter & Grease*
* ❖ *Farmer John Didn't Kill Anyone Up Here: An Uneasy Autobiography*

Music:

* ❖ Lesley Littlefield's *Little Songs* debut album, featuring farmy and environmental songs with two music videos starring Farmer John.

Film:

* ❖ *The Real Dirt on Farmer John,* the award-winning feature documentary film by Taggart Siegel, about the dramatic failure of Farmer John's conventional farming operation and its resurrection into a thriving, organic CSA farm.

Online:

Visit www.AngelicOrganics.com for more about all of our publications.

The Crop

HARVEST WEEK 8, 1998, NEWSLETTER
We are astounded by what we have created on the farm this year; our fields are overflowing.

BIODYNAMICS

HARVEST WEEK 3, 1996, NEWSLETTER
The open house was a wonderful event. The black raspberries just recently ripened; shareholders emerged from the woods with berry baskets and berry faces. Hayrides, great food, a farm tour of the beautiful crops, and a congenial shareholder meeting created a most convivial and enthusiastic afternoon. A highlight of the day was a video on Biodynamics and the ensuing discussion on Biodynamics and Anthroposophy. Because of the obvious shareholder interest in the rather exotic-sounding farming practices outlined by Rudolf Steiner in his 1925 Agriculture lectures, we're now providing shareholders with more information about Biodynamics in our weekly newsletters. (We follow many Biodynamic practices at Angelic Organics. Perhaps they are contributing to some of our good fortune this year.)

Farmer John Writes

This is the image era. Photographs are marketed as memories. Intense personal moments are "like something in the movies." The image becomes the real thing. The wax on the apple becomes the message of health.

—FROM JOHN'S ESSAY "BLOOMINGDALE'S AND PRODUCE," PAGE 237

Angelic Organics in the Process of Becoming Biodynamic

What Angelic Organics has Accomplished in the Biodynamic Sphere

Angelic Organics strives to develop itself as a Biodynamic farm organism. This is a broad task, as it requires a synergistic blending of diverse elements—forest, orchard, flowers, grasses, vegetables, grains, legumes, bees, goats, chickens, ducks, cows, horses, birds, worms, wetlands, etc. In contrast, the economic reality of farming today favors specialization, not diversity. Yet we move continually in the direction of Rudolf Steiner's indications for agriculture, as outlined in

Overheard

Sure, farming is a noble profession, but so was being a gladiator back in ancient Rome.

Farmer John Writes

Now [the farmers] have shrunk to a tiny minority, just two or three, hunched over coffee and sausage and talking a dying language.

—FROM JOHN'S BOOK *FARMER JOHN ON GLITTER & GREASE*

The Biodynamic farming method results in food that is more imbued with spiritual forces than food grown conventionally.

Andrew Lorand's excellent article "Biodynamics Between Myth and Reality," page 34. The results of following Steiner's indications are healthier crops, healthier people who eat from the farm, a more vibrant, self-contained farm organism, and a more lively earth. We have worked extensively to develop a diverse animal component on our farm, restore our woodland, establish an orchard, seed several patches of prairie, reintroduce native species of trees and shrubs for beauty and wildlife habitat, and acquire an adequate land base so fertility can be maintained through fallow management of cover crops. We rotate our crops and spray our fields with Biodynamic preparations. We sometimes host study sessions in which we discuss an anthroposophical text. The Biodynamic vision offers a compelling opportunity for the renewal of agriculture, from which the renewal of society and of the earth can flow.

We Have More to Accomplish

Angelic Organics still has far to go in becoming a realized Biodynamic farm. For instance, we do not have a large enough animal population to supply our fields with adequate Biodynamic compost. We do not yet make our own Biodynamic preparations (remedies for enhancing the soil and our compost). We save very little of our own seed. We bring in many more off-farm inputs than we would like. We work so hard on production that we do not easily find the time to observe and contemplate. However, in spite of the constraints caused by the limitations of capital, labor, and the marketplace, we continually move in the direction of a more self-contained, more Biodynamic farm organism.

The Process of Becoming

Becoming an exemplary Biodynamic farm is a long process. I suspect that, even after many future decades of moving in the Biodynamic direction, Angelic Organics will seem as though it is still in the process of becoming Biodynamic. This is not a hopeless statement; it is the reality of a farm always in the process of becoming better, stronger, more self-sufficient, more spiritualized. I would never want that process to end.

Spiritual Forces in Food

The Biodynamic farming method results in food that is more imbued with spiritual forces than food grown conventionally. In order to illuminate this picture of forces in food, we are including several anthroposophical and Biodynamic articles throughout the cookbook that will introduce our readers to additional wonders of the food we eat. As Angelic Organics moves more towards a Biodynamic ideal, the food people receive from our farm will be increasingly infused with beneficial spiritual forces.

> In spite of the constraints caused by the limitations of capital, labor, and the marketplace, we continually move in the direction of a more self-contained, more Biodynamic farm organism.

A Shareholder

Last week I was struck by how alive and lifelike your Angelic Organics vegetables are. Prior to becoming a shareholder, I'd always thought of vegetables as inanimate objects. I now think of them as living things with a spirit and a life. Thanks for enlightening us.

Biodynamics Between Myth and Reality

by Andrew Lorand, M.D.

Dancing under the full moon, magic herbal sprays and planting by constellations are all part of the (sometimes sensational) lore around Biodynamics—as are the deep felt hopes for a holistic renewal of farming. Most folks in the alternative/organic farming movement have heard of Biodynamics, but not all have really looked into it very closely or they have felt that there were barriers in getting to know it better. In many ways a grandparent of western alternative agriculture, Biodynamics still maintains a certain mystique and is often shrouded in myth. Here is a brief introduction that hopes to help demystify.

A Metaphor

There are many ways to introduce a friend. Each kind of introduction has its own strengths and weaknesses. I often like to think of Biodynamics as a living plant: rooted in its philosophy and history; growing (stems and leaves) through education and demonstration offered by its organizations and teachers; flowering and fruiting uniquely on each individual farm, in each individual garden through the work of each farmer, each gardener. Using this metaphor, I'll try and describe Biodynamics as: 1) a theory or philosophy of agriculture; 2) an agricultural movement with leaders, organizations, purposes, etc. and 3) a set of practical methods that are used by individual practitioners.

Roots

As a theory of agriculture, Biodynamics owes its beginnings to the spiritual philosophy of Dr. Rudolf Steiner (1861–1925) an Austrian philosopher, educator, social activist and innovator in a variety of fields, such as architecture, childhood development, the fine and performing arts, medicine, economics and of course agriculture. He wrote about 30 books and gave many lectures, some 6,000 of which are available in book form. Steiner built buildings, wrote plays, carved statues, inspired a new kind of alternative medical paradigm including new approaches to pharmacopoeia and social therapy; he made efforts to ease the burden on working people and the poor through a deeper understanding of our common social responsibility; he inspired new understandings of the great religions; founded the well known Waldorf School movement as well as several other, lesser known alternative movements and he laid greatest value on the freedom of each individual to find their own paths to self-awareness, social engagement and a non-dogmatic spiritual development. He was not a charismatic guru type, preferring a rather modest, hardworking personal style. Twice married and very cosmopolitan, Steiner had early on made friends in a wide variety of circles. He studied natural science, technology and philosophy and held a Ph.D. in the philosophy of science. Also a student of the classics and literature, Steiner admired greatly the artistic and scientific work of Goethe upon which he would later build much of his own outlook.

Steiner's philosophy, also known as "Anthroposophy," has several distinguishing elements. One of them is the understanding that life is not just physical, but also spiritual. In this case, he did not mean a vague spirituality, but a reality as tangible as the physical and perceptible with our wide-awake mind. Steiner believed in each individual's capacity to understand consciously the spiritual dimension(s) of life and in fact to interact with it practically. Imagine here a kind of physical-spiritual matrix in which the spiritual is the initial cause for and to varying degrees carrier of the physical. Steiner believed that all religions have their place and value. He also believed that the individual has the ability to gain direct knowledge of the spiritual world that is in and around us all the time. Such direct knowledge can be gained by anyone, according to Steiner, regardless of race, religion, gender, socio-economic status or formal education. On the other hand, the path of inner development he describes as "modern" (i.e. based on the freedom of individual choice and initiative) is very disciplined, rigorous, comprehensive and requires great dedication to truth. This path of inner development was also described by Steiner as "spiritual science" as he ascribes the same kind of empirical, disciplined rigor to the study of matters spiritual as science does to the physical realm. He spent much time in his books, lectures and other presentations describing in detail this particular path, this science of spiritual development. By the time Steiner died in 1925, there were organizations in many countries, including the United States, that promoted Anthroposophy as well as many of the practical activities that he inspired.

> I often like to think of Biodynamics as a living plant: rooted in its philosophy and history; growing (stems and leaves) through education and demonstration offered by its organizations and teachers; flowering and fruiting uniquely on each individual farm, in each individual garden through the work of each farmer, each gardener.

Stems and Leaves

Late in his life Steiner was asked by some of his students (who happened to be farmers and gardeners) if he could assist them with their concerns about deteriorating crop and animal health. He began a series of experiments with a small handful of farmers and gardeners around 1922 and in the summer of 1924 gave a more extensive series of lectures and workshops, known simply as the "Agriculture Course." There he laid down some fundamental principles and practices of a new kind of farming system that is both ecological and spiritual, resting squarely on the common sense won from centuries of agriculture, informed by modern science and at the same time infusing new, spiritual perspectives on what makes a farm healthy. A couple of years later, the farmers and gardeners using Steiner's ideas began calling the effort: "the biological-dynamic method of agriculture."

Initially a small group, in time the movement grew. Within a few years Biodynamics was being practiced in many countries and the movement had regional and international meetings on a regular basis. In 1929 the Demeter Association was formed and created the first certification for alternative foods setting high standards that to this day remain more comprehensive than most. Early pioneers of Biodynamics included Ernst Stegeman with whom Steiner had some of his first conversations about new farming methods; Count and Countess Keyserlingk upon whose farm and through whose persistence and support the Agriculture Course was given; Lili Kolisko, who had the first Biodynamic research laboratory and was asked by Rudolf Steiner to carry out experiments to verify and explore his indications; and Ehrenfried Pfeiffer, who carried the impulse to the Netherlands, inspiring many people including Lady Eve Balfour (founder of the Soil Association in England), and eventually brought Biodynamics to the United States in the late 1930s. It was in Kimberton, PA, in 1938 that Pfeiffer started the "North American Bio-Dynamic Farming and Gardening Association" and the "Kimberton Farm School" which was to be the first organic farm school in the U.S. There too, he had a strong influence on several early organic farmers, including Paul Keene of Walnut Acres fame. Although J. I. Rodale visited Pfeiffer and they supposedly had many lively talks, Rodale eventually rejected Biodynamics for what he perceived as its "mystical philosophy."

Despite this rejection of the philosophical nature of Biodynamics, which was not limited to Rodale or to folks in the U.S., Biodynamics pioneered the return of many regenerative, biologically and ecologically sound farming practices such as improved crop rotations, cover and multi-cropping, mulching, integrated animal production, and composting. Biodynamics also introduced several new methods, including an emphasis on aligning with natural rhythms, a focus on pest prevention rather than just management and on the use of "alternative medicine" for the farm as a whole. Fundamental to Biodynamics has always been the concept of the whole farm and self-sustainability. Biodynamic farmers look to create all the natural fertilizers and feed necessary to create and maintain a highly vibrant, diverse, and healthy operation.

Today, there are Biodynamic and Demeter associations worldwide, including such countries as Egypt, India, Brazil, South Africa, New Zealand, Australia and the Philippines. However, Biodynamics is still strongest in Europe, especially in Germany, where there are over 1,300 Demeter Certified farms and gardens producing over 3,000 Demeter certified products. In the U.S. there are estimates of roughly 50,000 acres in Biodynamic management. Each country, each region, has a different relationship to the various organizations and guidelines, and there are many farmers and gardeners who practice some form of Biodynamics without getting certified.

Flowering and Fruiting

The foundation of the actual Biodynamic practices still rests in "good farming

> Biodynamics pioneered the return of many regenerative, biologically and ecologically sound farming practices such as improved crop rotations, cover and multi-cropping, mulching, integrated animal production, and composting.

practices." These are practices we would today call sound ecological activities: the reduction and appropriate reuse of wastes; recycling of materials, energy, nutrients; an understanding and protection of natural archetypes (no genetic manipulation, thank you) and their normal metamorphoses through the seasons; perceiving, honoring and supporting "ecological succession" in nature (think here of the role of weeds, the significance of pastures, fallows and forestation); and seeking of "dynamic equilibrium"—the optimal state of well-being for soils, crops and animals—thus able to find a healthy balance in the face of constant change. These might be referred to as supporting the natural immunological functions in soil, plant and animal.

Today, there are Biodynamic and Demeter associations worldwide, including such countries as Egypt, India, Brazil, South Africa, New Zealand, Australia and the Philippines.

The "Bio" and the "Dynamic"

Biodynamics has methods that seem at least at first glance to be purely ecological, despite their spiritual/philosophical origins, some of which are mentioned above and below. We can attempt to organize these as follows. First, on the "bio" side:

1. Biodiversity (multi-cropping versus monocropping as well as the integration of "wild" and nonproductive habitat, emphasis on protecting and growing older, rare, or endangered species, emphasis on growing lots of different things);

2. Soil Fertility (the focused development of persistent, stable humus, not just temporary nutrient availability, through careful soil preparation, mulching, appropriate crop rotations, composts, herbal and mineral preparations/teas);

3. Integrated Cropping and Animal Systems (the search for farm-wide symbiosis through the integration of domestic animals, their manures and the influence of their biology as well as the reciprocal relationship with the plants that feed them);

4. Integrated Pest Prevention and Management (emphasis on prevention, least invasive/most natural methods including herbal, homeopathic and anthroposophical remedies)

Some of the more "dynamic" ideas/methods include:

1. Understanding the farm not just as a part of a local bioregion, but also as a place between heaven and earth, and itself as a living being: a real, living, distinct, conscious organism with both biological and spiritual qualities.

2. Learning to observe and work with the rhythms of the cosmos, such as: daily, monthly and seasonal growing patterns; learning to eat with the seasons; observing and researching the influence of the sun, moon, planets and constellations on the growth and health of soil, plants, and animals.

3. Developing a therapeutic mentality for what Steiner called the "farm individuality" including gaining the ability to diagnose health and ill health, recognizing that it is the balance of many qualities and activities that keeps the whole healthy.

Farmer John Writes

Bob and I are back from Las Vegas. On my arrival there, everything seemed so fake. I was appalled. On my second day, it seemed funny. By the third day, it all started to seem real.

We went into a shopping mall that was fourteen acres—that's over half the land we have in vegetable production [1996]. The mall brought the outdoors inside by having its own sky. We thought it was the real sky. It was very high and blue like the real sky and it had its own clouds. It was such a convincing sky that we actually debated whether it was a real sky. Then I remembered it should be almost dark by this time, so if this was the real sky, it should be getting dark too. But this blue sky was bright as day.

4. Using natural remedies, homeopathy and anthroposophical medical preparations for the farm, such as the manure and mineral preparations and field sprays, herbal and compost teas; bark and vine pastes; alternative veterinary care.

5. Seeking to strengthen the natural (but also weakening) forces of growth and reproduction on the one hand and ripening/nutritive quality on the other (in plant and animal) through a combination of points 1 through 4.

This last point may seem a little odd at first glance, but a key and implicit (not so obvious) assumption in Biodynamics is that not only is the Earth a living being, but that her natural forces are waning. In particular Steiner singled out two sets of complementary forces needing attention and support. On the one hand we have the growth and reproductive capacities of plants and animals—on the other their ability to mature and ripen and be of nutritive quality for themselves and other species. It was Steiner and his initial student's observation that the fundamental decline in soil, plant and animal health was due to an overall decline in the basic health giving forces in nature. Much of Biodynamics is about supporting, restoring, and regenerating those forces, processes, and phenomena in nature using a natural, holistic and spiritual approach.

Social Engagement

A description of Biodynamics would be incomplete without a word about social responsibility. Like many people involved with Steiner's ideas, Biodynamic practitioners are often searching for improved socio-economic conditions as an integral complement to the natural care and spiritual quality they value. Many Biodynamic farms today are directly, closely or at least to some high degree asso-

> A key and implicit assumption in Biodynamics is that not only is the Earth a living being, but that her natural forces are waning.

ciated with other care giving, social institutions such as homes for the handicapped or the elderly, educational schools for children and adolescents, group homes, colleges, hospitals and clinics and/or other community organizations. In the '60s and '70s Biodynamic farms in Europe pioneered new kinds of internal and external socio-economic relations with "community farms." In the mid-1980s in the U.S. "Community Supported Agriculture" was born out of the Biodynamic movement and quickly spread to many organic growers. In many cases like these, Biodynamics has renewed healthy methods and or pioneered new ones, both agricultural and social and in its own quiet way "spread the wealth."

Myths

Although it is true that Biodynamic practitioners make an effort to discern the

> Biodynamic practitioners . . . are by no means a wacky group of star-dazed, pie-in-the-sky wishful-thinkers, but a rather sober group of keenly awake agricultural professionals making an effort to be more in synch with the universe.

subtle influences of the universe on the development and health of their soils, plants and animals, they are by no means a wacky group of star-dazed, pie-in-the-sky wishful-thinkers, but a rather sober group of keenly awake agricultural professionals making an effort to be more in synch with the universe. There's a distinct difference worth noting. Naturally, there are always one or two folks who claim to be part of the latter group who really belong in the former. However, the gross over-generalization that one pundit wrote about "liking Biodynamics if you're into dancing naked by the moonlight" seems both vicious and revealing: people often dislike and fear what they don't understand. Biodynamics is a serious effort, sustained now for almost 80 years in a wide variety of ecosystems and socio-economic conditions. It is a spiritual philosophy, an agricultural movement and available to each individual as a set of farming and gardening methods meant to enhance the quality of life.

The Next Steps

Although some may find the study of Anthroposophy akin to studying a new religion, with its complex spiritual ideas and disciplined inner path, unlike most religions, Biodynamic practitioners (and Anthroposophists in general) don't do much evangelizing or self-promoting. There is a certain, genuine modesty about many if not most Biodynamic practitioners. Biodynamics is developing and evolving slowly as farmers and gardeners find its practical and spiritual value and add their experiences to the mix. One does not need to be an Anthroposophist or a serious student of Steiner to begin practicing Biodynamics, but over time many will find his ideas helpful, interesting and well grounded . . . to use a metaphor.

ANDREW LORAND'S BIOGRAPHY APPEARS ON PAGE 360.

An Introduction to Anthroposophical Nutrition

(An excerpt from Rudolf Steiner's report to Members of the Anthroposophical Society after the Agriculture Course, Dornach, Switzerland, June 20, 1924)

With regard to the Agriculture Course, the first consideration was to outline what conditions are necessary in order for the various branches of agriculture to thrive. Agriculture includes some very interesting aspects—plant life, animal husbandry, forestry, gardening, and so on, but perhaps most interesting of all are the secrets of [composting], which are very real and important mysteries. We began by discussing the basic principles and relationships, which are especially relevant nowadays because under the influence of our modern philosophy of materialism, it is agriculture—believe it or not—that has deviated furthest from any truly rational principles. Indeed, not many people know that during the last few decades the agricultural products on which our life depends have degenerated extremely rapidly. In this present time of transition from the Kali Yuga* to a new Age of Light, it is not only human moral development that is degenerating, but also what human activity has made of the Earth and of what lies just above the Earth.

This degeneration can be confirmed statistically and is the subject of discussion in agricultural organizations, and yet it seems that nothing can be done about it. Even materialistic farmers nowadays—if they don't just live from day to day but give some thought to what is happening on a daily basis, or at least a yearly basis—can calculate in approximately how many decades their products will have degenerated to such an extent that they can no longer serve as human nourishment. It will certainly be within this century. This is a cosmic issue as well as an earthly issue. Precisely from the example of agriculture, we can see how necessary it is to derive forces from the spirit, forces that are as yet quite unknown. This is necessary not only for the sake of somehow improving agriculture, but so that human life on Earth can continue at all, since as physical beings we depend on what the Earth provides.

---

* Kali-Yuga: according to some spiritual traditions, Kali Yuga is a 5,000 year period which ended in 1899, during which the spiritual world increasingly withdrew its accessibility to humanity. The point of this was to encourage humanity to develop spiritual capacities out of its own internal efforts. (It's the spiritual version of having a big, cushy trust fund that is gradually depleted and then having to work for a living.)

Overheard

FARM INTERN #1: Those flowers are amazing! It's like straight out of your imagination! Imagine telling someone you thought of inventing these bright-colored, circular beautiful things that smell really good—they'd think you were nuts!

FARM INTERN #2 : Yeah, and what if you told someone about this big blue thing we're all gonna live underneath—not pink or purple or green—blue with billowing floating white things passing through, that changes color during different times of the day . . . or, hey, how about a black-and-white-striped animal that runs through the savannah, or a polka-dotted huge cat, or any one of those insane crazy insects that how the heck got thought of?

SPRING

AN EMPHASIS ON PLANTING
EARLY MARCH to MID-JUNE

"The vision we have for Angelic Organics draws some of its inspiration from Biodynamics. Rudolf Steiner recommended using specific potentized herbal preparations to invigorate and harmonize the soil and plants. He also advocated a reintegration of agricultural enterprises (which are very specialized in mainstream agriculture), such as livestock, perennial, and vegetable operations. Steiner claimed these life forms each attract and emanate specific cosmic energies. By putting them in proximity to one another, cosmic energies are enhanced and enter into a state of synergy. Steiner's suggestions about farming in a way that truly contributes to the earth include the establishment of woodlands, beehives, orchards, pastures for livestock, birds, flowers, trees, soil microorganisms, earthworms, cows, pigs. All these living things offer vitality, balance, and life force to one another. When these different influences mingle, the individuality of the farm comes forth."

—FARMER JOHN PETERSON

Farmer John Writes

When the time is right to plow or plant, my body registers some mysterious sensation, an irresistible beckoning . . . I am all surrender.

—FROM JOHN'S BOOK *FARMER JOHN ON GLITTER & GREASE*

Spring Farming

Spring heralds the renewal of farm life. The planning and strategizing of winter are brought to a close, infrastructure projects are wound down, veteran workers arrive to start seedlings in the greenhouse, farm equipment is greased and inspected. The frozen ground of winter gives way to mud. Hints of balmy air occasionally waft through the farm, reminding us of the lush warmth and bright sunshine soon to follow. Rains replenish the fields. The silty clay soil of Angelic Organics dries slowly. Phantom-like tinges of green begin to appear in the fields and woodlands. By early April, we apply compost, till the fields, seed cover crops . . . and quickly the pace accelerates. We transplant, mulch, cover. Tens of thousands of seedlings are raced from the greenhouse into the fields, making room to establish more waves of seedlings in the greenhouse, more transplanting. Irrigation systems are put in place. By mid-May, our fields are showing the promise of the season. Mechanical and hand weeding are well under way. Fences are built to keep out the deer. Crops such as spinach, carrots, and mesclun mix are emerging from the dark soil in faint lines on their march towards the kitchens of our shareholders.

Farmer John Writes

HARVEST WEEK 3, 2004, NEWSLETTER

As I plunged into fieldwork in early April, I became more and more driven as the weather got drier and warmer. The clear, western skies somehow spoke more ominously of rain to me than brooding thunderheads would have. I remembered so clearly the heat and dryness of early spring, 1974, and so I became increasingly relentless with tillage and cover crop planting. I felt like a madman: "It's going to rain! Look at those nice skies. It's going to start raining and not stop." We were in great shape when the rains finally came.

Farmer John Writes

An hour saved can mean the difference between getting three thousand lettuce seedlings in on time or two weeks late.

—FROM JOHN'S BOOK *FARMER JOHN ON GLITTER & GREASE*

Overheard

FARMER: I smell the spring in the winds coming through San Miguel, Mexico, and I ache for the fields of the farm. How can I ever stop this yearning?

WOMAN: You've instilled the same yearnings in me too. It has been 70 to 80 degrees the whole month of February here in Mississippi, and my cravings to plant things are out of control. I planted beets today. I'm planning my seed order this weekend, though I vowed not to have a garden this year. Last week when I drove through the Delta, being around so much farmland put me into a trance. I want my own little Kubota tractor and a cow.

Spring Eating

For those who crave the first fresh vegetables off the farm, spring is a period of tantalizing waiting. Angelic Organics begins deliveries of vegetables in mid-June. Until that time, the rains, sunshine, and warmth that bless both city and country alike are reminders of the bounty to come. What to eat until the first vegetables of the season arrive? If you diligently preserved last year's vegetables and herbs, and carefully rationed them through the winter, you may still be smugly enjoying your farm's delights from a previous year as you watch your neighbor across the street lugging in bags of vegetables from the grocery store. But frankly, it's likely that you didn't preserve last year's bounty, and your squash, potatoes, and onions from last season are probably gone by now. You're probably foraging at the store, too, just like your neighbor, anxiously awaiting the new season's cascade of vegetables.

A Shareholder

This is the third season my husband and I are enthusiastically awaiting the delivery of the first box. The visual pleasure and eating pleasure of your vegetables are truly some of life's greatest moments. The smell of the basil brings tears to my eyes every time. Thanks for your hard work.

A Shareholder

We look forward to getting our new share! It's been marked on the calendar for weeks! We're excited about this year's crops and all of the wonderful meals to make with your fabulous vegetables . . .

Overheard

GIRL: I love springtime in the Midwest!
FARMER: Ohh, mmmmm, yeah, me too. It brought me back to the farm, onto the tractor again.
GIRL: I mean, spring to me is walking through the flowers, not driving a big thing over them.

The Crew

FARM NEWS, 1999

The crew get up really early; they start when it's just getting light. They start whether it's cold, or raining, or windy. They just get started because the work has to be done. And then they work through the day, regardless of what the weather throws at them, regardless of machinery problems, or greenhouse setbacks, or quality challenges; regardless of "I don't want to" or "I'm not in the mood." They stoop, bend, squat, lift, lug, sort, wash, pack, weed, thin, seed, sweep, weigh, bunch, bag, pack. They get paid little. There is a lot of harmony and good will among them. Go figure.

—FARMER JOHN

EARLY SEASON

AN EMPHASIS ON LEAFING
MID-JUNE to LATE JULY

"How can we create the proper soul mood to prepare for a meal? This question is especially pertinent if we realize the close relationship between the body and the soul-spiritual. Modern behavioral science has hardly recognized (in fact it has not even noticed) the importance of the "table prayer"—the saying of grace.

Rudolf Steiner supplied a prayer which is valid for persons of all ages and also meets the needs of modern man. This prayer addresses the soul which sprouts within as do the plants outside which provide our nourishment. It points to the relationship of the germinating, sprouting, ripening of this earth food with the soul-spiritual sprouting and ripening process.

In the darkness of the earth the seed is awakened.
In the power of the air the leaves are quickened.
In the might of the sun the fruit is ripened.
Thus in the shrine of the heart the soul is awakened.
In the light of the world the spirit is quickened.
In the glory of God man's power is ripened.

One can readily feel the harmonizing force that flows from these words and unites the soul in the right way with earth nourishment. And it will soon be recognized as a matter of fact in a proper nutritional hygiene that such a table prayer should be said when man sits down to eat.

Rudolf Steiner allegedly said once that through these words, if spoken in the proper manner, a health-giving element will affect man down into his digestive processes."

—GERHARD SCHMIDT, *DYNAMICS OF NUTRITION*

Overheard

Won't that be a distraction from the spiritual world?
Life is a distraction from the spiritual world.

We're Not an Eco-Novelty

by John Peterson

(FARM NEWS, 1998)

I was in Mexico recently. My friend, Monica, and I drove east from Mexico City into the Yucatan Jungle. We visited famous and obscure Mayan ruins, the spectacular waterfalls of Playa Azul, and the beautiful Spanish colonial town of San Cristóbal de las Casas in Chiapas near the Guatemalan border. Near San Cristóbal we visited the little Mayan town of San Juan Chamula, where a church without seats reverberates with Mayan chants, and Coca-Cola is regarded as a spiritual drink.

At the spectacular Mayan ruins of Palenque I had a conversation with two tall, thirty-ish tourists from Mexico City. His name was Juan. Hers was Ana.

JOHN: So where are you going from here?

ANA: To an Ecology Village near Mérida. They have solar panels. They make drinking water from the ocean. It's all built with nontoxic materials.

JOHN: What do you do in Mexico City?

JUAN: I market agricultural chemicals to the farmers—fungicides, insecticides, things like that.

JOHN: I farm, but I'm an organic farmer.

JUAN: I guess organic farming is fine, for a few people. It will never take care of everyone, but a few could benefit. To take care of everyone, we need chemicals.

JOHN [gazing at the great Mayan temples in the background]: There were great civilizations before there were farm chemicals. Those people ate. Do you really think people are taken care of today?

JUAN: We just don't have the right chemicals yet. We have to develop the right chemicals. It is our only hope.

JOHN: Our farm feeds a lot of people without chemicals. Feeding people well is not about chemicals. It's about paradigms.

> Our farm feeds a lot of people without chemicals. Feeding people well is not about chemicals. It's about paradigms.

I sat there in the dense, tropical air of the Yucatán Jungle, on the site of a once thriving agricultural and spiritual culture. I thought about the Angelic Organics shareholders, how they believe living well and eating well is not something that occurs only in an eco-museum, how they bring this conviction into their lives and make it a part of their daily existence. I thought about the farm—it's not an eco-novelty; it is a place that has come to life out of shareholders' commitment to eating well on a daily basis. I felt really blessed to have Angelic Organics shareholders in my life.

45

Overheard

My father-in-law is having open heart surgery tomorrow. He's getting a new valve. It will be out of a cow, a pig, or plastic. I told him that it might be out of the cow he shipped last week.

Anthroposophical Nutrition

There is a very materialistic picture of food embedded in the modern consciousness. The following article provides a different picture of food. It steps outside the material realm and looks at food in a more cosmic context.

The Relation of Foodstuffs to Man

from The Evolution of Earth and Man and Influence of the Stars
by Rudolf Steiner

That, I would say, is the secret of human nutrition: that if I want to work upon my head, I have roots or [grains] for dinner. If I want to work upon my heart or my lungs, I make myself a green salad. And in this case, because these substances are destroyed in the intestines and only their forces proceed to work, cooking is not so necessary. That's why leaves can be eaten raw as salad. Whatever is to work on the head cannot be eaten raw; it must be cooked. Cooked foods work particularly on the head. Lettuce and similar things work

Reprinted with permission from the Biodynamic Farming and Gardening Association, Inc. Rudolf Steiner's biography appears on page 360.

particularly on heart and lungs, building them up, nourishing them through the fats.

But now, gentlemen, the human being must not only nurture the head and the middle body, the breast region, but he must nurture the digestive organs themselves. He needs a stomach, intestines, kidneys, and a liver, and he must build up these digestive organs himself. Now the interesting fact is this: to build up his digestive organs he needs protein for food, the protein that is in plants, particularly as contained in their blossoms, and most particularly in their fruit. So we can say: the root primarily nourishes the head particularly [see page 48]; the middle of the plant, stem and leaves, primarily nourishes the chest particularly; and fruit nourishes the lower body.

When we look out at our grain fields we can say, Good that they are there! for that nourishes our head.* When we look down at the lettuce we've planted, all those leaves that we eat without cooking because they are easily digested in the intestines—and it's their forces that we want—there we get everything that maintains our chest organs. But cast an eye up at the plums and apples, at the fruits growing on the trees—ah! those we don't have to bother to cook much, for they've been cooked by the sun itself during the whole summer! There an inner ripening has already been happening, so that they are something quite different from the roots, or from [grains] (which are not ripened but actually dried up by the sun). The fruits, as I said, we don't have to cook much—unless we have a weak organism, in which case the intestines cannot destroy the fruits. Then we must cook them; we must have stewed fruit and the like. If someone has intestinal illnesses, he must be careful to take his fruit in some cooked form—sauce, jam, and so forth. If one has a perfectly healthy digestive system, a perfectly healthy intestinal system, then fruits are the right thing to nourish the lower body, through the protein they contain. Protein from any of the fruits nourishes your stomach for you, nourishes all your digestive organs in your lower body.

You can see what a good instinct human beings have had for these things! Naturally, they have not known in concept all that I've been telling you, but they have known it instinctively. They have always prepared a mixed diet of roots, greens and fruit; they have eaten all of them, and even the comparative amounts that one should have of these three different foods have been properly determined by their instinct.

> If I want to work upon my heart or my lungs, I make myself a green salad.

*Steiner elaborates on root forces: When I eat bread, the bread works upon my head because the root elements of a plant work up into the stem [of the grain]. The stem, even though it is stem and grows above the ground in the air, still has root forces in it. The question is not whether something is above in the air, but whether it has any root forces. Now the leaf, the green leaf, does not have root forces. No green leaf ever appears down in the earth. In late summer and autumn, when the sun forces are no longer working so strongly, the stem can mature. But the leaf needs the strongest sun forces for it to unfold; it grows towards the sun. So we can say, the green part of the plant works particularly on heart and lungs, while the root strengthens the head. —Rudolf Steiner, from his lecture *The Evolution of Earth and Man and Influence of the Stars.*

Welcome to the Early Season

An Emphasis on Leafing

Mid-June to Late July

Harvest Weeks 1 to 7

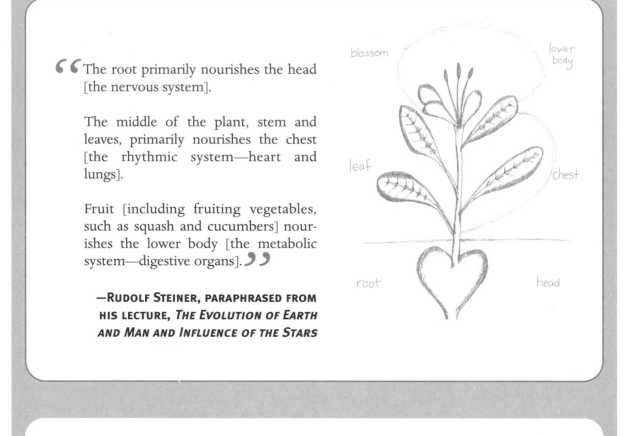

"The root primarily nourishes the head [the nervous system].

The middle of the plant, stem and leaves, primarily nourishes the chest [the rhythmic system—heart and lungs].

Fruit [including fruiting vegetables, such as squash and cucumbers] nourishes the lower body [the metabolic system—digestive organs]."

—Rudolf Steiner, paraphrased from his lecture, *The Evolution of Earth and Man and Influence of the Stars*

Forces in Food

When we look down at the lettuce we've planted, all those leaves that we eat without cooking because they are easily digested in the intestines—and it's their forces that we want—there we get everything that maintains our chest organs.

—Lecture by Rudolf Steiner, *The Evolution of Earth and Man and Influence of the Stars*

Early Season Vegetables

The contents of a vegetable box will vary from week to week and from year to year with changes in the weather, among other factors. Some of the vegetables listed below are also harvested at other times of the year. (See Vegetable & Herb Availability from Angelic Organics, page 334, and the Illustrated Vegetable Identification Guide, page 336.)

Asparagus

Beets

Chicories

Choi

Cooking Greens

Cucumbers

Herbs

Onions and Scallions

Radishes and Young Turnips

Salad Greens

Sugar Snap Peas

Zucchini and Summer Squash

A Diary of Early Season Weather

Notice the variability from year to year.

Late June	Mid-July	Late-July
HARVEST WEEK 2, 1996, NEWSLETTER One of the numerous downpours this week at Angelic Organics prompted a spontaneous mud party. Details of the event are missing.	**HARVEST WEEK 5, 1997, NEWSLETTER** Extreme heat and no rain for weeks. The crew starts at 5:30 in the morning and flies through most of the outside work by lunch. The heat is hard on people and crops, and especially on greens.	**HARVEST WEEK 7, 1997, NEWSLETTER** Cool and dry in the first part of the week. Seriously dry. Then hot and drier.
HARVEST WEEK 2, 1998, NEWSLETTER Hot and humid. Over two inches of rain and howling winds Thursday evening.	**HARVEST WEEK 5, 1998, NEWSLETTER** Dry weather! Relatively mild (in the 80s) and humid.	**HARVEST WEEK 7, 1998, NEWSLETTER** Hot and sticky. Some welcome rain.
HARVEST WEEK 2, 1999, NEWSLETTER Dry! Cool, dipping into the 40s at night and barely reaching 70 during the day.	**HARVEST WEEK 5, 1999, NEWSLETTER** It was too wet and now it's too dry. High temperatures ranged from the upper 90s early in the week to the mid-80s by Friday.	**HARVEST WEEK 7, 1999, NEWSLETTER** Did we say "drought" last week? We received 3 inches of rain this week, and on several days we experienced a heat index above 100 degrees.

NO MATTER WHAT

HARVEST WEEK 2, 2000, NEWSLETTER

There is a one-pointedness that takes over us farmers this time of the year. When the weather clears, there is only one thing to do—get the crops in. When that time arrives, there is nothing other than the work. Food, rest, talk are all immaterial. The clock is immaterial. Problems are, oddly, immaterial; problems cannot exist.

The Crop

HARVEST WEEK 6, 1998, NEWSLETTER

It's extraordinary to have sweet corn this early. Our second planting is also coming on very fast. It is challenging to raise organic sweet corn. Bugs, weeds, deer, and raccoons are especially troublesome. It's also tough to maintain high enough fertility and get timely rains for ear formation. This year we started all our sweet corn in the greenhouse and transplanted it. Rains were on time. The days were hot and humid. Nights were cool. We're happy.

Early Season Eating

Peek into early season boxes, and the color green will burst forth. Green lettuce, mesclun mix, spinach, kale, and chard dominate the harvest at this time of year. Looking at these leafy vegetables, it's easy to see where the term greens comes from. In fact, green is probably the best way to characterize this first part of the growing season. To help keep your eating lively and varied, we've included oodles of greens recipes in this section.

Even though we enjoy growing greens and even though you might enjoy eating them, we don't want you to blow away with all that feathery, leafy fare. To round out a vegetable share, we encourage our fields to offer some early fruiting and root crops like zucchini and cucumbers, beets and radishes, and later in the early season, bulb onions. With cooler spring temperatures, we're also able to sneak in some of those crops that love the fall, like broccoli and cabbage. Eating these early season vegetables eases both the physical and mental heaviness that we tend to acquire in winter. These foods are as cleansing and enlivening as spring itself. (If you do eventually find yourself getting tired of spring greens, just remember that the summer heavyweights—melons, tomatoes, sweet corn, and peppers— are loved and tended early in the season, in preparation for mid-season harvests.)

Early Season Farming

For several months the crew has been busy with pre-harvest tasks of greenhouse work, transplanting, weeding, seeding, hoeing, tilling, preparing and repairing tools, maintaining and building infrastructure, and learning to work and live together. Now that the harvest season has begun, those other activities don't stop but are accompanied by harvesting, washing, packing, and delivering vegetables. The first weeks of harvest typically start out slowly as veteran crew members train newcomers in the procedures for getting each crop into your box and delivered to you on time. By July we're really into the swing of things and we usually fly through harvest and packing with enough time left over for the other projects that must go on to keep Angelic Organics operating.

Farmer John Writes

HARVEST WEEK 2, 1997, NEWSLETTER

Rains came with wind—gales of wind—shredding spinach and choi. The curved roofs of our barns created wind tunnels, accelerating these smashing blasts of wind. They whooshed down, zinging shingles. They slapped at the blue tarp on our outdoor coolers. They teased the bungees. A bungee snapped. All bungees snapped. The winds sucked the 4-by-8-foot panels of insulation from the cooler roofs. The foam rectangles bobbed and careened like kites struggling into the sky. The white panels whipped through the air, first one, then three, four more. They sashayed across our potato field, spun high into the sheets of rain. They twirled and wobbled over the neighbor's cornfield, a geometric dream of white. They are gone.

If you got a soggy vegetable box last week, please reread the previous paragraph. Don't despair; we'll repair the cooler's leaky roof in a jiffy.

Farmer John Writes

On my farm, we had great celebrations. . . . Our Queen of Spring sat in her shrine, lights blinking atop her head, popcorn exploding at her feet. The popcorn slowly engulfed her.

—FROM JOHN'S BOOK *FARMER JOHN DIDN'T KILL ANYONE UP HERE: AN UNEASY AUTOBIOGRAPHY*

Asparagus

One of the earliest and most celebrated of spring vegetables, asparagus pokes its green crowns out of our kitchen garden several weeks before we have enough produce ready to give to our shareholders. If you volunteer at Angelic Organics early enough in the season, you might spot our small asparagus patch. Even though we don't distribute asparagus to our shareholders, we're including it here because of its springtime availability at farmers markets and in shops selling quality food. Although you won't receive it from Angelic Organics, don't let that deter you from finding other local sources of asparagus or from growing it in your own garden.

Commonly Grown Asparagus

Some varieties of asparagus are thoroughly green. Others have a more purplish color or are purple-green. European white asparagus, which is blanched underground until it is totally white, is esteemed for its delicate flavor and tender texture.

Storage

Asparagus spears are best eaten shortly after harvest when their tips are still firm. If you must store asparagus, trim the base of the stalks and place the stalks upright in a jar filled with an inch of water. An alternative method is to wrap the cut ends of the stalks in a moist paper towel or damp tea towel, cover the bundle loosely in plastic, and put it in the refrigerator. Refrigerate asparagus for up to two weeks.

Handling

Rinse asparagus under cold running water. If you will be eating it raw, peel the stems with a sharp knife instead of lopping off the tough base of the stalks. Start peeling at the base of the stalk, making your cut more shallow as you go upward. Stop peeling when you are two or three inches from the crown. Under the tough exterior you'll find tender, crisp flesh.

Culinary Uses

- ❖ Include plain, raw asparagus on a vegetable platter, or drizzle whole or thinly sliced asparagus with a vinaigrette.
- ❖ Blanch or steam asparagus (steam in an upright asparagus steamer or in a steamer basket) until bright green and just tender. Top with butter and salt.
- ❖ Add asparagus to soups, stews, or mixed vegetable dishes during the last minutes of cooking.
- ❖ Use leftover or mature asparagus in soufflés or omelettes.
- ❖ Substitute it where a recipe calls for leeks.
- ❖ Roast asparagus in olive oil at 500° F for 5 to 10 minutes depending on the thickness of the asparagus.

Our Cook

Here at Angelic Organics, asparagus is a special treat to be handled judiciously. When I arrived here in March, the cooler was filled with last year's beets, carrots, potatoes, and cabbage. Being a believer in eating seasonally and in the value of delayed gratification, I served lots of storage roots when I started cooking. So when the first precious asparagus stalks graced the table, everyone appreciated the meal even more.

Partners for Asparagus*

- ❖ Curry, dill, ginger, mint, mustard, parsley, tarragon, white pepper;
- ❖ Lemon juice, olive oil, peanut oil, sesame oil, soy sauce or tamari, white wine vinegar;
- ❖ Butter, cream, eggs, Muenster cheese, Parmesan cheese, pecorino cheese;
- ❖ Sesame seeds, slivered almonds;
- ❖ Garlic, scallions, shallots;

*See Louise Frazier's Complementary Herbs & Spices chart, page 345, for suggestions.

Asparagus and White Bean Salad

with Feta and Lemon Dressing

Served with crusty bread, this salad makes a terrific meal. White beans provide a delectable hearty-tenderness, without overwhelming the delicate asparagus. Tangy feta, zesty lemon, and a touch of mint give this salad a bright and refreshing flavor. If you have a special steamer just for asparagus, in which the asparagus is steamed standing upright, cut the asparagus into pieces after steaming. *Friend of the Farm.*

SERVES 4

1 pound	asparagus, cut on an angle in 1-inch pieces (about 3 cups)
1 tablespoon	extra virgin olive oil
2 teaspoons	freshly squeezed lemon juice
1 teaspoon	chopped fresh mint
1/2 teaspoon	freshly grated lemon zest
1/4 teaspoon	salt
1/8 teaspoon	freshly ground black pepper
1 cup	cooked or canned white beans, drained and rinsed
1/2 cup	crumbled feta cheese
1/2 cup	thinly sliced radishes
2 tablespoons	thinly sliced scallions

1. Place the asparagus in a steamer basket, set over 1 1/2 inches boiling water, and cover. Steam until the spears are tender-firm, 4 to 7 minutes depending on thickness. Drain and place in an ice water bath (or under cold, running water) for a moment to stop the cooking.

2. Put the olive oil, lemon juice, fresh mint, lemon zest, salt, and pepper in a small bowl and whisk until well combined. Drain asparagus.

3. Combine the beans, feta, radishes, and scallions in a large bowl. Add the asparagus pieces. Pour on the dressing and gently toss. Serve at room temperature or chilled.

A Farm Friend

Here in Mexico you can buy really cheap tin and enamel narrow pots with steamer inserts that are designed especially for steaming asparagus. This in a country where everything but everything else gets cooked in pig fat on the comal.

The Crop

Asparagus is usually easy to grow, but sometimes it gets rusty. Though not the same kind of rust that weakens machinery or tools left in the rain, asparagus rust is aggravated by the same damp weather as the rust that eats metal. Rust in the garden is a fungus that shows up on asparagus ferns in dark green, scaly scabs or reddish areas. Many organic farmers select rust-resistant varieties to yield the healthiest asparagus possible.

Our Cook

Asparagus is an exciting vegetable, the first thing in the garden to poke its head through the earth in the spring. Back home in Kansas, the asparagus bed is my father's pride and joy. In late April and May, the refrigerator always contains a pan of marinating spears and several jars of strange-looking bouquets. (We place the asparagus upright in jars of water after harvest and before cooking.)

Steamed Asparagus
with Balsamic Butter and Pine Nuts

Perhaps the best way to honor the delectable simplicity of tender-crisp, just-steamed asparagus spears is to prepare them with a light touch. In this recipe a touch of butter makes the bright green spears glisten, a sprinkling of tangy-sweet balsamic vinegar brings out their sweetness, and a scattering of crispy nuts complements their unique silky-firm texture. This is elegant—and a cinch to prepare. *Friend of the Farm.*

SERVES 3 TO 4

1½ tablespoons	pine nuts or slivered almonds
1 pound	asparagus, tough ends peeled or snapped off
2 tablespoons	butter, melted
2 teaspoons	balsamic vinegar
	salt
	freshly ground black pepper

1. Place a heavy skillet over medium heat. Add the pine nuts or slivered almonds. Toast the nuts on the dry skillet, stirring constantly, until they are lightly browned and begin to smell toasty, 3 to 5 minutes. (Be careful not to overtoast them, as they will burn very quickly once toasted.) Remove the skillet from heat and immediately transfer the nuts to a heatproof dish. Set the dish aside to let the nuts cool completely.

2. Place the asparagus in a steamer basket, set over 1½ inches boiling water, and cover. Steam until the spears are tender-firm, 4 to 7 minutes depending on thickness. Remove spears from the water and arrange on individual plates.

3. Combine the melted butter and balsamic vinegar in a small bowl and whisk until well combined. Pour this mixture over the asparagus and sprinkle on the toasted nuts. Season with salt and pepper to taste. Serve immediately.

Chilled Asparagus
with Mustard-Yogurt Sauce

Asparagus's natural sweetness is more noticeable when it is served cold. In this refreshing recipe, the spiciness of mustard and the slight astringency of plain yogurt accentuate this sweetness. *Friend of the Farm.*

SERVES 4

1 pound	asparagus, tough ends peeled or snapped off
1 cup	firm plain yogurt
⅓ cup	prepared Dijon mustard
¼ cup	mayonnaise
2 heaping tablespoons	minced fresh dill
2 heaping tablespoons	minced fresh chives
	salt
	freshly ground black pepper
4	cherry tomatoes, quartered (optional)

1. Place the asparagus in a steamer basket, set over 1½ inches boiling water, and cover. Steam until spears are tender-firm, 4 to 7 minutes depending on thickness. Drain; place in an ice water bath to stop the cooking.

2. Mix the yogurt, mustard, and mayonnaise in a medium bowl. Add the dill and chives; mix until well combined. Season with salt and pepper to taste.

3. Drain the asparagus and place in a large bowl. Pour in the yogurt mixture and combine well—your hands work best here, though you can use a wooden spoon or spatula.

4. Garnish with cherry tomato pieces if desired. Serve cold.

Beets

Sweet, earthy, and brilliantly colored, beets are one of the star crops on our farm. Our early summer beets are especially sweet and succulent, almost like candy, and not at all like the canned concoctions you may have endured. This said, we want all you recalcitrant beet-avoiders to give them a try. If you need some encouragement, this chapter offers recipes to satisfy both beet-lovers and beet-bashers. You might want to consult the Cooking Greens chapter, page 81, for tips and recipes using beets' tangy stems and leaves.

Beets Grown by Angelic Organics

Red beets have the crimson color, sweet flavor, and red-veined leaves that are usually associated with beets.

Golden beets have yellow skin and flesh. Because they have a delicate flavor and their color doesn't run all over, they are a good choice for more decorous meals.

Chiogga beets are pinkish red on the outside and have pretty stripes of white and red on the inside. They don't retain their stripes after cooking but turn pinkish throughout.

Storage

If your beets still have greens attached, cut them off, leaving an inch of stem. Keep these greens unwashed and refrigerated in a closed plastic bag. Store the beet roots, with the rootlets (or "tails") attached, unwashed, in a plastic bag in the

BEETS—YOU LOVE 'EM OR HATE 'EM

As far as popularity goes, beets are the most polarizing common vegetable. Most CSAs find that about half their shareholders want beets, and half don't. When surveyed, many of you indicated that beets were your "least desired" vegetable, yet we put them in your vegetable boxes fairly often. Big beets—big bunches of beets. Giving you beets when you say you don't desire them seems a little insensitive of us. So why do you get beets if you don't want them? Because so many of you *do* want them.

A Shareholder

I'm trying to talk Kara into fashioning me a beet costume for Halloween. Last year Kara and I dressed as genetically engineered farm animals. I was a cow with a gigantic udder and lots of teats made from pink spandex. Also I had three tails and wore a baseball cap with the logo "Body by Monsanto." Kara was much better—a carrot with chicken wings and beak.

crisper bin of your refrigerator. They will keep for several weeks, but their sweetness diminishes with time; so try to use them within a week.

Handling

Just before cooking, scrub beets well and remove any scraggly leaves and rootlets. If your recipe calls for raw beets, peel them with a knife or vegetable peeler, then grate or cut them according to your needs.

Culinary Uses

❖ Grate peeled, raw beets into salads, or use as an attractive garnish to various other dishes. Serve the most tender baby beet greens raw in salads.

❖ Bake beets in a covered roasting pan with ¹/₂ cup water at 400° F, or boil them, until easily pierced with a sharp knife. Both methods take 45 minutes to 1 hour, depending on beet size. Season cooked beets with butter, salt, and pepper; or with cream and chopped fresh herbs; or with a vinaigrette.

❖ Use peeled and sliced roasted beets in soup, or grate them and toss with extra virgin olive oil and salt over pasta.

❖ Roast beets with other root vegetables at 400° F with olive oil, garlic, herbs, and salt.

❖ Disguise cooked beets in baked goods and eat them for dessert (see Chocolate Beet Cake, page 62.)

❖ Lightly steam or stir-fry beet greens as you would their close botanical relatives, spinach and chard.

Partners for Beets*

❖ Allspice, basil, caraway, cilantro, coriander, cumin, curry, dill, fennel leaves or seeds, ginger, horseradish, lemon balm, mint, nutmeg, parsley, tarragon;

❖ Citrus juice, mustard oil, olive oil, prepared mustard, vinegar;

❖ Butter, cream, yogurt;

❖ Apples, oranges;

❖ Capers, celery, chiles, endive, onions, root vegetables, shallots, walnuts.

*See Louise Frazier's Complementary Herbs & Spices chart, page 345, for suggestions.

Julienned Beet Salad with Fresh Dill
and Umeboshi-Soy Vinaigrette

Many people love the summery-fresh taste of dill. In this recipe, dill is paired with an Asian-inspired combination of sweet and salty ingredients that gives it a richer, deeper undertone. Toss the dressing with delicate sticks of sweet beets, and the result is a wonderful salad or side dish that tastes both familiar and new. Umeboshi vinegar, a deliciously salty Japanese plum vinegar, is readily available in specialty stores and many supermarkets; it has an entirely unique flavor and no true substitute. *Friend of the Farm.*

SERVES 6

4 large	beets, scrubbed, trimmed
1 tablespoon	finely chopped fresh dill
3 tablespoons	Umeboshi vinegar
1 tablespoon	barley malt or rice syrup
1 tablespoon	soy sauce or tamari
1¹/₂ teaspoons	olive oil

1. Put the beets in a medium pot and cover with water. Bring to a boil over medium-high heat. Reduce to a simmer and cook, uncovered, until tender, about 45 minutes.

2. Drain beets in a colander and run cold water over them. When they are cool enough to handle, rub off the skins. Cut into matchstick-size julienne strips.

3. Put the beets in a large bowl; add the fresh dill.

4. Whisk the Umeboshi vinegar, barley malt or rice syrup, soy sauce or tamari, and olive oil in a small bowl. Pour this mixture over beets and toss until well combined. Set aside at room temperature to marinate for at least 30 minutes.

Sautéed Beet and Potato Hash

with Onion and Thyme

This is an easy, hearty side dish. The key is giving it a peppery punch. It's delicious with steamed beet greens (or other greens) and seasoned, baked, or broiled tofu. *Shareholder.*

SERVES 4

3 tablespoons	vegetable oil
2 small	onions, diced
4 medium	red or white potatoes, peeled, grated
2 medium	beets, peeled, grated (2–3 cups)
2 teaspoons	fresh thyme leaves or
1 teaspoon	dried thyme
1 teaspoon	minced garlic (about 2 medium cloves)
	salt
1/2 teaspoon	freshly ground black pepper

1. Heat the oil in a large skillet over medium heat. Add the onions; cook and stir until soft and translucent, 5 to 7 minutes.

2. Stir in the potatoes, beets, thyme, and garlic. Season with salt to taste. Cook, turning it occasionally, until the potatoes and beets are tender and slightly crispy, 15 to 20 minutes.

3. Remove the skillet from heat. Season generously with pepper, and more salt if desired, to taste.

Beet and Brown Rice Salad

with Toasted Sesame Seeds and Sesame Dressing

In this nutritious dish, sesame oil and spices subdue the flavors of beets and arame seaweed. It is quick to make once the rice and seaweed are cooked. Shareholder Heidi adds that the salty tartness of Umeboshi plum vinegar and the mellow smoothness of brown rice vinegar combine to create a distinctive and tasty blend. *Shareholder.*

SERVES 2 TO 4

4 cups	cooked brown rice
1 large	beet, grated (2–3 cups)
1 cup	arame seaweed
1/4 cup	sesame seeds
1/2 cup	thinly sliced scallions (about 3 scallions)
1/2 cup	toasted sesame oil
1/3 cup	brown rice vinegar
1 tablespoon	Umeboshi vinegar
3 cloves	garlic, minced (about 1 1/2 teaspoons)
	salt
	freshly ground black pepper

1. Put the rice and beets in a large bowl. In a separate bowl, cover the arame with water and soak for 15 minutes.

2. Place a small, heavy skillet over medium heat. Add the sesame seeds and stir them on the dry skillet just until lightly browned and fragrant, 3 to 5 minutes, watching closely to avoid burning them. Immediately remove from heat and transfer the toasted seeds to a dish to cool.

3. Bring 1 quart of water to a boil. Reduce to a simmer and lower undrained arame into the pot. Simmer, uncovered, until tender, 8 to 10 minutes.

4. Meanwhile, combine the scallions, sesame oil, brown rice vinegar, Umeboshi vinegar, and garlic in a large jar. With the lid tightly screwed on, shake the jar vigorously until the oil and vinegar no longer separate. Season with salt and pepper to taste.

5. Drain the seaweed in a colander; add it to the beets and rice and toss briefly. Add the oil and vinegar mixture and toss thoroughly.

6. Chill at least 1 hour or overnight. Serve chilled.

Sautéed Beets

with Turmeric and Toasted Black Mustard Seeds

Nippy, freshly toasted black mustard seeds are a familiar ingredient in Indian cooking. In this Indian-inspired recipe, their pungent flavor brings out the natural sweetness of the beets. You can use vegetable oil instead of ghee, though ghee is the preferred oil for Indian cooking. Before you add the seeds to the skillet, be sure you have a lid or a large piece of foil handy, as they will hop and pop while you toast them. Shareholder Laura once said: "I'm not usually a lover of beet dishes, but this recipe brings out our pink friend's best characteristics." *Shareholder.*

SERVES 4 TO 5

1 1/2 pounds	beets, peeled, cut into matchsticks
1/2 teaspoon	turmeric
2 tablespoons	ghee or vegetable oil
1/2 teaspoon	black mustard seeds
1 teaspoon	salt
1 teaspoon	sugar

1. Put the beets and turmeric in a large pot. Fill with enough water to barely cover the beets. Bring to a boil over medium-high heat. Cook, uncovered, until tender but still firm, 5 to 10 minutes.

2. Drain beets and set them aside to cool.

3. Heat the ghee or oil and the mustard seeds in a large skillet. As the mustard seeds begin to pop, place a lid over the skillet for a few seconds (to prevent the seeds from popping out), then add the beets. Cook and stir constantly, uncovered, for 1 minute.

4. Sprinkle the salt and sugar over beet mixture and cook for 1 minute more. Remove the skillet from heat. Season with more salt to taste if desired. Serve hot, at room temperature, or chilled.

Beet Slices

in Creamy Mustard Sauce

The pungent flavor of mustard is wonderful with the sweetness of beets. For this recipe, tender cooked beets are sliced and warmed in a creamy and delicious mustard sauce. If you cook the beets ahead of time, this becomes a low-fuss, high-impact side dish you can prepare and serve almost instantly. *Angelic Organics Kitchen* (adapted from *Greene on Greens*).

SERVES 4

1 1/2 pounds	beets, scrubbed, trimmed
3 tablespoons	unsalted butter
1/4 cup	chopped shallot or red onion
1 tablespoon	all-purpose flour
1/2 cup	vegetable or chicken stock
1/4 cup	milk
3 tablespoons	prepared Dijon mustard
	salt and freshly ground black pepper
	chopped fresh parsley

1. Preheat the oven to 400°F.

2. Place beets in a small roasting pan with 1/2 cup water. Cover with foil and bake until beets are easily pierced with a sharp knife, 45 minutes to 1 hour depending on size. Allow beets to cool slightly, then run under cold water and slip off their skins. Slice the beets in half; cut each half into 1/4-inch wedges.

3. Melt the butter in a large skillet over medium-low heat. Add the shallot or red onion; cook, stirring, for 4 minutes. Add flour and stir constantly for 2 minutes. Whisk in the stock, milk, and mustard. Cook and stir the mixture until slightly thickened. Add the beets, continuing to cook and stir until they are warmed through, about 10 minutes.

4. Remove the skillet from heat. Season with salt and pepper to taste and garnish with parsley.

Hot or Cold Creamy Beet Soup
with Buttermilk and Hard-Cooked Eggs

"This soup always makes me feel that summer has officially arrived," says recipe-tester Jone. For a heartier soup, you can add boiled, cubed potatoes or cooked shrimp. *Shareholder.*

SERVES 4 TO 5

3 medium	beets, scrubbed
5	scallions, both white and green parts, finely chopped
3	eggs, hard-cooked, diced
1 medium	cucumber, peeled if thick-skinned, seeded, diced
4 cups	buttermilk
4 cups	whole milk
1 tablespoon	finely chopped fresh dill plus more for garnish

salt
freshly ground black pepper

1. Preheat the oven to 400° F.

2. Place beets in a small roasting pan with 1/2 cup water. Cover with foil and bake until easily pierced with a sharp knife, 45 minutes to 1 hour depending on size. Allow beets to cool slightly, then run under cold water and slip off their skins.

3. Grate the beets into a large pot. Add the scallions, eggs, cucumber, buttermilk, milk, and dill; stir until well combined. Season with salt and pepper to taste. Serve immediately, or warm over low heat before serving. Garnish with fresh dill if desired.

Grated Raw Beet Salad
with Fresh Dill and Mustard Vinaigrette

Marinating raw beets tenderizes them very slightly, transforming their hearty crunch to a delectable tender-crispness. Serve this tangy-sweet salad on lettuce, over cottage cheese, or as an unusual and colorful condiment. You can make the dish a day ahead of time and let it marinate in the refrigerator to concentrate the flavor. *Angelic Organics Kitchen*

SERVES 6

4 medium	beets, peeled, coarsely grated (3–4 cups)
1/2 cup	olive oil
3 tablespoons	white wine vinegar
1 tablespoon	finely chopped shallot
1 teaspoon	prepared Dijon mustard
1 small clove	garlic, minced or pressed (about 1/2 teaspoon)
	salt
	freshly ground black pepper
1–2 tablespoons	finely chopped fresh dill

1. Put the grated beets in a large salad bowl.

2. Combine the olive oil, vinegar, shallot, mustard, and garlic in a large jar. With the lid tightly screwed on, shake the jar vigorously until the oil and vinegar are thickened (an easy, surefire way to get a good, thick vinaigrette).

3. Pour the dressing over the beets and toss until well coated. Season with salt and pepper to taste. Transfer beet mixture to the refrigerator to marinate for at least 1 hour.

4. Add the fresh dill, toss again, and serve chilled.

Baked Beet-and-Carrot Burgers

with Brown Rice, Sunflower Seeds, and Cheddar Cheese

If you like veggie burgers, you'll love this recipe. Sweet beets and carrots give luscious flavor to these patties—together with pungent onion, snappy Cheddar cheese, and lots of toasty nuts and seeds. Recipe-tester Lisa says these burgers are good on wheat buns with mayo and tomato. Lisa also mentions that additional flour and egg could be substituted for the rice. Cooks who dislike frying will appreciate this recipe, which calls for baking the patties in the oven. *Angelic Organics Kitchen* (adapted from the *Rose Valley Farm Food Book*).

MAKES 12 PATTIES

	butter for greasing the baking sheet
1/2 cup	sesame seeds
1 cup	sunflower seeds
2 cups	peeled, grated beets (1–2 medium beets)
2 cups	grated carrots (about 4 carrots)
1/2 cup	minced onion (about 1 medium onion)
2 eggs,	lightly beaten
1 cup	cooked brown rice
1 cup	grated Cheddar cheese
1/2 cup	vegetable oil
1/2 cup	finely chopped fresh parsley
3 tablespoons	flour
2 tablespoons	soy sauce or tamari
1 clove	garlic, minced or pressed (about 1/2 teaspoon)
1/8–1/4 teaspoon	cayenne pepper

1. Preheat the oven to 350°F. Lightly coat a baking sheet with butter.

2. Place a small, heavy skillet over medium heat. Add the sesame seeds and stir them on the dry skillet just until lightly browned and fragrant, 3 to 5 minutes, watching closely to avoid burning them. Immediately remove from heat and transfer the toasted seeds to a dish to cool.

3. Return the skillet to the heat. Add the sunflower seeds and stir them on the dry skillet just until lightly browned and fragrant, 3 to 5 minutes, watching closely to avoid burning them. Immediately transfer them to the dish with the sesame seeds.

4. Combine the beets, carrots, and onion in a large bowl. Stir in the toasted sunflower and sesame seeds, eggs, rice, Cheddar cheese, oil, flour, parsley, soy sauce or tamari, and garlic (your hands work best here). Add cayenne (use 1/4 teaspoon for spicier burgers) and mix until thoroughly combined.

5. Using your hands, shape the mixture into 12 patties and arrange them in rows on the baking sheet.

6. Bake the patties until brown around the edges, about 20 minutes. Unless they are very large and thick, it should not be necessary to turn them. Serve alone or on buns.

The Crop

HARVEST WEEK 1, 1995, NEWSLETTER

Welcome to our summer garden—our slow summer garden. As I began writing these newsletter notes, I glanced at our first newsletter from last summer to compare the goods. Then I pouted. The herbs and greens are about the same this year as they were last year. But I miss beets. Our teensy beets are hiding underground. I imagine them hanging out at their pedicurist's getting their toenails painted red as some token of their intention to display their color. For some of you who aren't so fond of beets, it's a relief that they are taking their time.

—FARM WORKER

Broiled Beet Slices
with Maple-Teriyaki Sauce

In this dish, tender slices of baked beets are coated in a garlicky-sweet teriyaki sauce and placed under the broiler. Shareholder Judy affirms that the results are irresistible. *Angelic Organics Kitchen* (adapted from the *Winter Harvest Cookbook*).

SERVES 4 TO 6

12 small or	
6 medium	beets, scrubbed, trimmed
1/4 cup	butter
2 tablespoons	maple syrup
1 tablespoon	minced or pressed garlic (about 6 cloves)
1 tablespoon	finely chopped or grated fresh ginger
1 tablespoon	soy sauce or tamari

1. Preheat the oven to 400° F.

2. Place beets in a small roasting pan with 1/2 cup water. Cover with foil and bake until beets are easily pierced with a sharp knife, 45 minutes to 1 hour depending on size.

3. Preheat the broiler.

4. Allow beets to cool slightly, then run under cold water and slip off their skins. Slice into 1/4-inch rounds.

5. Melt the butter in a small pan over medium heat. Stir in the maple syrup, garlic, ginger, and soy sauce or tamari. When the ingredients are thoroughly combined, remove from heat.

6. Put the beets in a shallow baking pan and pour the maple syrup mixture over them. Broil, stirring occasionally, until tender, 5 to 10 minutes.

Overheard

Our Field Manager: I dreamed that I was playing football in a grocery store with a bunch of beets. These people came running down the aisle. My mom went for a touchdown. Being a small person, she jumped into an empty meat cooler lined with green Astroturf to score.

The Crew

HARVEST WEEK 4, 1998, NEWSLETTER

Rescued the tomatoes from the onslaught of weeds. Uncovered melons. Planted the second succession of zucchini and summer squash and the third succession of cucumbers. Trellised tomatoes. Cultivated melons, cucumbers, carrots, and lettuce. Seeded more fall beets in the greenhouse. Prepared the first fall brassica field for planting. Frantically transplanted one bed of lettuce and seeded mesclun as the storm rolled in on Friday. Got rained on. Harvested and packed more than 600 boxes.

The Crop

HARVEST WEEK 1, 1995, NEWSLETTER

Welcome to our summer garden—our slow summer garden. As I began writing these newsletter notes, I glanced at our first newsletter from last summer to compare the goods. Then I pouted. The herbs and greens are about the same this year as they were last year. But I miss beets. Our teensy beets are hiding underground. I imagine them hanging out at their pedicurist's getting their toenails painted red as some token of their intention to display their color. For some of you who aren't so fond of beets, it's a relief that they are taking their time.

—FARM WORKER

Chocolate Beet Cake

Even confirmed beet-bashers will love this cake. The beets give it their moisture, their sweetness, and their rich color—but none of their beet flavor. If you don't have a double boiler, you can easily rig one up with what you have in your kitchen; try using a sauté or omelette pan that fits over the edges of a small pot filled with water. And if you don't have a Bundt pan, you can bake the batter in two loaf pans, checking for doneness after about 25 minutes and covering the pans with foil if the cakes brown too quickly. *Angelic Organics Kitchen*.

SERVES 10 TO 12

	oil and flour for preparing the pan
4 ounces	unsweetened chocolate
1 cup	mild-flavored vegetable oil, divided
3	eggs
1³/₄ cups	sugar
2 cups	puréed cooked beets (3 medium beets)
1 tablespoon	vanilla extract
1¹/₂ cups	all-purpose flour
¹/₂ cup	whole wheat pastry flour
2 teaspoons	baking soda
¹/₄ teaspoon	salt
	powdered sugar

1. Preheat the oven to 375° F. Lightly coat a 10-cup Bundt or tube pan with oil and dust it with flour.

2. Partially fill the bottom of a double boiler with water and bring to a boil over high heat; reduce to a simmer. Put the chocolate and ¹/₄ cup of the oil in the top of the double boiler. Heat just until the chocolate melts; remove from heat and stir until well combined.

3. Combine the eggs and sugar in a large bowl and beat with an electric mixer until fluffy. Slowly beat in the remaining ³/₄ cup oil, chocolate mixture, beets, and vanilla.

4. Sift the all-purpose flour and whole-wheat pastry flour into a large bowl. Stir in the baking soda and salt. Gently stir the flour mixture into the egg and chocolate mixture just until flour is mixed in. Pour batter into the prepared pan.

5. Bake until a toothpick inserted near the center comes out clean, about 45 minutes. Remove the pan from the oven and set it on a wire rack to cool for 30 minutes.

6. Carefully remove the cake from the pan and let cool on the rack. When completely cool, dust with powdered sugar.

Chicories

Endive, Escarole, Radicchio

The somewhat bitter-tasting greens of the chicory family can be wonderfully refreshing during the hot days of late spring and summer. In the same way that a squeeze of lemon can bring a dish to life, these snappy greens will accent whatever milder or sweeter ingredients they are mixed with, adding an exciting complexity and depth to the flavors. When chicories are cooked, they reveal a softer side, becoming tender and surprisingly sweet. Cooked or raw, a chicory dish is a delightful component of any meal.

Chicories Commonly Grown

Endive, also known as frisée, has coarse, frilly, dark green leaves that are pleasantly tangy and delicious eaten raw or lightly steamed.

Escarole has thinner, wavy, broad leaves with a tart, bittersweet taste that makes it a pungent addition to salads. Escarole also is a fantastic ingredient in cooked recipes.

Radicchio, with its compact head of white veined, purple-red leaves, looks like a small red cabbage and has a bitter, peppery taste. Raw radicchio provides an interesting and pretty accent for a green salad, while cooked radicchio gives a wonderful savory-sweetness to a dish.

Storage

Keep unwashed chicories in a perforated plastic bag in the refrigerator's vegetable bin for up to a week.

Farmer John Writes

They stand around, discussing the merits of cosmic pipes and energy wheels in their drawls and twangs. They debate the intricacies of rain machines and free energy. They lumber about the exhibition hall, muttering in farmer dialects, their big, chunky hands swinging pendulums, trying to figure out which product to buy or which booth to visit.

—FROM JOHN'S BOOK *FARMER JOHN ON GLITTER & GREASE*

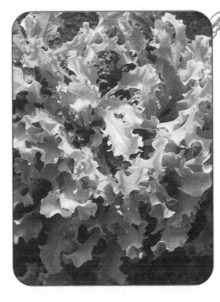

Overheard

I know almost nothing about chicories. Almost nothing. I like cookies, and chicories are not cookies.

Our Cook

Endive and escarole both have a slightly bitter flavor, endive more so than escarole. These greens are perfect partners in a raw salad, especially if a sweeter green—such as red leaf lettuce—is mixed in. Herbs like parsley, fennel, mint, and basil and even young and tender mesclun mix can add sweetness as well. Endive and escarole can also be cut into strips and added to soups. My favorite way to indulge in their romantic flavors is to use the younger inner leaves in a salad and have the larger, more bitter leaves in a cooked dish at the same meal. Cooking tends to bring a sweet flavor to the leaves. I also usually add roasted nuts and something sweet—like raisins, anise hyssop, or chopped sun-dried tomatoes—to any salad that contains anything slightly bitter.

In the West we haven't seemed to develop the same affinity for bitter flavors that other cuisines include. The Italians like to sauté bitters with pasta, garlic, and olive oil. In Greece bitter cooked salads are quite popular.

A Shareholder

I work on a cardiac unit in the hospital here, and I brought our busy report session to a halt on Wednesday by going on and on about how buoyed I was that morning knowing my first box was on its way. We all started talking about cooking from scratch and the joy of fresh, unpoisoned veggies. One nurse had been in the Philippines and reminisced about the open-air markets and cooking there.

We were dragged back soon to the realities of our urgency ridden surroundings, but we had all enjoyed the earthy time of nourishment that we had talking about Angelic Organics.

Handling

Since chicory leaves bruise where cut, prepare them as close to serving time as possible. Slice endive and escarole at the base with a sharp knife and let the leaves fall open. Discard or compost the outer leaves if they are withered or damaged. Wash endive and escarole in a large basin of cold water, being sure to thoroughly clean the base of the leaves, which sometimes hoards grit and dirt. For radicchio, discard any old or limp outer leaves and wash the head thoroughly in cold water. Drain or dry the chicory and cut it according to the specifications of your recipe.

Culinary Uses

❖ Eat the larger, outer leaves raw if you relish more bitter flavors.

❖ To cut the leaves' bitterness, boil them until just tender and dress them with lemon juice or vinegar and salt.

❖ Make a milder salad from fresh, uncooked chicories by combining the younger, inner leaves with lettuce and any combination of richer ingredients like olives, spicy cheeses, and hard-cooked eggs. Or, toss the greens with something sweet, like apples or raisins, or a sweet dressing.

❖ Slice any chicories into strips and sauté or stir-fry them in oil or butter.

❖ Roast radicchio: quarter the tight heads, lightly coat them in oil, and roast at 425° F for 20 minutes, turning halfway through cooking.

❖ Grill marinated radicchio: serve cooked chicories with risotto, white beans, polenta, or hearty whole-grain pasta.

Partners for Chicories

❖ Basil, cilantro, garlic, lemon balm, parsley, red pepper flakes, thyme;
❖ Balsamic vinegar, lemon juice, olive oil, red wine vinegar;
❖ Asiago cheese, butter, cream, Gruyère cheese, hard-cooked egg, Parmesan cheese;
❖ Grilled vegetables, lettuce, mesclun, scallions;
❖ Capers, fresh shell beans, nuts, olives, pasta, rice.

Lettuce—bed preparation, transplanting, growing, harvesting

Broccoli seedlings

Fennel, scallions, hearts of radish, turnips

Weeding, weeding, weeding . . . do these kids really want to farm?

Cucumber harvest, flying chard, Farmer
John in sweet clover cover crop

Parsley and anise hyssop, herb harvest

Onions growing, hoeing squash,
sweet onions

Mesclun harvest, turnip topping, kale

Farmer John and Assistant Editor Lesley
Littlefield Freeman, Allis G tractor, metal
meets metal

Steamed Chicory
with Pine Nuts and Raisins

This lovely, simple recipe accentuates the bittersweet taste of cooked chicory by pairing it with fruits and nuts. The plump, juicy raisins and silky-crisp pine nuts strike a perfect note with the simply prepared greens. You can make a terrific and very pretty variation on this dish by substituting dried cranberries for the raisins and slivered almonds for the pine nuts. Or try chopped dried apricots (use unsulfured for a deeper flavor) and toasted chopped pecans or walnuts. *Friend of the Farm.*

SERVES 4

3 tablespoons	raisins
1 pound	chicories, such as endive, escarole, or radicchio, leaves separated but left whole (if you're using radicchio, simply cut it into quarters)
1/4 cup	extra virgin olive oil
2 cloves	garlic, peeled, thinly sliced
3 tablespoons	pine nuts
	salt
	freshly ground black pepper

1. Put the raisins in a bowl and cover with boiling water. Set aside to plump, then drain.

2. Put the chicory in a steamer basket, set over 1½ inches boiling water, and cover. Steam just until wilted, 2 to 4 minutes. Transfer the greens to a colander to drain.

3. Heat the oil in a large skillet over medium-high heat. Add the garlic and pine nuts and cook, stirring constantly, until the pine nuts begin to brown in spots, about 3 minutes.

4. Give the greens a few chops on a cutting board, then add them to the skillet and stir until the greens are well coated with the oil. Remove from heat and stir in the raisins. Season with salt and pepper to taste.

Roasted Radicchio
with Gorgonzola and Balsamic Vinegar

Roasting brings out a concentrated, natural sweetness in radicchio. This dish is unusual, elegant, simple—and delicious. Served on a bed of risotto, it makes an attractive meal. If you're not a Gorgonzola fan, this is equally delicious with Brie, Swiss, aged Cheddar, or smoked Gouda. You can substitute lemon juice for the balsamic vinegar. *Friend of the Farm.*

SERVES 4

1 medium head	radicchio, cut into 2-inch wedges
1/4 cup	olive oil
	salt
	freshly ground black pepper
	balsamic vinegar
4–6 ounces	Gorgonzola (or other cheese), sliced

1. Preheat the oven to 400° F. Lightly oil a 2-quart baking dish.

2. Using a pastry brush, brush the radicchio generously with olive oil and place in a single layer in the baking dish. Season with salt and pepper.

3. Bake the radicchio for 20 minutes, turning wedges over once midway through cooking. Drizzle with balsamic vinegar and top with cheese. Return to the oven until cheese is melted, about 5 minutes.

> ## A Shareholder
> Sincere thanks for such a warm introduction to "vital vegetables." I thoroughly enjoy the surprises in my weekly box. I can feel the difference wellness-wise.

Puffy Endive Frittata

Lighter and more sophisticated than an omelette, but a great deal less fussy than a quiche, a frittata is a brilliant solution for an easy and elegant egg-based meal. Our Farm Cook asserts that the secret to flavor in this dish is long, slow cooking, which deepens and sweetens the flavors. You can substitute escarole or radicchio for the endive in this recipe, but because of their heartier textures, they might require slightly longer cooking before they yield their sweet flavor. *Angelic Organics Kitchen.*

SERVES 6

2 tablespoons	extra virgin olive oil or butter
1 large	onion (red or white), thinly sliced
1	endive, chopped
1 clove	garlic, minced (about 1/2 teaspoon)
8	eggs
4 tablespoons	finely chopped fresh herbs (any combination of parsley, basil, cilantro, or thyme)
1/4 teaspoon	salt
1/4 teaspoon	freshly ground black pepper
1 cup	grated Gruyère cheese
2 tablespoons	freshly grated Parmesan cheese, divided

1. Heat the oil over low heat in a medium (preferably nonstick) skillet with an ovenproof handle. Add the onion; cook, stirring occasionally, until it is soft but not browned, about 15 minutes.

2. Add the chopped endive; cook, stirring occasionally, until it is tender and the moisture has cooked off, about 15 minutes. Add the garlic.

3. Lightly beat the eggs in a large bowl. Stir in the herbs, salt, and pepper. Pour the egg mixture into the skillet. Add the Gruyère and 1 tablespoon of the Parmesan.

4. Preheat the broiler.

5. Cook the mixture in the skillet over very low heat, without stirring, until the eggs are set on top but still a little moist, 10 to 15 minutes. Remove the skillet from heat.

6. Sprinkle the remaining 1 tablespoon of Parmesan on top of the frittata. Place the skillet under the broiler; broil the frittata until it is lightly browned on top, about 1 minute. If not brown to your satisfaction after 1 minute, continue cooking under the broiler, checking every 30 seconds.

7. Remove the skillet from the broiler. Slice the frittata into wedges and serve. Wrap any leftovers and store at room temperature up to one day.

The Crew

HARVEST WEEK 1, 1996, NEWSLETTER

We just caught up with planting in a great flurry of machines, people, water, and dust, and now we've plunged into the first week of harvest and packing.

Baked Chicory and Rice
with Crispy Parmesan Crust

This dish makes a terrific grain-based side dish or a complete meal. It is full of wonderful texture (tender escarole, firm rice, and crispy-melty crust) and bright flavor (savory cooked chicory, lemony sorrel, tangy Parmesan) and is delicious served hot or cold. The sorrel infuses this dish with an irresistible lemony aroma. If you cannot find sorrel, you might like to try a few chopped lemon balm leaves. *Friend of the Farm.*

SERVES 6 TO 8

	butter for greasing the baking dish
1/3 cup plus 3 tablespoons	olive oil, divided
1 medium	onion, chopped
2 teaspoons	finely chopped or pressed garlic
2 1/2 pounds	escarole or radicchio, chopped
1/2 cup	chopped sorrel leaves (optional)
1/2 cup	uncooked white rice
	salt
3/4 cup	freshly grated Parmesan cheese, divided
	freshly ground black pepper
1/2 cup	fresh bread crumbs

1. Lightly coat a medium baking dish with butter.

2. Place a large pot over medium heat. Heat 1/3 cup of the olive oil in the pot. Add the onion. Cook until the onion is wilted, about 5 minutes.

3. Add the garlic and cook, stirring, for 30 seconds. Add a large handful of the chopped escarole and stir until it is thoroughly coated with oil. Continue adding handfuls of escarole and stirring them in until all of the escarole is added and wilted. Add the sorrel and continue to cook the mixture, stirring occasionally, until the escarole is tender, 7 to 8 minutes.

4. Preheat the oven to 400° F.

5. Fill a medium pot with water and bring it to a boil over high heat. Add the rice and a dash of salt. Boil the rice for 5 minutes, then drain the rice in a colander. Put the rice back into the pot and set over low heat.

6. Transfer the cooked escarole along with 1/2 cup of the cooking liquid to the pot with the rice. Add 1/2 cup of the Parmesan cheese. Stir the ingredients until combined. Season with salt and pepper to taste.

7. Transfer the escarole mixture to the prepared baking dish and smooth the top with a spatula. Sprinkle the bread crumbs and the remaining 1/4 cup Parmesan cheese on top. Drizzle the remaining 3 tablespoons of olive oil over the topping. Bake until the rice is tender, 30 to 40 minutes. Serve warm.

The Crew

HARVEST WEEK 7, 1997, NEWSLETTER
Worked on shade construction in packing area. Transplanted 2,700 lettuces and 5,000 kohlrabi. Seeded beets, spinach, cilantro, and mesclun mix. Hand weeded 13,000 row-feet of leeks, herbs, beets, and carrots. Thinned 5,400 row-feet of carrots. Tractor cultivated brassicas. Constructed a new electric fence. Sprayed Biodynamic Preparation 501 (potentized silica) on all flowering plants. Seeded 2,700 lettuces and 2,000 choi in the greenhouse. Hosted a gathering of farmers and interns from various Wisconsin farms. Harvested and packed 500 boxes.

Choi

Choi (also spelled choy) has been cultivated in China for centuries and is now commonly found in markets in the United States. With good reason, this member of the cabbage family is becoming a favorite among chefs and health-conscious cooks worldwide. Choi grows in elongated, upright heads of dark green leaves with large, white (or sometimes green) stems. Since the texture of the leaves differs from that of the stems, choi is practically two vegetables in one. The leaves can be cooked and eaten like spinach, while the crisp stems—sweet and mild in flavor—can be used like celery or asparagus.

Storage

Refrigerate unwashed choi in a plastic container or loosely wrapped in a plastic bag. Choi keeps for over a week but is firmest and tastiest if used within a few days.

Handling

Just before using, rinse choi under cold running water and gently shake it dry. Because the thick stems and tender leaves will require different cooking times and will usually be added separately, cut the stems from the leaves. Cut the stems into 1-inch pieces and slice, shred, or tear the leaves. If you will be eating the stems raw, slice or julienne them.

Culinary Uses

A small choi is mild enough to eat raw. The stems resemble celery without the "strings."

❖ Include small choi leaves as a tasty addition to a raw vegetable platter.

❖ Add the uncooked, shredded leaves of a small choi to salads.

❖ Full-grown choi have a sharper flavor and texture that softens with cooking.

❖ Steam choi and top with toasted sesame oil, butter, salt, or vinaigrette.

❖ Add it to stir-fries or other cooked dishes: put the stems in first, for 1 to 2 minutes near the end of cooking, then add the leaves for the last 1 to 3 minutes.

❖ Use the shredded leaves as a last-minute garnish for soups.

Partners for Choi*

❖ Basil, chili powder, cilantro, coriander, curry, fennel, garlic, ginger, lemon balm, rosemary, tarragon;

❖ Lemon juice, peanut oil, sesame oil, soy sauce or tamari, vinegar;

❖ Butter, coconut milk;

❖ Sesame seeds, roasted cashews;

❖ Asparagus, baby corn, broccoli, carrots, celery, hot peppers, mushrooms, shallots, snow peas, zucchini;

❖ Beans, rice, water chestnuts.

*See Louise Frazier's Complementary Herbs & Spices chart, page 345, for suggestions.

Stir-Fried Choi with Mushrooms and Cashews
over Rice Noodles

Choi is an Asian vegetable, so it's no surprise that it features prominently in many excellent Asian and Asian-inspired recipes. A traditional soy-sesame-rice combination is the base for this delicious noodle salad, which pairs succulent cooked choi with earthy mushrooms and sweet cashews. This is a perfect dish for a balmy summer day; it is light and refreshing but substantial and satisfying, too. Readily available in Asian grocery stores and many supermarkets, delicate rice noodles are quick to prepare and taste wonderful chilled. *Angelic Organics Kitchen* (adapted from *Judy Gorman's Vegetable Cookbook*).

SERVES 4 TO 6

1/4 cup	coarsely chopped, unsalted cashews
8 ounces	dry rice noodles
6 tablespoons	peanut oil or mild-flavored vegetable oil, divided
1 medium	choi (any kind), stems cut diagonally into 1/4-inch pieces, leaves sliced into 1/2 inch strips
8	fresh shiitake mushrooms, sliced, OR
8	dried shiitake mushrooms, rehydrated in hot water for 20 minutes, strained and sliced, water reserved
3	scallions, sliced in half lengthwise, then sliced crosswise into 1-inch pieces
1/4 cup	water (if you're using dried shiitakes, use 1/4 cup of the soaking water instead)
2 tablespoons	rice vinegar
2 tablespoons	soy sauce or tamari
1 teaspoon	toasted sesame oil
	sugar (optional)
1 tablespoon	chopped fresh cilantro leaves

1. Preheat the oven to 350° F.

2. Toast the cashews in a heavy (preferably cast iron) dry skillet over high heat until they begin to brown slightly. Transfer the nuts to a dish to cool.

3. Cook the rice noodles according to the directions on the package.

4. Meanwhile, heat a wok over high heat for 2 minutes. Add 3 tablespoons of the peanut oil and let heat for 30 seconds. Add the sliced choi stems and stir-fry for 2 minutes.

5. Add the mushrooms, scallions, and choi leaves. Add the water (or shiitake soaking liquid). Cook, stirring constantly, until most of the liquid has evaporated, 8 to 12 minutes.

6. In a small bowl, whisk the remaining 3 tablespoons of peanut or vegetable oil, rice vinegar, soy sauce or tamari, and toasted sesame oil. Add a little sugar to taste, if desired. Pour this mixture over the vegetables in the wok and toss until well combined.

7. Drain the noodles and add them to the wok along with the sauce. Toss to thoroughly combine. Serve warm or chill for 1 to 2 hours. Garnish with the cashews and cilantro just before serving.

Our Cook

Succulent oval leaves around bright white, crisp, juicy stems. The leaves of the mild greens are good in salads, with the stem chopped finely like celery. My favorite way to prepare this soothing and watery vegetable, however, is stir-fried. It can be good all by itself, but I prefer to mix it with something sweet, like carrots—plus some garlic, broccoli, peas, beans, ginger, some tamari or shoyu—and a splash of lemon juice or rice vinegar. Choi is also a classic green for soups. To roast choi, cut the whole head lengthwise into quarters and roast them for 15 minutes on each side. Brush the open sides with a little extra oil as well. After removing them from the oven, salt to taste and serve.

Choi Salad with Fruit
and Creamy Poppy Seed Dressing

If you enjoy the tangy-sweet taste that comes from adding mandarin orange segments, raisins, or chunks of apple to a salad, then you already know how delicious fruit and salad dressing can be. In this salad, choi provides a succulent base for a mixture of apples, grapes, mild onion, and freshly toasted almonds, all smothered in a luxurious poppy seed dressing. (The sneaky secret to the dressing's impossible smoothness is silken tofu, which purées beautifully and makes an exceptional, flavorless base for soups, sauces, and dressings. Don't tell anyone it's in there; they'll never guess.) This recipe yields more than 2 cups of dressing, so you'll have plenty left over for other salads. Silken tofu is widely available in grocery stores and health food stores. *Friend of the Farm*.

SERVES 4 TO 6

1/2 cup	slivered, blanched almonds
1 cup	mild-flavored vegetable oil
1/2 cup	honey
1/2 cup	white vinegar
4 ounces	soft silken tofu
2 tablespoons	poppy seeds
1 1/2 teaspoons	dry mustard
1 1/4 teaspoons	salt
1 teaspoon	paprika (optional)
2 tablespoons	minced onion
1	pac choi or other white-stemmed choi, trimmed, stems cut diagonally into thin slices, leaves sliced into thin strips
1 large	sweet apple, peeled, cored, diced
1 cup	red or purple seedless grapes, halved
	salt
	freshly ground black pepper

1. Toast the almonds in a heavy (preferably cast iron) skillet over high heat until they begin to brown slightly. Transfer the nuts to a bowl to cool.

2. Put the oil, honey, vinegar, tofu, poppy seeds, dry mustard, salt, and paprika in a food processor or a blender. Process or blend the ingredients until smooth. Pour the mixture into a bowl and stir in the onion. Cover the dressing and store it in the refrigerator until you are ready to serve the salad.

3. Toss the choi, apple, and grapes in a large bowl.

4. Pour the dressing over the ingredients; toss until everything is thoroughly combined. Cover the bowl and set it aside at room temperature for 15 minutes to let the flavors develop.

5. When you're ready to serve, stir in the toasted almonds. Season with salt and pepper to taste.

Choi Relish
with Mustard and Yogurt

With the bite of mustard and as much fiery chile as you care to add, this relish definitely has heat. At the same time, its succulent morsels of cooling choi and a base of refreshing yogurt quench the very fire it sets. Enjoy this as you would any spicy or cooling condiment: on a veggie burger, baked potato, or bratwurst; with steamed vegetables or spicy wilted greens; or on hot or cold soups. Be adventurous. *Friend of the Farm.*

MAKES ABOUT 1¼ CUPS

2 tablespoons	plain yogurt
½ teaspoon	prepared Dijon or Chinese mustard
⅛ teaspoon	freshly ground black pepper
1	scallion, thinly sliced
½–1 teaspoon	finely chopped hot chile pepper (remove stems, seeds, and membranes before chopping)
½	small choi (any kind), stems finely diced, leaves finely chopped (about 1 cup)

1. Combine the yogurt, mustard, black pepper, and scallion in a small bowl. Add ½ teaspoon chile pepper or more if you prefer a hotter relish.

2. Stir in the choi. Serve immediately or cover and store in the refrigerator for up to 8 hours.

HISTORY OF CHOI

Choi has been grown in China since the fifth century, and from there it was introduced throughout Asia. Obscure in Europe, choi later became a more commonly used vegetable when seeds arrived in the late eighteenth century. Chinese migrants who moved to Australia during the Gold Rush brought oriental vegetables with them. When the rush for gold lost its luster, Chinese would-be gold miners became market gardeners growing choi and other leafy greens. Today choi can be found growing on all continents except Antarctica.

The Crop

HARVEST WEEK 3, 1997, NEWSLETTER

The long, cool spring gave way to torrid weather last weekend. Eighteen thousand row-feet of spinach (that's over three feet of spinach for each box) was of fine quality last Friday. By the following Monday, the leaves were scorched, brown, unusable. Tightly budded broccoli on Friday were shocked into flowering over the same weekend. Sweet, succulent lettuces veered toward bitter during the 95-degree days. The choi and first spinach planting, beautiful crops throughout the spring, were shredded by pounding rain and hail and a wind of almost hurricane proportions. These gales also snapped off many zucchini plants at the stems.

Let us add now (before you decide that there won't be any vegetables in your boxes for the rest of the season) that our fields, as a whole, look the best ever. We've learned to roll with the wild 90-degree weather. If a crop is ruined by storm or heat, we have a lot more crops to choose from. If a sweet corn planting doesn't come up due to the cool spring soil, we venture to our greenhouse and start it in flats. If the carrots get pounded off by torrents of rain, we replant them. If the broccoli bolts, we've got cauliflower on line, and cabbage.

Farmer John Writes

"[Andy Warhol] died?" she gulped. "I was thinking about him in the mountains. Andy is dead?"

"Yeah."

"I was planning what to cook. I figured it out when I was skiing."

"He can't come, Isa," I said gently.

Long silence.

"I'm looking around the apartment now. Wherever I look, I see things Andy gave me."

"I'm sorry you didn't have your dinner, Isa. Andy would have liked it."

—FROM JOHN'S BOOK *FARMER JOHN ON GLITTER & GREASE*

Choi with Gingery Butter

Here succulent strips of choi are blanched and then briefly cooked in a delicious, gingery sauce. The sauce has characteristically Asian-inspired flavors, but this recipe uses butter instead of oil for added richness. Don't be fooled by how simple this is; it is an interesting and wonderfully flavorful side dish. If you prefer, you can steam the choi instead of blanching it. Try serving this with rice. *Angelic Organics Kitchen* (adapted from *Judy Gorman's Vegetable Cookbook*).

SERVES 4 TO 6

2 medium	choi (any kind), sliced crosswise into 1-inch strips
6 tablespoons	butter
2 tablespoons	soy sauce or tamari
1 tablespoon	grated or finely chopped fresh ginger
1 clove	garlic, minced or pressed (about 1/2 teaspoon)
1 tablespoon	finely chopped fresh cilantro
	salt
	freshly ground black pepper

1. Bring a large pot of water to a boil. Add the choi; cook until the choi is tender but still crisp, 2 to 3 minutes. Drain the choi in a colander and immediately run under cold water. Drain well.

2. Melt the butter in a large skillet over medium heat. Add the soy sauce, ginger, garlic, and choi; cook, stirring constantly, until the choi is well coated and heated through.

3. Remove the skillet from heat. Stir in the cilantro. Season with salt and pepper to taste. Serve immediately.

> *A Shareholder*
>
> I'm a first-year shareholder, and I love getting my vegetable box each week. I'm pleased to receive wonderful organic produce and support a farm that is very local.

Creamy Choi Soup

This recipe takes the flavors of a Japanese clear vegetable soup and gives them a spin . . . in the blender . . . with a potato and a touch of sour cream. The soup ends up thick and slightly creamy—and, incidentally, a lovely shade of jade green. This is easy to make and truly delicious. You will find toasted sesame oil, sometimes called dark sesame oil, in supermarkets and specialty stores. It has a distinct toasty flavor that will remind you of the best Chinese or Japanese meals you've eaten out. Untoasted or light sesame oil will not impart the same flavor. *Friend of the Farm*.

SERVES 4

1 tablespoon	peanut oil
1/2 cup	chopped scallions (about 3 scallions), divided
3 cloves	garlic, minced (about 1 1/2 teaspoons)
2 teaspoons	coarsely chopped fresh ginger
1 pound	choi (any kind), chopped
1 large	potato, peeled, diced
3 cups	vegetable stock or water
3/4 teaspoon	salt
1/4 teaspoon	freshly ground black pepper
	hot pepper flakes
1 teaspoon	toasted sesame oil
2 tablespoons	sour cream

1. Heat the peanut oil in a medium pot over medium-high heat. Set aside a couple tablespoons of scallions for a garnish. Add the remaining scallions, garlic, and ginger to the pot. Cook, stirring, until fragrant, about 1 minute.

2. Add the choi and potato. Pour in the stock or water and add the salt, pepper, and hot pepper flakes to taste. Increase the heat and bring to a boil; cover, reduce heat, and simmer until the potato is tender, about 20 minutes. Remove the pot from heat. Stir in the toasted sesame oil.

3. Transfer the soup to a food processor or a blender and purée. Ladle soup into individual bowls.

4. Garnish each bowl with a dollop of sour cream and some chopped scallion. Serve immediately.

Collards

Chard

Tetragonia

Cooking Greens

A bunch of cooking greens is strikingly distinct from a bag of salad. Salad greens are so petite that you can almost forget that what you're about to eat is, in fact, a pile of leaves. Not so with cooking greens! Most cooking greens are big. Kale and chard leaves, for example, might grow to be longer than your forearm. Some greens, like those of beets and turnips, come attached to the roots, and you can take the "tops" off yourself. You'll find lots of recipes in this chapter to help you prepare a variety of cooking greens. Don't forget, though, that some cooking greens, like spinach, are excellent raw as well as cooked. To find recipes for salads made with raw "cooking" greens, page through the Salad Greens chapter, page 136.

After eating them a few times, you'll learn why cooking greens are essential to so many cuisines. Their short cooking time, versatility, flavor, and nutritional benefits make for a winning combination. A side dish of greens always rounds out a meal, and, in main dishes, a few tender ribbons of greens curled among vegetables enhances a meal.

Cooking Greens Grown by Angelic Organics

Varieties of cooking greens are basically interchangeable in the kitchen, but when replacing one green with another, be aware that some are stronger in flavor than others, and some have different cooking times. You'll achieve the best results by making substitutions within the same family.

Brassica Family

Collards have large, smooth, paddle-shaped leaves. They contain almost as much calcium as milk. The thick stems require longer cooking than the leaves. Season collards with vinegar, hot pepper sauce, garlic, onions, chile peppers, or lemon.

Kale

*Red
Russian
Kale*

Kale comes in blue-green, reddish green, and red varieties and may have flat or curly leaves. All varieties of kale have jagged-edged leaves and thick stems. Kale has a mild cabbage flavor and aroma when cooked. A longer cooking time is usually best, as it tends to bring out the natural sweetness of these greens. Kale is such a hearty vegetable that a little longer cooking shouldn't result in a mushy texture. Complementary flavors for kale are caraway, dill, thyme, marjoram, tarragon, nutmeg, allspice, and coriander.

Turnip greens are coarse, have a slight bite, and look very similar to radish leaves. It is good to blanch them before cooking. They do well combined with other greens and cooked lightly with oil, vinegar, hot sauce, ground red pepper, sugar, garlic, or onions.

Goosefoot Family

These tangy, tender leaves have a shorter storage life than those of the brassica family, so they should be used promptly to avoid spoilage. They are best cooked lightly, just until the leaves turn bright green and limp. The leaves tend to discolor if heated in aluminum or iron pans, so use stainless steel when cooking greens of the goosefoot family.

Beet greens are medium-sized leaves, and, except for our golden variety (see the chapter on beets, page 57), have bright red veins. Large leaves can be cooked like chard, and small, tender leaves are good in salads. Sauté the greens in butter or steam them, and complement their flavor with tarragon, fennel seeds, caraway, basil, horseradish, ginger, allspice, or coriander. Store the leaves and roots in separate bags.

Swiss chard has expansive, pocketed leaves with stems in a spectrum of colors: red, white, green, yellow. Its leaves are more tender and delicate than other greens. Eat small leaves raw in salads and blanch or steam larger leaves. Season them with marjoram, parsley, lovage, savory, nutmeg, allspice, or paprika.

Spinach has small leaves with thin stems. It can be served raw in salads or lightly cooked. The best spinach results come from briefly blanching, steaming, or sautéing until it turns bright green. Experiment by combining spinach with dill, thyme, lovage, chives, basil, nutmeg, or allspice.

Tetragonia, also known as New Zealand spinach, is not botanically related to spinach but is sometimes grown as a spinach substitute during hot months. Nutritionally, tetragonia contains less iron than spinach but about the same amount of other vitamins and minerals. The small, spade-shaped leaves are more crisp and coarse than spinach and have more stem. Tetragonia is delicious with dill, thyme, lovage, chives, basil, nutmeg, or allspice.

Storage

Cut beet and turnip greens from their roots; store roots separately. Keep dry, unwashed greens in a sealed plastic bag in the refrigerator. Thicker greens will keep up to two weeks, but tender ones like spinach and beet greens should be eaten within a week.

Handling

Just prior to use, swish leaves in a large basin of lukewarm water. After any grit has settled to the bottom, lift the leaves out carefully. Additional rounds of washing may be necessary—especially with spinach, which you may want to wash leaf by leaf. If the sink is full of dirt or if a leaf you sample tastes gritty, the greens probably need to be rinsed again.

How you prepare greens for cooking can make or break a dish. It's fine to leave the stems on small baby greens, but many greens (choi, chard, collards, kale) have thick stems that cook more slowly than the leaves. If stems are not removed, you wind up with either soggy greens or raw stems. Fold each leaf in half and slice out the stem. De-stem several leaves, then stack them up and slice them diagonally into 1-inch-wide ribbons. If you want to use the stems in your dish, slice them ¼ inch thick and begin cooking them before you add the greens.

Culinary Uses

❖ Sauté greens until tender (with the water still clinging to them from their washing), in a covered pot or large sauté pan with olive oil, a pinch of salt, and garlic or onion.

❖ Blanch greens until they wilt, 3 to 10 minutes depending on size, freshness, and type of green. Thinly sliced kale and collards blanch in 3 to 10 minutes; whole leaves blanch in 15 to 20 minutes.

❖ For richer, more lavish greens, dot the cooked greens with butter or cream and season with fresh herbs or salt and pepper.

❖ Serve cooked greens alone as a side dish or use them in soup or with pasta, beans, rice, or potatoes.

❖ Add a few sliced kale greens to soups and stews during the last 10 to 15 minutes of cooking time.

❖ Use cooked spinach and chard in enchiladas, quesadillas, crepes, lasagna, and macaroni and cheese.

❖ For breakfast, sauté slivered greens and garlic in the frying pan before adding to eggs for scrambling. Use leftover cooked greens in omelettes, quiches, or soups.

Partners for Cooking Greens*

❖ Allspice, basil, caraway, celery leaves or seed, chives, coriander, dill, fennel, garlic, ginger, nutmeg, oregano, parsley, paprika, red pepper flakes, sage, savory, tarragon, thyme;

❖ Mustard oil, olive oil, roasted peanut oil, sesame oil, vinegar;

❖ Asiago cheese, butter, cream, Parmesan cheese, Monterey Jack cheese;

❖ Celery, leeks, mushrooms, onion, potatoes;

❖ Hard-cooked eggs, legumes, pasta, rice.

*See Louise Frazier's Complementary Herbs & Spices chart, page 345, for suggestions.

Spinach

Spinach or Tetragonia
and Coconut Banana Curry

The pairing of banana and spinach in the same recipe may seem peculiar at first. However, if you consider all these ingredients as being flavor elements in a good curry, suddenly it makes sense. In fact, the ingredients in this dip truly are the disparate ingredients of a sweet curry dish—and while their texture may become homogenized, their flavors don't. It's worth getting your mind around this one, because the results are special. Serve this with raw or slightly blanched vegetables, crackers, or chips. Try tossing this with rice for a delightful side dish, or serve it with curried chicken. To prepare the curry faster, you can use a 6-ounce can of green lentils (drained) instead of dried lentils. *Friend of the Farm.*

MAKES ABOUT 2 CUPS

1/2 cup	dried green lentils
1 1/2 teaspoons	salt
3/4 pound	spinach leaves, trimmed, chopped (about 2 cups)
2 small ripe	bananas, broken into chunks (about 1 cup)
1 cup	canned coconut milk
6 ounces	cream cheese, softened
2	eggs, hard-cooked
1 small or medium	red onion, cut into wedges
1 clove	garlic, peeled
2 tablespoons	butter, softened
1 tablespoon	curry powder
1 teaspoon	freshly ground black pepper

1. Put the lentils in a medium skillet and cover with water. Bring to a boil over high heat, add the salt, cover, and reduce heat. Cook at a steady simmer until the lentils are soft, about 45 minutes. Add more water if it starts to dry up. Drain.

2. Combine the cooked lentils with the remaining ingredients in a food processor and purée until smooth.

3. Transfer the mixture to a bowl; cover and refrigerate for at least 1 hour. Serve cold or at room temperature.

Shareholders' Serving Suggestions for Tetragonia

*Make gomai (Japanese chilled spinach): steam the tetragonia, then add tamari or soy sauce, sesame seeds, and a sprinkle of sugar or drizzle of honey.

*Use it in a spinach-rice-cheese casserole. It's indistinguishable from spinach and easier to clean, too.

*Stir-fry it with eggplant, kohlrabi, onions, and peppers, and serve it over couscous. It cooks down well while keeping a good texture.

*Clean it and steam it for about ten minutes. Yum!

*Make an omelette filled with sautéed tetragonia, red onion, tomato, pepper, and Kasseri cheese.

*Use it in macaroni and cheese.

*Sauté it with garlic, onions, almonds, scallions, and/or sesame seeds in olive or sesame oil.

*Put it in a sweet-and-sour wilted greens salad.

*Try it on pizza.

*Juice it.

*Put it in a salad or on a sandwich.

*Put it in a quiche.

*Add it to soup.

Shareholders Approve Tetragonia

The early votes are in: based on your postcards, tetragonia is being well received. On her comment card, one shareholder said that even her three-year-old thought it was great. Her nine-year-old had this to say: "It isn't as slippery as spinach when you cook it."

Creamy Spinach and Tarragon Soup
with Apple and Toasted Almonds

Here's a spectacularly fresh perspective on what it takes to make a cream of spinach soup. First, skip the cream. Next, refrain from boiling the spinach and potatoes—and refuse to fry any onions. Then get two lovely crisp apples out of the refrigerator. Set one on the counter next to an avocado, and take the other with you to munch on while you enjoy a little more of your summer's day—perhaps outside on a bench, on a swing, up a tree . . . you've got lots of time. This sumptuously creamy, savory-sweet, and super-fresh raw-ingredients soup won't take more than a moment to prepare. *Friend of the Farm.*

SERVES 2

2 tablespoons	chopped or slivered almonds or other nuts
1	apple, peeled, cored, cut into chunks
1 cup	water
2 cups	coarsely chopped spinach (about 3/4 pound)
1 tablespoon	chopped fresh tarragon, plus 2 small sprigs for garnish
1	ripe avocado, peel and pit removed, quartered
	freshly squeezed juice of 1/2 lemon (about 1 1/2 teaspoons)
1 tablespoon	almond oil or olive oil
1/2 teaspoon	salt (or more, to taste)

1. Toast the almonds in a heavy, dry skillet (preferably cast iron) over medium-high heat, stirring constantly, until they are lightly browned and begin to smell toasty. (Be careful not to overtoast them, as they will burn very quickly once they are toasted.) Transfer nuts to a dish to cool.

2. Put the apple chunks and water in a blender and purée. Add the spinach and tarragon; pulse the blender a few times to partially blend in the leaves. Add the avocado pieces, lemon juice, oil, and 1/2 teaspoon salt. Blend the ingredients until smooth, thinning with more water if necessary (add 1 tablespoon at a time). Add more salt to taste if desired.

3. Pour the soup into two bowls, top with the toasted almonds, and garnish each with a fresh tarragon sprig.

A Shareholder

My husband picked up our first basket of veggies on Wednesday while I was at work, and Thursday morning was as good as Christmas as I went poking through the fridge. I am positively thrilled! I had read in a newsletter that many people try something for the first time because it was in the basket, and I am so grateful you put a list of contents and recipes in the newsletter, or I would have tossed the kale out. Instead, I considered it a challenge. So I made two things I never made before. I started with Sautéed Kale, and while the kale was sautéing, I made Basil Pesto. I didn't have any pine nuts or walnuts, so I made it with sunflower seeds. It was such a success that when I saw that the kale simply wasn't going to cook down enough for me to feel safe eating it, I decided to make Kale Pesto too. Wonderful! And my husband's lips are still smacking. Consider me one happy customer!

Kale and Walnut Pesto

While your Italian grandmother might cringe at this being called a pesto, reassure her that this is just a contemporary spin on that classic dish and that you will continue to also make it with basil and pine nuts. But still, make this dish for her—she will certainly be won over. This version of pesto is particularly good over roasted potatoes, but it works great over pasta, too. You can freeze it, but if you do, don't add the cheese; simply mix it in after the pesto has thawed, when you are ready to serve. *Shareholder* (adapted from the *Seed Savers Calendar, 1998*).

MAKES ABOUT I CUP

¹/₄ cup	chopped walnuts
1 tablespoon plus	
¹/₂ teaspoon	salt, divided
¹/₂ pound	kale, coarsely chopped
2 cloves	garlic, minced (about 1 teaspoon)
¹/₂ cup	extra virgin olive oil
¹/₂ cup	freshly grated Parmesan cheese (about 1¹/₂ ounces)
	freshly ground black pepper

1. Toast the chopped walnuts in a dry, heavy skillet (preferably cast iron) over high heat, stirring constantly, until they start to brown in spots and become fragrant. (Be careful not to overtoast them, as they will burn very quickly once they are toasted.) Immediately transfer the walnuts to a dish to cool.

2. Bring two quarts of water to a boil. Add 1 tablespoon salt, then add the kale. Cook kale until tender, about 10 minutes. Drain.

3. Put the garlic, walnuts, and kale in a blender or food processor; pulse until well combined. With the blender or food processor running, pour in the olive oil in a steady, smooth, pencil-thin stream.

4. When the ingredients are thoroughly combined, transfer to a bowl. Stir in the Parmesan, remaining ¹/₂ teaspoon salt, and pepper. Serve hot.

Mediterranean Summer Greens Sauce

This versatile recipe has many applications. You can use this sauce to stuff ravioli, mushroom caps, or a roast. Present it as an elegant side dish by pouring it onto rounds of fresh, ripe tomato and cooked eggplant, setting it briefly under the broiler, and then sprinkling it with a little fresh lemon juice. Toss the sauce with warm baby potatoes, let cool, and serve as a side salad. It's an ideal sauce for 1 pound of fusilli (corkscrew) pasta (if tossing with pasta, add 2 extra tablespoons of olive oil in step 8). The Mediterranean ingredients of olives, capers, and anchovies, combined with your favorite greens, give this dish a wonderful complexity and depth of flavor. If you don't have a food processor, you can chop the ingredients with a large chef's knife (some might say that this is the preferred way). *Friend of the Farm*.

MAKES I ¹/₂ CUPS

1¹/₂ tablespoons	chopped raisins (optional)
1 tablespoon	salt
2 pounds	spinach, tetragonia, escarole, chard, collard greens, or other greens (or a mixture), stems removed (if you are using chard, chop and reserve the stems)
2–4 tablespoons	extra virgin olive oil, divided
2 cloves	garlic, peeled, smashed (don't use a garlic press; you want the cloves flattened, but still more or less whole)
4–6	anchovy fillets, drained, mashed
2 teaspoons	rinsed, drained capers
10	fresh black olives, pitted, cut in half
¹/₈ teaspoon	hot pepper flakes
¹/₃ cup	grated Parmesan cheese (about 1 ounce)

1. Soak raisins in hot water until plump, about 15 minutes.

2. Bring a large pot of water to a boil. Add the salt, then add the greens. Simmer until tender, 3 to 10 minutes. (Spinach will need only a few minutes, while collard greens will take the full 10 minutes.)

3. Drain the greens in a colander and run cold water over them to stop the cooking. When cool, squeeze out excess water with your hands.

4. If you are using Swiss chard, heat 2 tablespoons of the oil in a sauté pan. Add the chopped chard stems and sauté over medium heat until tender, 5 to 7 minutes. Remove from the pan and set aside.

5. Wipe the pan clean; return it to the burner and heat 2 more tablespoons of oil. Add the garlic and cook, turning often, until lightly browned and fragrant, 3 to 5 minutes. Remove the garlic and discard it.

6. Add the cooked and drained greens (and the chard stems if using) to the pan with the garlic-infused oil and cook for 1 minute, stirring constantly. Add anchovies to taste; add capers. Stir to combine and continue to cook for 30 seconds. Remove the pan from heat. Set the mixture aside to cool for 10 minutes. Transfer the greens mixture from the skillet to a food processor (do not use a blender).

7. Drain raisins and squeeze out excess moisture. Add the raisins, olives, and hot pepper flakes to the processor. Pulse process just until mixture is finely chopped and combined (but not puréed). (You can also chop the ingredients using a large chef's knife, without the risk of overprocessing.)

8. Stir in the Parmesan cheese. Serve immediately or at room temperature. This sauce is best if used the day it's made.

Simple Cooked Greens

Cooking greens in oil or butter over high heat until they are just wilted is a great way to give them an added richness while preserving their fresh taste and delicate texture. Wilted greens mix well with almost anything. They add sophistication to cooked grain or pasta. Topped with grated cheese, a cream sauce, or toasted nuts, they make a complete side dish; dressed with a vinaigrette they become a delicious warm salad. Wilted greens also make a great bed for any meat. They are also wonderful served on their own, simple and elegant, as in this recipe. If you are using greens with hearty stems, such as Swiss chard, cut out the stems, chop them, and sauté them before cooking the leaves to give them enough time to cook. *Angelic Organics Kitchen.*

SERVES 4

3 tablespoons	butter or olive oil
1 teaspoon	minced garlic (about 2 medium cloves) (optional)
1 pound	greens, rinsed, torn or chopped into bite-size pieces
	salt

freshly ground black pepper
extra virgin olive oil

1. Heat the butter or olive oil in a large skillet or pot over medium heat. Add the garlic, sauté for 1 minute.

2. Add the greens immediately after rinsing them, with the water still clinging to the leaves. Cover; cook for 1 minute. (If you are using heartier greens, such as kale or collard greens, add a cup of water to the skillet. Cover; cook for 5 minutes.)

3. Uncover the skillet, add salt to taste (this will ensure the greens stay a bright green), and give the greens a good flip and stir. Cover the skillet again and continue cooking the greens until they are bright green, tender, and wilted to your taste. (For spinach this will be only another minute or two, for Swiss chard 3 to 5 minutes, and for kale or collard greens, depending on their maturity, this could be up to 20 minutes. Be sure to add more water if it boils away.) Season with pepper and olive oil to taste.

Chard
with Sweet-and-Sour Ginger Sauce

In this recipe, the natural, salty tang of chard is intensified by cooking the chard in stock; the same stock is then used as a base for the wonderful sauce, thus ensuring that none of the precious nutrients from the leaves are lost. For a unique touch, try adding a handful of raisins or currants to the boiling stock, allowing them to plump and soften for a minute or so before adding the chard; then cook, strain, and serve them right along with the greens. Lisa, shareholder and recipe-tester, says she created a terrific variation on this recipe by substituting honey for brown sugar and balsamic vinegar and cooking sherry for white vinegar. *Angelic Organics Kitchen.*

SERVES 4

1 cup	vegetable, chicken, or beef stock or water
1/2 pound	chard, stems and ribs removed (save them for another recipe), leaves torn into bite-sized pieces
4	scallions, thinly sliced (about 1/3 cup)
	salt
	freshly ground black pepper
2 tablespoons	white vinegar
1 tablespoon	light brown sugar
1 tablespoon	finely chopped or grated fresh ginger
1 teaspoon	red pepper flakes

1. Bring the stock or water to a boil in a large skillet or pot. Add the chard and cook, stirring, until it is wilted, about 1 minute.

2. Drain the chard, saving the cooking liquid. Transfer the chard to individual plates and garnish with the scallions. Season with salt and pepper to taste.

3. Pour the reserved cooking liquid back into the skillet or pot and bring to a boil over high heat. Boil it until it is reduced to 1/3 cup, about 8 minutes. Add the vinegar and brown sugar. Stir in the ginger and red pepper flakes. Boil for 30 seconds. Remove from heat and spoon the mixture over the chard. Serve immediately.

Steamed Greens
with Ginger Tempeh and Brown Rice

This tasty dish highlights the vibrancy of lightly steamed greens with a snappy ginger sauce. A touch of soy sauce and toasted sesame oil give it deep flavor, and nutty tempeh, hearty potatoes, and sweet brown rice make it a satisfying full meal. The complex taste of fresh horseradish root will surprise and delight you—

Cooking greens are a backbone vegetable in so many cuisines, perhaps because they have a winning combination of attributes: they are easy to prepare, quick to cook, and very healthful. Greens usually round out a meal by adding texture and color to other dishes. We grow many types of greens, but they can all be used similarly—just adjust the cooking time to the density of the greens. Spinach, chard, and beet greens are mild, tender, and require brief cooking. Collards and turnip greens—with their more assertive flavor and texture—require longer cooking, while kale falls between the two groups. Kale and chard are two staples of the farm; you're sure to receive lots.

but if you can't find it, you can substitute bottled (not creamed) horseradish, rinsed. (Treat fresh horseradish as you would hot chiles, being careful not to get it near your eyes and washing your hands immediately after handling it.) Tempeh is available in Asian markets and many health food stores. It has a more assertive flavor and texture than tofu and is equally nutritious. *Shareholder.*

SERVES 4

2¹/₂ cups	vegetable, chicken, or beef stock or cold water
1 cup	uncooked brown rice, rinsed until the water is clear
³/₄ tablespoon	mild-flavored vegetable oil
8 ounces	tempeh, cut into ¹/₂-inch cubes
2 medium	red potatoes, scrubbed, cut into ¹/₄-inch cubes
3 to 4 cloves	garlic, minced or pressed (about 2 teaspoons)
2 tablespoons	grated fresh horseradish
1 tablespoon	grated fresh ginger
	ground cayenne pepper
¹/₂ teaspoon	toasted sesame oil
6–7 large	leaves cooking greens (about ³/₄ pound), stems removed (if using chard, thinly slice the stems or reserve them for use in another recipe)
2 teaspoons	soy sauce or tamari

1. Combine the stock or water and rice in a 2-quart pot and bring to a boil. Reduce the heat to low so that the water continues at a gentle simmer. Cover; cook until the rice is tender and all the water is absorbed, 45 to 60 minutes depending on the type of rice you are using.

2. About midway through the rice cooking time, heat the oil in a large skillet over medium-high heat. Add the tempeh, potato cubes, garlic, horseradish, ginger, chard stems if you're using them, and a pinch of cayenne. Cook, stirring frequently, until the potato cubes are tender and golden brown, about 8 minutes. Stir in the toasted sesame oil and cook for 2 minutes more. Remove the skillet from heat.

3. Put the chopped leaves in a steamer basket set over 1¹/₂ inches boiling water, cover, and steam the greens until they are just tender, 3 to 8 minutes for spinach or chard and 20 minutes or longer for kale and collard greens.

4. Transfer the greens to the skillet. Add the soy sauce or tamari. Stir to combine.

5. When the rice is cooked, remove it from the heat. Let stand, covered, for 5 to 10 minutes.

6. Serve the rice on individual plates and top with the greens.

The Crop

HARVEST WEEK 3, 1995, NEWSLETTER

The cool, wet weather that lingered through May discouraged rapid growth in our fields. (We began to get flashbacks to the morbidly soggy summer of 1993.) Just about when the warmth started, the rain stopped cold. Stopped hot, rather. The farm has been hot, dry, dusty—Sahara-esque. Plants prefer a balance of elements. The heat told them to get moving, but the skies provided no rain-fuel to help them get moving. It's confusing for youthful plants to receive so many mixed messages. In this confused state, the crops are proceeding slowly, cautiously. With our constant irrigation efforts (through twelve miles of drip tape), we've been trying to instill confidence in the reluctant crops. Unfortunately, the dry air sucks the moisture to the sky after it has barely teased the plants' roots. Because of the weird weather this spring, herbs, salad greens, and cooking greens will dominate the first few weeks of our harvest. We hope you enjoy green leafy things or that you at least see this as an opportunity to develop your taste for greens.

Steamed Collards
with Lemon Balm Cream

No matter how bitter your collards may be feeling, the cheerful tang of fresh lemon balm is bound to brighten them up. And who wouldn't be mellow after a steam and a bath in a sumptuously smooth and creamy sauce? *Friend of the Farm*

SERVES 4

1 pound	collard greens, stems removed and discarded, sliced crosswise into 1/2-inch strips
1/4 cup	butter
2 tablespoons	flour
1 cup	half-and-half or heavy cream
1 tablespoon	chopped fresh lemon balm
1 teaspoon	salt
1 teaspoon	freshly ground black pepper

1. Place the chopped collards in a steamer basket over 1 1/2 inches boiling water, cover, and steam until just tender, about 20 minutes or longer depending on the thickness of the leaves.

2. Meanwhile, melt the butter in a medium skillet over medium-low heat. Sprinkle in the flour and stir it in to form a thick paste. Stir in 1/4 cup of the cream, then gradually add the rest of the cream, stirring it in thoroughly, so that the mixture slowly changes from a thick to a thin, runny sauce.

3. Stir in the lemon balm and add salt and pepper to taste. Continue cooking, stirring constantly, until thick again. Remove the skillet from heat.

4. Pour the sauce over the collards; toss to coat well.

Braised Collard Greens
with Sweet-and-Sour Sauce

Cooking collards in an Asian-style sweet-and-sour sauce is a case of inspired culinary cheekiness. It may seem almost blasphemous to pair the definitive southern vegetable with soy sauce and five-spice powder; yet the signature bitterness of the collards is in such harmony with the layered Asian seasonings that we think wontons-and-grits can't be far behind. This is a simply terrific way to enjoy collards. Chinese five-spice powder is a traditional blend of highly flavorful spices (usually a mixture of fennel, cinnamon, cloves, star anise, and Szechwan peppercorns) that is readily available in most supermarkets and specialty stores. *Friend of the Farm*

SERVES 4 TO 6

1/4 cup	water
1/4 cup	sweet sherry
3 tablespoons	soy sauce or tamari
2 teaspoons	sugar
1/2 teaspoon	Chinese five-spice powder
2 1/2 pounds	collard greens, stems removed and discarded, sliced crosswise
	rice vinegar

1. Bring the water, sherry, soy sauce or tamari, sugar, and five-spice powder to a boil in a large, heavy pot.

2. Add the collard greens; cover. Reduce to a simmer and cook until very tender, 15 to 20 minutes. Add more water if necessary to keep mixture from drying out.

3. Uncover the pot and continue simmering until the mixture no longer resembles a soup, 3 to 4 minutes. Remove the pot from heat.

4. Stir in a dash of rice vinegar. Season to taste with more sugar, soy sauce, or rice vinegar.

Radish or Turnip Greens
with Miso Sauce

This recipe is a take on a classic from Japan that uses daikon radish greens. Of course, if you still have some of those tasty roots attached to your leaves, they will be delicious cubed and cooked to tender-crisp succulence right along with the leaves. You will find miso paste in the refrigerated section of most specialty stores, health food stores, and many supermarkets. If you are unfamiliar with its distinct flavor, start with a light-colored variety for a milder, sweeter taste. Toasted sesame oil, also widely available, has a deep, roasted sesame flavor that makes any dish taste unique. Untoasted, or "light," sesame oil will not impart the same flavor. *Friend of the Farm*

SERVES 2

1 bunch	radish or turnip greens or both
1 tablespoon	miso paste
1 tablespoon	peanut oil
	sugar
1 teaspoon	toasted sesame oil
2 cups	hot cooked rice

1. Bring 2 cups of water to a boil in a medium pot. Add the greens and boil for 1 minute.

2. Drain the greens in a colander and run cool water over them to stop the cooking. Let drain again, then gently squeeze out any excess water with your hands. Transfer the greens to a cutting board. Chop finely and set aside.

3. Put the miso paste in a small bowl. Stir in 2 tablespoons water; then add a little more water so that the miso is thinned just enough to stir into other ingredients.

4. Heat the peanut oil in a large skillet over medium heat. Add the chopped greens; cook, stirring, until they are tender and heated through. Add the thinned miso paste. Add sugar to taste; stir the ingredients until thoroughly combined. Remove from heat; stir in the toasted sesame oil. Serve over rice.

Overheard

Customer at a Chinese Restaurant: I went to a health food restaurant. That's a place where they serve food that's good for you, all natural. I had alfalfa sprouts and avocado on my sandwich. Avocado is green and kind of gooey and creamy. It's high in fat, but the things at this health food restaurant weren't necessarily low in fat. They were just good for you. They made a spinach lasagna that was so delicious. It tasted like it had meat in it.

Swiss Chard
with Raisins and Pine Nuts

This classic Mediterranean preparation of Swiss chard is one of our favorite ways to enjoy greens. The chard's silky, earthy flavor is nicely balanced in taste and texture with the pine nuts and raisins. This dish sits comfortably on the side of just about any entrée. It makes a great bed for grilled meats, it's wonderful stuffed in roasted portabella mushrooms, and it makes an outstanding pizza topping. It's even been known to find its way inside a grilled cheese sandwich. You can make the same recipe with spinach. *Friend of the Farm.*

SERVES 4 TO 6

1/4 cup	extra virgin olive oil, divided
1/2 cup	thinly sliced onion
1 clove	garlic, minced (about 1/2 teaspoon)
1 1/2–2 pounds	Swiss chard, rinsed, coarsely chopped
1/3 cup	raisins
1/4 cup	pine nuts, toasted
1 tablespoon	freshly squeezed lemon juice
	salt
	freshly ground black pepper

1. Heat 3 tablespoons of the oil in a large skillet over medium-high heat. Add the onion; cook, stirring occasionally, until golden, about 15 minutes. Stir in the garlic and cook for 1 minute more.

2. Add the chard in batches, adding more as each batch wilts (the only water you will need is the water clinging to the leaves from rinsing), and keep the pan covered between batches. When all the chard is added and the leaves are wilted, stir in the raisins, pine nuts, lemon juice, and the remaining 1 tablespoon oil. Season with salt and pepper to taste.

Wilted Greens and Basil
with Tomato, Garlic, and Ginger

Delicate pieces of fresh basil mingle with the wilted greens in this dish (quick-cooking greens like spinach or Swiss chard are best here), giving a sweetly fragrant note to each savory bite. Garlic and onion add depth and pungency, and ginger adds just a slight nip. Shareholder Laurel says she was pleasantly surprised when she tasted this easy and intensely flavorful dish. If you are using Swiss chard, cut the stems out and sauté them, chopped, ahead of the leaves to give them enough time to cook. To make your tomatoes virtually peel themselves, score a very shallow X on the bottom of each one, put them in a heatproof bowl or measuring cup, and pour boiling water over them. Leave them in the boiling water for a minute or so if necessary; the peel will loosen completely. *Angelic Organics Kitchen* (adapted from *Greene on Greens*).

SERVES 4

2 tablespoons	olive oil or unsalted butter
1 large	onion, finely chopped (about 3/4 cup)
1 large clove	garlic, minced or pressed (about 1/2 teaspoon)
2 medium	tomatoes, peeled, stems and seeds removed, chopped (about 2 cups)
1/4 teaspoon	ground ginger
4–5 cups	chopped greens (any kind)
1/2 cup	chopped fresh basil
	salt
	freshly ground black pepper

1. Heat the oil or butter in a large pot over medium heat. Add the onion; cook until soft, about 5 minutes. Add the garlic and cook, stirring frequently, until the garlic is fragrant and golden, about 5 minutes more.

2. Add the tomatoes and ginger. Continue cooking the mixture, stirring occasionally, until slightly thickened, about 5 minutes.

3. Stir in the chopped greens. Cover the pot and continue to cook until the greens are wilted and tender, 3 to 4 minutes. Stir in the basil just before removing the greens mixture from heat.

4. Remove the pot from heat. Season with salt and pepper to taste. Serve hot or at room temperature.

The Crop

HARVEST WEEK 4, 1996, NEWSLETTER

Abundance! We just can't fit everything that's ready into the vegetable box this week. This is the first time this has ever happened, and it's the kind of problem we like at Angelic Organics. The kale is threatening to turn into palm trees; the cucumbers are pummeling us; thousands of lettuces are eager to storm your boxes; after the rain, the beets suddenly got larger than we'd ever seen them; and we have cabbages, some of which would fill half your box. Let's hope the cabbages can hold off until next week because there's no room for them this week. We're going to cram everything else in, but it's "no" to the cabbages. You'll get them next week.

The Crew

HARVEST WEEK 7, 1998, NEWSLETTER

The farm team made a slow recovery from the extra effort needed to set up, host, and prepare for (1) the Sunday land investor breakfast (for about fifty people) and (2) the summer open house (for the more than two hundred people who attended). We also weeded kale, herbs, and tomatoes; transplanted chard; trellised tomatoes; and seeded kohlrabi in the greenhouse. Harvested and packed more than 600 boxes.

Kale and White Bean Soup
with Sun-dried Tomatoes and Saffron

Sun-dried tomatoes lend their deep, sweet flavor to this wonderful and easy-to-prepare soup, and fennel seeds and saffron add a little mystery. A shareholder recipe-tester informed us that this is a wonderful spring or fall soup. Our Farm Cook adores using sun-dried tomatoes and saffron together in this recipe, and the crew just loved gobbling down the tasty results. What a wonderful, hearty soup for farmers and everyone else! *Shareholder* (adapted from *The Moosewood Restaurant Kitchen Garden*)

SERVES 4 TO 6

3 tablespoons	olive oil
2 cloves	garlic, minced or pressed (about 1 teaspoon)
1/2 teaspoon	ground fennel seeds
1 1/2 cups	chopped onion (about 3 small onions)
1 medium	potato, diced into 1/2-inch pieces
1 small	carrot, chopped
1 small	parsnip, chopped
1 1/2 cups	peeled (see page 92), chopped fresh tomatoes or canned tomatoes
6 cups	vegetable or chicken stock
2	bay leaves
1 tablespoon	chopped fresh oregano or 1 teaspoon dried oregano
6 7	large leaves kale, chopped (3 to 4 cups)
3/4 cup	cooked or canned (rinsed, drained) white beans
1/2 cup	chopped oil-packed sun-dried tomatoes, drained
pinch	saffron
	salt
	freshly ground black pepper

1. Heat the olive oil in a large pot over medium-high heat. Add the garlic and fennel seeds; cook, stirring constantly, for 1 minute. Add the onion and cook, stirring constantly, for 2 minutes. Add the potato, carrot, and parsnip and cook, stirring constantly, for 5 minutes more.

2. Add the fresh or canned tomatoes. Pour in the stock. Stir in the bay leaves and oregano. Bring the mixture to a boil, then immediately reduce the heat so that it continues at a simmer.

3. Add the kale, beans, and sun-dried tomatoes. Simmer until the vegetables are just tender, 15 to 20 minutes. Remove the pot from the heat; add the saffron. Season with salt and pepper to taste.

Spinach or Tetragonia with Yellow Split Peas

and Saffron-Coconut Sauce

The heady aroma of saffron gives intoxicating flavor to this Indian dish. For this recipe, split peas and spinach are combined with a mixture of pungent and spicy ingredients and cooked in creamy coconut milk. For a sensational complete meal, serve this with rice that has been cooked in a mixture of orange juice and water. Don't be afraid to use the fresh jalapeños in this recipe; even a very moderate amount will mix with the saffron and the rich coconut milk to produce a wonderfully complex flavor. Mango chutney is a delicious condiment for this dish. *Shareholder.*

SERVES 4

1 large	onion, chopped (about 2 cups)
2/3 cup	yellow split peas, rinsed well and picked over to remove any pebbles
4–8 thin slices	fresh jalapeño pepper, seeded (use 4 for a milder version and more for a hotter version)
2 cloves	garlic, minced or pressed (about 1 teaspoon)
	pinch saffron
1 cup	coconut milk
1 teaspoon	salt
1 cup	coarsely chopped spinach or tetragonia (1/4–1/2 pound)
4 cups	hot cooked basmati rice

1. Combine the onion, split peas, jalapeño, garlic, and saffron in a large pot. Fill the pot with enough water to cover the peas; bring to a boil. Reduce the heat and simmer, partially covered, for 45 minutes.

2. After 45 minutes of simmering, the peas will start to break apart and mush up as you stir them. Add the coconut milk and salt; stir. Add the spinach on top, but do NOT stir. Cover the pot and cook the spinach with the split pea mixture for 10 more minutes. Uncover the pot and stir the spinach to combine with the peas. If it looks too soupy, continue to simmer, uncovered, until it reaches a thicker consistency. Serve warm over rice.

Easy Greens with Peanuts

Fuss-free and full of taste and texture, this stunningly simple dish will put your fancy recipes to shame. *Angelic Organics Kitchen* (adapted from *Judy Gorman's Vegetable Cookbook*).

SERVES 4

1/2 pound	chard or beet greens or kale, stems and ribs removed (save them for another recipe)
1/2 cup	peanuts (toasted, if desired)
3 tablespoons	olive oil or butter
	salt
	freshly ground black pepper

1. Place the greens in a steamer basket set over 1 1/2 inches boiling water, cover, and steam until just tender, 5 to 10 minutes for chard or beet greens and 15 to 20 minutes for kale, depending on the thickness of the leaves.

2. Transfer the greens to a colander and run cold water over them to stop them from cooking. When cool enough to handle, gently squeeze out the excess water from the greens and chop coarsely.

3. Place the peanuts in a plastic zip-top bag and crush them with a rolling pin or heavy skillet.

4. Heat the olive oil or butter in a large skillet over medium heat. Add the greens; sauté, stirring constantly, until thoroughly coated and glossy, about 2 minutes.

5. Remove the skillet from heat; sprinkle the peanuts over the greens. Season with salt and pepper.

Cucumbers

Although cucumbers require a lot of care in the field, they are usually not demanding in the kitchen. It's easy to find a home for them in salads and sandwiches. The challenge occurs when you get more cucumbers than will fit into your salad or sandwich comfortably. This is an excellent opportunity to vine out into the exciting world of cucumber cookery. Having been around the world a time or two—from India to Rome to the Americas—cucumbers are featured in a plethora of ethnic dishes, some of which are included in this chapter. Still greater options exist if you are adventurous enough to actually apply heat to a cucumber. (Refer to Cucumbers with Risotto, page 100, or Baked Cucumbers in Basil Cream, page 101, for inspiration with cooked cucumbers.)

Storage

Most cucumbers found in supermarkets have endured a journey of hundreds of miles from where they were grown. To keep them from drying out on their long trip, their skins are usually waxed. We don't like the idea of feeding shareholders wax, so we leave our farm-fresh cucumbers in their natural, wax-free state. Because they dehydrate faster than the waxy kind, be sure to get them into the refrigerator right away. If you store unwashed cucumbers in a sealed plastic bag in the vegetable crisper bin, they'll hold for at least a week. Cucumbers store best at around 45° F, but refrigerators are usually set cooler than this. Keep cucumbers tucked far away from tomatoes, apples, and citrus—these give off ethylene gas that accelerates cucumber deterioration.

Handling

You can do a lot of fancy things to the skin of a cucum-ber, and when it is young, fresh, and unwaxed, it really only needs to be thoroughly washed. However, if the skin seems tough or bitter you can remove it; if the seeds are bulky, slice the cucumber lengthwise and scoop them out. Scoring the skin of a cucumber with a fork or citrus zester gives it attractive stripes (and may help release any bitterness). Slice, dice, or cut a cucumber into chunks according to specifications given in your recipe.

Culinary Uses

* Eat cucumbers raw in sandwiches or salads.
* Try cucumber rounds topped with vegetable, egg, or tuna salad, or simply sprinkle with salt.
* Marinated cucumbers are popular at picnics.
* Use cucumbers in chilled summer soups, such as cold borscht.
* Many ethnic cuisines feature cucumbers in condiments like raita (an Indian yogurt salad), page 97.
* Try the succulence and mild flavor of cooked cucumbers (see page s 100-101).

Partners for Cucumbers*

* Allspice, basil, cilantro, coriander, cumin, dill, garlic, horseradish, lemon balm, mint, mustard, oregano, parsley, tarragon, toasted sesame seeds;
* Lemon, prepared mustard, sour cream, soy sauce or tamari, vinegar,
* Cream cheese, yogurt;
* Sunflower seeds, sprouted beans and seeds;
* Onions, peppers, scallions, tomatoes.

*See Louise Frazier's Complementary Herbs & Spices chart, page 345, for suggestions.

Curried Rice and Cucumber Salad
with Walnuts and Raisins

Because they are so mild and refreshing, cucumbers are often used as a foil to more assertive or fiery ingredients. This recipe pairs juicy cucumber slices with rich curry seasoning but forgoes the heat, instead letting the freshness of the cucumber feature prominently. Mixed with golden raisins and tender, aromatic rice, the result is sweet succulence. Of course, if you like your curry spicy you can certainly add some hot pepper to this dish, and it will be differently delicious. You can use vegetable oil or butter instead of ghee, though ghee is the preferred oil for Indian cooking. You can make this dish up to two days in advance, store it in the refrigerator, and toss it with freshly toasted nuts just before serving. *Friend of the Farm.*

SERVES 6

3 cups	cooked basmati or jasmine rice
1/3 cup	sliced scallions (about 2 scallions)
1/3 cup	golden raisins
3 tablespoons	freshly squeezed lemon juice (about 1 lemon)
	salt
1/2 cup	coarsely chopped walnuts
1 tablespoon	ghee
1 tablespoon	curry powder
1 large	cucumber, peeled, halved length wise, seeds scooped out, thinly sliced
	paprika

1. Combine the cooked rice, scallions, raisins, and lemon juice in a large bowl and stir. Season with salt to taste.

2. Toast the walnuts in a dry, heavy skillet (preferably cast iron) over high heat until they turn brown in spots and smell fragrant. Transfer the nuts to a dish and set aside to cool.

3. Quickly wipe the surface of the skillet with a clean towel; melt the ghee in the skillet over medium heat and stir in the curry powder; stir for 30 seconds.

4. Add the cucumber slices. Cook, stirring constantly, until cucumber is tender, 3 to 4 minutes. Remove the skillet from heat.

5. Add the cucumber to the rice mixture and toss to combine. Refrigerate for at least 1 hour.

6. Toss the toasted walnuts with the salad, then sprinkle a generous amount of paprika over the top. Serve chilled or at room temperature.

Spiced Raita

Traditionally used as a cooling complement to spicy Indian foods, raita also makes a refreshing dip or sauce for raw or cooked vegetables. This recipe calls for whole cumin and whole coriander seeds, freshly toasted and ground. If you use preground spices, your raita will be lovely. However, if you take the extra step and work with the whole seeds, your raita will be spectacular, alive with the astonishing subtleties from the just-released volatile oils. Either way, be sure to toast the spices on a dry skillet before you add them to the other ingredients. You can use parsley instead of cilantro. And remember to keep your hands away from your face and eyes when you handle the chile pepper in this recipe! *Angelic Organics Kitchen* (adapted from *Rodale's Garden Fresh Cooking*).

SERVES 4 TO 6

3 medium	cucumbers, peeled, seeds removed, coarsely grated
1/2 teaspoon	cumin seeds
1/2 teaspoon	coriander seeds
2 cups	plain yogurt
1 medium	tomato, halved, stem and seeds removed, cut into thin strips
1	green chile pepper, stem, seeds, and membranes removed, thinly sliced (optional)
1/2 cup	finely chopped scallions (about 3 scallions)
1/8 teaspoon	ground white pepper
1 tablespoon	finely chopped fresh cilantro

1. Place a large strainer over a bowl or a pot. Put the grated cucumber in the strainer; set aside to drain for 30 minutes.

2. Place a dry, heavy skillet (preferably cast iron) over medium heat. Add the cumin and coriander seeds and stir constantly until toasted and fragrant, 3 to 5 minutes, watching carefully to avoid burning them. Immediately transfer seeds to a mortar and pestle and grind (or use the back of a wooden spoon to crush).

3. Pour the yogurt into a strainer lined with several layers of cheesecloth or a coffee filter. Set it aside for 10 minutes to drain.

4. Remove the drained, grated cucumber from the strainer with your hands and gently squeeze out the excess moisture. Spread the grated cucumber on clean dish towels and pat it dry.

5. In a medium bowl, gently combine the cucumber, crushed cumin and coriander seeds, yogurt, tomato, chile pepper, scallions, and white pepper. Garnish with cilantro. Serve immediately or refrigerate for 1 hour.

A Shareholder

I imagine that picking a cucumber for every box is a prickly event, so I want to say thanks. I got to eat mine today, and it was the best cucumber that I have ever eaten. It tasted of sun and clean water and reminded me of my dad's vegetable patch when I was a kid.

Marinated Cucumber Salad with Dill

This delicious salad from Denmark has no sauce, no oil, no dressing—yet each delicate slice of cucumber is bursting with tangy-sweet juiciness. The secret is an initial draining step that partially dehydrates the cucumbers, ensuring they will soak up lots of the flavorful marinade. This recipe makes a wonderful salad or side dish. You can also use the slices as you would any sweet pickles—in an egg salad sandwich or layered on a veggie burger, and of course, this dish is great with hotdogs. This takes a bit of time to prepare from start to finish, but most of that time is unattended. For a unique twist, replace dill with the feathery leaves of fennel. *Angelic Organics Kitchen*

SERVES 6 TO 8

3 large	cucumbers (about 2 pounds), peeled, very thinly sliced
1 tablespoon	coarse sea salt or kosher salt
2/3 cup	white or apple cider vinegar
1/2 cup	water
1/2 cup	sugar
1/2 teaspoon	salt
1/4 teaspoon	white pepper
2 tablespoons	finely chopped fresh dill or 1 tablespoon dried dill

1. In a large bowl, use your hands to thoroughly but gently mix the cucumbers and salt.

2. Place a plate on top of the cucumbers, then place a 2- or 3-pound weight (such as a large can of vegetables) on the plate to weigh it down (this helps release the salt). Set the cucumbers aside to marinate at room temperature for several hours or in the refrigerator overnight.

3. Drain the cucumbers thoroughly in a colander and pat them dry on a clean dish towel. Rinse and dry the bowl, then return the cucumbers to the bowl.

4. Mix the vinegar, water, sugar, salt, and pepper in a small pot over medium heat and bring to a boil. Reduce the heat and simmer, stirring often, until the sugar is dissolved, about 3 minutes. Remove from heat.

5. Pour the hot vinegar mixture over the cucumber slices. Sprinkle with the dill and mix to combine.

6. Chill for at least 3 hours. Drain and serve.

A Shareholder

I made the most fabulous chilled cucumber soup with the cucumbers, and the best zucchini fritters with the zucchini! Best wishes to all of you who work so hard to give us the very best organic vegetables, week after week.

Marinated Cucumber Salad

in Honey-Cider Vinegar

Marinated in a tangy nectar and accented with onion and a choice of flavorful seasonings, these delicate cucumber rounds are irresistibly good. This salad is like a time-lapsed version of classic Danish marinated cucumbers, requiring no advance preparation and only half an hour to marinate. If you have a mandoline or a food processor to make an easy job of the slicing, it is almost absurdly easy to assemble. *Angelic Organics Kitchen* (adapted from *American Wholefoods Cuisine*).

SERVES 4

1/4 cup	apple cider vinegar
2 tablespoons	water
1–3 teaspoons	honey
1/4 teaspoon	prepared Dijon mustard OR
	1 1/2 teaspoons caraway seeds OR
	1 teaspoon celery seeds OR
	1 teaspoon chopped fresh dill
4 medium	cucumbers, peeled, thinly sliced
6 thin slices	onion

1. Mix the vinegar, water, honey to taste, and mustard (or other choice of seasoning) in a glass mixing bowl. Add the cucumber and onion; toss until well combined.

2. Marinate for at least 30 minutes at room temperature or refrigerate overnight. Serve cold or at room temperature.

Chilled Cucumber-Mint Soup

with Yogurt or Sour Cream

Everything about this dish is summery and fresh—including the cook, who hasn't had to hover over a steamy stovetop to achieve this surprisingly intense blend of flavors. A shareholder recipe-tester says the sour cream gives this soup lovely richness and suggests using a little finely chopped fresh dill for a pretty garnish. *Angelic Organics Kitchen* (adapted from *The New Moosewood Cookbook*).

SERVES 4 TO 6

4	cucumbers, peeled, seeded, and chopped (about 4 cups)
1 to 2 cups	water
2 cups	plain yogurt (or 1 cup plain yogurt combined with 1 cup sour cream)
1 clove	garlic, peeled and smashed several fresh mint leaves
2 tablespoons	fresh dill or 1 teaspoon dried dill
1 tablespoon	honey
1 to 2 teaspoons	salt
2	scallions, finely chopped (about 1/3 cup)

1. Combine the chopped cucumber, 1 cup water, yogurt, garlic, mint, dill, honey, and 1 teaspoon salt in a blender or food processor. Purée the ingredients, adding more of the water until the soup is a consistency you like. Season with more salt to taste.

2. Transfer the soup to a large bowl and chill for several hours. Garnish each serving with chopped scallions.

One of our fields was soupy all spring. Our second planting of cucumber seedlings had no place to go, because the crew couldn't work the bed without sloshing. That's the simple version; here's the whole story. The first batch of cucumbers had no place to go because of the rain. They unfurled in the greenhouse, growing bigger and bigger. Much to our chagrin we eventually had to throw them out, because mature cucumbers will not transplant successfully. In another attempt, we seeded more cucumbers in the greenhouse, but the ground stayed wet and sadly we had to throw them out, too. The third batch went in so late that we decided not to plant another succession. Despite all our struggles with transplanting them, it turns out to be a good year for cucumbers. Now that they are in the ground, we find that we are totally inundated with them. Maybe you won't miss that second succession of cucumbers after all.

Cucumbers with Risotto

The light, succulent texture of cooked cucumber is a surprising and satisfying accent in this rich and creamy risotto. If you must substitute another rice for the Arborio rice, choose a medium-grain variety, not long-grain. Allow it to continue cooking in the pan for a few minutes after you remove it from the heat. Shareholder Gwen says this recipe serves two as an entrée or four as a side dish. *Angelic Organics Kitchen* (adapted from *Greene on Greens*).

Serves 2 to 4

2 tablespoons	unsalted butter, divided
$3/4$ cup	minced onion (about 1 large onion)
1 clove	garlic, minced (about $1/2$ teaspoon)
$3^1/2$ cups	peeled, seeded, diced cucumbers (about $3^1/2$ cucumbers)
$1/2$ cup	uncooked Arborio rice
$1/8$ teaspoon	crushed dried red chile peppers
$1^3/4$ cups	hot vegetable stock or chicken stock, divided
	salt
	freshly ground black pepper
1 tablespoon	chopped fresh dill or $1^1/2$ teaspoons dried dill

1. Melt 1 tablespoon of the butter in a large skillet over medium heat. Add the onion; cook for 2 minutes. Add the garlic and continue cooking for 1 minute. Stir in the cucumbers, rice, and chile peppers. Continue to stir until everything is well combined and the rice is shiny and well coated.

2. Pour $3/4$ cup of the hot stock over the rice mixture and stir it in. Cook the mixture, stirring constantly to prevent sticking, until the liquid is absorbed, about 15 minutes. If necessary, reduce the heat so that the rice does not cook too fast. Repeat the process with the remaining stock, adding $1/2$ cup at a time until all the liquid is absorbed and the rice is tender but still slightly firm to the bite, about 40 minutes. (If there is too much liquid, increase the heat to cook off some of it. If there is too little liquid and the rice is tough, pour in some additional stock.)

3. Stir in the remaining 1 tablespoon of butter. Season with salt and pepper to taste, and garnish with dill just before serving. Serve hot.

Baked Cucumbers in Basil Cream

When cucumbers are baked, their characteristic crispness gives way to a silky succulence. Bathed in a fragrant and creamy sauce, they become almost unrecognizably luxurious. Though you may be afraid that a dish based on cooked cucumber will taste watery, you will find that the marinated slices in this recipe are full of sweetly tangy flavor. Garnish this dish with thin slices of fresh basil for added color and taste. *Angelic Organics Kitchen.*

SERVES 4 TO 6

1½ tablespoons	red wine vinegar
1 teaspoon	salt
¼ teaspoon	sugar
4–5	cucumbers, peeled, halved lengthwise, seeds removed, cut into 1-inch slices
2 tablespoons	unsalted butter, melted
1	scallion, finely chopped
1 cup	heavy cream
3 tablespoons	chopped fresh basil leaves
	salt
	freshly ground black pepper

1. Preheat the oven to 375° F.

2. Mix the vinegar, salt, and sugar in a medium glass bowl. Add the cucumber slices and toss to combine. Set aside to marinate for 30 minutes.

3. Drain the cucumber slices in a colander, then pat them dry with a clean dish towel.

4. Put the cucumber slices in a shallow baking dish. Pour the melted butter over them and add the scallion; toss to combine. Bake the cucumbers, stirring occasionally, until tender, about 45 minutes.

5. Meanwhile, heat the cream in a small pot until it comes to a light boil. Continue to cook the cream, stirring frequently, until it is reduced to ½ cup, about 20 minutes. Stir in the basil and turn off the heat; let mixture steep for 2 minutes.

6. Pour the basil cream sauce over the cooked cucumber slices. Season with salt and pepper to taste.

A Shareholder

Cucumbers—you're testing my creativity. Learned from an old cooking encyclopedia (Wise) that cooked cucumbers are tasty served with salt, pepper, cream, and nutmeg. One night I cut them in half, scooped out the seeds, coated them with a little pesto (from your basil, of course), wrapped them in foil, and threw them on the grill for about 10 minutes. Drizzled cream down the center to serve. Yum. Thanks for all your hard work!

Overheard

My new jar of pickles fell to the ground and shattered, sending glass shards and baby cucumberettes all around my feet.

Herbs

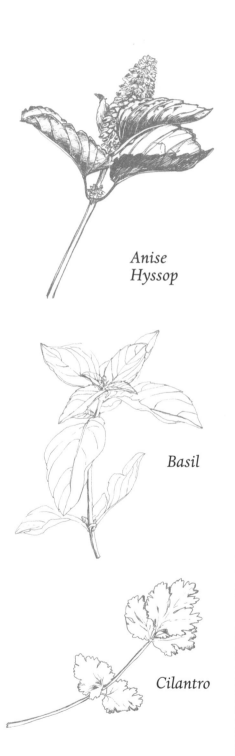

Anise Hyssop

Basil

Cilantro

Conventional supermarkets might lead us to believe that herbs in their natural state come dried and prepackaged in little jars or tins. For the many consumers who are accustomed to shaking on a little onion salt or lemon pepper, cooking with fresh herbs can be intimidating. Occasionally we get calls from new shareholders who have herbal anxiety about those unfamiliar bouquets that arrive from the farm week after week. For the uninitiated, this chapter offers concrete suggestions and recipes using fresh herbs.

The recipes in this chapter focus on herbs as the main attraction; vegetables are not a prominent feature here. If you are looking for herbs in combination with other vegetables, check the index or refer to the vegetable chapter of your choice to seek out herb pairings. In this chapter you will find ideas for an exciting array of herb-based dips, condiments, beverages, dressings, and desserts—even ice cream! You will also find delicious, herb-flavored baked goods and a terrific selection of herbed grain and vegetarian protein dishes. Once you discover (or rediscover) the sheer joy of using fresh, fragrant herbs in your cooking, you'll never want to do without them. In fact, you may soon join the leagues of happily dependent cooks who supplement their shares and fill their year-round needs by growing potted herbs on every available ledge, windowsill, and doorstep.

Herbs Grown by Angelic Organics

Anise hyssop has crinkly, serrated, heart-shaped leaves that look like mint and have a sweet, licorice flavor. Your bunch may come with edible purple flowers that, like the leaves, are good in teas, vegetable and fruit salads, and baked goods and waffles. The flowers are slightly stronger and sweeter than the leaves, so if you are substituting all of one for the other in a recipe, you will need to adjust accordingly. Try using anise hyssop in baked desserts, homemade ice cream, sorbet, or as a garnish for melons. It combines well with fruit, carrots, and spinach.

Basil is graced with shiny, oval leaves that range in color from yellow-green to dark green. Basil has a heady, spicy, clovelike fragrance and taste. Popular in Mediterranean dishes and Thai curries, basil pairs readily with almost every summer vegetable, especially tomatoes, eggplant, peppers, green beans, and summer squash. Basil is the main ingredient in a classic pesto and is an extraordinary complement in both tofu and tempeh marinades. Basil is also excellent in egg dishes. Basil is fairly fragile, so unless it is to be eaten raw, it is best added near the end of a dish's cooking time. Do not refrigerate basil. See storage notes below.

Cilantro is used in many ethnic cuisines, including Asian, Indian, and Mexican. It has flat, delicate, lacy-edged leaves and a bold, almost citrus aroma, with an overall freshness similar to parsley. Since it doesn't stand up to much heat, it is usually added to a dish right before serving. Cilantro's delicate leaves can be sensitive to moisture, so be sure to keep the bunch upright with the stems in a jar as described below in the "Storage" section.

Dill has feathery, blue-green leaves with a bright, clean, summery taste. It has an assertive but clear aroma like celery, with a freshness like parsley and a hint of aniselike sweetness. It is common in European cooking and is the standard flavoring for pickles. It also combines well with green beans, broccoli, cabbage, carrots, cauliflower, tomatoes, parsnips, potatoes, spinach, squash, eggplant, and eggs. Try adding it to yogurt sauces or baking it in bread.

Fennel is valuable as both a vegetable and an herb. Its leaves are deep green and feathery with a licorice flavor that is especially good with potatoes, tomatoes, eggplant, beets, rice, eggs, and fish. See the chapter on fennel, page 181, for recipes and more suggestions.

Lemon balm resembles mint in appearance, with its broad, heart-shaped leaves, but is characterized by a soft yet distinct lemon flavor. It is commonly used in teas, vegetable and fruit salads, baked goods, and desserts. It is excellent paired with asparagus, broccoli, corn, and fruit. Adding a few leaves to any recipe calling for lemon juice will brighten the flavor. Fresh lemon balm is a good substitute for lemon zest and fresh lemon grass.

Oregano has small, fuzzy leaves and a peppery flavor that can be substituted for marjoram. It is an Italian classic used in pizzas and pastas and is also commonly used in Mexican and Greek dishes. It enhances breads, dried beans, broccoli, eggplant, mushrooms, potatoes, squash, tomatoes, and eggs.

Parsley comes in two varieties at Angelic Organics. Flat-leaf parsley, also known as Italian parsley, has leaves that look like those of celery. Curly-leaf parsley is the frilly type you find on your plate as a garnish in restaurants. Both varieties can be used to flavor most foods—except sweets. Parsley's gentle flavor blends well with other foods and is used in many American and European dishes, especially with dried beans, carrots, cauliflower, eggplant, parsnips, potatoes, tomatoes, stuffing, and eggs.

Rosemary has dark green needlelike leaves, a distinctive evergreen scent, and a bold, savory-sweet flavor. It is used in many cuisines but in particular is associated with Mediterranean countries, especially Italy and France. Because rosemary will not lose flavor when it is exposed to long or high-temperature cooking, it is an ideal herb for roasting, frying, and grilling. Layer and cook whole sprigs with vegetables such as potatoes, eggplant, summer and winter squash, tomatoes, mushrooms, cauliflower, onions, garlic, and sweet potatoes. Toss some whole sprigs on your barbecue coals for a delicious, fragrant smoke. Cook whole sprigs in soups, stews, and sauces, then remove them afterwards. Chop the leaves very finely and add sparingly to beans, rice, peas, egg dishes, batters, doughs, spreads, and purées. Rosemary is wonderful in herb butters and breads. It makes a classic-flavored olive oil, and it partners well with bay, parsley, sage, and thyme.

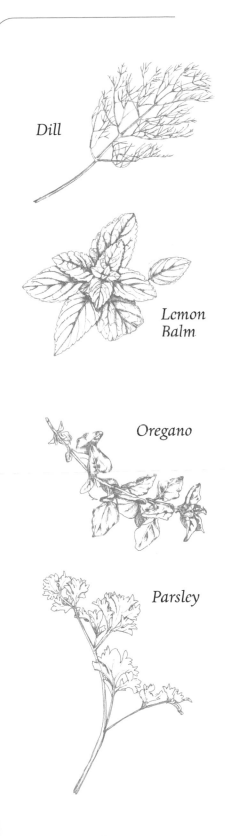

Dill

Lemon Balm

Oregano

Parsley

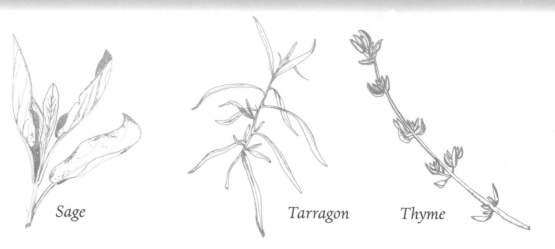

Sage   Tarragon   Thyme

Sage has velvety, pebbly, gray-green leaves with a pleasantly bitter lemon taste. It is a good complement for asparagus, dried beans, cabbage, carrots, corn, eggplant, potatoes, squash, tomatoes, stuffing, cheese, and eggs. Pan-fry a few leaves until they become crisp, and then crumble them into soup, scrambled eggs, or on an extra-special grilled cheese sandwich. Use sage sparingly, as too much of its intense aroma will produce an unpleasant, musty taste.

Tarragon has long, narrow, light green leaves with a distinctive lemon-licorice flavor. It is widely used in French cuisine and pairs with broccoli, cooking greens, beets, carrots, cauliflower, mushrooms, peas, potatoes, rice, lentils, tomatoes, and eggs. It is the main seasoning in a basic tartar sauce, and when combined with oil and white wine vinegar it makes a classic salad dressing.

Thyme is excellent in bean dishes, soups, and pasta sauces. It has tiny, smoky-green, diamond-shaped leaves with a subtle clove taste. Since thyme leaves are so small, it's easiest to cook with whole sprigs; remove them from the pot after cooking. Thyme complements rice, dried and green beans, broccoli, carrots, corn, eggplant, mushrooms, parsnips, peas, potatoes, spinach, tomatoes, stuffing, and eggs.

Storing Fresh Herbs

Except for basil, set unwashed bunches of fresh herbs (with stems) upright into small jars filled with 1 to 2 inches of water. Then cover the herbs loosely with plastic wrap and refrigerate for up to two weeks. Roll up unwashed smaller sprigs or loose herbs in a dry towel, place the bundle in a plastic bag, and store it in the refrigerator's vegetable bin for up to a week.

Now for fresh basil. It is a warm-weather crop and is very sensitive to cold temperatures. Do not refrigerate fresh basil; it will turn black very quickly. To keep just-harvested basil fresh for several days, strip the lower leaves off the stems and place the stems in a glass of water on the kitchen counter. Wrap the stripped leaves (or all your basil, if your fresh basil arrives without adequate stems) in a dry paper towel (damp leaves will quickly turn black) and keep in an airtight container at about 50 degrees. (Room temperature is also okay.) If you have more basil than you can use in a few days, try chopping it and adding it to butter, cream cheese, or your favorite pasta sauce. Make a batch of pesto—or simply purée extra basil with a bit of olive oil and freeze it in ice cube trays.

Long-Term Herb Preservation

Herbs taste best when eaten fresh, but you may not be able to use all that you receive, and you might want to preserve some for colder months. Drying and freezing are two ways to preserve herbs by themselves, without adding other ingredients. Consult our recipes to learn to preserve herbs in butter, vinegar, sauces, pestos, jellies, and other condiments.

Drying Herbs

Herbs that dry most effectively are basil, parsley, cilantro, dill, fennel, oregano, sage, thyme, and summer and winter savory. 1 teaspoon of dried herbs is equivalent to 1 tablespoon of fresh herbs.

The simplest way to dry herbs is to spread them on a tray and place it in the oven at its lowest setting with the door ajar. Stir the herbs periodically. When the leaves crumble when pinched, they are dried.

You can also hang bouquets of fresh herbs to dry. Puncture a large paper bag with air holes. Tie the stalks of herbs into skimpy bunches with cotton string and place the bunches upside down in the bag. Tie the neck of the bag tightly around the base of the bunch and hang it with the leaves facing down in a warm, ventilated place. (Optimum conditions for drying herbs are temperatures of about 85 degrees with humidity below 60 percent.) Check the herbs daily until they are dry, about two weeks. When the herbs crumble when pinched, remove the stems and store the leaves in a sealed glass jar—away from heat and light—for up to a year. Crush them just before using.

Freezing Herbs

Freezing herbs is a nearly foolproof way to store them. Frozen herbs retain their full aroma and are just as easy to use as dried herbs. Frozen herb cubes are ideal for flavoring soups, sauces, gravies, stews, and casseroles. One frozen herb cube is equivalent to 1 tablespoon fresh or about 1 teaspoon of dried herb. Just add a cube when your recipe calls for the herb. The water will evaporate during cooking, leaving the herb to flavor the dish.

To prepare herbs for freezing, rinse them gently in cool water. Chop the leaves fairly coarsely. (Don't freeze stalks or flowers, or particularly delicate leaves like cilantro or basil.) Spoon 1 tablespoon of the desired chopped herb into each compartment of an ice cube tray, add about 1 inch of water to each compartment, and place the tray in the freezer.

Remove the frozen herb cubes from the trays and bundle all the cubes containing the same herb in a plastic freezer bag. Remove as much air as possible, seal the bag, and store it in the freezer for up to a year.

> ### Farmer John Writes
>
> In anthroposophical cooking there is the premise that grains move towards completion as they are growing, but they never complete. Certain spices and herbs complete the process, which is why well-seasoned grains sometimes can impart a deeply satisfying experience.
>
> **—FROM JOHN'S ESSAY "THE PIG COMPLETES THE BUNNY," PAGE 348**

An alternative method: rinse whole herb leaves and place them on a large tray in a single layer. Freeze, then store in plastic freezer bags for up to a year.

Converting Between Fresh and Dried Herbs

To substitute fresh herbs in recipes calling for dried herbs, use this ratio:

1/4 teaspoon dried ground herbs: 1 teaspoon dried crumbled leaves: 1 tablespoon finely chopped fresh herbs.

Handling

If your herbs seem dusty when you get them home, brush them gently with a dry pastry brush or paintbrush, but do not wash them. Damp herbs will get brown spots and rot during storage. Immediately before using, gently wash the herbs in cool water. Cut or pinch herbs from the stems, or if you don't have the time, drop whole sprigs into the dish and remove them before serving. To release the flavor of fresh herbs, rub them between your hands before mincing or chopping. To cut larger herbs into strips, roll the leaves into little tubes and make several parallel slices across the tube.

Culinary Uses

❖ Make beautiful garnishes for soups, salads, main dishes, and even frosted cakes using whole or chopped fresh herbs.

❖ Make herb condiments ahead of time for use throughout the week to flavor pizza, pasta, grains, roasted vegetables, and eggs. Besides contributing to other dishes, herbs can stand on their own in condiments such as pesto. Fresh herb condiments make even the simplest dishes gourmet.

❖ Soak or sauté fresh or dried herbs in the butter, oil, or vinegar called for in your recipe to increase the herbs' potency.

❖ Freeze or dry herbs for later use (see above instructions).

❖ Use frozen or dried herbs in teas, salad dressings, or wherever herbs are called for in cooking.

*See Louise Frazier's Complementary Herbs & Spices chart, page 345, for suggestions.

Rosemary Lemonade

Rosemary adds a lovely herbal note to homemade lemonade. For an extra summery kick, garnish each serving with a sprig of fresh lemon balm or mint. *Friend of the Farm.*

SERVES 2 TO 4

4 cups	water
6 sprigs (each about 5 inches long)	fresh rosemary
3/4 cup	sugar (or more, to taste)
1/2 cup	freshly squeezed lemon juice (about 3 large lemons)

1. Bring the water to a boil in a medium pot, and then reduce the heat so that the water barely simmers. Add the rosemary sprigs; cover and steep the rosemary for 45 minutes. Remove the pot from heat and remove the rosemary sprigs. (If necessary, strain the mixture to remove loose leaves.) Add the sugar; stir until dissolved. Set aside to cool.

2. Put the lemon juice into a large plastic or glass container and add the cooled rosemary syrup; stir until well combined. Taste the lemonade and sweeten it with additional sugar if desired. Refrigerate until cold.

Orange and Mint Punch
with Ginger Ale

This is a delightful punch to serve at a summer lunch or picnic—it's refreshing and full of citrus zing and minty zip. Ginger ale makes it light and sparkly and gives it just the right amount of sweetness. This looks especially beautiful in a punch bowl with fresh mint sprigs or mint ice cubes. When zesting the orange for this recipe, be sure to avoid the white pith beneath the colored skin, as the pith can impart a strong, bitter flavor. *Friend of the Farm.*

MAKES 4 QUARTS

3 3/4 cups	water
2 1/4 cups	sugar
3 cups	freshly squeezed orange juice (about 9 medium oranges)
1 3/4 cups	freshly squeezed lemon juice (about 7 lemons)
1 1/4 cups	fresh mint leaves
1 tablespoon	freshly grated orange zest
8 cups	cold ginger ale

1. Combine the water and sugar in a large pot and bring to a boil, stirring until the sugar is completely dissolved. Remove the pot from heat.

2. Put the orange juice, lemon juice, mint, orange zest, and sugar water in a 4-quart glass bowl or pitcher; stir. Cover the container and set it aside at room temperature for 1 hour to let the flavors develop.

3. Strain the orange-lemon juice mixture. Refrigerate until you are ready to serve.

4. Add the ginger ale to the orange-lemon mixture when you are ready to serve.

Creamy Tarragon Dressing

Tarragon and creamy things really like each other—and most people really like what happens when they get together. Here's a fantastic, creamy-rich tarragon dressing for a green salad, potato salad, or egg salad. This is great over sliced tomatoes on a bed of alfalfa sprouts or spooned onto a fluffy baked potato. You can also use this the way you would a tartar sauce, offering it with fish. *Friend of the Farm.*

MAKES ABOUT ³/₄ CUP

1/2 cup	mayonnaise
1/4 cup	milk
2 tablespoons	olive oil
1 1/2 tablespoons	finely chopped fresh tarragon
1 tablespoon	apple cider vinegar
1 clove	garlic, minced or pressed (about 1/2 teaspoon)
1/8 teaspoon	curry powder (or more, to taste)
	salt

1. Stir the mayonnaise, milk, and olive oil in a medium bowl until smooth. Add the tarragon, apple cider vinegar, garlic, and curry powder; whisk until thoroughly combined.

2. Cover and refrigerate for at least 3 hours to let the flavors develop. Season with salt to taste. Serve chilled or at room temperature.

Soy-Ginger Dressing
with Honey, Lemon, and Cilantro

The pungent and distinctly "green" flavor of fresh cilantro is a staple in many world cuisines. In this recipe, cilantro mixes with classic Asian flavors for a dressing that is delicious over hot or cold vegetables, greens, pasta, or potatoes. It also makes a great marinade for chicken or tofu in a stir-fry. Toasted sesame oil, available in Asian grocery stores and many supermarkets, imparts a wonderfully intense and nutty flavor; if you cannot find it, peanut oil or untoasted sesame oil is an acceptable substitute. *Angelic Organics Kitchen* (adapted from *Fit for Life*).

MAKES ABOUT 1¹/₂ CUPS

2/3 cup	finely chopped fresh cilantro
1/2 cup	freshly squeezed lemon juice (about 3 lemons)
1/4 cup	finely chopped red onion
1/4 cup	light vegetable oil
3 tablespoons	peanut oil
1 tablespoon	Worcestershire sauce
1 tablespoon	tomato paste
1 tablespoon	soy sauce or tamari
1 tablespoon	toasted sesame oil
2 teaspoons	grated fresh ginger
2 teaspoons	honey
2 teaspoons	hot chile oil (optional)
1/2 teaspoon	salt

Combine all the ingredients in a large glass jar. With the lid screwed on, shake the jar vigorously until the oil and lemon juice have combined and thickened. Store the dressing in the refrigerator for up to 2 weeks. Shake again just before serving.

> *Overheard*
>
> **FARMER:** How often do you like to fall in love?
>
> **INTERN:** Whenever I want to lose weight.

Sage and Butter Sauce

In Italy this classic sauce is called *burro oro e salvia,* or "golden butter and sage." It is one of the most intense ways to experience the wonders of this herb. The heat from the butter releases the penetrating flavor and aroma of the fresh sage. Cooking this fragrant sauce is a heady experience. Like a pesto, this sauce is "light" but not at all shy. For an easy meal, toss with pasta and season with freshly ground black pepper and Parmesan cheese. It is also superb with cooked carrots or winter squash such as acorn or spaghetti. This recipe is sufficient for 1 pound of pasta. *Friend of the Farm.*

MAKES 1/2 CUP

7 tablespoons	butter
10 large	fresh sage leaves
	freshly ground black pepper

1. Melt the butter in a small sauté pan over medium heat. Monitor closely until the foam subsides and the color is a rich gold. Do not to let the butter brown.

2. Add the sage leaves (they should sizzle—if not, your butter is not hot enough). Cook the leaves in the butter, turning them once, for 15 seconds. Immediately remove the skillet from the heat and serve.

PARSLEY AND PESTO

The most common pesto is made from basil, but it can be made from a variety of fresh herbs. Parsley is added to pesto because its flavor does not compete with the main herb. Rather, it extends and complements it. Parsley also reduces the "blackening" that traditional basil pesto undergoes when in contact with air.

Some Pesto Combos

❖ Oregano Pesto: 1 part oregano to 3 parts parsley
❖ Cilantro Pesto: 1 part cilantro to 1 part parsley
❖ Tarragon Pesto: 1 part tarragon to 2 parts parsley
❖ Mint Pesto: 2 parts mint to 1 part parsley

Creamy Lemon Balm Soup
with Spinach or Tetragonia

You can throw this recipe together in no time for a quick first course. Lemon balm and spinach are a delicate yet delicious match. This soup is fairly thin, but it's loaded with flavor and sophistication. *Friend of the Farm.*

SERVES 4

1 tablespoon	extra virgin olive oil
1 small	onion, quartered and thinly sliced
2 cups	finely chopped spinach or tetragonia leaves
1/2 cup	finely chopped lemon balm leaves
4 cups	light vegetable or chicken stock
3/4 cup	sour cream
1/2 teaspoon	salt
1/4 teaspoon	freshly ground black pepper
	small lemon balm sprigs or freshly grated lemon zest or paper-thin slices of lemon

1. Heat the olive oil in a medium pot over medium heat. Add the onion; cook, stirring often, until lightly golden, 15 to 20 minutes.

2. Add the spinach or tetragonia and lemon balm; stir the ingredients until combined. Cover; cook until the greens are wilted, about 3 minutes.

3. Pour in the stock and bring to a simmer. Add the sour cream, salt, and pepper; heat, stirring, until warmed through. (Avoid boiling the soup, as this will curdle the sour cream.)

4. Top each serving with a fresh grinding of black pepper and garnish with a small lemon balm sprig, a pinch of lemon zest, or a thin slice of lemon.

Cilantro Spread — Two Versions

Both versions of this terrific spread are easy and fantastically flavorful. Try one with a platter of grilled vegetables or thickly sliced ripe tomatoes. Both are great on rice noodles or rice, and you might like to try the peanut version with grilled eggplant. Remember to keep your hands away from your face when you are handling hot chile peppers. *Angelic Organics Kitchen.*

MAKES 1 CUP

2 packed cups	very finely chopped fresh cilantro
2 cloves	garlic, minced (about 1 teaspoon)
	finely grated zest of 1 lime

Spicy Cilantro-Peanut Version

	freshly squeezed juice of 2 limes (3 to 4 tablespoons)
1 to 2	chile peppers, stems and seeds removed, coarsely chopped
1 tablespoon	peanuts
	salt
	freshly ground black pepper

Cilantro-Ginger Version

1/2 cup	extra virgin olive oil
1 tablespoon	freshly squeezed lime juice
1 teaspoon	finely chopped or grated fresh ginger

Put the cilantro, garlic, and lime zest in a bowl. Add the next three ingredients for the version you are making (either oil, lime juice, and ginger; or lemon juice, peppers, and peanuts). Mix well with a fork or whisk until well combined. Season with salt and pepper to taste. Serve immediately or store in the refrigerator for up to 2 days.

A Shareholder

Every Saturday marks the beginning of a weeklong celebration. The food nourishes and inspires me, and the pain I always experience while shopping in supermarkets falls away.

Mixed Herb Butter

Delicious spread on bread, melted over vegetables, or slathered over fish or a grilled steak, this sweet or savory herb butter will instantly enliven even the simplest dishes. Try combinations of two or three complementary herbs or make each stick a different flavor. Try keeping one stick aside for immediate use and freezing the others to have on hand when you next need a quick and delicious flavor hit. *Angelic Organics Kitchen*

MAKES 4 1/2-CUP STICKS

2 cups	salted or unsalted butter, softened
1/4 cup	finely chopped fresh herbs (such as anise hyssop, basil, dill, lemon balm, marjoram, oregano, tarragon, parsley, sage, thyme)
1 tablespoon	minced garlic (about 6 cloves) (optional)

1. In a medium bowl, cream the butter with an electric mixer until very soft and fluffy. Add the herbs and garlic and mix until thoroughly combined. (If you don't have an electric mixer, you can simply mix the herbs into softened butter with a fork.) Cover and refrigerate until the butter is just firm enough to shape into sticks.

2. Working quickly, use your hands to shape the butter into 4 sticks or logs, each about 1 inch thick. Transfer one or more of the sticks to a covered butter dish and place in the refrigerator or wrap the logs in waxed paper and store them in the freezer for up to 6 months.

Basil-Garlic Cream Cheese

The possibilities for this classic, creamy dip-spread-sauce are endless. Use it as a spread on crackers or bread, as a dip for vegetables, or as a sauce for warm pasta with artichoke hearts and sliced black olives. Stir it into warm tomato soup, scoop it over a steaming-hot baked potato, or pipe it into halved cherry tomatoes and arrange them on a salad plate. Vary the texture and flavor by changing the amount of olive oil or by using the oil from preserved sun-dried tomatoes or anchovies, or experiment with using cottage cheese, ricotta, or yogurt cheese in place of the cream cheese. It's fresh basil—you can't go wrong. *Angelic Organics Kitchen*

MAKES 1 1/3 CUPS

8 ounces	cream cheese, softened
1/2 cup	coarsely chopped fresh basil
1/4 cup	coarsely chopped fresh chives
2 cloves	garlic, minced (about 1 teaspoon)
2 tablespoons	extra virgin olive oil
1/2 teaspoon	salt
	freshly ground black pepper

Stir all the ingredients in a medium bowl with a wooden spoon until smooth. (You can also do this in your food processor.) Transfer the herbed cheese to a small dish and put it in the refrigerator to let the flavors develop for about 1 hour.

A Shareholder

I'd been looking forward with great enthusiasm to the delivery of the first box. And it was true to form! The smell of the basil brought tears to my eyes. The visual pleasure and eating pleasure of your vegetables are truly one of life's greatest moments.

Creamy Dill Sauce

This versatile dill sauce is wonderful in egg salad, or tossed with cucumbers, or as a sauce for fish or crab cakes. It also makes a delicious salad dressing. We like it on just about anything. The method for making this sauce is similar to that for making your own mayonnaise (see recipe on page 332). You can use a food processor or make it by hand; the food processor method is quicker and works well, but the hand method, which gives your forearm a good workout, results in a nicely lighter sauce. *Friend of the Farm* (adapted from *Mastering the Art of French Cooking*).

MAKES ABOUT 3/4 CUP

1/3 cup	extra virgin olive oil
2 tablespoons	white wine vinegar or sherry wine vinegar
1/2 teaspoon	minced shallot
1/4 teaspoon	prepared Dijon mustard
	pinch salt plus more to taste
	freshly ground black pepper
1	egg yolk
1/4 cup	sour cream
3 tablespoons	minced fresh dill
	lemon juice

1. Combine the oil, vinegar, shallot, mustard, pinch of salt, and pepper to taste in a large jar. Cover tightly and shake the jar vigorously until the oil and vinegar have thickened.

2. Beat the egg yolk with the sour cream in a separate bowl until well combined.

3. If you're using a food processor: Process the yolk and sour cream for 30 seconds and then, with the machine still running, pour in the vinaigrette in a very thin stream in about three additions, letting the sauce thicken before each addition.
If you're making the dressing by hand: Using a good whisk, beat the yolk and sour cream; then add the vinaigrette a scant tablespoon at a time, whisking thoroughly after each addition, until the vinaigrette is fully combined with the egg yolk and sour cream.

4. Once you've incorporated the last of the vinaigrette and the sauce is very thick, thin it either with a little lemon juice (1 to 2 teaspoons) or by vigorously stirring in 1 tablespoon boiling water.

5. Stir in the dill. Add salt and pepper to taste.

The Crew

HARVEST WEEK 2, 1998, NEWSLETTER
Hoed herbs, potatoes, leeks, and carrots. Trellised four more beds of tomatoes. Transplanted lettuce. Seeded lettuce and mesclun. Cultivated two fields of winter squash and two fields of sweet corn. Added reinforcements to the deer fence. Finished clearing out and setting up the new packing room. Drove the tractor on Angelic Organics North, the land you shareholders acquired for us, to knock down some thistles. What a sight to be on the other side of the fence! Trained the crew in the harvesting, washing, and packing process. Harvested and packed more than 600 boxes with vegetables and herbs.

Fried Herb Topping
with Garlic and Cheese

Herbs, like most foods, develop rich and mellow flavors when they are cooked in hot oil. They also become irresistibly crispy. There is no better showcase for this topping than a bed of simple al dente pasta—though it would also be delicious over cooked potatoes or tomatoes or a plate of steamed or grilled vegetables. Parsley, tarragon, sage, and oregano leaves are good choices for frying. A small amount of lemon balm or mint would add an interesting, bright flavor in a mix with other herbs. Rosemary and thyme are also delicious fried, but both need their leaves removed from their stems or their whole sprigs removed from the skillet before serving the topping. *Shareholder.*

SERVES 2 TO 3

1/4 cup	extra virgin olive oil
1 cup	chopped fresh herb or a combination of herbs
1–2 cloves	garlic, minced (1/2–1 teaspoon)
1/2 pound	hot cooked pasta or vegetables
1/2–1 cup	freshly grated Parmesan or Asiago cheese (11/2-3 ounces)

1. Heat the oil in a small skillet over medium heat until it is very hot but not smoking. Add the herbs and garlic; cook until the garlic is fragrant and slightly golden and the herbs are crisp but not burned. (You may need to sample a leaf. Some herbs, such as sage, take longer to mellow than others.)

2. Remove the skillet from the heat. Pour the fried herbs and flavored oil immediately over warm cooked pasta or vegetables of your choice. Top with grated cheese. Serve immediately.

Fresh Sage in Polenta

In this version of polenta, the assertive flavor of fresh sage adds a savory accent to cornmeal's gentle sweetness. Fresh Parmesan cheese is the perfect tangy complement. Enjoy this polenta accompanied by thick and juicy tomato-eggplant stew or a hearty bean dish. *Angelic Organics Kitchen.*

SERVES 8

61/2 cups	vegetable or chicken stock
	salt
2 cups	coarse-grained cornmeal (polenta)
2 tablespoons	chopped fresh sage leaves
2 tablespoons	unsalted butter
	freshly ground black pepper
1/4 cup	freshly grated Parmesan cheese (about 3/4 ounce) (optional)

1. Bring the stock to a boil in a large pot over high heat. Add salt to taste. (The amount you use will depend on the saltiness of your stock. The seasonings will concentrate as the polenta cooks, so if you are in doubt, use less.) Reduce to a simmer.

2. Slowly pour the cornmeal into the simmering stock, stirring constantly with a wooden spoon. Continue to cook the cornmeal, stirring constantly to prevent sticking on the bottom, until it pulls away from the sides of the pot and is thick enough for the spoon to stand upright, 5 to 7 minutes.

3. Stir in the sage and butter. Season generously with salt and pepper. Stir in the Parmesan cheese. Serve warm.

Asian Noodle Stir Fry
with Cilantro and Broccoli

You might find yourself making this flavorful Asian noodle dish over and over again. It is delicious served hot for dinner, or cold for lunch on a warm summer day. Cellophane or rice noodles work best, as they are perfect for soaking up the tangy, salty-sweet sauce, and their texture is just right with the broccoli and red pepper. A garnish of gomashio (a mixture of toasted sesame seeds and sea salt, found in specialty stores or Asian markets) provides just the right amount of extra flavoring to make this dish a staple in your kitchen. *Shareholder.*

SERVES 4 TO 5

8 ounces	Asian noodles, such as cellophane noodle or rice noodle
1 tablespoon	peanut oil
2 large cloves	garlic, minced (about 1 teaspoon), divided
3 teaspoons	grated ginger, divided
1/4 teaspoon	hot pepper flakes
1 pound	broccoli (about 1 medium head), cut into bite-size florets
1 large	red bell pepper, sliced into thin strips
1/4 cup	soy sauce or tamari, divided
3 tablespoons	water
1/4 cup	chopped scallions (about 2 small scallions)
1/4 cup	freshly squeezed lime juice (about 2 limes)
1 tablespoon	toasted sesame oil
1/4 cup	chopped fresh cilantro plus more to taste
	gomashio or toasted sesame seeds for garnish

1. Cook the noodles according to package directions.

2. Meanwhile, heat the peanut oil in a wok or large deep skillet over very high heat. Test to see if the oil is ready by dropping in a small piece of the ginger. If it sizzles vigorously upon contact, the oil is ready. Add half the garlic, 1/2 teaspoon of the ginger, and all of the hot pepper flakes; cook, stirring with a spatula, for 30 seconds. Add the broccoli and red bell pepper; cook, stirring, for 3 minutes. Add 1 tablespoon of the soy sauce and 3 tablespoons water; stir, reduce heat to medium-high, cover, and cook until the vegetables are tender, 3 minutes. Transfer the vegetables, along with any juices still in the wok, to a large bowl.

3. Combine the remaining soy sauce or tamari, garlic, and ginger in a small bowl. Add the scallions, lime juice, and toasted sesame oil. Stir to combine.

4. Place the cooked noodles in a large bowl. Pour the soy mixture over the noodles and toss to allow the noodles to soak up the sauce. Add the vegetable mixture and toss again. Add the cilantro and toss. Garnish each serving with the gomashio and more cilantro if desired. Serve immediately or chill before serving.

WELCOME TO THE HARVEST

HARVEST WEEK 1, 1996, NEWSLETTER

This season has been dominated by floods and persistent cloud cover. That's made it tough to get the crops in on time. This week we finally caught up on planting. Catching up is just about impossible in a complex produce operation like ours. It's akin to going back in time and seizing a lost opportunity.

Even though the crops we planted this week went in about four weeks later than scheduled, the recent sunshine has made your vegetables jump. We can sometimes see this growth happening on a daily basis. Yes, daily.

Herb and Fruit Jelly

Perfect for gifts, this is as pretty as it is tasty. With a delightful sweet-savory aroma, herb jelly on crackers or bread makes a wonderful base for almost any cheese. It's also a neat trick for adding amazing flavor to a salad dressing (just dissolve or blend it in) or for glazing sautéed or baked foods (dissolve it over low heat and use it as you would honey). Experiment with the recommended combinations of herbs and juices, or invent your own. You will need three clean, sterilized 1-pint jelly jars with new lids (to sterilize, place jars and lids in a large pot, cover with water, and boil for 15 minutes). *Angelic Organics Kitchen.*

MAKES 5 TO 6 CUPS

3 cups	apple or grape juice
1 cup	chopped fresh herbs
2 tablespoons	freshly squeezed lemon juice or vinegar
1 package (1³/4 ounces, or ¹/₃ cup)	powdered pectin
¹/₂ teaspoon	butter
4 cups	sugar
3 fresh	herb sprigs, rinsed and dried (optional)

1. Heat the juice and herbs to a low simmer in a large, nonreactive pot. Remove the pot from heat, cover, and let stand for 20 minutes to let the flavors develop.

2. Strain the juice and herbs into a large bowl; discard the herbs. Pour the strained juice back into the pot over medium-high heat and add the lemon juice or vinegar. Stir in the pectin and butter. Continue to heat the mixture, stirring constantly, until it comes to a full boil. Add the sugar and continue stirring until it returns to a full boil. Cook the mixture at a rolling boil for exactly 1 minute.

4. Remove the pot from heat and skim off the foam with a clean metal spoon. Drop a fresh herb sprig into the bottom of each jar if desired and immediately pour or ladle the hot jelly into the warm jars, leaving a ¹/4-inch space at the top.

5. Seal the jars with the lids. Any jars that do not seal should be reprocessed in a boiling water bath for 5 minutes or stored in the refrigerator—or enjoyed immediately!

Tabbouleh — Two Versions

The standard debate about this classic Middle Eastern dish is whether it should be prepared as a bulgur salad with some parsley, or as a parsley salad with some bulgur. We think there's no debate; who can resist the aromatic pleasure of herbs, herbs, herbs? Below you will find two recipes for herb-laced tabbouleh. The first is a traditional Lebanese version that successfully makes a case for using masses of fresh parsley and mint. The second is an ingenious variation that features the sweet, licoricey flavor of anise hyssop. Both recipes can be served either as side dishes or, in the traditional manner, on a large platter surrounded by crisp romaine lettuce leaves or pita bread to use as scoops. Bulgur is simply cracked wheat; you will find it in your grocery store or health food store. You can make tabbouleh up to four hours ahead of time; just add the tomatoes about 20 minutes before serving. *Friend of the Farm.*

A Shareholder

I'm a new shareholder and I just picked up my first box of the season. I spent forty-five minutes deliriously sniffing and tasting and generally admiring my greens and herbs—until I finally had to put them in the refrigerator.

Parsley and Mint Version

This version is moist and refreshing. It has lots of juicy tomatoes and dressing, as well as lots of fresh green parsley and mint. Don't worry if you don't have exact quantities; as long as you remember to keep things in balance by cutting back the mint (and perhaps the onion), it won't matter if you use a little less of the other ingredients. You may also make this a drier tabbouleh by using a larger proportion of bulgur.

SERVES 6

1 cup	hot water
1/2 cup	bulgur
3 cups	chopped fresh parsley
2	tomatoes, seeded, finely diced (about 2 cups)
1/2–1 cup	chopped fresh mint leaves
1/2 cup	finely diced onion (about 1 medium onion)
2 large	scallions, halved lengthwise, thinly sliced
2/3 cup	freshly squeezed lemon juice (about 2 lemons) plus more to taste
1/2 cup	extra virgin olive oil
1 teaspoon	salt
1/2 teaspoon	freshly ground black pepper
1/2 teaspoon	ground allspice

1. Combine the water and bulgur in a large bowl. Cover and set aside until the bulgur has completely absorbed the water, 30 minutes to 1 hour. (If after 1 hour the grains are plump and there is still water in the bowl, strain the bulgur and squeeze out any excess water.)

2. Stir the parsley, tomatoes, mint to taste, onions, and scallions into the plumped bulgur. Add the lemon juice, olive oil, salt, pepper, and allspice; toss until thoroughly combined. Add lemon juice to taste (this salad should be lemony but not unpleasantly tart).

3. Cover and let stand for 20 minutes to let the flavors develop. Serve at room temperature.

Anise Hyssop Version

This drier tabbouleh is refreshing and delicious and richly perfumed with the fascinating essence of anise hyssop. If you enjoy the flavors of this but prefer your tabbouleh more saladlike, you can easily reduce the quantity of grain and add more tomatoes and dressing (and herbs to taste). As long as the flavors stay in balance, the ingredients are flexible. Trust yourself, and have fun!

SERVES 6

2 cups	hot water
1 cup	bulgur
2–3 medium	tomatoes, seeded, diced (2–3 cups)
2/3 cup	fresh anise hyssop leaves (and blossoms, if available)
2/3 cup	chopped fresh parsley
1/4 cup	extra virgin olive oil
	freshly squeezed juice of 1/2 lemon plus more to taste
1 teaspoon	salt
	freshly ground black pepper

1. Combine the water and bulgur in a large bowl. Cover and set aside until bulgur has completely absorbed the water, 30 minutes to 1 hour. (If after 1 hour the grains are plump and there is still water in the bowl, strain the bulgur and squeeze out any excess water.)

2. Stir the tomatoes, anise hyssop, and parsley into the bulgur. Add olive oil, lemon juice, salt, and pepper to taste; toss until thoroughly combined. Add lemon juice to taste (this salad should be lemony but not unpleasantly tart).

3. Cover and let stand for 20 minutes to let the flavors develop. Serve at room temperature.

Baked Tofu
with Orange and Thyme

The Crop

HARVEST WEEK 2, 1997, NEWSLETTER

We planned to put beets and lemon balm into your first week's vegetable box. However, we were under duress due to the heat, wind, and harvest learning curve, so we decided it was a pretty nice first box without the beets. The last crop we planned to harvest was lemon balm, but rains came.

This splendidly tasty tofu is a snap to prepare. The fresh herbs balance the intriguing, tangy-sweet flavor of the orange marinade. You can use these tofu strips in sandwiches or dice them and include them in salads, pastas, or soups. If you can find whole nutmeg, grating it fresh (a lemon zester works nicely) will add a strong, sweet, nutty flavor. This dish will also work with rosemary or oregano. *Friend of the Farm.*

SERVES 4

1 pound	firm tofu, cut into $1/2$-inch slices
3 tablespoons	freshly squeezed orange juice (about $1/2$ large orange)
2 tablespoons	soy sauce or tamari
1 tablespoon	balsamic vinegar
2–3 tablespoons	extra virgin olive oil
6 sprigs	fresh thyme
$1/2$ teaspoon	freshly grated nutmeg

1. Arrange the tofu slices in a single layer on a cutting board lined with several clean dish towels; cover with another clean dish towel. Press the water from the tofu by weighing it down with a heavy pan or some other heavy object; let drain for about 30 minutes, wringing out the towels if they get too wet.

2. Preheat the oven to 350° F.

3. Stir the orange juice, soy sauce or tamari, and balsamic vinegar in a small bowl.

4. Coat a baking dish evenly with olive oil. Arrange the thyme sprigs evenly in the dish.

5. Arrange drained tofu slices in a single layer on top of the thyme in the baking dish. Pour the orange juice mixture over the tofu and sprinkle with nutmeg.

6. Bake until tofu is golden brown and all the marinade has been absorbed, 30 to 40 minutes. Serve warm or at room temperature.

The Crew

HARVEST WEEK 4, 1997, NEWSLETTER

July is a month that easily gives way to pandemonium at Angelic Organics. Three to four full days each week are taken up by harvest. In the time that remains, we must conduct many other field activities to ensure that you will be loaded with veggies through the rest of the season. By now our crew has expanded to ten people, who are managing quite admirably to keep up. In fact, we have never been so current with the work as we are this July.

Herb-Flavored Vinegar

Herb-infused vinegars are a great way to preserve the flavor and beauty of fresh herbs. They give a hint of summer to a winter salad or marinade. The best vinegars for herbs are wine, champagne, and cider vinegars. *Friend of the Farm.*

MAKES 2 CUPS

1/2 cup   chopped fresh herbs
2 cups   vinegar (wine, champagne, or cider vinegar)

1. Put the herbs in a pint jar.

2. Heat the vinegar in a medium, nonreactive pot over medium-low heat until it reaches almost a simmer (be careful not to boil it, as this will greatly reduce the flavor of your vinegar). Pour the hot vinegar over the herbs and cover tightly with a nonmetallic lid or with two layers of plastic wrap and a metal lid. Set the jar aside in a cool, dark place for 2 to 3 weeks.

3. Strain the vinegar through a coffee filter or a strainer lined with several layers of cheesecloth. Repeat until the vinegar is completely clear.

4. Pour the strained vinegar into a clean, sterilized, nonmetallic jar or bottle. For a pretty touch, add a clean and dry sprig of the fresh herb with its flowers. Cap the jar or bottle with a plastic or plastic-lined lid or with a brand new cork (available in some grocery stores or at wine- or beer-making supply stores). Tightly sealed and stored in the refrigerator, the herb-flavored vinegar will keep for several months.

Lemon Balm and Sun-Dried Tomato Tapenade

Lemon balm gives this condiment a vivid and lively character. It works beautifully as a salad topper and is terrific with cream cheese on crackers and on grilled vegetables, fish, or chicken. For a spectacular bean salad, toss black beans with this salsa, and let the mixture sit for about an hour before you serve it. You can use packaged sun dried (or your own oven-dried) tomatoes for this recipe if you prefer; just soak them in boiling water first until they are plump and juicy. It's a good idea to rinse diced or chopped onions that will be eaten raw; rinsing takes away some of their bite. *Friend of the Farm.*

SERVES 4

2 tablespoons   sunflower seeds
8   oil-packed sun-dried tomatoes, drained, chopped
1 medium   red onion, diced, rinsed in cold water
1/2 cup   chopped kalamata olives
1/2 cup   extra virgin olive oil
3–4   anchovy fillets, finely chopped (optional)
3–4 tablespoons   chopped fresh lemon balm
    freshly squeezed juice of 1 lemon (about 3 tablespoons)
1 tablespoon   capers
    salt
    freshly ground black pepper

1. Toast the sunflower seeds in a dry, heavy skillet (preferably cast iron) until lightly browned and fragrant. Transfer the seeds to a dish to cool completely.

2. Combine the sun-dried tomatoes, onion, olives, olive oil, optional anchovies, lemon balm, lemon juice, and capers in a medium bowl; toss to combine. Season with salt and pepper to taste.

3. Chop or coarsely grind the sunflower seeds (do not overprocess) and stir them into the mixture. Cover and refrigerate to let the flavors blend for at least 30 minutes before serving.

Chocolate and Anise Hyssop Butter Cookies

Anise hyssop is a brilliant addition to chocolate. These cookies are melty-smooth and bewitchingly good. If you have a food processor, you can use it to easily and thoroughly mix the unchopped anise hyssop with the salt and flour. If you are in a hurry, you can cut the chilling time for the dough in half by chilling it in the freezer. And you can easily rig up a double boiler with what you have in your kitchen. Try using a sauté or omelette pan that fits over the edges of a small pot filled halfway with water. If anise hyssop is not available, you can use 1 tablespoon of lightly crushed whole fennel seeds in its place. The farm crew went absolutely nuts over this one. These cookies are just so good. *Friend of the Farm.*

MAKES 4 TO 5 DOZEN COOKIES

2 cups	flour
1/3 cup	very finely chopped fresh anise hyssop blossoms and/or leaves
1/2 teaspoon	salt
2 ounces	unsweetened chocolate
1 1/2 cups	unsalted butter, softened
1 cup	sugar
1	egg, beaten

1. Stir the flour, anise hyssop, and salt in a medium bowl.

2. Partially fill the bottom of a double boiler with water and bring to a boil, then reduce to a simmer. Fit the top on, put the chocolate in, uncovered, and heat until just melted. Remove from heat and set aside to partially cool.

3. In a large bowl, cream the butter with an electric mixer until pale and creamy. Gradually add the sugar, beating until the mixture is light and fluffy. Beat in the egg and chocolate until combined.

4. Mix in a little of the flour mixture on low speed. Gradually mix in the rest of the flour until the ingredients form a soft dough.

5. Place a square of wax paper on a flat surface. Transfer about half of the dough to the center of the square. Pat the dough into a long, thin log and roll it so that you end up with a cylinder of dough about 1 1/2 inches in diameter. Roll up the cylinder in the wax paper. Repeat the process with the remaining dough. Chill both logs in the refrigerator for 1 hour.

6. Preheat the oven to 350° F.

7. Unwrap the dough and cut it into 1/4-inch slices. Arrange the slices on ungreased baking sheets, spacing them well apart. Bake cookies until brown, about 10 minutes. Immediately transfer cookies to racks to cool.

Anise Hyssop Tea Bread

with Lemon and Walnuts

This is the perfect accompaniment to a midday cup of tea—it's tender, moist, and full of flavor but not too sugary or rich. The natural essence of the anise hyssop gives this loaf a delicious sweetness that doesn't need enhancing. However, if you would like to serve this bread as a dessert, it's sensational topped with fresh berries and one of the sweet syrups or sauces from this chapter. Or you can give the loaf a delectable, lemony-sweet glaze by mixing the juice of two lemons with enough powdered sugar to form a thick, pourable paste to spread over the bread when you've just removed it from the pan. *Friend of the Farm.*

MAKES 1 LOAF

	butter for greasing the pan
1 cup	all-purpose white flour
1 cup	whole wheat flour
1 tablespoon	baking powder
1/2 teaspoon	salt
1/2 cup	butter, softened
1/2 cup	sugar
1/2 cup	chopped fresh anise hyssop blossoms and/or leaves

2   eggs, at room temperature, beaten
     freshly grated zest of 1 lemon
       (about 1 teaspoon)
¹/₂ cup   finely chopped walnuts
¹/₂ cup   freshly squeezed lemon juice
       (about 3 lemons)

1. Preheat the oven to 350° F. Lightly coat a loaf pan with butter.

2. Sift the white flour, wheat flour, baking powder, and salt into a medium bowl.

3. In a large bowl, cream the butter with an electric mixer on high speed until pale and creamy. Gradually add the sugar, beating until the mixture is light and fluffy. Add the anise hyssop, beaten eggs, and lemon zest; beat until thoroughly combined.

4. Stir in the nuts and lemon juice. Gradually add the sifted flour, stirring it into the mixture just until the ingredients are thoroughly combined.

5. Pour the batter into the prepared pan and bake until a toothpick inserted in the center comes out clean, 50 to 55 minutes.

6. Set the pan on a wire rack and let cool for 10 minutes. Unmold the bread and put it on the rack to cool completely. Serve the bread at room temperature or wrap it and store it for up to 5 days.

Baked Lemon Balm Pudding-Soufflé

We apologize for the ambivalent title of this recipe, but we just couldn't choose! Well, actually, we could —but we didn't think "spongy-creamy-oozy-silky-lemony-puddingy-poof" was very clear, either. But we figured that once people started swooning over this, no one would give a hoot what it's called. The farm crew sure didn't, when they taste-tested it! Make sure to get the lemon balm very finely minced; we wouldn't want the texture of the leaves distracting you from the pudding's deliciousness. *Friend of the Farm.*

SERVES 4 TO 6

3¹/₂ tablespoons   butter, softened
1 cup   sugar
2   eggs, yolks and whites separated
1 cup   minced lemon balm leaves
¹/₄ cup   flour
1 cup   milk
¹/₈ teaspoon   salt
    freshly whipped cream (optional, but encouraged)
small sprigs   lemon balm

1. Preheat the oven to 350° F. Place a 7- or 8-inch baking dish inside a larger baking pan. Pour enough water into the larger pan to come ¹/₂ inch up the sides of the smaller dish.

2. In a medium bowl, cream the butter with an electric mixer until it is light and fluffy. Add the sugar, a little at a time, creaming it into the butter. Beat in the egg yolks (reserve the whites). Add the lemon balm and run the beaters just enough to mix it in. Wash the beaters and dry them thoroughly. Stir in the flour with a wooden spoon, then stir in the milk. Set aside.

3. Using the cleaned and dried beaters, beat the egg whites and salt in a medium bowl until stiff.

4. Fold one-quarter of the beaten egg whites into the butter mixture. Add the rest of the beaten egg whites, and with as few strokes as possible, gently fold them in. (Avoid overmixing the batter, as this will make your pudding flat.)

5. Pour the mixture into the small baking dish. Transfer the filled dish, together with the surrounding larger pan and water, to the oven. Bake until the pudding is set and golden brown, 45 minutes to 1 hour.

6. Remove the baked pudding from the oven. Transfer the pan to a wire rack and let cool for at least 10 minutes. Serve warm or cold. Top each serving with a dollop of freshly whipped cream and a small sprig of lemon balm.

Basil Cheesecake

This is a classic, rich, smoother-than-sin cheesecake with a sweet, touch-of-vanilla, touch-of-lemon flavor to rival the best. It has a classic pressed-crumb crust. What that whole cupful of fresh basil contributes to this recipe is a captivating savory-sweet aroma, a sophisticated dimension that makes this an especially elegant dessert. This recipe is made entirely with a food processor, which makes it particularly easy. (If you don't have a food processor, slice the basil into chiffonade by stacking several leaves at a time, rolling them tightly, and slicing across the rolls as thinly as you can. Then mix the ingredients with an electric mixer at low speed.) This cake will keep, tightly covered in the refrigerator, for up to one week; it also freezes very well. For a tasty variation lower in fat, try using fat-free sour cream, 1 pound fat-free cream cheese, and 1 pound Neufchâtel cheese. *Angelic Organics Kitchen* (adapted from *From Asparagus to Zucchini*).

SERVES 10 TO 12

1¹/₂ cups	crushed vanilla wafers or graham crackers (about 45 wafers or 24 crackers)
6 tablespoons	butter, melted, divided
³/₄ cup plus 1 tablespoon	sugar, divided
2 pounds	cream cheese, softened, divided
pinch	salt
2 large	eggs, at room temperature, lightly beaten
2	egg yolks, at room temperature, lightly beaten
1 cup	finely sliced fresh basil
1 cup	sour cream
2 tablespoons	cornstarch
2 tablespoons	freshly squeezed lemon juice
1¹/₂ teaspoons	vanilla
	fresh basil leaves for garnish

1. Preheat the oven to 325° F.

2. Mix the crumbs with 5 tablespoons of the melted butter and 1 tablespoon of the sugar in a small bowl.

3. Grease a 9-inch springform pan with the remaining 1 tablespoon of butter. Press the crumb mixture into the bottom of the pan and press with the bottom of a glass to form a solid, tight crust.

4. Bake until light brown, about 10 minutes. Remove the pan from the oven and let cool. Turn the oven up to 450° F.

5. Put the cream cheese in a food processor in half-pound batches; process at low speed to break it up. (You can also do this with a large bowl and electric mixer.) When all the cream cheese has been processed, add a pinch of salt and process for a few seconds more. Add the eggs and egg yolks, basil, sour cream, remaining ³/₄ cup sugar, cornstarch, lemon juice, and vanilla; process on low speed just until thoroughly combined.

6. Pour the batter into the prepared crust. Bake the cheesecake until it is set and slightly puffed around the edges but still slightly moist and "jiggly" in about a 3-inch circle at the center, 30 to 40 minutes. (The cake will continue to cook and set after you remove it from the oven, so don't worry about that center part. If you bake it until it is solid, your cake will be overcooked.) Remove the pan from the oven and place it on a rack to cool for 30 minutes.

7. Carefully run a knife around the outside of the partially cooled cake to loosen it from the sides of the pan. Leave the cake in the pan, on the rack, to cool completely, about 1 hour. Cover with plastic wrap and transfer to the refrigerator to set for at least 4 hours, preferably overnight.

8. At least 1 hour before serving, remove the cake from the refrigerator. While the cake is still cold, carefully and gently remove the sides of the springform pan. With a sharp knife dipped in hot water and dried, or with a long strand of waxed dental floss, divide the cake into 10 or 12 wedges. (You will need to dip and dry the knife, or wipe the floss clean, several times.) Garnish each serving with a fresh basil leaf.

Onions and Scallions

Nothing makes a home more inviting than the smell of sautéing onions. Even if the bulk of the meal is conspicuously waiting, boxed in Styrofoam and wrapped in plastic bags printed with the name of the closest take-out restaurant, everyone who enters the kitchen will say, "Oh, it smells delicious!" Many a successful recipe begins with that familiar first step: "Sauté the onions . . ." But onion cookery doesn't have to end there. Year round, onions can lend warmth and spunk to breads, soups, and salads.

Scallions, or bunching onions, are precocious young onions that are considered "bulbless." Also called green onions, scallions can range from sweet to spicy, but in general their flavor is milder than a full-grown onion's. Their round, hollow tops are almost always sweet. Scallions can bring as much color, texture, and life to your taste buds as they do to our fields.

Onions Grown by Angelic Organics

Sweet mild onions are large, juicy, and pale white or yellow. You may receive them with their edible green tops. Mild onions are best eaten raw or gently sautéed to keep their juices and delicate texture from cooking away.

Red and yellow storage onions are usually cured (dried) in our fields or greenhouse. Their tops are removed during harvest to make them more resistant to spoilage. Sometimes we give our shareholders uncured storage onions, with

or without their tops. These fresh onions are milder than when cured but less mild than sweet onions. Storage onions have a pungency that cooks away to reveal a sweet flavor.

Scallions are plentiful for the first six or seven weeks of the season. There is no noticeable difference in taste between the white- and purple-skinned varieties, and both have white flesh. They are mildly pungent and have undertones of sweetness.

Storage

Sweet mild onions should be kept in a plastic bag in the refrigerator, but beware the fatal moisture accumulation that causes them to spoil. Eat them within a week or two.

Red and yellow storage onions will keep in any cool, dark, dry place with adequate air circulation for several months if they have been cured. (Angelic Organics typically cures storage onions.) Uncured storage onions should be stored like sweet mild onions. (Be sure to store onions and potatoes in separate places. Moisture given off by potatoes can cause onions to spoil.)

Scallions should be stored unwashed and wrapped loosely in a plastic bag. Put them in the refrigerator, where they will keep for a week. To keep scallions longer, chop off about three-quarters of the tender green tips; the end closest to the root is less perishable.

Handling

When the sulfur in cut onions meets the water in your eyes, it turns into sulfuric acid—hence those infamous onion-induced tears. To reduce the sulfur assault, use a very sharp knife, or chill your onions before cutting

Our Cook

Onions. These old friends hardly need an introduction. They have a place in so many recipes. Their dual nature—zippy when raw, sweet when slowly braised and caramelized—makes them indispensable for a wide range of dishes. The green (uncured) onions that our shareholders receive in the early season are milder and more succulent than the dried versions that come later. Make the most of this time by storing green onions in the refrigerator and using them as quickly as you can.

them. If you're planning to use chopped or sliced onions raw, it's a good idea to rinse them in water before use, as this takes away the unpleasant bite.

Cutting boards can retain the flavor of alliums, so unless you want their pungency invading your next apple pie, make sure to reserve a separate cutting board for onions, scallions, leeks, and garlic.

Onions

Slice or chop onions depending on the specifications given in your recipe. Anytime you cut an onion, be careful to tuck your fingertips slightly inward to keep them out of the path of the blade. Also remember that a little rot is not the kiss of death. If you encounter some while you're slicing or chopping an onion, just cut away the bad sections. If there are a few black spots, thoroughly rinse the whole onion in cool water while rubbing the spots with your thumbs.

To peel and slice an onion, first cut off both the root and stem ends. Set the onion upright on either end and cut it in half. Now the onion is easy to peel. Place the halves on the cutting board, flat edges down, and proceed to slice as thinly as needed.

To peel and chop an onion, slice off the stem end and just the very end of the root. Stand the onion upright on either end and slice from top to bottom through the middle of the onion. Peel the onion. Place each half on your cutting board, cut-side down. Without slicing through the root end, which will hold the onion together, make three parallel slices that are perpendicular to the ends. Now slice across the cuts you just made, and the onion will fall into small pieces.

Scallions

Except for any damaged leaves, you can eat the entire scallion. You can even eat the roots—try roasting them for a crunchy flourish. Rinse scallions in cold water and snip off anything that's floppy. Leave scallions whole if your recipe says so, or display their circular structure by slicing the cylindrical leaves and bulb crosswise. This yields beautiful miniature concentric rings that are perfect for garnishes.

Culinary Uses

Onions

❖ Try sliced or chopped raw onions in salads or sandwiches.
❖ Add cool, crisp, diced raw onions to burritos or quesadillas or to hot tomato-based soups as an especially tasty condiment.
❖ Sauté chopped onions in oil with chopped carrots until soft and golden. Add this mixture to soup near the end of preparation time.
❖ Onions can star in dishes such as risotto, omelettes, frittatas, tarts, gratins, and conserves. The sharp, water-soluble sulfur compounds in onions and scallions get milder as you cook them.
❖ Grill, bake, broil, or stir-fry onions and scallions with a little oil to concentrate their sweetness and flavor.

Scallions

❖ Use chopped scallions as a garnish; they are less pungent than onions. The minced greens of scallions are an especially good substitute for chives.
❖ Use scallions in almost any recipe that calls for onions, raw or cooked, and you'll have great results.
❖ Scallions are excellent in soups and stew, especially when added late in cooking.
❖ Try brushing scallions (and other fresh vegetables) with sesame oil, salt, and pepper, then put them on the grill or under the broiler.

Partners for Onions and Scallions*

❖ Anise seed, basil, bay leaf, chile, cilantro, cinnamon, cloves, curry, dill, garlic, nutmeg, oregano, paprika, parsley, rosemary, sage, thyme;
❖ Dijon mustard, honey, olive oil, sesame oil, vinegar, sugar;
❖ Butter, cream;
❖ Carrots, cooking greens, mushrooms, peppers, tofu, tomatoes;
❖ Apples, lemon, raisins;
❖ Bread crumbs, rice.

*See Louise Frazier's Complementary Herbs & Spices chart, page 345, for suggestions.

Onion Poppy Seed Drop Biscuits

Poppy seeds lend their distinctive flavor and pop pop-pop texture to these delightful biscuits. They go well with soup and salad for a light lunch or supper. For a different but equally distinctive flavor and texture, try using sesame seeds. *Angelic Organics Kitchen* (adapted from *Roots: A Vegetarian Bounty*).

MAKES 40 SMALL BISCUITS

	oil or butter for greasing the baking sheets
2 large	eggs
1/2 cup	canola oil
2 large	yellow onions grated over a dish, liquid reserved
3 cups	unbleached all-purpose flour
1/2 cup	poppy seeds
2 tablespoons	water
2 teaspoons	baking powder
1 1/2 teaspoons	salt
1 teaspoon	sugar

1. Preheat the oven to 400° F. Lightly coat 2 baking sheets with oil or butter.

2. Beat the eggs in a large bowl. Stir in the oil and the grated onions with their liquid. Sift in the flour, then add the poppy seeds, water, baking powder, salt, and sugar. Stir the ingredients just until they are moistened but not completely smooth. (Do not overmix the batter, or it will become stretchy and your biscuits will be tough.)

3. Drop the mixture by the tablespoonful onto the prepared baking sheets. Bake until golden brown, 10 to 15 minutes. Serve warm.

Onion or Scallion and Orange Salsa

Refreshing, juicy, and sweet, oranges are a delightful accompaniment to crisp and pungent raw onions. This salsa is fantastic on anything grilled. It's also great as an addition to a salad plate, over lettuce, or over cottage cheese. The milder scallion version is fantastic on lettuce or endive cups with a salty and creamy cheese such as soft feta, chèvre, or blue. For either version, you can adjust the amount of chile pepper to suit your palate. *Friend of the Farm.*

MAKES 2 CUPS

1/2 cup	minced scallions or onions (about 3 scallions or 1 medium onion)
2 large or 3–4 medium	oranges peeled, seeds removed, diced
2 tablespoons	chopped fresh cilantro
1 1/2 tablespoons	finely chopped chile pepper (or more or less, to taste)
1/4 teaspoon	ground cumin

1. Put the chopped scallion or onion in a strainer and run under cold water. Drain well.

2. Stir all the ingredients in a medium bowl. Serve immediately or cover and refrigerate for up to 1 day.

Spicy Onions and Bell Peppers in Yogurt Sauce
over Corn Bread

The key to the creamy sauce in this recipe is yogurt, which perfectly balances the intense flavors of the onion, garlic, and spices. You may make this dish as hot or as mild as you like by varying the amount of cayenne. For great corn bread, refer to the Fresh Sweet Corn Bread recipe, page 226, or just use your favorite one. Recipe-tester Larry says that whole-grain bread works well in place of the corn bread and that nondairy yogurt can be substituted. The sauce also goes well with curried basmati rice. *Angelic Organics Kitchen* (adapted from *The Moosewood Cookbook*).

SERVES 4

1 loaf	corn bread
2 tablespoons	extra virgin olive oil or butter
2 cups	thinly sliced onion (about 3 medium onions)
1/2 teaspoon	salt
3 medium	bell peppers, stems and seeds removed, thinly sliced
1/2 teaspoon	ground cumin
	freshly ground black pepper
	cayenne pepper
3 cloves	garlic, minced (about 1 1/2 teaspoons)
1/2 – 3/4 cup	yogurt

1. Set the oven to its warm setting or preheat it to 200° F. Wrap the corn bread in aluminum foil and place it in the oven to warm.

2. Heat the oil or butter in a large skillet over medium heat. Add the onion and salt; cook, stirring frequently, until the onion is very soft and just beginning to brown, 10 to 15 minutes.

3. Add the bell peppers, cumin, and black pepper and cayenne to taste. Cook until the bell peppers are tender, about 10 minutes. Add the chopped garlic and cook until fragrant, 1 minute more.

4. Remove the skillet from heat. Stir in 1/2 cup of the yogurt. If you would like a creamier sauce, add the rest of the yogurt.

5. Tear the warm bread into chunks and place it on individual plates. Spoon the onion sauce over the bread. Serve immediately.

The Crew

HARVEST WEEK 9, 1999, NEWSLETTER
Tilled the western half of the new land in preparation for a second rotation of cover crops. Lifted the rest of the onions. Seeded fall chois and lettuce. Set up irrigation lines. Weeded. Trellised tomatoes. Harvested and packed 625 boxes.

A Shareholder

At the beginning of the onion season you sent us a big sweet onion that I cooked into a casserole with the summer squash, garlic, and parsley from that week's box. It's a nice casserole usually, but this onion transformed it into something irresistible.

Scallion-Garlic Chickpea Spread
(Hummus)

A tangy, garlicky, and delicious chickpea purée from the Middle East, hummus is a perfect dip or sandwich spread. This variation introduces the delicate pungency of scallions. Preparation is easy and quick in a food processor, but you can also do the mincing and mashing by hand, with slightly more textured results. If you choose to use canned chickpeas, two 15.5-ounce cans provide the right amount. Recipe-tester Laurel recommends garnishing hummus with chopped parsley or Aleppo pepper and drizzling it with extra virgin olive oil before serving. *Angelic Organics Kitchen* (adapted from *The Moosewood Cookbook*).

MAKES ABOUT 3 CUPS

3 cups	cooked chickpeas, fresh or canned, rinsed
1/2 cup	coarsely chopped scallions (about 3 scallions)
1/2 cup	tahini plus more to taste
1/2 cup	freshly squeezed lemon juice (about 3 lemons)
1/3 cup	fresh parsley
2 cloves	garlic minced (about 1 teaspoon)
3/4 teaspoon	salt plus more to taste
1/4 teaspoon	ground cumin plus more to taste (optional)
pinch	cayenne pepper (optional)

1. Put all of the ingredients in a food processor and process until they form a thick paste. (Alternately, mash and mix everything together with a potato masher, or run the beans through a food mill and stir in the remaining ingredients.)

2. Season to taste with extra salt, cayenne, and cumin. If you like your hummus creamier, stir in more tahini. Serve at room temperature or chilled.

Scallion and Ginger Fried Rice
with Bean Sprouts

This Cantonese-inspired recipe gets its wonderful flavor from a combination of soy sauce, toasted sesame oil, sake, and lots and lots of tasty scallions. Served with stir-fried seafood or tofu and a steamed green vegetable, this makes a delicious feast. Recipe-tester Pamela says, "This recipe is hearty but surprisingly light for a fried rice. And the ginger is prominent and permeates the dish in a great way!" If you do not have a wok, you can use a large skillet. *Friend of the Farm.*

SERVES 6

3 tablespoons	vegetable or chicken stock
1 tablespoon	soy sauce or tamari
1½ teaspoons	toasted sesame oil
1½ teaspoons	salt
⅓ teaspoon	freshly ground black pepper
2 tablespoons	mild-flavored vegetable oil
2½ cups	finely chopped scallions (about 18 scallions)
3 tablespoons	finely chopped or grated fresh ginger
1½ cups	bean sprouts, rinsed and drained
⅓ cup	rice wine or sake
5 cups	cooked rice

1. Stir the stock, soy sauce or tamari, toasted sesame oil, salt, and pepper in a small bowl until well combined.

2. Place a wok over high heat and heat for 1 minute. Add the vegetable oil and swirl it until the bottom and sides of the wok are coated and the oil is very hot. Add the scallions and ginger; stir-fry, tossing them constantly with a spatula, until they are fragrant, about 20 seconds. Add the bean sprouts and rice wine. Continue stir-frying for 1 minute. Toss in the cooked rice and stir-fry until the rice is heated through, about 2 minutes. Remove the wok from heat.

3. Pour the stock mixture over the ingredients in the wok and toss until everything is well coated. Serve immediately.

Ari the Cook and I headed way up into Michigan to get a couple of bunch washers for cleaning scallions. It was an eighteen-hour round trip in our big delivery truck to bring back these two little devices that look like push brooms hooked to an electric motor. Let's hope they were worth the trip. Sometimes these exotic pieces of vegetable equipment make an enormous difference to the operation. Sometimes they bomb.

Grilled Scallions with Sesame Oil

The intense heat of the grill or broiler caramelizes the natural sugars in scallions as they cook, making them exquisitely sweet and tender. Toasted sesame oil gives them a special nutty flavor. Serve these whole as a delicious side dish or slice them for a garnish to enhance the rest of your meal. *Friend of the Farm.*

SERVES 2

8	scallions, greens trimmed to 5 inches, cut in half lengthwise
	toasted sesame oil
	salt
	freshly ground black pepper

1. Preheat the broiler or lightly oiled grill to medium-high heat. Arrange the scallions on a shallow baking sheet or a piece of aluminum foil.

2. Pour a little toasted sesame oil into a small bowl. Use a pastry brush to completely coat the scallions with a thin layer of oil. Season with salt and pepper. Place the scallions under the broiler or on the grill and broil until they are golden brown on all sides, 3 to 5 minutes.

Scallion and Potato Patties

Mashed potatoes make these patties moist and irresistible, and succulent pieces of cooked scallions give them a gentle sweetness that is enhanced by freshly grated nutmeg. Recipe-tester Laurel finds this recipe great for using up leftovers. She says that these patties are excellent when made with flavored mashed potatoes, such as wasabi or garlic mashed potatoes, and her kids love them. *Angelic Organics Kitchen* (adapted from *Greene on Greens*).

SERVES 4

1 tablespoon	butter
1 cup	chopped scallions, white parts and about 2 inches of the pale green parts (about 10 scallions)
2	eggs
1½ cups	cold mashed potatoes
¼ cup	dried bread crumbs
½ teaspoon	salt
¼ teaspoon	freshly grated nutmeg
¼ teaspoon	freshly ground black pepper
3 tablespoons	vegetable oil

1. Melt the butter in a medium skillet over medium heat. When the foam subsides, add the scallions; sauté until tender, 3 to 5 minutes.

2. Beat the eggs in a medium bowl. Add the sautéed scallions, mashed potatoes, bread crumbs, salt, nutmeg, and pepper. Stir until well combined.

3. Place a baking pan in the oven and preheat the oven to 250° F.

4. Heat the oil in a large skillet over medium-high heat. Shape the scallion and potato mixture into manageable patties. Sauté the patties in the skillet, turning them once, until they are golden brown on both sides, 2 to 3 minutes per side. Transfer the cooked patties to the baking pan in the oven to keep them warm while you sauté the next batch. Serve warm.

Onion, Feta, and Parmesan Frittata
with Balsamic Reduction

A frittata is an omelette that thinks it's a quiche, minus the cream. Partway through its cooking time, it's placed under the broiler—and the result is an irresistible puffy-firm texture with a delectable "sealed" exterior. In this spectacular recipe, the sweetness of caramelized onions is accentuated by the saltiness of feta and Parmesan cheeses and heightened by a final coating of balsamic vinegar. A nonstick skillet works best for this recipe; otherwise, you might have difficulty unmolding the frittata during the final steps. Also, be sure to use a skillet with an ovenproof handle. *Angelic Organics Kitchen*, (adapted from *Fields of Greens*).

SERVES 6 TO 8

1 tablespoon	olive oil
3	large onions, thinly sliced
1/2 teaspoon	salt
1/8 teaspoon	freshly ground black pepper
3 cloves	garlic, minced or pressed (about 1 1/2 teaspoons)
8	eggs
1/3 cup	freshly grated Parmesan cheese (about 1 ounce)
1 tablespoon	finely chopped fresh sage
2 tablespoons	butter
3 ounces	feta or mild goat cheese, crumbled
6 tablespoons	balsamic vinegar

1. Heat the oil in a large, nonstick skillet over high heat. Add the onions, salt, and pepper; cook, stirring constantly, until onions start to brown, 3 to 5 minutes. Reduce the heat to very low.

2. Continue to cook, stirring occasionally, for 30 minutes. Add the garlic; cook, stirring occasionally, until onions are very brown and soft, about 10 minutes more. Remove the skillet from heat; transfer the onion mixture to a bowl and set it aside to cool.

3. Preheat the broiler.

4. Beat the eggs in a large bowl. Stir in the cooled onion mixture, Parmesan cheese, and sage.

5. Place a large, ovenproof skillet or pan over medium-high heat and melt the butter. When the foam subsides, reduce the heat to low, pour in the egg mixture, and crumble the feta or goat cheese on top. Cook over low heat until the frittata firms up around the edges and moves easily in the pan when you give it a good shake, 8 to 10 minutes.

6. While the eggs are cooking, heat the balsamic vinegar to a rolling boil in a small pot over high heat; boil until it reduces by half.

7. Transfer the skillet or pan to the broiler and broil until the frittata starts to firm up on top and is lightly golden, 30 to 90 seconds. Be sure to check every 30 seconds. If you find that the eggs are still not cooked to your satisfaction in the center, and the top is in danger of burning, turn the broiler off and leave the pan in the hot oven to set the eggs for another minute or two.

8. Slide the frittata from the skillet onto a large plate or round cutting board. (If you're not using a nonstick skillet, swipe a heatproof rubber spatula around the sides of the frittata to help loosen it from the skillet. Place a large, flat plate over the skillet and, holding the plate firmly against the skillet, flip the plate and skillet together so that the plate ends up on the bottom. Set this flipped combo on the counter and carefully lift the skillet away to uncover the frittata.)

9. Brush the top of the frittata with the balsamic vinegar. Cut into wedges and serve.

Radishes and Young Turnips

With their bright colors, tidy size, and zesty, satisfying flavor, radishes might make a fun snack food for your family. A bowl of these raw pink, white, black, purple, and red gems left on the counter will gradually disappear—and not spoil anyone's appetite for dinner. Sliced or grated, radishes add a wonderful fresh-peppery note to a large range of salads and dishes—yes, even cooked. Once you've discovered the incomparable succulence of tender cooked radish pieces, suspended, say, in a creamy radish-leaf soup, you may take to hiding your radishes from the snackers in your household.

By contrast, if you're used to thinking of turnips as "cooking vegetables," you are in for another delightful discovery. Our tender young turnips have a mild flavor and a delectable, juicy crispness that can be enjoyed raw, much like a radish. In fact, the two are interchangeable in several of the recipes included in this chapter. Of course, young turnips are also wonderful cooked, especially in simple recipes that highlight their delicate taste and texture.

Note: Daikon radishes are actually members of the far-flung cabbage family and look like white, overgrown carrots and taste like mild radishes. Daikon radishes are described in their own chapter, page 274.

Storage

Remove radish or turnip leaves if they are still attached. Store the unwashed greens in a loosely wrapped plastic bag in the vegetable bin of your refrigerator. Because of their high water content, turnips and radishes deteriorate quickly. Store them dry and unwashed in a plastic bag in the refrigerator. Young turnips and most radishes should keep for a week. Black radishes will keep slightly longer.

Handling

Scrub radishes and young turnips well to remove any lingering dirt. Trim off the stems and rootlets. Slice, chop, or mince the roots or leave them whole.

Culinary Uses

❖ Eat radishes and young turnips raw, with room-temperature or melted butter (common in parts of Europe).
❖ Grate radishes and turnips into slaws and salads.
❖ Make canapés: arrange thinly sliced radishes or young turnips on a buttered baguette or on triangular slices of thinly sliced bread and season with salt.

Easter Egg Radish

French Breakfast Radish

Turnip

❖ Blanch whole radishes in boiling, salted water for 5 to 10 minutes (depending on their size), or steam them until just tender, 8 to 12 minutes. Top with butter, salt, and pepper or with a vinaigrette.

❖ Boil whole young turnips for 15 to 20 minutes, or steam them until just tender, 20 to 25 minutes. Top with butter, salt, and pepper or with a vinaigrette.

❖ Try small, young radish and turnip leaves in salads; they are perfectly edible and have a terrific earthy taste similar to watercress.

❖ Cook larger leaves as you would any cooking greens, perhaps mixing them with milder varieties.

Partners for Radishes and Young Turnips*

❖ Basil, borage, chives, cilantro, curry powder, dill, lovage, marjoram, mint, oregano, parsley, rosemary, thyme;

❖ Honey, lemon juice, orange juice, sesame oil, soy sauce or tamari, vinegar;

❖ Butter, cream, cream cheese, feta cheese;

❖ Cucumbers, onions, scallions, sugar snap peas.

*See Louise Frazier's Complementary Herbs & Spices chart, page 345, for suggestions.

Young Turnip Salad
with Apples and Lemon Dressing

Raw young turnips are sweet, with a tender-firm crunch. In this refreshing salad, lemon juice and tart, crispy apples accentuate both of these qualities. For a sweet treat, try tossing in some raisins. Farm friend Andy suggests topping this salad with chopped and freshly toasted pecans or walnuts. This salad was a hit at recipe-tester Laurel's house. She recommends serving it on its own as a dip. *Friend of the Farm.*

MAKES ABOUT 2 CUPS

1 cup	peeled and grated raw young turnips (about 2 medium turnips)
1 cup	peeled and grated tart apples (Granny Smith or greenings) (about 1 large apple)
1/2 cup	finely chopped fresh parsley
3 tablespoons	fresh lemon juice
1 tablespoon	vegetable oil
	salt
	freshly ground black pepper

Toss the turnips, apples, parsley, lemon juice, and vegetable oil in a large bowl. Season with salt and pepper to taste. Cover and refrigerate for 1 hour.

Radish and Cucumber Salad

with Tofu and Soy Vinaigrette

Tender cubes of cold, barely cooked tofu are a wonderful treat in this salad. They provide a satisfying, soft complement to the crispy vegetables—similar to cubes of mild cheese. As for taste, with nippy radish slices and a delicious salty-sweet dressing, this salad has flavor to spare. Try adding a few drops of toasted (dark) sesame oil or tossing in some toasted sesame seeds for a deeper, more "authentically Asian" note. Ginger fans will enjoy a grating of fresh ginger in the dressing. *Friend of the Farm.*

SERVES 4

1/2 pound	firm or medium-firm tofu, cut into 3/4-inch cubes
2 tablespoons	rice vinegar
2 tablespoons	peanut oil or 2 tablespoons untoasted sesame oil
1 tablespoon	tamari or soy sauce
1/2 teaspoon	sugar
	freshly ground black pepper
8	radishes, thinly sliced
2	cucumbers, peeled, quartered lengthwise, seeded, cut into 1/2-inch slices

1. Bring 2 quarts of water to a boil in a medium pot. Add the tofu cubes; boil for 1 minute. Transfer the cubes to a clean dish towel to drain and cool.

2. Stir the rice vinegar, oil, and tamari or soy sauce in a small bowl. Stir in the sugar and pepper to taste. Whisk until well combined.

3. Transfer the cooled tofu cubes to a serving bowl. Add the radish slices and cucumber; briefly toss. Add the dressing; toss again until the salad is thoroughly combined.

Sautéed Radishes

with Radish Greens or Arugula

Radish greens and arugula both have a peppery bitterness that mellows slightly when they are cooked. The succulence of sautéed whole radishes will make you wonder why we don't cook these feisty little roots more often. You can use either radish greens or arugula, or both, for this recipe. Or if you don't have either, you can substitute any cooking green, and perhaps stir in a little prepared mustard or horseradish or a dash of cayenne to compensate for the missing "bite." *Angelic Organics Kitchen.*

SERVES 4

1/4 cup	butter
1 pound	radishes, quartered
4 cups	radish greens or arugula
2 tablespoons	freshly squeezed lemon juice (about 1 small lemon)
	salt
	freshly ground black pepper

1. Melt the butter in a large skillet over medium heat. Add the radishes; cook, stirring constantly, until tender but still crisp, about 5 minutes depending on size. Transfer to a bowl to cool. Return the skillet to stove.

2. Put the greens or arugula in the skillet with the wash water still clinging to the leaves. Cook over medium heat, stirring constantly, just until wilting, 2 to 3 minutes.

3. Turn off the heat. Add the lemon juice and radishes to the skillet; stir until well combined. Season with salt and pepper to taste. Serve immediately.

Sautéed Radishes with Hard-Cooked Eggs
and Spiced Yogurt Sauce

This dish is based on a recipe from Nepal. Cooked radishes add their peppery succulence to pieces of hard-cooked egg in an intricately flavored, currylike (but not spicy-hot) yogurt sauce. Served at room temperature with basmati rice on the side, this makes a marvelous lunch or dinner. For an attractive presentation, add 1/2 teaspoon of turmeric or saffron powder to your rice while cooking. This will turn the rice yellow and make for a prettier plate. Also, if the eggs are overcooked an unpleasant greenish coating will form around the yolks. Lowering room-temperature eggs into barely boiling water, cooking for 10 minutes, then transferring to an ice water bath for 5 minutes will result in perfect hard-cooked eggs every time. *Friend of the Farm.*

SERVES 4

6 large	hard-cooked eggs, halved, each half quartered
1	scallion, chopped
	salt
	freshly ground black pepper
2 tablespoons	ghee or butter, divided
1 bunch	radishes (about 1/2 pound), quartered
1 teaspoon	ground cardamom
1 teaspoon	crushed coriander seeds
1 teaspoon	crushed sesame seeds
1 teaspoon	ground cumin
1 1/4 cups	plain yogurt
1/3 cup	chopped fresh cilantro
	freshly squeezed juice of 1 lemon (about 3 tablespoons)
1 teaspoon	paprika

1. Arrange the hard-cooked egg pieces in a shallow serving dish. Scatter the scallion over the eggs and season with salt and pepper.

2. Melt 1 tablespoon of the ghee or butter in a medium skillet over medium heat. Add the radishes; cook, stirring, until tender, about 8 minutes. Transfer the radishes to a plate and set aside to cool.

3. Let the skillet cool for a couple minutes, then return it to the stove over low heat. Melt the remaining ghee or butter in the skillet. Add the cardamom, coriander, sesame seeds, and cumin; cook, stirring constantly to prevent them from burning, until they are fragrant, 3 to 4 minutes. Scrape the spices into a small bowl and set aside to cool.

4. Put the yogurt in a medium bowl. If it is firm yogurt, beat it vigorously with a fork or whisk until creamy. Add the cooled spices, cilantro, lemon juice, and paprika; stir to combine. Season with salt and pepper to taste.

5. Arrange the cooked radishes over the eggs and scallions in the serving dish. Pour the yogurt sauce evenly over the dish. Serve immediately.

Farmer John Writes

HARVEST WEEK 2, 1996, NEWSLETTER

There were very few days this spring when we could do fieldwork. It was a challenge to approach the really short, drier periods knowing they probably wouldn't last, that rain would fall again immediately and continue for weeks on end. To approach the weather as though it will not support farming—well, that smacks of paranoia and pessimism. It's lucky that your farmer is thoroughly capable of both. I rallied every ounce of help I could muster, headed into the fields before they were dry, and we raced through the work—sometimes skipping lunch, working in shifts, working straight though some weekends, doing whatever it took.

Young Turnip and Apricot Salad with Toasted Walnuts
and Creamy Greens Dressing

Crisp young turnips mixed with dried apricots and toasted walnuts, then tossed with a refreshing, flavorful yogurt-based dressing, make for a unique and special salad that will delight your dinner guests. This recipe is a great way to use up any leftover turnip or radish greens. A tarragon-infused vinegar goes well here; see the recipe for Herb-Flavored Vinegar, page 117, if you'd like to make your own. *Friend of the Farm*

SERVES 4 TO 6

¹/₂ cup	walnut pieces
4–5	young turnips, cut into matchstick-size sticks
¹/₂ cup	finely sliced dried apricots (preferably unsulfured)
1	small bunch parsley, chopped
1	bunch young turnip greens or radish greens (or both), coarsely chopped
¹/₂ cup	mild-flavored vegetable oil
¹/₂ cup	extra virgin olive oil
¹/₃ cup	vinegar
¹/₄ cup	plain yogurt
2	shallots, quartered
1–2	jalapeños or other chile peppers, stems and seeds removed, quartered
1 clove	garlic, quartered
2 teaspoons	dry mustard
1 tablespoon	grated horseradish
1 teaspoon	soy sauce or tamari
	salt
	freshly ground black pepper
	salad greens of your choice

1. Toast the walnuts in a dry, heavy skillet (preferably cast iron) over medium-high heat, stirring constantly, until lightly browned and fragrant. (Be careful not to overtoast them, as they will burn very quickly once toasted.) Transfer the walnuts to a dish to cool.

2. Combine the turnips, apricots, and walnuts in a large bowl and stir to combine.

3. Put the parsley, chopped greens, vegetable oil, olive oil, vinegar, and yogurt into a blender; process briefly, until the ingredients are just combined. Add the shallots, chile pepper, garlic, dry mustard, horseradish, and soy sauce or tamari; process until thick and creamy. If necessary, thin the dressing with a little extra yogurt or a tablespoon of cold water.

4. Pour the dressing over the turnip-apricot-walnut mixture; toss until well combined. Season with salt and pepper to taste.

5. Line individual plates with a generous amount of salad greens; spoon the turnip mixture on top. Serve immediately.

The Crew
HARVEST WEEK 10, 1998, NEWSLETTER

Seeded radishes, spinach, mesclun, and lettuce mix and transplanted two beds of lettuce and two beds of kohlrabi all in one afternoon. Reworked the entire onion cleaner and cleaned our first two beds of onions. Hoed over 15,000 row feet of fall carrots, beets, and rutabagas. Harvested and packed more than 700 boxes.

Radishes are crisp, pungent, and refreshing. They come in myriad shapes, colors, and sizes. While they are most often eaten fresh and uncooked, radishes can also be served braised, steamed, sautéed, in soups, or—my favorite—thinly sliced in stir-fries. If you do cook them it's best to allow just a hint of tenderness; that crispness is worth keeping. Tangy and tasty radish greens are great in salads, stir-fries, and soups.

A Shareholder

We got our first box yesterday, and cooked out with our veggie-sharing partners and other friends—what a perfect way to spend the first day of summer! I've never liked radishes—until last night. We ran through the herbs and squash in no time and loved every bite. Thanks so much for the great work you do.

Ginger-Glazed Young Turnips
with Cider and Raisins

This is a spectacular way to serve young turnips. Their refreshing taste and texture is enhanced, but not overwhelmed, by an exciting, sweetly pungent sauce made from fresh ginger and juicy sweet raisins. Ginger lovers will want to use lots of ginger, but even in its mildest version, this dish is superb. To make the most of the great flavors in this recipe, serve it over jasmine rice. *Friend of the Farm.*

SERVES 4

1/2 teaspoon	salt plus a dash, divided
1 bunch	young turnips, trimmed
1/4 cup	sugar or honey
1/8 cup	white vinegar
1–2 teaspoons	freshly grated ginger (or more, to taste)
2 tablespoons	cornstarch
1/4 cup	apple or grape cider
1/2 cup	raisins
2 tablespoons	finely chopped fresh parsley
	finely chopped crystallized ginger (optional garnish)

1. Bring 2 quarts water to a boil in a large pot. Add a dash of salt, then the young turnips. When the water returns to a boil, cover and reduce heat. Simmer the turnips gently until tender but not mushy, 10 to 15 minutes depending on size. Remove the pot from heat and transfer the turnips to a dish to cool.

2. Meanwhile, transfer 1/2 cup of the hot cooking water to a medium pot. Stir in the sugar or honey, vinegar, and ginger to taste. Add 1/2 teaspoon salt.

3. Combine the cornstarch and cider in a small glass or bowl; let stand until cornstarch is dissolved.

4. Slice the turnips to your desired thickness.

5. Place the pot with the ginger mixture over medium heat. Stir in the cider mixture and adjust the heat so the ingredients simmer. Cook, stirring constantly, until the mixture is smooth and thickened, 2 to 3 minutes.

6. Remove the pot from heat; stir in the raisins and sliced turnips and continue to stir for 2 minutes, until the mixture reaches a thick, gravylike consistency. If necessary, stir in a bit more cider to reach the desired consistency. Stop stirring and let stand for 2 minutes. Garnish with parsley and crystallized ginger.

Young Turnip Galette with Cardamom

A galette can be any manner of flat, round cake or tart. In this case, it is an exquisite arrangement of buttery-thin turnip slices, glazed and sealed together in an overlapping pattern like the surface of a fine apple tart. This sophisticated galette, however, is quite easy to make; it has no pastry—no fussy ingredients or procedures—and it cooks right on your stovetop. Farmer/caterer Jennifer suggests serving it "as a component of a menu featuring dainty spring vegetables, or as a side with an Indian vegetable curry, or even as a light, not-too-sweet dessert to impress your vegetable-leery friends!" Shareholder Matt suggests trying this with grilled lamb chops or a roasted chicken. Because cardamom loses much of its flavor once it is ground, you might like to grind it fresh: split the whole pods and grind the seeds with a mortar and pestle (or in a shallow bowl with the back of a sturdy spoon). About twelve cardamom pods yields 1/2 teaspoon of ground cardamom. Because of the more intense flavor, you will want to make it a scant measurement. *Friend of the Farm.*

SERVES 4

1 tablespoon	cornstarch
1 tablespoon	powdered sugar
1/2 teaspoon	freshly ground cardamom
2 tablespoons	cold water
3	young turnips, preferably of similar size, sliced into very thin rounds
6 tablespoons	butter
	salt
	cinnamon sugar (if serving as a dessert)
	whipped cream (if serving as a dessert)

1. Whisk the cornstarch, powdered sugar, and cardamom in a medium bowl. Whisk in the water until it forms a thin paste. Stir in the turnips and coat evenly.

2. Melt the butter in a large skillet over medium heat, then remove the skillet from heat.

3. Place one of the turnip rounds in the center of the skillet. Then add 4 more, slightly overlapping the first round, so that you end up with a four-petaled flower shape in the center of the skillet. Add the rest of the slices, overlapping them in concentric circles, until you have used them all to form a large single circle that fills the bottom of the skillet. (Ideally, there should be no skillet showing through between the overlapping slices.)

4. Place the skillet over medium heat; cook until slices are golden brown on the bottom, about 10 minutes.

5. If you are serving the galette as a side dish: Carefully flip the galette with a large spatula. Continue to cook the galette until it is golden brown on the second side, about 10 minutes. Remove the skillet from heat, season galette with salt to taste, and slice into triangles.

If you are serving the galette as a dessert: Sprinkle the top surface of the galette with a generous layer of cinnamon sugar, then flip it with a large spatula. Continue to cook until a caramelized crust forms on the bottom, 5 to 8 minutes. Remove the skillet from the heat, slice galette into triangles, and top each slice with a dollop of whipped cream.

FORCES IN FOOD

If one needs to stimulate one's thinking then one should use especially the salty stimulant of the radish for instance. If someone is not very active in the head it is good for him to add some radish to his food which will activate his thoughts a little. So you see the strange fact emerges: One can say radishes stimulate thinking. And one does not even need to be very active oneself, the thoughts simply come when one eats radishes—such strong thoughts that they even generate powerful dreams.

—**RUDOLF STEINER,** *NUTRITION AND STIMULANTS*

Salad Greens

We grow and distribute several varieties of head lettuce as well as seasonal combinations of leaf lettuce and mustard greens. The salad greens start early and keep coming throughout the season. Our shareholders are sometimes salad greens connoisseurs who ache for more. Some of them, however, may have serious trouble keeping up with the steady supply of fresh salad greens. But we ask that, instead of feeling overwhelmed, they think of salad greens as their medium. Because each week they receive supplies in their vegetable boxes perfect for salad building.

Experiment with salad building! You can top greens with fruit, nuts, seeds, pasta, and whole grains in addition to the numerous dressings and salad suggestions we've included in this chapter. You can find dressing recipes in other chapters as well, including the Asparagus, Beets, Cooking Greens, Herbs, Sugar Snap Peas, and Tomatoes chapters. Additionally, this chapter will show you how to mix a few cooking greens (like spinach, for example) into your salads, adding variety and complexity to them. As nineteenth-century editor and author Charles Dudley Warner once wrote, "You can put everything, and the more things the better, into a salad, as into a conversation; but everything depends on the skill of mixing."

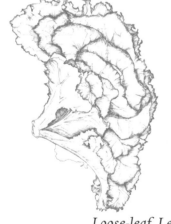

Loose-leaf Lettuce

Summer Crisp

Butterhead Lettuce

Romaine

Salad Greens Grown by Angelic Organics

Loose-leaf lettuce has soft, open heads of loosely joined, tender leaves. It requires a lighter dressing and more delicate handling than other lettuces.

Summer crisp lettuce forms a compact head or bunch. Its thick leaves are crisp, sweet, and juicy and are more tolerant of hot weather than other lettuces.

Butterhead lettuce has ruffled outer leaves and a soft, folded heart. It has a tender, elegant rosette-shaped head.

Romaine lettuce has long, broad, upright leaves that bunch as they mature. The strong taste and snappy texture combine well with heavier dressings.

Mesclun mix from our farm is composed of seasonal combinations of the following baby-sized greens: arugula, hon tsai tai, mibuna, mizuna, Osaka purple, Red Russian kale, tatsoi, ruby red chard, and several varieties of tender young lettuces. On a rare occasion you may find a bunch of arugula or tatsoi making a solo appearance in your box, without their usual mesclun mix counterparts. When using these tangy greens in delicious cooked recipes, don't forget to refer to the Cooking Greens chapter, page 81, for more suggestions.

place them loosely in a mesh bag or thin towel, then go outside and swing the bundle around your head.)

Culinary Uses

❖ For a simple salad, drizzle greens with a light dressing.

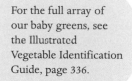

Hon Tsai Tai

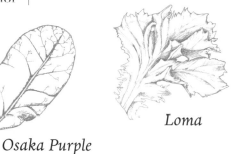

Osaka Purple

Loma

For the full array of our baby greens, see the Illustrated Vegetable Identification Guide, page 336.

Tatsoi

Marvel of Four Seasons

Storage

Store unwashed lettuce or mesclun in a plastic bag in the refrigerator. To store lettuce or mesclun that you have already washed and dried, roll the leaves loosely in a kitchen towel, put the towel in a plastic bag, and place the package in the vegetable crisper bin. (Wet greens will spoil quickly, so make sure they are truly dry before refrigerating them.) If you have a salad spinner, wash and spin the greens before refrigerating them. Eat mesclun mix within three or four days, and use lettuce within a week.

Handling

Salad greens bruise easily, so be sure to handle them gently. For lettuce, slice the head at its base with a sharp knife and let the leaves fall open. Discard any damaged or leathery outer leaves and tear large leaves into bite-size pieces. Both lettuce and mesclun mix can be washed by swishing them around in a basin of cold water. (If a lot of dirt collects in the water, wash them a second time.) Dry the greens in a salad spinner. (Or

❖ For a richer salad, include combinations of greens and lettuce with grapefruit, pear, avocado, raw or roasted nuts, flax or sunflower seeds, olives, fine cheeses, cooked grain, pasta, croutons, or edible flowers like nasturtium.
❖ Add milder, sweeter lettuces to the mix if you find the flavor of mixed greens strong (especially in the heat of summer).
❖ In many cultures it is common to cook lettuces. The tender succulence of the delicate cooked leaves adds a special elegance to all manner of dishes.
❖ Add a few leaves of mesclun mix to a soup or a stir-fry late in cooking.
❖ See recipes for cooked lettuce and mesclun in this chapter to further spark your creativity.

Partners for Salad Greens

❖ Anise hyssop, basil, black pepper, dill, fennel leaves, garlic, lemon balm, mint, parsley, tarragon;
❖ Dijon mustard, lemon juice, oils, vinegars;
❖ Cheeses, hard-cooked eggs;
❖ Chicories, raw vegetables, edible flowers, grated root vegetables (beets, celeriac, kohlrabi, turnips, etc.), mushrooms, sprouted seeds and beans, watercress;
❖ Apples, dried fruits and berries, oranges, pears, peaches, raisins, raw or roasted nuts;
❖ Capers, croutons, olives, pasta, tofu.

Arugula is a mustard. Picked young, it has a nutty (some say sesame) flavor succeeded by a "horseradish-y" bite. Arugula, which is rich in vitamin C and minerals, adds much nutritional value to your salads. Chard, ruby red chard, and Red Russian kale are better known at maturity as cooking greens but are as nutritious an addition to mesclun as baby greens. Mizuna, tatsoi, and mibuna are Asian greens from the brassica family. Mizuna has an attractive pale green, jagged-toothed leaf. Tatsoi has a round leaf and grows to a symmetrical flower-shaped head at maturity. Mibuna has a long, green, slender leaf reminiscent of dandelion. Hon tsai tai and Osaka purple, both brassicas as well, are Asian greens with a red or purple tinge to their stems and leaves.

Our Cook

In Provence, France, *salade de mesclun* means a mixed-up mess of wild baby greens. Mesclun gained popularity in the United States in the early to mid-'90s. Today you can buy it at farmers markets, upscale grocery stores, and even at restaurants that feature quality local produce. Mesclun varies depending on where it's sold. Some growers include more lettuce, others favor mustards, and some add herbs and edible flowers. For me, mesclun is a word packed with potential for a confetti of delightful flavors and textures.

Sweet Maple and Balsamic Vinegar Dressing

Try this dressing over a mesclun mix or tossed with grilled or steamed vegetables. You might like to add some bitter greens such as endive, radicchio, or arugula to your salad mix to complement the sweetness of the dressing. *Angelic Organics Kitchen.*

MAKES ABOUT 1 CUP

1 cup	extra virgin olive oil
3 tablespoons	maple syrup
2 tablespoons	balsamic vinegar
2 tablespoons	finely sliced fresh basil
1 tablespoon	freshly squeezed lemon juice
1 teaspoon	dry mustard
1 clove	garlic, minced (about 1/2 teaspoon)
	salt
	freshly ground black pepper

1. Combine the oil, maple syrup, balsamic vinegar, basil, lemon juice, dry mustard, and garlic in a large jar. With the lid tightly screwed on, shake the jar vigorously until the oil and vinegar have thickened. Add salt and pepper to taste and shake again to combine.

2. Store the dressing in the refrigerator for up to 2 weeks. To serve, toss it with salad greens or grilled or steamed vegetables.

A SHAREHOLDER ON HOMEMADE SALAD DRESSINGS

We make our own salad dressing in the bottom of the salad bowl. Each time it's a little different. Since we shy away from dairy products, we use raw sesame tahini for a creamy texture. Then we add oil, vinegar, and something salty. The salty item could be tamari or miso or umeboshi plum paste or sea salt. Spices are always nice. We use whatever we feel like that day. Sometimes it's basil, oregano, or fennel from the little herb garden in our front yard. Or we might use dried herbs. Then, for a little tang, we add spicy mustard or fresh garlic or both. If we feel like a smoky flavor, we use a drop or two of toasted sesame oil. We put the greens on top and don't toss it all together until just before we eat it. Even the kids get into the act. Our Coco, who is nine years old, is a great salad dressing chef.

Spiced Bitters Dressing

Allspice and a few dashes of Angostura bitters give this lovely dressing an intriguing spiced note. Angostura bitters is a specialty food and beverage flavoring made from a secret combination of tropical herbs and spices. First invented as a remedy for digestive troubles by a German doctor stationed in the port town of Angostura, Venezuela, it is now widely used to lend flavor to a variety of food and drinks. You can find it at liquor stores and some health food stores. This dressing is especially delicious over a salad of greens mixed with a mildly bitter leaf, such as mizuna or arugula. It's also an excellent dressing for mesclun mix. *Angelic Organics Kitchen*.

MAKES 3/4 CUP

1 teaspoon	sugar
1/2 teaspoon	prepared Dijon mustard
1/2 teaspoon	freshly ground black pepper
1/4 teaspoon	salt
1/8 teaspoon	allspice
2 tablespoons	red wine vinegar
3 dashes	Angostura bitters
1/2 cup	peanut oil or other vegetable oil

1. Combine the sugar, mustard, pepper, salt, and allspice in a small bowl. Whisk in the red wine vinegar and bitters. Continue to whisk, adding the oil in a slow, thin stream, until the dressing is thick and the oil and vinegar no longer separate.

2. Store the dressing in the refrigerator indefinitely. To serve, toss it with salad greens or grilled or steamed vegetables.

OUR COOK
ON HOMEMADE SALAD DRESSINGS

Salad dressings are easy to make but can seem mystifying. A rule of thumb for vinaigrettes is to use 1 part vinegar to 3 parts oil; then you can adjust the balance based on the acidity of the vinegar. A good dressing can be as simple as fruity olive oil and lemon juice sprinkled over greens—or it can include herbs and salty cheese for a stronger taste. Salad dressings keep well in the refrigerator, and when made with herbs and other strong seasonings, their flavors actually deepen over time. When tasting a salad dressing it's best to sample it on what it will be eaten with, like a piece of lettuce; otherwise it can be hard to judge its intensity. It's fun to experiment by adding various ingredients to a basic vinaigrette.

Farmer John Writes

The notes were popping, streaming from the inside outward. . . . They began to acquire forms, shapes. The music emerged into my consciousness as numerous varieties of baby greens and lettuce. . . . The impeccably groomed leaves sauntered, twisted, and whirled down the Runway of Celestial Greens in exquisite choreography.

—FROM JOHN'S BOOK *FARMER JOHN ON GLITTER & GREASE*

The Crop

HARVEST WEEK 1, 1999
Our growing manager said to me last night, "What are we going to do with all the lettuce? We've got so much lettuce, and it's all big and beautiful." I said, "Give it all. The shareholders won't mind. It's the first box—they're not tired of anything yet. Just cram it in somehow."

—FARMER JOHN

A Shareholder

There is no salad to compare with the greens from Angelic Organics. The mesclun is sweet! The flavors vary and mingle, blend and stand out all at the same time. I forget how wonderful a salad is until the first box of the season . . . I remember and I'm hooked all over again.

Arugula Pesto

Here is a saucy way to use up a bunch of late-season arugula. In this recipe, the strong, peppery snap of mature arugula finds its counterpart in Asiago cheese. Blended to creamy smoothness with garlic, olive oil, and toasted pine nuts, this vibrant pesto will make something brilliant of a basic pasta meal. You can also try it tossed with roasted potatoes or steamed vegetables. Store extra pesto in either the refrigerator or the freezer; if you plan to freeze it, don't add the cheese until after the pesto has thawed. *Angelic Organics Kitchen.*

MAKES ABOUT 1½ CUPS

¼ cup	pine nuts
2 cups	mature arugula
½ cup	freshly grated Asiago cheese (about 1½ ounces)
½ cup	extra virgin olive oil
1 clove	garlic, smashed
	salt
	freshly ground black pepper

1. Preheat the oven to 350° F.

2. Toast the pine nuts in a dry, heavy skillet (preferably cast iron) over high heat until they start to brown in spots and become fragrant. Transfer the nuts to a dish to cool.

3. Combine the arugula, Asiago cheese, oil, garlic, and pine nuts in a blender or food processor; process until thoroughly combined and smooth. Season with salt and pepper to taste.

Braised Lettuces

Tired of munching bunny food? Don't be afraid to add heat to lettuce. In this recipe, small heads of lettuce are carefully bundled and cooked like whole vegetables—first blanched to tender succulence, then braised to give them a buttery golden glow. Cooking lettuce this way brings out a natural, delicate sweetness in the leaves. The bunnies don't know what they're missing. *Shareholder.*

SERVES 3 TO 4

3 to 4 small	heads lettuce, rinsed whole under running water, tough or bruised outer leaves removed
½ teaspoon	salt
1–2 tablespoons	butter
	freshly ground black pepper

1. Tie a piece of string around each head of lettuce, just tightly enough to hold the leaves together and promote even cooking.

2. Bring 2 quarts of water to a boil; add the salt and reduce the heat to a simmer. Add the lettuce heads and boil for 3 minutes.

3. Drain the lettuces in a colander and let cool. When cool enough to handle, gently squeeze them in your hands to remove any excess water. Remove the string.

4. Melt the butter in a large skillet over medium heat. Add the lettuce heads; cook until lightly browned, about 3 minutes. Continue to cook, turning them carefully, for another 3 minutes. Season with salt and pepper to taste. Serve immediately.

FORCES IN FOOD

What lives in the leaves of the plants has a rather similar connection with the lungs, and all that belongs to that system . . . a person whose breathing system requires strengthening is well advised to eat as much leaf food as possible. These things have their close connection with the healing forces which are in the world in the kingdoms of nature, for those parts of individual plants that have a definite relationship to such organs contain forces of healing for these regions of the human organism. Thus . . . leaves . . . contain great forces of healing for the lung system.

—RUDOLF STEINER

The Crop

HARVEST WEEK 14, 1997, NEWSLETTER

When our field manager and I took a jaunt to assess the winter squash, we discovered that the storm had shredded half the lettuce. It looked more like it had been ripped by a sandstorm than pelted by a fall downpour. I had frequently marveled at this crop of about ten thousand heads, which would have been twelve or thirteen heads for each of you this fall. It was among the most beautiful lettuce we had ever raised.

We're sad about the lettuce loss, but we remind ourselves that it is not a farm catastrophe. This is farming. Farming is beautiful crops, decimated crops, parched crops, bountiful crops. We plan our vegetable production with setbacks in mind. We anticipate weather terrors. We overplant. As we moved past the lettuce field, I felt fortunate to have a couple thousand chois under row cover, another bed of mesclun mix, and a new bed of spinach.

—FARMER JOHN

A Shareholder

My husband picked up our box on Wednesday, and going through all the goodies was so exciting. I felt like a kid in a candy shop but so much healthier. We've been eating salads every night. It seems extravagant. Saturday night dinner was the best so far. I mixed up a salad of mesclun, spinach, radishes, and onions with a light dressing. Then I sliced the beets, yellow squash, and zucchini and marinated them in olive oil flavored with finely chopped oregano, basil, and garlic tops (which I'd never seen before). I grilled the veggies and served them hot over the cold salad.

Mesclun Soufflé

The delicate texture and complex array of tastes in mesclun mix make it a particularly suitable soufflé ingredient. Creamy goat cheese is the perfect accent, providing lots of lively flavor that highlights but does not overwhelm the exquisitely piquant young greens. Shareholder Carolyn says this makes a beautiful presentation. She suggests experimenting with a variety of soft cheeses. *Angelic Organics Kitchen* (adapted from *Greene on Greens*).

SERVES 4 TO 6

	butter for greasing the baking dish
1/4 cup	dried bread crumbs
5	egg yolks
4 ounces	soft goat cheese
1/2 cup	ricotta cheese
1 cup	mesclun mix
3 tablespoons	finely chopped scallions or chives
3/4 teaspoon	salt
pinch	freshly grated nutmeg
6	egg whites
pinch	salt

1. Preheat the oven to 425° F. Lightly coat a 6- to 8-cup soufflé dish with butter and dust with bread crumbs.

2. Combine the egg yolks and goat cheese in a large bowl; mash with a fork or potato masher until smooth. Add the ricotta cheese and beat the mixture with an electric mixer until well combined.

3. Stir in the mesclun and scallions or chives. Season with the salt and nutmeg. Wash and thoroughly dry the beaters.

4. Beat the egg whites with the electric mixer (or by hand) in a medium bowl with a pinch of salt until they form stiff peaks. Add 1/4 of the beaten egg whites to the cheese and greens mixture. Gently stir them in, just enough to lighten the mixture. Carefully fold in the remaining beaten egg whites. Pour this mixture into the prepared soufflé dish. Gently smooth out the top with a spatula.

5. Bake the soufflé until it has puffed, 25 to 30 minutes. Serve immediately.

Sugar Snap Peas

We farmers can't live without a few sugar snap peas fresh from our kitchen garden. But because they are exceedingly laborious to harvest and are ready to harvest before we begin delivering our vegetables, we don't grow them for distribution to shareholders. Even so, they are an important early season vegetable that you'll find readily available from sources like farmers markets, food co-ops, and home gardens. Fresh or lightly cooked, sugar snap peas can be enjoyed pods and all.

Storage

Eat sugar snap peas as fresh as possible, within four or five days of harvest. To store them, put whole, unwashed peas in a perforated plastic bag in the crisper drawer of your refrigerator.

Handling

Rinse sugar snap peas in their pods and pat them dry. To string both sides at once, hold the top stem-end and pull down toward the flat side of the pea. Alternatively, string peas after cooking to retain sweetness.

Culinary Uses

❖ Arrange raw, fresh sugar snap peas atop salads or on a tray with other spring vegetables.
❖ Add raw sugar snap peas to a stir-fry or soup in the last minutes of cooking.
❖ Steam sugar snap peas until just tender-crisp, 3 to 5 minutes. Toss with butter, olive oil, cream, vinaigrette, or pesto.
❖ Add leftovers to omelettes or to chilled vegetable or pasta salads.

Partners for Sugar Snap Peas*

❖ Basil, chervil, chives, cilantro, curry, dill, garlic, ginger, lovage, mint, nutmeg, parsley, rosemary, sage, tarragon, thyme;
❖ Lemon juice, toasted sesame oil, olive oil;
❖ Butter, cream;
❖ Almonds, pine nuts, sesame seeds;
❖ Carrots, celery, cucumbers, leeks, mushrooms, onions, pasta, potatoes, rice, turnips.

*See Louise Frazier's Complementary Herbs & Spices chart, page 345, for suggestions.

Our Cook

Peas are so cute. They always remind me of little kids, maybe because I remember many mornings spent picking peas as a child. And I remember evenings shelling them, the tight green balls pinging against the sides of the bowls. Unfortunately, the shell type my parents grew, while yielding many grocery sacks full of pods, diminished to a few small bowls of green peas. Now I know about sugar snap peas, which are currently flourishing in the kitchen garden. These don't need to be shelled, thus reducing labor and producing higher volume. Just toss them into a stir-fry, steam them lightly, or simply crunch them raw.

Farmer John Writes

When I was little, my mom happily toiled amongst her vegetable and flower gardens on our farm; occasionally, I helped her—obediently, with little enthusiasm or interest. I remember my sister was usually assigned the task of shucking the peas. My mom would often be disappointed at the few peas that resulted from my sister's efforts; being the loyal brother, I would never show my mom the site amongst the pine trees where my sister was throwing the unshucked peas when she got tired of shucking. But Mom found the pile eventually.

—FROM JOHN'S BOOK *FARMER JOHN ON GLITTER & GREASE*

Sugar Snap Pea and Cucumber Salad
with Walnut-Dill Dressing

Delicate cucumber slices and refreshing dill are wonderful companions for crispy-sweet sugar snap peas. The robust flavor of a walnut dressing adds depth to the bright flavors in this summery salad. Recipe-tester Pamela recommends this recipe for its "refreshing and rich combination." Though some people find they need to string their peas, you might find you can skip the process altogether. *Friend of the Farm.*

SERVES 4

1 pound	sugar snap peas
1	cucumber, peeled if thick-skinned, halved lengthwise, seeded, thinly sliced
1 tablespoon	walnut oil or peanut oil
2 tablespoons	chopped walnuts
1 1/2 teaspoons	freshly squeezed lemon juice (about 1/2 lemon)
1 tablespoon	water
1 tablespoon	fresh dill or 1 teaspoon dried dill
1/8 teaspoon	cayenne pepper
	salt
	freshly ground black pepper

1. Remove the strings from both edges of the pea pods (start by gently pulling from the stem).

2. Place the peas in a steamer basket set over 1 1/2 inches boiling water, cover, and steam until they are just crisp-tender, 3 to 5 minutes.

3. Drain the peas in the sink and immediately run cold water over them. Transfer the peas to a clean, dry dish towel and pat them dry. Place them in a large bowl and add the cucumber.

4. Put the oil, walnuts, lemon juice, water, dill, and cayenne pepper into a blender. Blend until smooth.

5. Pour the walnut dressing over the cucumbers and peas. Toss until well combined. Season with salt and pepper to taste.

Steamed Sugar Snap Peas
with Papaya Salsa

This is an exceptionally pretty and great-tasting way to serve sugar snap peas. It's easy enough to make as a side dish for a regular meal and elegant enough to serve as an appetizer at a dinner party. *Friend of the Farm.*

SERVES 4

1 cup	peeled, seeded, diced papaya (about half a large papaya)
1/2 cup	chopped fresh cilantro
1 tablespoon	minced onion
2 teaspoons	freshly squeezed lime juice
2 teaspoons	rice vinegar
1/8 teaspoon	salt
1/8 teaspoon	ground white pepper
1 pound	sugar snap peas

1. Combine the papaya, cilantro, onion, lime juice, rice vinegar, salt, and white pepper in a medium bowl. Gently toss the ingredients until well combined.

2. Remove the strings from both edges of the pea pods (start by gently pulling from the stem).

3. Place the peas in a steamer basket set over 1 1/2 inches boiling water, cover, and steam until they are just crisp-tender, 3 to 5 minutes.

4. Drain the peas and immediately run cold water over them. Transfer the peas to a clean, dry dish towel and pat them dry.

5. Arrange the sugar snap peas on individual plates and top with the papaya salsa. Serve immediately.

> *Farmer John Writes*
>
> The land has a feel underfoot that melts me to it.
>
> —FROM JOHN'S BOOK *FARMER JOHN ON GLITTER & GREASE*

It's been a spectacular season so far, in spite of frequent, heavy rains and erratic machinery. Usually we are running a bit behind by now; the spring planting and weed control overlap scarily with the first harvest weeks. This spring, we've stayed on top of all the work. This sets the tone for the whole season. Timeliness is probably the most important aspect of farming. We make sure to have a big crew. We keep an arsenal of machinery on hand. We try to get work done early to make sure it gets done on time. When the weather is right, we work a little later and get up a little earlier. And we have an occasional raucous party, which is a great reminder that all of life can't be scripted.

The Crop

Peas, like all legumes, are great soil enhancers. Their leaves gather nitrogen from the air, and their roots thread that nitrogen into the soil, right where we want it. Another way to put nitrogen in soil is to inject fields with anhydrous ammonia. We prefer to let our plants do it in their organic, silent, and splendid way.

A FAR-OUT TREAT

The '70s brought forth many righteous trends: the *Brady Bunch*, hotpants, and halter tops. A little-known fact is that the '70s also yielded sugar snap peas, a hybrid crop that combines the sweetness of green peas with the crunch of snow peas. Far from a passing phase, sugar snap peas are still the bomb.

KIDS AND PEAS

Sugar snap peas are beloved by kids. You can string them and eat them whole or split them open and eat the tiny, baby peas. You can eat the pod too, which makes a satisfying snap when you bite it. You can put them in a pocket or in a plastic bag and save them for later.

Sautéed Sugar Snap Peas
with Carrots and Honey Glaze

The fresh, summery flavor of sugar snap peas is set off by the sweetness of lightly cooked carrots and a honey glaze. Sweet simplicity. *Friend of the Farm.*

SERVES 3 TO 4

1/2–1 pound	sugar snap peas
2 medium	carrots, peeled
2 tablespoons	butter
1 tablespoon	honey
	freshly ground black pepper

1. Remove the strings from both edges of the pea pods (start by gently pulling from the stem).

2. Cut each carrot into thirds. Slice each third, lengthwise, into quarters so that the slices are about the size and shape of the sugar snap peas.

3. Place the carrots in a steamer basket set over 1 1/2 inches boiling water, cover, and steam until they are just crisp-tender, 3 to 5 minutes. Drain the carrots in a colander.

4. Melt the butter in a large skillet over medium heat. Add the sugar snap peas; cook, stirring frequently, for 5 minutes. Add the carrots. Continue to cook and stir until the peas are bright green and crisp-tender, about 3 minutes. Add the honey and cook for 1 more minute, stirring constantly, until the peas and carrots are thoroughly glazed with the honey.

5. Remove the skillet from heat. Season generously with pepper.

Zucchini and Summer Squash

Zucchini and summer squash are kind of like the rabbits of the vegetable world: once they start reproducing, there's no turning back. The vines unfurl rapidly, displaying extravagant flowers. The bees buzz around and, before we know it, the flowers give way to mature squash. If we didn't visit the plants daily with our knives and buckets, they'd overtake the farm. With such abundance of this springtime bounty, it's a good thing zucchini and summer squash have so many desirable attributes. They are tender, juicy, and versatile, arriving at shareholders' homes in a variety of shapes and colors throughout the early season.

Zucchini and Summer Squash Grown by Angelic Organics

Squash that produces in summer generally falls into two categories: (1) zucchini and (2) everything else, collectively known as summer squash. There are subtle differences, but zucchini and summer squash are generally interchangeable when cooking.

Zucchini are smooth and cylindrical with a stem that is just about as thick as the fruit. While most zucchini are deep green, we also grow a yellow zucchini with a flavor and texture that is milder than the green variety.

Summer squash come in many shapes, but the most common is narrow at the top with a wider, bulb-shaped base. The stems are more brittle and much skinnier than zucchini stems. We usually grow yellow straightneck and crookneck summer squash plus one half-green, half-yellow straightneck variety.

Storage

Our unwaxed farm-fresh zucchini and summer squash respire through their skins, so they need to be refrigerated as soon as possible. Store them unwashed in a perforated plastic bag in the vegetable bin, or refrigerate them in a sealed plastic container that you've lined with a kitchen towel. In the refrigerator they keep for about a week and a half.

Handling

Rinse zucchini and summer squash under cool running water to remove any dirt or prickles; then slice off the stem and blossom ends. According to the specifications of your recipe, slice the vegetable into rounds, quarters, or chunks.

Culinary Uses

Since their flavor and texture aren't overpowering, zucchini and summer squash are a valuable addition to almost any recipe.

❖ Slice tender, young zucchini and summer squash raw into salads.
❖ Try them in stir fries, with pasta, and in Mediterranean vegetable stews.

Summer Squash

Zucchini

- Lightly steam zucchini and summer squash and dress them with fresh herbs or pesto.
- Coat zucchini lightly in oil and roast them at 350° F, whole or sliced in half, for 15 to 45 minutes depending on size (an overgrown zucchini can take even longer).
- Stuff zucchini with your favorite stuffings (try a variation of bread crumbs with Parmesan cheese, beaten egg, herbs, and scallions) and bake at 350° F.
- Don't let the summer pass without tossing a few marinated squash on the grill.
- Coat thinly sliced zucchini in your favorite batter mix and fry them.
- Use overgrown zucchini or summer squash (some- times found in the "Swap Boxes" at our share holders' delivery sites) in baked goods or grated and cooked like hash browns.

Partners for Zucchini and Summer Squash*

- Basil, chives, coriander, dill, garlic, marjoram, mint, oregano, parsley, pepper, sage, thyme;
- Lemon, olive oil;
- Butter, cream, goat cheese, Gruyère cheese, Parmesan cheese, yogurt;
- Pecans, pine nuts, walnuts;
- Chile peppers, corn, eggplant, onions, sweet pep- pers, tomatoes.

*See Louise Frazier's Complementary Herbs & Spices chart, page 345, for a suggestions.

Our Cook

I grew up with summer squash, which is very popular in the South. It was amazing how bags of squash came out of the woodwork in the summer—whether by way of my grandparents' neighbor, a customer at my dad's store, or one of my mother's students. The donors were probably as glad to give them away as we were to receive them, and I remember the happy anticipation of washing and slicing loads of fresh, fresh squash. Southern squash is long cooked, which results in a creamy purée that has the emotional significance of mashed potatoes. Up here people seem to prefer their squash crunchy-fresh, which has its own appeal and is defi- nitely quicker and preserves more nutrients. The flavor of fresh squash is more delicate, since a long cooking evaporates the water in squash and concentrates its flavor. Enjoy squash while you can. Like summer itself, summer squash doesn't last forever.

Creamy Zucchini-Cumin Dip

Treat your zucchini like cucumbers! As in many classic cucumber recipes, the grated raw zucchini for this salad is salted and drained before being used. Salting tenderizes the zucchini, mellowing its "raw edge," and prepares it to absorb the flavors from the other ingre- dients in the dish. We know the classic combination of sour cream and onion is grand, and lime, cumin, and a touch of paprika give it character. This works great as an all-purpose party dip—double the recipe if you're making it for a party. Or use it as a stylish garnish for tacos or chili. *Friend of the Farm.*

MAKES 1½ TO 2 CUPS

4 small or 2 medium	zucchini, coarsely grated
2 teaspoons	salt
1 cup	sour cream
2 tablespoons	finely chopped onion
1 tablespoon	freshly squeezed lime juice
1 teaspoon	cumin seeds or ½ teaspoon ground cumin
	freshly ground black pepper
	paprika

1. Place the zucchini in a medium bowl; add the salt and mix well. Transfer to a colander and set in the sink to drain for at least 15 minutes, up to 30 minutes.

2. Meanwhile, put the sour cream, onion, lime juice, and cumin in a large serving bowl; stir until well com- bined. Season with pepper and paprika to taste.

3. Squeeze as much moisture as you can from the zuc- chini with your hands; add the zucchini to the sour cream mixture. Stir until thoroughly combined.

4. Cover and refrigerate for at least 2 hours. Serve cold or at room temperature.

Zucchini, Summer Squash, and Bulgur Salad
with Fresh Parsley and Dill

This is an interesting and delicious variation on the Middle Eastern bulgur-and-parsley salad known as tabbouleh. Bulgur, which is simply cracked wheat, has a nutty taste and satisfying, chewy texture similar to brown rice, but it is finer and lighter, which makes it perfect for a summery salad. Former farm cook Kristen found this recipe ideal to make use of dill and summer squash. This dish is wonderfully refreshing and very simple to make. *Angelic Organics Kitchen*.

SERVES 6

1¼ cups	water
1 cup	bulgur
2 small or 1 medium	zucchini, finely diced
2 small or 1 medium	yellow summer squash, finely diced
1	bell pepper, stem and seeds removed, finely diced
½	red onion, minced, or 2 scallions, minced
¼ cup	chopped fresh dill
¼ cup	chopped fresh parsley
2 tablespoons	extra virgin olive oil
	freshly squeezed juice of 1 lime (about 2 tablespoons)
	freshly grated Parmesan cheese (optional)

1. Bring the water to a boil in a small pot, then add the bulgur. Leave uncovered; cook the bulgur for 1 minute. Remove the pot from heat, cover, and set aside until the bulgur has absorbed the rest of the water, about 15 minutes.

2. Fluff the cooked bulgur with a fork until the grains are well separated; transfer to a large bowl. Add the zucchini, yellow squash, bell pepper, and onion or scallions. Toss until well combined.

3. Whisk the dill, parsley, olive oil, and lime juice in a small bowl. Pour the dressing over the bulgur and toss until thoroughly combined. Sprinkle with Parmesan cheese just before serving. Serve at room temperature.

Chilled Zucchini and Avocado Soup
with Yogurt and Coriander

Puréed avocado combined with the unique silky texture of puréed raw zucchini makes for a soup so smooth it defies description. Freshly ground whole coriander seeds give this soup a slightly exotic citrus aroma. You can crush the seeds in a mortar and pestle or use the back of a sturdy spoon to grind them into the bottom of a shallow bowl. This makes a perfect, refreshing dinner on one of those sweltering summer days when the idea of eating anything hot seems absurd. *Angelic Organics Kitchen*.

SERVES 2 TO 4

4 small or 2 medium	zucchini, coarsely chopped
2	avocados, peeled, pits removed, coarsely chopped
3 medium	scallions, coarsely chopped
2 cloves	garlic, peeled, halved
½ teaspoon	chili powder
½ teaspoon	coriander seeds, crushed
1 cup	plain yogurt
	salt
	freshly ground black pepper
¼ cup	chopped fresh cilantro

1. Put the zucchini, avocado, scallions, garlic, chili powder, and coriander seeds into a food processor; process until smoothly combined.

2. Transfer the mixture to a medium bowl; stir in the yogurt. Refrigerate for at least 1 hour. Season with salt and pepper to taste; garnish with cilantro.

We are a bit surprised at how full the boxes are. It was a challenge to close them last week. The first few years we were doing a CSA, we were usually in a panic the first couple weeks of delivery. Some of you probably remember the hefty potted herb plants we put in your boxes to give you more value. No room for a potted plant this year. We think that with the spinach behind us and the broccoli winding down in another week the boxes will be just pleasantly full for a while.

The Crop

HARVEST WEEK 4, 1995, NEWSLETTER

The recent hot spell seems to be affecting even the usually impervious zucchini plants. Most boxes contain normal-looking samples, but a few of you may see a weird blossom end on your zucchinis. Occasionally the blossom end just didn't seal up. Oh well. The weather's cooler now, so less stress and more normal zucchinis will ensue.

WEED? WRITE?

HARVEST WEEK 4, 2001, NEWSLETTER

I was asked to write a 1,200-word column this week. It was such an appealing prospect (I love to write), but I fought weeds instead. Farming requires this kind of nimbleness. We think we'll harvest the kale, but the broccoli comes on so fast that we harvest more broccoli, no kale. We think that we will excavate for a concrete pour with the 656 International, but the 656 doesn't run. We think the problem is in the carburetor, but the problem is not in the carburetor—it's in the fuel shutoff solenoid. We think it won't rain, and it rains. I guess a lot of life is like that. Sometimes I graciously accept the changes of plans that farming sends my way; sometimes I am ungracious.

—**FARMER JOHN**

Baked Zucchini Halves
Stuffed with Wild Rice and Quinoa

In this hearty recipe the classic combination of onion, celery, and cheese give plenty of robust flavor to the mixed grains, while zucchini provides the perfect juicy-firm base. Both wild rice and quinoa have a firm outer layer that splits during cooking to expose a soft kernel inside. In the case of quinoa, this layer twists and rolls so that each tiny, tender nugget ends up surrounded by a delicately crispy ring. Remember to rinse your quinoa thoroughly before you cook it, as rinsing will remove all traces of a naturally occurring coating that can make it taste bitter. This satisfying dish is an excellent accompaniment to roasted chicken or grilled fish. This recipe serves four to six as a side dish, and two to three as a main course. *Friend of the Farm.*

SERVES 4 TO 6

1 large	zucchini, halved lengthwise
1 1/2 cups	cooked quinoa
1/2 cup	cooked wild rice
1/4 cup	freshly grated Parmesan cheese (about 3/4 ounce)
1 1/2 teaspoons	olive oil
1/2 cup	chopped onion (about 1 medium onion)
1 rib	celery, chopped
3/4 cup	fresh bread crumbs
1 teaspoon	salt
	butter (optional)

1. Preheat the oven to 350° F.

2. Cut out the center from each half of the zucchini with a paring knife, being careful not to puncture the bottom or the sides; reserve the centers. Transfer the hollow halves, cut-side up, to a baking dish.

3. Coarsely chop the zucchini centers and put them in a large bowl. Add the quinoa, wild rice, and Parmesan. Stir until well combined.

4. Heat the oil in a medium skillet over medium-high heat. Add the onion and celery; cook for 5 minutes, stirring frequently. Stir in the bread crumbs and salt. Continue to cook, stirring constantly, until the bread crumbs are well mixed in and heated through, about 1 minute.

5. Add the bread crumb mixture to the quinoa/rice mixture and combine well.

6. Stuff hollow zucchini halves with the quinoa/rice mixture. Cover with aluminum foil; bake for 40 minutes.

7. Remove the foil. If you wish, dot each half with a pat of butter. Continue baking until zucchini is very tender and the filling is golden brown, 10 to 20 minutes. Serve warm.

Sweet Zucchini Crumble

Silky smooth baked zucchini is the surprising filling in this sweet dessert. Like the best apple crumble, this dessert has a tender, lemony-sweet, spiced filling just waiting to be discovered beneath its irresistible, crunchy crust. Don't count on having leftovers. *Shareholder.*

SERVES 6 TO 8

4$\frac{1}{2}$ cups	flour
3 cups	sugar, divided
$\frac{1}{2}$ teaspoon	salt
1$\frac{1}{2}$ cups	shortening, softened, or butter, cold
6–8 cups	thinly sliced zucchini (about 4 large zucchini)
$\frac{2}{3}$ cup	freshly squeezed lemon juice (about 3 lemons)
1 teaspoon	ground cinnamon
$\frac{1}{4}$ teaspoon	ground or freshly grated nutmeg

1. Preheat the oven to 350° F.

2. Stir the flour, 2 cups of the sugar, and salt in a large bowl until well combined. Add the shortening or butter and cut it into the flour with a pastry blender or your fingertips until the mixture looks like coarse oatmeal.

3. Pour half of the mixture into a 9x13-inch cake pan. Using your fingers or a rubber spatula, press the mixture evenly into the bottom of the pan. Bake for 10 minutes. Remove the pan from the oven and set it aside.

4. Combine the zucchini and lemon juice in a large pot over high heat and cook until zucchini is tender, 8 to 10 minutes. Stir in the remaining 1 cup of sugar, cinnamon, and nutmeg. Simmer for 1 minute more. Stir in $\frac{1}{2}$ cup of the reserved flour mixture and continue to cook, stirring constantly, until mixture thickens. Remove the pot from the heat to cool for 10 minutes.

5. Pour the zucchini mixture over the baked crust and sprinkle with the remaining flour mixture. Return the pan to the oven and bake until it is lightly browned and bubbly, 40 to 45 minutes.

The cucumbers, zucchini, and summer squash are finished. Zucchini and summer squash have been harvested daily for many weeks, cucumbers every other day. Our crew is relieved it's over. That was a lot of bending.

I was disturbed at how right the truck looked, sitting in our yard. Sometimes things show up, and I know they are just a dense version of what is already there. If I look out of the corner of my eyes, I see that thing just plunking itself into an etheric outline, an Akashic unfolding.

—FROM JOHN'S BOOK *FARMER JOHN ON GLITTER & GREASE*

In this recipe, individual slices of squash get a crispy cornmeal coating to seal in their juices. You can vary the flavor by adding a couple tablespoons of your favorite fresh herbs (such as basil, oregano, onion, chives, or dill), a few grindings of black pepper, or a teaspoon of toasted and crushed coriander seeds to the cornmeal. Our recipe testers have commonly recommended paprika and garlic. You might like to see Louise Frazier's Complementary Herb & Spices chart, page 345, for additional flavor ideas. *Angelic Organics Kitchen* (adapted from *American Wholefoods Cuisine*).

SERVES 4

1 cup	cornmeal
	salt
	freshly ground black pepper
2 small or 1 medium	yellow summer squash, halved crosswise, each half sliced lengthwise into 1/4-inch thick strips
2 small or 1 medium	zucchini, halved crosswise, each half sliced lengthwise into 1/4-inch thick strips
1 cup	all-purpose flour
1	egg, beaten
	olive oil

1. Mix the cornmeal with salt and pepper to taste in a shallow bowl (mix in any herbs and/or spices at this time, if you are using them).

2. Working with one piece of zucchini or squash at a time, coat it lightly in flour and shake off any excess. Next, dip the floured zucchini or squash in the beaten egg, letting the excess drip off, then dip it in the cornmeal and coat well. Set the coated zucchini or squash aside. Repeat the process with the remaining zucchini and squash pieces.

3. Line a plate with a paper towel. Pour enough oil into a large skillet to thoroughly cover the bottom and heat over medium-high heat. Transfer as many of the coated slices to the skillet as will easily fit and cook until they are brown, about 5 minutes. Flip the slices and cook until brown, about 5 minutes more. Transfer the cooked slices to the paper towel to lined plate to drain and cool.

4. Scrape off any leftover burning pieces of cornmeal from the skillet, add more oil if necessary, and repeat the cooking process with the next batch of squash and zucchini.

5. Season with additional salt to taste and serve slightly warm or at room temperature.

MID-SEASON

AN EMPHASIS ON FRUITING
EARLY AUGUST to EARLY SEPTEMBER

Lilipoh asks Dr. Williams, Can you say something about "spiritual nutrition?"

"There is not only the digestion of food but the digestion of ideas. Our current academic life tends to foster memory of other's ideas rather than the contemplation that is needed to form our own position or idea. Ideally we must digest our instruction—breaking it down and then resynthesizing it into our own mental substance or concept in a way very comparable to the physical digestion of food. . . .

This leads us to the social aspects of nourishment. We all recognize the importance of the surroundings where we eat and especially the people with whom we eat. Both have a real influence on our enjoyment of the meal and the inner satisfaction we feel as we leave the table.

Families soon find that what is talked or even thought about at the table can make the meal heavenly or distressing. We are told, and many of us recognize, that the attitude and love of the cook adds something precious to the food. These are also spiritual aspects to digestion and nutrition as well as the grace before the meal and, in the case of some religious groups, after the meal also."

—INTERVIEW WITH DR. WILLIAMS, FROM *LILIPOH*

Overheard

In my early religious training, I substituted the word *nature* for *God*. Whenever we were supposed to say God in a song or a reading, I said *nature* really loud so everyone would hear. When it was time to get bat mitzvahed, I went to Rabbi Goldberg and said, "Rabbi, I don't believe God exists. I don't want to get bat mitzvahed." He said, "This is great, to really examine what your feelings are about God. Take your time. You can get bat mitzvahed at any time, in your 80s if you want." The other girls reminded me of all the gifts I would get if I went through the ceremony. I didn't care about the gifts.

Heat

by John Peterson

(FARM NEWS, 1995)

It is Sunday morning. Marci, Kimberely, and Frédérique are in Chicago at a birthday party for Judy, the farm cook. It is 9:30 a.m., and it is already hot—90 degrees. I flinch as I lower myself onto the tractor seat; the seat almost sizzles from the sun. I start the tractor. Spark plugs synapse. Gasoline vapors ignite. They pound the pistons of my 656 Farmall engine. The combustion seems redundant in the blistering heat. I drive to a field, lower my disc into the crust of the clay soil. The disc swirls weeds into the dirt. The hard clay on the surface mixes with the powdery soil underneath. A cloud of dust floats into the air. I lurch across the bumpy field, wincing in the blast of engine heat. I finish discing and head home, the disc jouncing behind me. I gaze at our nice onion field near the woods; I take note of its light green upright stalks. I park the tractor, shut down the engine. The sudden silence is eerie in the horrific heat. The silence closes in on me, heavy, suffocating.

I carry the little red Earthway seeder to the field. I load it with carrot seed. I spin carrot seed into the dust—ten thousand seeds in a row. Plumes of dust swirl about my feet. I take off my sandals. The soil burns my feet. I put my sandals back on. I imagine the carrots growing towards our boxes of vegetables: the air will be cool when these carrots fall into the boxes of our shareholders; oak leaves will be brown.

Judy pleaded with me to come to her birthday party.

"No, Judy, I'm sorry I can't come to your birthday party. I must plant for the shareholders. The boxes must always be full."

The sun arcs higher. It slams heat at the farm. I squint at the stubble

> "No, Judy, I'm sorry I can't come to your birthday party. I must plant for the shareholders. The boxes must always be full."

across the draw to the south, where Jack Dwyer has harvested his wheat.

"Can I get a few bales of wheat straw for our hay ride?" I asked Jack before our open house. Jack, his wife, Joanne, and I sat at his kitchen table.

Jack squinted at me as he chewed tobacco. "It's all put away."

"You still milk, Jack?"

Jack's eighty-five.

"Grandkids do   forty seven cows."

"They like it?"

"Nope."

"Going to keep doing it?"

"Yup," he snorted, as though I had asked a stupid question.

Jack's wife, Joanne, looked at him adoringly. "Jack does the field work," she said. "Gets up at 5. That's early enough."

"You see who sprayed my beans?" Jack asked. A scowl swept over his wizened face. His eyes narrowed. "They went around the field one and a half times, then they left. Must have figured out they were in the wrong field. Killed fifteen acres."

"We don't know who did it," Joanne added.

I hear the soft whir of the seeder. The soil at my feet looks white in the sun. I think of earthworms, cooling themselves deep in their burrows.

I wonder if Judy and the crew found each other for the party.

"Sometimes the rains come and they don't stop," I told Judy. "If the seed isn't in the ground when the rains come, then the boxes will have no carrots, no kohlrabi, no beets at the end of the season. I can't plant in the mud. I have to plant when the ground is ready."

I consider whether our shareholders would have wanted me to attend Judy's birthday party, at the risk of their not receiving beets and carrots later in the season. I imagined some of our shareholders saying, "You go and have fun. You don't want to die in this heat." I imagined other shareholders saying, "Forget the party, John. I want my fall carrots, my beets."

I finish seeding the carrots. Now the Earthway whisks tiny arugula seeds into the dirt.

"We are proudly celebrating our 125th year of service," the National Weather Service announced this morning. "For today, Sunday, there is a livestock advisory in affect. Actual temperatures may exceed 105 degrees. Heat index will be over 110 degrees. Keep livestock cool and in shade, if possible. Starting in September, due to funding cutbacks, there will no longer be agricultural weather forecasts."

Southeast of us a ramshackle farm bursts with hogs and manure. I think of the husky farmer, walking amongst his crumbling barns, belonging there, like the oaks in his front yard. I hear he is quitting.

"Your party would be such fun, Judy." The thought of her party made me think of the movie

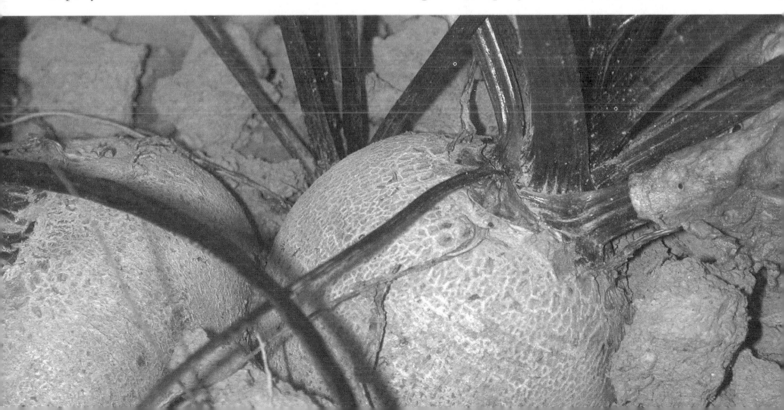

I wanted to see last winter. The desire to see the movie seemed like a movie.

Now the Earthway is metering beet seed into the dust.

"Only two beets this week?" a shareholder had asked two weeks earlier.

Row upon row of beet seeds whirl into the powdery soil. Sweat sops my shirt.

"Due to the diminishing farm population, the census bureau will no longer keep separate statistics on farm families," the farm paper stated.

A Chicago family walks into the field. They are shareholders. They seem an apparition in the white heat. The mother talks about her son's shoes. He holds up a foot. I am in a blister of heat. I do not understand shoes. Are the shoes too big, too little, too stylish for the scorched dirt? Are they orthopedically hopeless? I listen politely. I comprehend nothing. The family seems cool. They speak as though we are in the evening. Sweat drips down my legs. I hallucinate carrots in boxes. The carrot vision lures me back to the field.

I plant Purple Danube kohlrabi. The Earthway puffs dust at my knees.

I study our onion field. The onions have turned from light green to grayish white in the last few hours. The stalks, upright this morning, have flopped.

"Avoid the sun," the Ayurvedic doctor told me. "You are the most pitta [fiery] patient I have ever diagnosed. Walk in the moonlight. Be around sweet things—flowers and sweet people."

I glance across my fields as White Danube kohlrabi seed cascades into the powder of clay. The crops shimmer. They look crisp, rigid, shiny. Suddenly, the crops look frozen solid; it seems as though the heat has transformed into frigid cold. The crops look brittle, as though they will shatter in the next moment, as though they will crackle like ice. I feel I am in a prison of heat, heat so hot it has become frigid, the way bad suddenly becomes good, the way love abruptly becomes hate. I am so hot, I am cold. I am in a prison of vegetables, the most beautiful prison in the world.

"I want to support your farm, but I don't want it to cost me any more than it would cost at Whole Foods," I was told.

I see hands clutching onions, ramming bunches of onions into a machine in California. The bunch goes in one direction, gets clenched by a rubber band, goes in the other direction—rubber band. It happens fast by these hands, hands that get paid by the bunch. My imagination blurs with the speed of the hands. Beyond the blurry hands are more blurs; a raft of hands slams onion bunches into rubber banding machines. The Pacific Ocean sends cool air to the packing room.

We have no bunching machine, no ocean.

"Some weeks I hardly ate anything out of your box. I was hardly ever home," a shareholder told me. "I was just so happy knowing that it was grown in a healthy way; I didn't even care when I didn't eat it."

I imagine the girls glittering at Judy's party. I want to lean into their glamour, to say reckless things.

To the north, my neighbor's barn roof shimmers in the white heat.

I called him before our open house.

"Got a few bales for our hayride?" I asked.

Six minutes later he and his boy delivered fifteen bales of straw to our barn.

"It takes longer than that to get a pizza delivered," I said. "Bad year for crops, isn't it?"

"I've lost money the last four years out of six," he said, shaking his head. "If it happens again this year, I'm going to throw in the towel."

"He ain't going to quit," his teenage son whispered behind his dad's back.

"I'm all done, if this keeps up," my neighbor said. "Little roots on the corn—half the usual size, corn shooting tassels already in this heat. What's the point of taking money out of my pocket to keep farming? As much as I love it, I'm just not going to keep doing it until I'm broke."

The son caught my eye again. He was shaking his head. "Dad won't quit, no matter what."

Cilantro marches into the dust, in long rows.

On Monday night the rain will come. On Friday it will still be raining. The beets and arugula will already be up.

Next winter, the neighbor who brought me the straw will sell out.

> I think of the husky farmer, walking amongst his crumbling barns, belonging there, like the oaks in his front yard. I hear he is quitting.

Thoughts on Nutrition

by Thomas Cowan, M.D.

WITH RESEARCH ASSISTANCE FROM LOUISE FRAZIER AND SHERRY WILDFEUER

When you participate in the act of growing or processing your own food, almost every meal becomes an occasion to experience gratitude for this miracle. I have had the opportunity for most of my adult life to work with the connection between food and consciousness, and I am continually amazed at just how profound is this connection. I am also keenly aware of the major controversies that exist in the American public as to what constitutes a healthy diet. These controversies exist even within the Biodynamic and anthroposophic communities. In this brief essay I offer a few thoughts to help towards an orientation in this complex question of humanity's relation to food.

> When you participate in the act of growing or processing your own food, almost every meal becomes an occasion to experience gratitude for this miracle.

Some people advocate what is called a paleolithic diet, which consists as much as possible of food that can be obtained in the wild. This pre-agriculture diet consists mainly of meat, fish, and wild fruits and vegetables. Advocates of this approach, which is similar in broad terms to all of the low-carbohydrate diets, claim that the medical problems of modern people fundamentally stem from the disparity between the

Overheard

MALE #1: Want to go with me to yoga this morning?

MALE #2: Yoga? I'd rather be a vegetarian than do yoga.

Overheard

You can drink all the bancha tea you want, be a vegan, say all the right stuff about diet and multi-national corporations and recy-cling and old growth forest, but if you lie to your friends, you dam-age the earth terribly, much worse than you would if you owned some IBM stock and had a malt every now and then.

dictates of our biology and our modern life. They assert that we grew and evolved for the majority of our time on earth eating these wild and unprocessed foods and are therefore biologically unable to digest or utilize foods that come through agriculture. Advocates of these diets eschew all grains, dairy products, and other products of modern agriculture.

On perhaps the opposite pole are the advocates of a totally vegan diet. Some claim that this is the future of humanity, as we evolve the consciousness that avoids the heavy earthiness that comes from the consumption of animal prod-ucts. More extreme elements of this vegan movement claim we should eat all of our food raw, thus preserving the natural and beneficial enzymes in the food.

I have come to value a diet that lies between these two poles, including some ani-mal products and some raw food, with grains in the middle. Humanity evolves slowly. We are still shedding our biological, hunter-gatherer roots, yet we have just as surely evolved to obtain our nourishment from cultivated plants and domesticated animals.

Rudolf Steiner taught that one of the most important guides for humanity was the great initiate Zarathustra. In Persia 8,000 years before Christ, it was his task to provoke a radical shift in the consciousness of humanity. This he did by introducing the cultivation of the grains. We find record of this in the ancient text of the Avesta, where Zarathustra asks: "O maker of the physical world, thou Holy One! Which is the third place where the Earth feels most happy?

Ahura Mazda answered: "It is the place where one of the faithful cultivates most grain, grass, and fruit, O Spitama Zarathustra! Where he waters ground that is dry, or dries ground that is too wet."

"Oh maker of the material world, thou Holy One! What is the food that fills the law of Mazda?"

Ahura Mazda answered: "It is sowing grain again and again, O Spitama Zarathustra! No one who does not eat has strength to do works of husbandry, strength to beget children. By eating, every material creature lives, by not eating it dies away.

He who sows grain, sows holiness: he makes the law of Mazda grow higher and higher."

When asked about nutrition, Rudolf Steiner acknowledged that this is an individual matter, owing to our very different constitutions. However, out of spiritual science he could offer insight into the effects of various foods. He pointed out that human beings are opposite to plants not only in relation to their breathing of oxygen and carbon but also in their metabolism. Humans gain strength through the inner activity of breaking down what they take in as food and then building up their own substance. To build one's body from a vegetarian diet requires more effort, but this in turn gives one an inner flexibility in thinking. Because the animal has already permeated its substance with its soul (astral) nature, this astral nature penetrates the nervous system of the person who eats meat.

> In the ancient text of the Avesta, Zarathustra asked: "O maker of the physical world, thou Holy One! Which is the third place where the Earth feels most happy? Ahura Mazda answered: "It is the place where one of the faithful cultivates most grain, grass, and fruit, O Spitama Zarathustra! Where he waters ground that is dry, or dries ground that is too wet."

We are not here making propaganda for vegetarianism. On the contrary, animal food was, for a time, necessary for man and is often still necessary today, because man must stand firmly on the earth and be well embedded in what is personal. Everything that has led man to personal interests is connected with meat eating. The fact that there have been men who have made war, who have had sympathies and antipathies and sensual desires for each other is [typically] due to eating meat. But when a person does not act out of narrow self-interest but can grasp the wider perspectives, he owes this to his connection with the plant world through food. Thus certain peoples who are mainly vegetarian have more of a leaning towards spiritual matters, while other peoples develop more bravery, courage and heroism which are also necessary in life. These qualities are not conceivable without the personal element and this is [typically augmented by] meat.

. . . It will be a step forward when man, if he is not able to produce his protein requirements in himself, will restrict himself to what in animal food is not permeated by emotions and desires—namely milk. . . .

. . . We must not be one-sided. An extreme vegetarian would say that we must not take milk, butter and cheese. But in the production of milk it is mainly the animal's etheric [life] body which is involved. The astral [emotional] body [of the animal] has hardly anything to do with [milk].

. . . What is given to the human organism in milk prepares him to be a human creature of the earth, unites him with the conditions of the earth, but does not really fetter him to the earth.[2]

Our task is to live a practical life on the earth while transforming our thinking into spiritual insight and opening ourselves to the forces that are contained in the whole solar system. Our food plays a central role in this transformation. It is the rare person today who would be served by an evolutionary step backwards of a predominantly meat diet. Likewise, it has been my experience that an all-vegetable diet calls on powers that not all of us actually possess. As the Buddha suggests, the right way is the middle way.

1. *Nutrition and Stimulants,* Rudolf Steiner, pages 135, 136, 137.

2. Ibid, page 163.

This article appeared first in *Stella Natura,* a planting guide published annually by the Biodynamic Farming and Gardening Association, which can be ordered by calling 888-516-7797. Thomas Cowan's biography appears on page 360.

(**Note from Farmer John:** There is much controversy today about the consumption of dairy products. It would say: To take a closer look, see Thomas Cowan's article "Raw Milk" at : www.angelic-organics.com/vegetableguide, and click on Outtakes)

Welcome to the Mid-Season

An Emphasis on Fruiting

Early August to Early September

Harvest Weeks 8 to 13

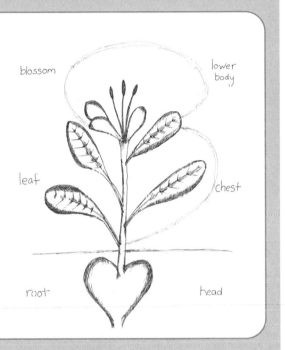

"The root primarily nourishes the head [the nervous system].

The middle of the plant, stem and leaves, primarily nourishes the chest [the rhythmic system—heart and lungs].

Fruit [including fruiting vegetables, such as squash and cucumbers] nourishes the lower body [the metabolic system—digestive organs]."

—RUDOLF STEINER, PARAPHRASED FROM HIS LECTURE *THE EVOLUTION OF EARTH AND MAN AND INFLUENCE OF THE STARS*

Forces in Food

If one has a perfectly healthy digestive system, a perfectly healthy intestinal system, then fruits [including fruiting vegetables, such as winter squash and cucumbers] are the right thing to nourish the lower body, through the protein they contain. Protein from any of the fruits nourishes your stomach for you, nourishes all your digestive organs in your lower body.

—LECTURE BY RUDOLF STEINER, *THE EVOLUTION OF EARTH AND MAN AND INFLUENCE OF THE STARS*

Overheard

I am tired of feeling the pain of my friends. They don't even tell me about their pains sometimes, and I start to feel the pain—in my gall bladder, in my back. They tell me later about their pain, where it is, and it is my pain exactly. I don't want to have all this empathy. It is too much.

Mid-Season Vegetables

The contents of a vegetable box will vary from week to week and from year to year with changes in the weather, among other factors. Some of the vegetables listed below are also harvested at other times of the year. (See Vegetable & Herb Availability from Angelic Organics, page 334, and the Illustrated Vegetable Identification Guide, page 336.)

Carrots	Kohlrabi
Celery	Leeks
Eggplant	Melons
Fennel	Peppers
Garlic and Garlic Scapes	Sweet Corn
Green Beans	Tomatoes

Farm News

HARVEST WEEK 10, 1999, NEWSLETTER

We have been getting some shareholder raves about the flavors of our vegetables this year. Perhaps this is due to changes in some of our cultural practices. For example, this year we turned more cover crops under for soil tilth and fertility. We did deep tillage to oxygenate the soil. We inoculated the soil with friendly microbes. We added trace minerals and gypsum (a.k.a. calcium sulfate, a rock powder). It's a challenge to figure out just what makes the difference in quality; there are so many factors to sort through.

A Diary of Mid-Season Weather

Notice the variability from year to year.

Early August	Mid-August	Late August	Early September
HARVEST WEEK 9, 1997, NEWSLETTER Mild and wet. We got an inch of rain! This will help our fall crops tremendously.	**HARVEST WEEK 10, 1997, NEWSLETTER** Warm and drizzly. Great for brassicas!	**HARVEST WEEK 11, 1997, NEWSLETTER** Mild. No rain.	**HARVEST WEEK 13, 1997, NEWSLETTER** Mild. No rain. The ground is very dry.
HARVEST WEEK 9, 1998, NEWSLETTER Weeds covered our rain gauge for a few days. We received a few inches of rain and then some.	**HARVEST WEEK 10, 1998, NEWSLETTER** Dry and mid-80s. One-third of an inch of rain fell Friday evening after our planting extravaganza.	**HARVEST WEEK 11, 1998, NEWSLETTER** Hot and incredibly sticky with occasional thunderstorms. A few crew members were almost carried away by the swarms of mosquitoes.	**HARVEST WEEK 13, 1998, NEWSLETTER** Cool and only a trace of precipitation.
HARVEST WEEK 9, 1999, NEWSLETTER Incredibly dry but much cooler with highs in the mid-80s and lows dipping into the 50s.	**HARVEST WEEK 10, 1999, NEWSLETTER** Dry and mild until Thursday morning when over two inches of rain fell while the crew fearlessly harvested your vegetables.	**HARVEST WEEK 11, 1999, NEWSLETTER** Cool and wet. Over two inches of rain fell.	**HARVEST WEEK 13, 1999, NEWSLETTER** Dry and mild with lows dipping into the 50s and highs in the 80s.

Overheard

I knew these people out West years ago. It got very hot out there in the summer. They kept a pitcher of water in their refrigerator. Problem was, during the hot part of the day, they wouldn't let anyone open the refrigerator door. They said all the cool air would fall out. The water was cold, but you couldn't get at it.

Overheard

CUSTOMER: You have no idea how hot it is outside.

INSURANCE PERSON: I sure do.

CUSTOMER: How's that? You're in this cool office all day long.

INSURANCE PERSON: I go outside and smoke.

HARVEST WEEK 12, 1999, NEWSLETTER

A lot of next year's ground will be new to vegetables. We are getting it ready now: tilling it to eradicate next year's weeds, subsoiling it to stimulate soil life, spritzing it with friendly soil microbes, energizing it with Biodynamic preparations, balancing it with rock powders. This fall we will install the pipe that will take water from our new irrigation well out to those new fields. We'll be ready to fling water on your vegetables when the Y2K rains refuse to fall.

MID-SUMMER

HARVEST WEEK 10, 1995, NEWSLETTER

We are now in the middle of the delivery season at Angelic Organics, the tenth week out of twenty. This week we will plant spinach and radishes in the fields. The field planting will be the last of the season. Soon we will be putting some fields to sleep with fall tillage and a planting of oats and vetch or clover. We are doing our last Biodynamic spraying of the season (silica to enhance ripening, valerian and apple cider vinegar to encourage some laggard peppers and heirloom tomatoes to flower and bear fruit). The days are shortening noticeably; even a 5:30 a.m. start is now difficult due to darkness. Although the afternoons are still fiercely hot, the mornings have a faint nip in them.

Mid-Season Eating

Mid-season is when the glamour crops, as we like to call them, begin to mature and waltz off our fields and into the boxes. The height of summer on our farm is dominated by these luscious, juicy fruiting crops. They are not what we typically think of as fruit. You won't find a single orange or pineapple growing on our farm, but crops like tomatoes, peppers, eggplant, and sweet corn can legitimately be classified as fruits, at least from a Biodynamic and a botanical perspective. A botanist would identify fruits as those crops that come into fruition, or actually set seed, before they are harvested. This also includes melons, those fruit-flavored botanical relatives of cucumbers.

Of course, there is still a nice backdrop of greens for adorning your fruit plate. They are present during the summer peak, though not as bountiful as before. And carrots begin arriving during this period. And garlic! And celery and fennel and more herbs and . . . Wow, how great to be a seasonal eater!

Mid-Season Farming

Most of the weeding, seeding, thinning, transplanting, and greenhouse work finally winds down as the mid-season begins. And that is a good thing, because the summer crops overwhelm the fields now, eager to return all the love and care we have given them so far this season. Most of our time in the field is spent harvesting, harvesting, harvesting.

Mid-season is also when we start to focus on the future. We prepare next season's ground through fallow tillage (a great form of weed control). We plant short-season cover crops, such as peas and oats or peas and triticale, to nourish the soil for next year's vegetables. We ask ourselves what's been working, and what hasn't.

Carrots

Carrots, flashes of vivid orange twisted up from the dark brown soil, are nearly as delightful to harvest as they are to eat. The magical experience of unearthing these brilliant roots is reason enough to plant them by the fieldful—but, oh, they're just so tasty, too. We notice that when ideal temperatures converge with ideal moisture levels, our carrots are of the utmost crispness and sweetness. Countless dishes, ranging from simple raw salads to elaborate curries, owe their sweet flavor, enticing color, and satisfying texture to this universally loved, crispy-sweet vegetable. You will find a selection of excellent carrot-based recipes in this chapter to guide and inspire you. Also be sure to check the index for other recipes containing carrots, since their characteristic sweetness is used as an accent in many other vegetable dishes as well.

Storage

Remove the leafy green tops, leaving about an inch of stems. Refrigerate dry, unwashed carrots in a plastic bag for two weeks or longer.

Handling

Organic carrots fresh from the farm generally don't need to be peeled—but should you decide to peel them, the nutrient loss is negligible. Peel carrots or scrub them well with a stiff brush just before using. Trim off any green spots, which can taste bitter. When slicing or chopping carrots for cooking, be sure to make all the pieces relatively the same size. With their tapered shape this can be a challenge, but your efforts will ensure an evenly cooked dish.

Forces in Food

Carrots are the most truly root of all vegetables. They contain many salts. Because they have the forces of the earth, they have the property, when they are taken into the stomach, of working right into the head by way of the blood. Only substances rich in salts are able to reach the head. Root substances rich in salts strengthen man through the head. This is extremely important. And it is particularly the carrot that makes the uppermost part of the head strong. So this is what one needs for man to become inwardly strong and firm, and not soft and delicate.

If you look at a carrot you will say: I can see something specific about this plant, its growth concentrates towards the root. The carrot is almost all root. The root holds one's interest if one looks at this plant. The rest of the plant only sits on top of it and is of no significance. So the carrot is especially suitable food to provide for the human head. If you have a sort of empty feeling in the head and cannot think very well, it would be good to add carrots to your diet for a time. But obviously it is of the greatest help to children.

Now you must say to yourselves, when I eat carrots my body can be a real lazy-bones, for only the saliva of the mouth is required to soften the carrot and then only the pepsin of the stomach and so on, and all the important part of the carrot goes to the head. Man needs salts. These are provided by all that is plant root, and particularly by such a root as the carrot.

—LECTURE BY RUDOLF STEINER, *NUTRITION AND STIMULANTS*

Culinary Uses

❖ Eat crunchy-sweet carrot spears plain or dipped in hummus, peanut butter, or a creamy dressing.

❖ Slice or grate raw carrots into salads.

❖ Cooking accentuates carrots' sweetness. Just be sure to remove them from the heat while they still have some firmness to them.

❖ Steam whole or halved carrots in a steamer basket for 15 to 20 minutes.

❖ Boil 2-inch chunks of carrots in rapidly boiling salted water, uncovered, for 7 to 10 minutes.

❖ Stir-fry thinly sliced carrots in a hot wok for 2 to 4 minutes.

❖ Place sliced carrots in a single layer in a covered sauté pan with enough water or stock to come halfway up the carrots. Braise until there is no more liquid in the pan, 15 to 20 minutes. When the pan is dry, season with your favorite fresh or dried herbs and butter to taste.

❖ Purée carrots as a classic winter soup.

❖ Combine carrots with other root vegetables for a winter gratin or roasted vegetable platter (lightly coat in oil and salt and roast at 400° F until vegetables start to brown all over, about 45 minutes), or serve them with a grain, such as millet, for a simple evening meal.

Partners for Carrots*

❖ Anise hyssop, basil, chervil, chile, cilantro, coriander, cumin, dill, fennel leaves, ginger, lemon balm, lovage, mace, mint, parsley, rosemary, sage, tarragon, thyme;

❖ Butter, cream, olive oil, roasted peanut oil, toasted sesame oil;

❖ All root vegetables;

❖ Brown sugar, honey, maple syrup, mustard.

*See Louise Frazier's Complementary Herbs & Spices chart, page 345, for suggestions.

A Shareholder

FARM NEWS, 1996

A shareholder once told Bob and Farmer John that as she was carrying her CSA box home one afternoon, she passed a police officer. Half a block farther down the sidewalk she heard, "Miss! Miss! Can you tell me where you got that box?"

She turned to find the police officer behind her.

"Is that the box I saw on television? I wanna know where I can get those vegetables."

Jen gave her our phone number. "Do you want a carrot?" she offered.

"No, Ma'am. I can't take a carrot while I'm on duty."

Our Cook

I will never forget the summer that, thanks to an overgrown carrot, I gained a reputation among the kids on our block. First my older brother tried, then a neighbor's kid, then another, until everyone had tried. They tugged and tugged, but no one could unearth that stubbornly rooted carrot. Maybe my predecessors had loosened it up, or maybe I was lent some supernatural strength. When I stepped up to give it a try—Umph!—that carrot came up and I was flung backward by my own momentum. I actually gained some respect though—my own personal Excalibur event.

Spiced Carrot Salad

In this exotic recipe from Morocco, carrots are blanched until they are barely tender, then marinated in a lemony-sweet spiced dressing. Slivered dried prunes and/or chopped black olives (both common Moroccan ingredients) or a handful of currants make great additions to this recipe. *Angelic Organics Kitchen.*

SERVES 4 TO 6

2 cups	diagonally sliced or julienned carrots
3 tablespoons	finely chopped fresh parsley
2 tablespoons	finely chopped fresh cilantro
1 tablespoon	finely chopped fresh mint
2 tablespoons	freshly squeezed lemon juice
2 cloves	garlic minced (about 1 teaspoon)
1/2 teaspoon	ground cumin
1/2 teaspoon	ground cinnamon
1/2 teaspoon	paprika
1/8 teaspoon	cayenne pepper
1 teaspoon	sugar
1/3 cup	olive oil
	lemon slices

1. Bring a medium pot of water to a boil. Add the carrots; boil until barely tender and still brightly colored, 1 to 2 minutes.

2. Drain the carrots and immediately run cold water over them to stop the cooking. Drain well.

3. Transfer the carrots to a large salad bowl. Add the parsley, cilantro, and mint; toss to combine.

4. Mix the lemon juice, garlic, cumin, cinnamon, paprika, and cayenne in a small bowl. Stir in the sugar. Slowly pour in the olive oil in a thin stream, whisking constantly, until the dressing is thick and no longer separates.

5. Pour the dressing over the carrots and toss until well coated. Cover and refrigerate for at least 2 hours.

6. Let the salad come to room temperature before serving. Top each serving with a lemon slice.

Farmer John Writes

HARVEST WEEK 10, 1995, NEWSLETTER

It's a miracle that we got the carrots out of the ground. The tractor had a flat tire. I got it repaired in town, and returned to the farm and a brooding horizon. Primo and I raced to put the carrot lifter on the tractor. Winds started to blow, the sky went psychedelic, the morning night turned dark like night. I lowered the lifter into the hard clay. The tractor screamed through the wind. The lathe on the lifter sliced under the carrots. Workers converged from all over the farm. They raced down the row, yanking carrots from the ground. The clouds were shadows of themselves—low, swirling. Cold pellets of water pelted us. Carrots flew. Rain streamed. We reached the end of the row as the hard ground was turning to mud. Enjoy your carrots.

Forces in Food

The human infant also needs the carrot to stimulate the silica organization because his sense organs and his brain are still developing. He needs the proper salt process in order to stimulate the formation of his nerve-sense organization and also of his bones. For that reason carrots are especially important for infants and small children and should be part of the diet at regular intervals.

—**RUDOLF STEINER, *DYNAMICS OF NUTRITION***

Creamy Carrot and Rice Casserole

When rice is cooked to creamy tenderness in a silky carrot purée, the result is like a very sophisticated rice pudding. This is almost like having dessert for dinner —but don't let anyone tell you that you can't still have carrot cake! *Angelic Organics Kitchen.*

SERVES 4 TO 6

	butter for greasing the baking dish
2¹/₂ cups	vegetable or chicken stock
¹/₂ pound	carrots (about 3 medium carrots), roughly chopped
¹/₂ cup	heavy cream
¹/₂ cup	milk
1 tablespoon	unsalted butter
2 tablespoons	flour
¹/₄ teaspoon	freshly ground nutmeg
¹/₈ – ¹/₄ teaspoon	cayenne pepper
³/₄ cup	uncooked short-grain white rice
	salt
	freshly ground black pepper

1. Preheat the oven to 375° F. Lightly coat a 6-cup baking dish with butter.

2. Bring the stock to a boil in a medium pot. Add the carrots and reduce the heat to a simmer; cook, uncovered, until very tender, 10 to 12 minutes.

3. Drain the carrots, reserving the stock. Let the carrots cool for 5 minutes.

4. Transfer the cooked carrots to a blender or a food processor. Add the cream; process to a smooth purée. Heat the milk in a small pot over medium-low heat, stirring occasionally, just until bubbles form at the edge, but do not boil.

5. Melt the butter in a medium pot over low heat. Stir in the flour; cook, stirring constantly, for 2 minutes. Gradually whisk in the hot milk and then the stock. Add the carrot purée, nutmeg, and cayenne to taste. Turn the heat up to high and bring the mixture to a boil; add the rice, and season with salt and pepper to taste. Cover, reduce the heat to low, and cook for 12 minutes. Remove the pot from heat.

6. Transfer the ingredients to the prepared baking dish and bake for 15 minutes.

Carrot and Sweet Potato Soup with Ginger

This flavorful soup is full of aromatic spices and rich, nutty sweetness. Furthermore, it brightens the table with color. And served with a dollop of yogurt or sour cream in the center and garnished with fresh chives, it offers lovely presentation. This soup is heavier than you might expect, so if you're serving it as a first course, small cups are ideal. *Angelic Organics Kitchen.*

SERVES 4 TO 6

¹/₂ cup	chopped raw, unsalted cashews
3 tablespoons	butter
1¹/₂ cups	chopped leeks or onion (about 1 large or 2 small leeks or 1 large onion)
2 tablespoons	finely chopped or grated fresh ginger
¹/₂ teaspoon	ground cumin
¹/₄ teaspoon	ground cinnamon
¹/₄ teaspoon	ground fennel seeds
¹/₄ teaspoon	ground allspice
¹/₄ teaspoon	ground nutmeg
2 pounds	carrots, roughly cut into ¹/₂-inch chunks (10–12 medium carrots)
¹/₂ pound	peeled, diced sweet potato (about 1 large sweet potato)
4 cups	vegetable or chicken stock or water plus more to thin the soup
2 tablespoons	freshly squeezed orange juice
1 teaspoon	salt
	freshly ground black pepper or cayenne pepper
	plain yogurt or sour cream
	chopped fresh chives

1. Toast the cashews in a dry, heavy skillet (preferably cast iron) over high heat until they start to brown in spots and become fragrant. (Be careful not to over-toast them, as they will burn very quickly once they are toasted.) Immediately transfer the nuts to a dish to cool.

2. Melt the butter in a soup pot over medium-high heat. Add the leeks or onion; cook, stirring frequently, for 8 minutes. Add the ginger, cumin, cinnamon, fennel, allspice, and nutmeg; cook, stirring, for 1 minute more.

3. Add the carrots, sweet potatoes, and stock or water; stir to combine. Partially cover the pot, reduce the heat to medium, and bring to a simmer. Cook until the carrots and potatoes are tender, 15 to 20 minutes.

4. Transfer the mixture to a blender (you may need to work in batches). Add the toasted cashews and process to a smooth purée. If it seems too thick for soup, add a little more stock or water.

5. Transfer the soup back to the pot. Add the orange juice, salt, and pepper to taste.

6. Gently heat the soup over medium heat, stirring frequently, until hot. Ladle the soup into individual cups and place a dollop of yogurt or sour cream in the center of each. Garnish with chives.

Carrot Apricot Muffins

It's hard to imagine anything more tempting than a batch of freshly baked muffins. The kitchen smells sweet and spicy, and those steamy little gems look so comforting, so tasty, so easy-to-eat-more-than-one . . . *Angelic Organics Kitchen.*

MAKES 12 MUFFINS

	butter for greasing the muffin pan
2 cups	all-purpose flour
1/2 cup	sugar
1/4 cup	brown sugar
2 teaspoons	baking powder
1/2 teaspoon	salt
2	large eggs
1/2 cup	butter, softened
1/3 cup	buttermilk
2 teaspoons	orange juice concentrate
1/2 cup	chopped dried apricots
1 1/2 cups	grated carrots
1/2 cup	chopped walnuts or almonds

1. Preheat the oven to 400° F. Generously coat a 12-cup muffin pan with butter or line it with paper muffin cups. Set the pan aside.

2. Mix the flour, sugar, brown sugar, baking powder, and salt in a large bowl.

3. In a separate large bowl, beat the eggs. Beat in the butter, buttermilk, and orange juice concentrate. Slowly add the flour mixture, stirring lightly and briefly, until just combined. (Avoid overmixing the batter, as this makes muffins dense and tough.)

4. Add the apricots to the flour mixture. Stir in the carrots and nuts until the ingredients are just combined.

5. Ladle the batter into the prepared muffin pan, filling each cup no more than three-quarters full. Bake the muffins until a toothpick inserted near their centers comes out clean, 20 to 25 minutes. Cool for 10 minutes on a wire rack before serving.

The Crop

FARM NEWS, 1994
We could have dug the carrots a couple weeks ago, but lured by the promise of increased size and sweetness (the starch-sugar conversion resulting from the colder temperatures), we opted to wait. Patience paid off beautifully this time.

The Crop

HARVEST WEEK 10, 1995, NEWSLETTER

The carrots you receive this week are from the same planting as last week's carrots: the same variety, the same field, a different row. At least half the carrots from this row are wildly misshapen; their most unifying attribute is their stubbiness. We suspect that earlier in the season, before the carrots were planted, the big tractor crossed the field where that row is and compacted the wet soil. The carrots did their darndest to lengthen into the ground, but their struggle made them fat and short. These mutants are great for juicing, but your kids might not want them in their lunch box.

Orange Curry Carrots

This dish is a nice accompaniment to a chicken curry; it's a fine side at a luncheon of sandwiches and makes a simple vegetarian meal on its own over a helping of basmati rice. The thick, sweet-savory sauce nicely complements the tender carrots. If you use the cardamom seeds, grind them with a mortar and pestle. And don't be shy adding the banana—that's what makes this dish unique and delicious. *Angelic Organics Kitchen.*

SERVES 4

1 cup	freshly squeezed orange juice (about 2 medium oranges)
1 cup	water
4 cups	1/4-inch-sliced carrots (about 6 medium carrots)
1/2 cup	raisins
2 tablespoons	ghee or butter
2 teaspoons	curry powder
1/2 teaspoon	turmeric
	seeds from 3–4 cardamom pods, freshly ground (optional)
2 tablespoons	flour
1	very ripe banana, peeled, mashed
1/2 teaspoon	salt
	freshly ground black pepper
	chopped fresh cilantro

1. Bring the orange juice and water to a boil in a medium pot. Add the carrots and reduce the heat to a simmer; cook, uncovered, until barely tender, about 6 minutes. Stir in the raisins and remove the pot from heat; let stand.

2. Melt the ghee or butter in a large skillet or pot over medium-high heat. Add the curry powder, turmeric, and cardamom seeds; cook, stirring constantly, just until fragrant, 1 to 2 minutes. Sprinkle the flour into the skillet and stir constantly until a smooth paste forms. Remove from heat.

3. Drain the carrots and raisins, reserving the orange liquid. Add about half of the liquid to the curry powder mixture in the skillet, return the skillet to medium heat, and stir to combine. When the sauce thickens nicely, slowly add in the rest of the liquid, and then stir in the mashed banana. Add the carrots and raisins and stir to combine. Season with salt and pepper to taste.

4. Garnish with cilantro and serve immediately.

Celery

Contrary to its prosaic reputation, celery has some unusual characteristics. It is a stem vegetable that is related to both parsley (which is cultivated for its leaves) and celeriac (which is cultivated for its root crown). There aren't many stem vegetables. In fact, the only other stem veggies we grow at Angelic Organics are fennel and kohlrabi. Native to the marshes of southern France, celery prefers moist, slightly acidic conditions. Unless we've just had torrents of rain, you won't find any marshes in our fields. Nevertheless, with the help of irrigation, we put water right where we need it and produce admirable celery.

Our celery may look and taste more vibrant than what you're accustomed to. (Some of you might even say it tastes "aggressive.") This is because we do not blanch our celery plants by hilling soil around them to exclude light. Blanching would make for paler, juicier stalks—but our deep green unblanched celery is especially wonderful for cooking. Save the light-colored, mild inner stalks for eating raw.

Storage

Wrap unwashed celery tightly in a plastic bag and place it in the coldest part of the refrigerator; it will keep for up to two weeks. Or, to keep celery extra crisp, place it upright in a container filled with an inch of water, cover with a plastic bag, and refrigerate for up to two weeks.

Handling

Separate the ribs and rinse them well, especially at the base, where dirt can accumulate. Trim off any roots and the leafy tips; be sure to save the leaves for soups and other dishes. If the people in your household feel they could do without the celery strings, remove the strings from the outer stalks with a vegetable peeler or paring knife by making a shallow cut across the base of the stalk and pulling the strings up, up, and away.

Culinary Uses

❖ Serve raw celery stalks stuffed with peanut butter, cream cheese (or other spreadable cheese), pesto, or hummus.

❖ Slice celery into vegetable salads and use the leaves as a substitute for parsley.

❖ Make an aromatic seasoning by sautéing celery along with onions, garlic, or ginger.

❖ Place sliced celery in a single layer in a covered sauté pan with enough water or stock to come halfway up the celery. Braise until there is no more liquid in the pan, 15 to 20 minutes. When the pan is dry, season the celery with lemon juice, your favorite fresh or dried herbs, and butter to taste.

❖ Use celery trimmings for soup stocks.

Partners for Celery*

❖ Basil, bay leaf, chervil, curry, dill, garlic, lovage, paprika, parsley, thyme;
❖ Lemon juice, olive oil, wine vinegar;
❖ Butter, cream cheese, feta cheese, goat cheese, Parmesan cheese, Roquefort cheese, Swiss cheese;
❖ Beets, potatoes, red onions, scallions, tomatoes;
❖ Bread crumbs, capers, Dijon mustard, hard-cooked eggs, hummus, legumes, peanut butter.

*See Louise Frazier's Complementary Herbs & Spices chart, page 345, for suggestions.

Chinese "Pickled" Celery

While not truly pickling, this recipe uses an abbreviated method of pickling, with wonderful results. This is such a tasty and refreshing snack you'll always want to have a jar of them in your refrigerator. The pale-green, inner stalks are the tender-tastiest, so you might want to use two heads of celery to get enough of them. But don't fret; if you only have one bunch of celery, the outer stalks work fine. *Friend of the Farm* (adapted from *The Modern Art of Chinese Cooking*).

MAKES ABOUT 3 CUPS

1 pound	celery, cut into pinky-size pieces
1 tablespoon	plus 1/2 teaspoon sugar
1 teaspoon	coarse salt

2 tablespoons	soy sauce
2 tablespoons	toasted sesame oil
1 tablespoon	sake or rice wine
1 tablespoon	minced scallion
2 teaspoons	peanut oil
2 teaspoons	rice vinegar
2 cloves	garlic, minced (about 1 teaspoon)

1. Combine the celery, sugar, and salt in a medium bowl. Let stand on the counter for 45 minutes, stirring every 15 minutes. The salt will draw a considerable amount of water from the celery.

2. Meanwhile, combine the soy sauce, sesame oil, sake or rice wine, scallion, peanut oil, vinegar, and garlic in a large jar, cover tightly, and shake vigorously until the mixture no longer separates.

3. Drain the celery in a colander and rinse under cold water to remove the salt and sugar. Drain well.

4. Rinse the bowl. Return the celery to the bowl. Shake the dressing once more and then pour it over the celery; stir to combine. Refrigerate for 4 hours, stirring the celery at least twice in that time. Store in the refrigerator for up to 1 week.

Celery Salad with Walnuts and Gruyère

This salad works for just about any occasion. It's simple enough to make for yourself at a moment's notice, and it's elegant enough to make as the salad course for a dinner party—just serve it over a bed of leaf lettuce. The interplay of tastes and textures in this great salad will have you making it countless times. Farm friend Andy always gets asked about it: "Nobody invites me to potlucks anymore," she exclaims. "They invite my salad." *Friend of the Farm.*

SERVES 4

3 ribs	celery, cut into matchstick-sized strips
1/2 cup	chopped toasted walnuts
8 ounces	Gruyère cheese, cut into matchstick-sized strips
1 teaspoon	minced shallot
1	scallion, thinly sliced
	salt
	freshly ground black pepper
2 tablespoons	prepared Dijon mustard
1 1/2 teaspoons	freshly squeezed lemon juice
1/2 cup	heavy cream
1 tablespoon	finely chopped fresh parsley

1. Combine the celery, walnuts, Gruyère, shallot, and scallion in a large bowl. Add salt and pepper to taste.

2. Whisk the mustard and lemon juice in a small bowl. Add the cream in a stream, whisking constantly, until everything is well combined.

3. Pour the dressing over the celery mixture and toss gently but thoroughly. Sprinkle with the parsley.

Aromatic Braised Celery

Talk about easy; this one-pot dish couldn't be more foolproof. Try this delicious recipe as a side to roasted meats or as an accompaniment to your lunchtime sandwich instead of the usual chips. *Angelic Organics Kitchen* (adapted from *Joy of Cooking*).

SERVES 4

1 large	bunch celery, including leaves (about 1 1/2 pounds), cut into 3-inch pieces
1/2 cup	chicken or vegetable stock
3 tablespoons	freshly squeezed lemon juice (about 1 lemon)
1	carrot, cut into thirds
1	bay leaf
1	large parsley stem, no leaves attached
3 tablespoons	butter, divided
1 tablespoon	sugar
1/2 teaspoon	salt
1/4 cup	chopped parsley

1. Place the celery, stock, lemon juice, carrot, bay leaf, parsley stem, 2 tablespoons of the butter, sugar, and salt in a medium saucepan and bring to a boil. Reduce the heat and simmer until celery is tender, about 25 minutes.

2. Using a slotted spoon, transfer the celery to a serving dish. Discard the bay leaf, parsley stem, and carrot (you can eat it!). Increase the heat and continue cooking the liquid in the pot until it is reduced to 1/2 cup, about 5 minutes.

3. Turn off the heat and stir in the remaining 1 tablespoon butter until it is completely melted. Pour the sauce over the celery and garnish with chopped parsley.

Celery Salad
with Roasted Red Peppers and Mozzarella

Our Cook

The *Harrowsmith Salad Garden* cookbook advises against trying to grow celery unless you have marsh-like conditions. Here at Angelic Organics the celery crop was a success despite our unmarsh-like fields. Louise Frazier, a farm friend and contributing writer, writes in her book *Louise's Leaves* that "Europeans have seen celery as an aphrodisiac and think this is why Americans chew celery at parties." She recommends filling celery with anything from nut-thickened basil pesto to lentils with pineapple and parsley.

Enjoy this refreshing salad at a summer barbeque along with your burgers and brats, or as a light lunch with some good bread. There is a wonderful play of texture in this salad between the celery, cheese, and egg—just be sure to slice the celery as thin as you can. Fresh provolone works well in this recipe in place of the mozzarella. If you'd like to roast your own peppers, see the recipe for Roasted Bell Peppers, page 217. *Angelic Organics Kitchen* (adapted from *Judy Gorman's Vegetable Cookbook*).

SERVES 6 TO 8

2 bunches	celery, with leaves, thinly sliced
2	roasted red peppers, cut into strips
4 ounces	mozzarella cheese, cut into strips
2 tablespoons	chopped fresh basil
6 tablespoons	extra virgin olive oil
2 tablespoons	freshly squeezed lemon juice
1	small clove garlic, minced (about 1/2 teaspoon)
1/2 teaspoon	salt
1/4 teaspoon	freshly ground black pepper
3	eggs, hard-cooked, sliced

1. Combine the celery, roasted red peppers, mozzarella, and basil in a large bowl.

2. Whisk together the oil, lemon juice, garlic, salt, and pepper in a small bowl. Pour the dressing over the salad; toss to coat.

3. Cover the bowl and chill for at least 2 hours. Toss again before serving; arrange the egg slices decoratively around the salad.

A Shareholder

Even the weekly Angelic Organics newsletter gently suggests that "real" celery from the farm is so much stronger than store-bought that we shareholders might want to use it in soups rather than eat it raw. But if you slather it with peanut butter or add it to an American-style potato salad, that strong, crisp, salty taste is perfectly balanced. And the color—greener than most conventional peppers or peas—stands out in any preparation. To think I used to consider celery a worthless vegetable!

Classy Celery Hors D'oeuvre with Roquefort

You may have had celery stuffed with peanut butter as a kid (perhaps this is still a favorite). This recipe, however, is a little more, shall we say, dainty. It's the perfect party or picnic food, and indeed it's not for dieters, so make sure you have a good hike to your picnic spot or backyard deck. A glass of red zinfandel or cold sauterne pairs well here. This is lovely presented on a bed of ice if you're serving it at a party. Eat with pinky extended toward the ceiling. *Friend of the Farm* (adapted from *German Cookery*).

SERVES 6 TO 8

1/2 cup	unsalted butter, softened
10 ounces	Roquefort cheese
1 teaspoon	paprika
1/4 teaspoon	salt
4 to 6	large celery stalks, trimmed and cut into 2-inch pieces
3 tablespoons	chopped chives

1. Cream the butter in a medium bowl. Crumble the cheese and mix it well into the butter. Stir in the paprika and salt.

2. Stuff the mixture into the hollows of the celery pieces and top with the chopped chives. Cover with plastic wrap and refrigerate until the filling firms up, 2 to 3 hours.

Creamy Celery Soup

Creamed soups are great comfort food, and they make a perfect course for whetting your appetite. For extra richness, substitute heavy cream for the milk. For a nice presentation and great texture, serve with home-made Garlic Croutons (page 187). *Angelic Organics Kitchen* (adapted from *Joy of Cooking*).

SERVES 2 TO 4

2 tablespoons	butter
1 1/2 cups	chopped celery with leaves (about 3 ribs)
1/2 cup	thinly sliced leek (about 1 small-medium leek, white and green parts)
2 cloves	garlic, minced (about 1 teaspoon)
3 cups	chicken or vegetable stock
1/2 cup	dry vermouth (optional)
2 cups	milk
1/2 teaspoon	salt
	freshly ground black pepper
	pinch freshly grated nutmeg
	chopped fresh parsley

1. Melt the butter in a pot over medium-high heat. Add the celery, leek, and garlic; sauté for 2 minutes. Add the stock and vermouth; simmer until the celery is tender, 10 to 15 minutes.

2. Place a mesh strainer over a large bowl or pan. Strain the soup through the strainer. Return the soup to the pan and bring to a boil. Add the milk and reduce the heat so the mixture barely simmers; simmer for 5 minutes. Add the salt and pepper to taste. Garnish with parsley.

Over-read

At Uncle Bud's Catfish Camp in Mississippi: Health food restaurants are where they add nothing to the food and 50 percent to the price.

Our Cook

Someone asked me the other day if eggplant is my favorite vegetable. That's a tough question. I said, "Well . . . yes . . . in season." But then what about the gorgeous rainbow of sweet bell peppers growing next to the eggplant? They seem to distill what is sweetest in summer. And then there are tomatoes. A world without salsa and pizza? Terrible! How about the alliums? I doubt if I have cooked a single meal this year that did not contain onions, garlic, or one of their cousins. And then there are my spring favorites. "What is my favorite vegetable?" That question ranks up there with "What do I want to do when I grow up?" After years of pondering, the answer remains elusive.

Eggplant

Although at various times throughout history the eggplant has been accused of causing everything from madness and leprosy to bad breath, it has also been appreciated for its exquisite beauty. In America its richly colored skin and elegant curves made it a favorite feature in still life arrangements and centerpieces until the eighteenth century—perhaps it took us that long to learn to cook it properly. Eggplant does not require a great deal of preparation in order to be delicious, but it does require the right preparation; otherwise it can be unpleasantly bitter, rubbery, or watery. In this section you will find a selection of recipes to guide you through preparation and to help you create some truly memorable dishes.

The recipes are remarkable for their wide range of ethnic influences. It seems that all over the world, at some point along the way, many cultures met and fell in love with the lovely appearance and creamy-smooth flesh of this surprisingly versatile vegetable. Eggplant is a pleasure to the senses, and, as you will see from the creativity and breadth of these recipes, it is a worthwhile and welcome addition to a cooking repertoire.

Storage

Eggplant prefers to be kept at about 50° F, which is warmer than most refrigerators and cooler than most kitchen counters. Wrap unwashed eggplant in a towel (not in plastic) to absorb any moisture and keep it in the vegetable bin of your refrigerator. Used within a week, it should still be fresh and mild.

Handling

Rinse eggplant in cool water and cut off the stem. Many people like to peel, salt, and drain their eggplant to draw out any bitter flavor; however, bitterness develops only in eggplant that has been stored for a while, so with farm-fresh specimens this is generally not necessary. Many recipes call for salting in order to make the vegetable less watery and more absorbent—much like draining tofu. Salting is not an essential step, but it can greatly enhance the taste and texture of your dish and is well worth the extra effort.

Eggplant's slick skin can be difficult to cut. Do so carefully with a sharp knife. The shape of an eggplant determines how it is best prepared. Slice a straight, narrow eggplant into rounds for grilling or broiling, and cut a rounded, bulbous eggplant into cubes for stews and stir-fries.

Culinary Uses

❖ Stir-fry or sauté 1-inch-cubed eggplant in a very hot wok or sauté pan with peanut (or other) oil until the eggplant has released much of its water and is very soft.

❖ Brush 1/2-inch to 1-inch slices of eggplant with olive oil or melted butter and broil or grill until brown; turn over and brown on the other side.

❖ Pierce a whole eggplant in a few places with a knife, lightly coat with olive oil, and bake at 375° F until the eggplant is very soft and has collapsed some, 30 minutes to 1 hour, depending on the size. One use for the baked interior is Baba Ghanouj, page 176.

❖ Coat 1-inch-cubed eggplant pieces in oil and salt and roast at 375° F until soft and nicely browned. Or, brush slices of eggplant with a thin layer of oil and bake or broil on an oiled baking sheet. The results are great on sandwiches or as an alternative to the fried eggplant slices called for in some dishes.

❖ Eggplant burns easily if you're not vigilant. Instead of adding water to prevent burning, add chopped green tomatoes. They are a perfect partner for eggplant; the flavors are compatible, and the tomato releases just enough juice to keep curries and stir-fries from sticking. You can substitute green tomatoes for about one-quarter of the eggplant in any recipe.

Partners for Eggplant*

❖ Basil, cilantro, cinnamon, cumin, curry, garlic, ginger, oregano, parsley, pepper, rosemary, saffron, savory, sesame seeds, thyme;

❖ Balsamic vinegar, lemon juice, olive oil, red wine vinegar, roasted peanut oil, sesame oil, soy sauce or tamari, goat cheese, coconut milk, cream, feta cheese, Gruyère cheese, Parmesan cheese, ricotta cheese, yogurt;

❖ Cashews, peanuts, pine nuts, tahini;

❖ Onions, peppers, potatoes, summer squash, tomatoes;

❖ Chickpeas, rice, tofu.

*See Louise Frazier's Complementary Herbs & Spices chart, page 345, for suggestions.

A Shareholder

This is our first season as shareholders, and we have really loved it so far. We have been seduced by the bounty and the flavor of the good food in the vegetable boxes. Count us as satisfied. We have been very happy with the quality and the cleanliness of the produce. With only two of us, it has been work to eat everything. Also, we never would have chosen some of the veggies in the box had we been shopping in a market, so we have been introduced to beets, chard, and eggplant. I used to detest eggplant, but this fresh eggplant is amazing.

Overheard

Seeds want to grow.

Baba Ghanouj

This is a traditional Middle Eastern recipe for baba ghanouj, a thick but light spread that is delicious as a dip for pita bread or vegetables or as a filling in a sandwich. Its distinct, nutty flavor comes from tahini, a sesame paste that is widely available in specialty stores and many supermarkets. Some traditional additions to baba ghanouj include diced and drained fresh tomatoes, finely chopped black olives, zahter (a Middle Eastern blend of marjoram, thyme, sesame seeds, and sumac seeds found in good Middle Eastern grocery stores), or pomegranate seeds. *Angelic Organics Kitchen* (adapted from *Fields of Greens*).

SERVES 4

3 tablespoons	extra virgin olive oil, divided
2 medium	eggplants (about 1¹/₂ pounds)
¹/₄ cup	pine nuts
¹/₄ – ¹/₂ cup	freshly squeezed lemon juice (1–1¹/₂ large lemons)
¹/₃ cup	tahini
1–2 cloves	garlic, minced (¹/₂ –1 teaspoon)
1 teaspoon	ground cumin (optional)
¹/₂ teaspoon	salt
¹/₄ teaspoon	cayenne pepper
3 tablespoons	chopped fresh cilantro or parsley

1. Preheat the oven to 375° F.

2. Rub 1 tablespoon of the oil over both whole eggplants and place them on a baking sheet. Roast, turning once or twice, until very soft, 30 to 45 minutes depending on size. Let cool.

3. Meanwhile, toast the pine nuts in a dry, heavy skillet (preferably cast iron) over high heat until they start to brown in spots and become fragrant. (Be careful not to overtoast them, as they will burn very quickly once toasted.) Immediately transfer the nuts to a dish to cool.

4. Cut the eggplants in half and scoop out the flesh. Purée the eggplant flesh in a food processor or finely chop it on a cutting board. Transfer to a bowl.

5. Add the lemon juice, tahini, garlic, cumin, salt, cayenne, and the remaining 2 tablespoons of olive oil. Mix until well combined.

6. Transfer to a serving bowl and garnish with cilantro or parsley and toasted pine nuts.

Roasted Eggplant and Tomato with Pine Nuts
in Mustard-Balsamic Vinaigrette

In this recipe, slices of eggplant and diced tomato are roasted until they are soft and deeply flavored and then topped with a tangy-sweet vinaigrette. The balance of deep and light flavors in this recipe merits words like *sophisticated* and *exquisite,* but you probably won't get much beyond mmmmm. You can slice the eggplant into thicker wedges for some added interest. This goes great topped with several lumps of creamy chèvre cheese. You can also serve it over greens or with toasted whole-grain bread or pita on the side. *Angelic Organics Kitchen* (adapted from *Vegetable Heaven*).

SERVES 4

¹/₄ cup	roughly chopped pine nuts or slivered almonds
	olive oil for greasing the pan
1 pound	eggplant (about 1 medium eggplant)
¹/₂ pound	ripe tomatoes (about 2 small or 1 large tomato), stems removed, seeds squeezed out, diced
¹/₄ cup	apple juice or white grape juice
3 tablespoons	balsamic vinegar
3 tablespoons	finely chopped fresh parsley
2 tablespoons	prepared grainy mustard
2 tablespoons	freshly squeezed lemon or lime juice

2 cloves	garlic, minced or pressed (about 1 teaspoon)
1 teaspoon	salt
1/2 cup	extra virgin olive oil
	salt
	freshly ground black pepper

1. Preheat the oven to 375° F.

2. Toast the nuts in a dry, heavy skillet (preferably cast iron) over high heat until they start to brown in spots and become fragrant, about 1 minute. (Be careful not to overtoast them, as they will burn very quickly once toasted.) Immediately transfer the nuts to a dish to cool.

3. Brush a baking sheet with a light coating of olive oil. If using a larger eggplant, quarter it lengthwise and cut each quarter into two or more long, narrow slices; if using a small eggplant, cut lengthwise into six or eight slices. Arrange the eggplant slices on the baking sheet. Pile the diced tomatoes around the eggplant. Transfer the baking sheet to the oven and roast until the eggplant is soft, 30 to 40 minutes.

4. Mix the juice, balsamic vinegar, parsley, mustard, lemon juice, garlic, and salt in a small bowl. Slowly pour in the olive oil in a thin stream, whisking constantly, until the dressing is thick and no longer separates.

5. Remove the vegetables from the oven and flip the eggplant pieces over with tongs. Spoon about two-thirds of the mustard dressing over the cut surfaces. Set the baking sheet aside to let the vegetables cool.

6. When the eggplant has reached room temperature, transfer several slices to four individual plates. Divide the tomatoes evenly among the plates and drizzle the remaining dressing over the tomatoes to taste. Sprinkle on the toasted nuts and season each serving generously with salt and pepper. Serve at room temperature.

Broiled Eggplant

with Crunchy Parmesan Crust

This is such an easy way to make a crunchy-crusted eggplant appetizer that you may even feel guilty about the raves it receives. You will not feel guilty, however, if you make your own mayonnaise, which will really make this dish shine (see our recipe for Homemade Mayonnaise, page 332). Recipe-tester Barbara suggests topping this dish with tomato sauce. *Angelic Organics Kitchen* (adapted from *Recipes from a Kitchen Garden*).

    oil for greasing the baking sheet
    mayonnaise
    eggplant, cut into 1/4-inch slices
    freshly grated Parmesan cheese (about 1/2 cup)

1. Preheat the broiler. Lightly oil a baking sheet.

2. Spread mayonnaise sparingly on both sides of each eggplant slice, then dip the slices in the grated Parmesan cheese, thoroughly coating both sides.

3. Arrange the slices in a single layer on the oiled baking sheet and place under the broiler until golden brown, about 3 minutes. Flip the slices and broil until golden brown and crunchy on top and the eggplant is soft, about 3 minutes more.

A Shareholder

I am a painter, and there is not a single eggplant that I haven't lusted over the color of, or a pepper I haven't looked at as a work of art.

Sautéed Eggplant Salad
with Red Wine Vinegar and Tomato Dressing

This is an authentic Mediterranean way to prepare eggplant—shareholder Terry got this recipe from a friend in Rome. The flavors in this dish are released by the heat of cooking and then left to develop over several hours of standing time; the resulting tangy-sweet salad is so deeply flavored that it can double as a relish. You might like to make 1½ cups of your own tomato puree for this recipe (see the recipe for basic Tomato Puree, page 333). For a surefire method for peeling tomatoes, see page 92. *Shareholder.*

SERVES 4

2 large	eggplants, cubed
2 tablespoons	salt
¹/₃ cup	mild-flavored olive oil
1 cup	tomato purée
2 teaspoons	red wine vinegar
2 teaspoons	sugar

1. Put the eggplant cubes in a large bowl. Fill the bowl with enough water to cover the cubes. Stir in the salt; let stand for 1 hour.

2. Drain the eggplant and gently squeeze the cubes to remove any excess water.

3. Heat the oil in a large skillet over medium-high heat. Add the eggplant; sauté, stirring frequently, until golden brown, about 5 minutes. With a slotted spoon, transfer the eggplant to a plate.

4. Reduce the heat to medium. Add the tomato purée to the remaining hot oil in the skillet. Stir in the red wine vinegar and sugar. Simmer, stirring frequently, for 5 minutes, then gently stir in the eggplant. Simmer for 5 more minutes. Remove the skillet from heat.

5. Set the skillet aside and let the flavors develop at room temperature for at least 2 hours. Stir before serving. Serve at room temperature.

Baked Eggplant "Lasagna"
with Olives, Bell Pepper, and Three Cheeses

With its creamy layers of sliced eggplant and ricotta, Parmesan, and mozzarella cheeses, this marvelous dish is a little like lasagna—without the pasta. Also featuring bell pepper, basil, and black olives, the result has a lusty, Mediterranean flavor. *Angelic Organics Kitchen* (adapted from *Food and Wine*, July 1995).

SERVES 4

	olive oil for greasing the pans and coating the eggplant and peppers
1 large	eggplant, cut into 1/2-inch slices
	salt
1	red or green bell pepper, sliced into 1/4-inch rings
1 cup	ricotta cheese
3 large	egg whites, lightly beaten
3/4 cup	freshly grated Parmesan cheese, divided
2 tablespoons	finely chopped fresh basil
2 tablespoons	finely chopped fresh parsley
	pinch cayenne pepper
1 cup	tomato sauce, divided
4 ounces	mozzarella cheese, grated
1/3 cup	pitted, finely sliced black olives

1. Preheat the oven to 400° F. Lightly grease an 8- or 9-inch square baking dish with olive oil.

2. Arrange the eggplant slices on the baking sheet, season with salt, and lightly brush the tops with olive oil. Bake until eggplant is soft and golden, about 20 minutes. Transfer the eggplant to a plate and set aside to cool.

3. Reduce the oven temperature to 350° F.

4. Toss the peppers with a few dashes of olive oil in a medium bowl. Spread on a baking sheet and bake for 10 minutes.

5. In a large bowl, mix the ricotta cheese, egg whites, 1/2 cup of the Parmesan, basil, parsley, cayenne pepper, and a generous dash of salt until all of the ingredients are well combined.

6. Arrange half of the eggplant slices in the baking dish. Spread the ricotta mixture evenly over the slices. Pour half of the tomato sauce evenly on top. Sprinkle with mozzarella cheese. Arrange the pepper and olives on top of the mozzarella. Top with the remaining tomato sauce. Add the remaining eggplant slices and sprinkle with the remaining Parmesan cheese. Bake until all the layers are heated through and the cheese is melted, about 45 minutes.

Overheard

FARMER #1: I haven't seen you for . . . gosh . . . I don't know how long. Your sale.

FARMER #2: Oh, okay. I don't remember that you were here for that—twenty years ago this last March. You buy anything?

FARMER #1: I bid on the corn planter. Didn't get it. Spent $5 though, on a tank. Might have been $2, but I think it was $5. It was supposed to hold water, but it didn't. But I used it to store feed. Worked real good for storing feed. Uh, yeah, and I almost bought a . . . what do you call it? From that real pretty girl with the black hair. Real dark thick coffee in a small cup.

FARMER #2: Espresso?

FARMER #1: Yeah, that's it. One of those. Real black and thick. I almost bought it, but I was afraid of it.

Thick Eggplant and Onion Soup
with Orzo

Eggplant becomes tender but less "silky" simmered in broth than when it is fried, giving it a slightly heartier texture that lends wonderful richness to a soup or stew. With a thick broth full of chunky vegetables and pasta, this stewlike soup is hearty, warming, and simply delicious—a complete and satisfying meal. The farm crew comes to expect this on rainy afternoons; it fills them with the spirit to get back out in the rain and tend to the many challenges of mid-season harvesting. You might like it with some bacon pieces sprinkled on top (but not if you're a vegan or a vegetarian). You can make this with oregano instead of basil, with equally good results. If you use oregano, use 3 tablespoons fresh or 1 1/2 tablespoons dried, and add it when you add the eggplant and zucchini. *Shareholder* (adapted from *Better Homes and Gardens Vegetarian Recipes*).

Overheard

The intern said that seeing eggplants grow on a plant satisfied him more than anything else in the world. Like most of the students he's working with in the garden, he'd never seen those glossy purple fruits attached to their greenery.

SERVES 4

2 tablespoons	butter
2 large	onions, thinly sliced (about 1 1/2 cups)
5 cups	vegetable or chicken stock
1 medium	eggplant, peeled, chopped (about 4 cups)
1 small	zucchini or yellow summer squash, thinly sliced (about 1 cup)
1/3 cup	tomato paste
1/4 cup	dry red wine
1 clove	garlic, minced (about 1/2 teaspoon)
1/2 teaspoon	sugar
1/4 teaspoon	salt
1/4 teaspoon	freshly ground black pepper
1 1/2 cups	uncooked orzo or other small pasta
3 tablespoons	fresh basil
	freshly grated Parmesan cheese

1. Melt the butter in a large pot over medium-high heat. Add the onions; cook until tender but not brown, 5 to 7 minutes.

2. Pour the stock into the pot. Add the eggplant, zucchini, tomato paste, wine, garlic, and sugar. Bring the ingredients to a boil, then reduce the heat to a simmer. Add the salt and pepper. Simmer until the vegetables are almost tender, 20 to 25 minutes.

3. Add the orzo and continue to simmer just until the pasta is tender, about 7 minutes. Remove the pot from heat; stir in the basil. Let stand for about 5 minutes to allow the flavors develop.

4. Ladle into bowls. Top with plenty of freshly grated Parmesan cheese.

Fennel

From a distance, fennel plants growing in the field look like a tall, rich, plush carpet. Their feathery green fingertips flutter with the breeze, reminiscent of a scene created by Dr. Seuss. Once you finish caressing fennel's fanciful fronds, you realize that it is a practical addition to the kitchen that can be used as both a vegetable and an herb. With a sweet, delicate anise flavor all its own, fennel can be used much like celery in soups, salads, stir-fries, and other dishes. When used raw, its distinct taste shines through. When cooked, it imparts a subtle but delicious quality to the finished dish.

Storage

Cut off the stalks where they emerge from the bulb, and if you want to use the feathery foliage as an herb, place the dry stalks upright in a glass filled with two inches of water. Cover the glass loosely with a plastic bag and store it in the refrigerator for up to five days. The unwashed bulb will keep in a plastic bag in the refrigerator for at least a week.

Handling

Use the fennel stalks and bulb separately. If the outer layers of the bulb are damaged, either trim off the bad spots or remove the layers altogether. Cut the bulb in half lengthwise and check the inner core. If it's tough, remove it with a paring knife. Fennel should be washed carefully, because dirt can lodge between the layers of the bulb. Chop or mince the leaves.

Culinary Uses

❖ To slice fennel, quarter it lengthwise, which displays its texture.
❖ Prevent raw slices from discoloring by rubbing the cut edges with lemon.
❖ Try raw fennel as it's done in Italy: brush raw slices with olive oil and lemon juice, sprinkle with salt and pepper, and serve as an appetizer.
❖ Use the fernlike tops as a licorice-flavored herb or garnish.
❖ Use the stems in soup stocks and other dishes in place of fennel's botanical cousin, celery.
❖ Grill, braise, and roast fennel.
❖ Make an aromatic seasoning by sautéing fennel along with, or instead of, onions at the beginning of a recipe to flavor a dish.

Partners for Fennel*

❖ Basil, bay, coriander, lemon balm, lovage, nutmeg, orange, paprika, parsley, rosemary, saffron, thyme;
❖ Olive oil, lemon;
❖ Butter, Parmesan cheese, goat cheese, Gruyère cheese;
❖ Garlic, olives, potatoes, tomatoes.

*See Louise Frazier's Complementary Herbs & Spices chart, page 345, for anthroposophical suggestions.

Our Cook

I admit it took me some time to warm up to fennel. I never really cooked it until this year. I knew that I would write about cooking with it, so I thought I'd better practice. It helped that the fennel was growing along the driveway, so on my way home at night I could just grab a few for dinner. And you know, fennel has really grown on me. Now I think of it as an exotic treat, like leeks and arugula. As Thomas Jefferson wrote in his *Garden Book*, "The fennel is beyond any vegetable delicious. . . . There is no other vegetable that equals it in flavor."

Rich Summer Fennel Soup

This hearty soup makes for a meal on its own, and it's even better the next day for lunch, though the farm crew seldom leaves any behind. This is one of those soul-filling soups that seems to enliven you with good spirits and energy—which is one reason why we serve it just before the melon harvest. To make your tomatoes virtually peel themselves, score a very shallow X on the bottom of each one, put them in a heatproof bowl or measuring cup, and pour boiling water over them. Leave them in the boiling water for a minute or so if necessary; the peel will loosen completely. *Angelic Organics Kitchen.*

SERVES 3

A Shareholder

I want to tell you about my least favorite vegetable—fennel. I had never seen or heard of it before it came in my box that first year as a shareholder in 1995. It's not that I didn't like the taste, though a licorice-flavored vegetable did take some getting used to. It's just that fennel seemed so cumbersome. I wasn't sure how to use the feathery fronds, the bulky bulb, or the skinny stalks that held the vegetable together. It took several tries and a few years before I finally figured out how to make the best use of fennel's unusual taste and diverse parts. I cut up the bulb and cook it in my clay pot at 400 degrees for 70 minutes with carrots, rutabaga, cabbage, or kale. I use the stalks like celery, and I've come to like the feathery fronds chopped up in a salad. Fennel is still my least favorite vegetable. Yet part of the fun and challenge of being an Angelic Organics shareholder is the opportunity to try new things and to be creative enough to make even my least favorite vegetable into something tasty.

Bouquet Garni

1 sprig	parsley, stem only
1	bay leaf
1 sprig	thyme

Soup

2 tablespoons	unsalted butter
2 tablespoons	vegetable oil
1 medium	onion, sliced
1 to 2 cloves	garlic, crushed
1 medium or large	fennel bulb, roughly chopped
1 large	carrot, chopped
1 medium	potato, peeled, cubed
2 medium	tomatoes, peeled, seeded, chopped
3 cups	vegetable or chicken stock
2 tablespoons	Pernod (licorice-flavored liqueur) (optional)
1/4 cup	heavy cream or silken tofu
	salt
	white pepper
	chopped parsley

1. To prepare the bouquet garni, tie together the parsley stem, bay leaf, and thyme sprig in a piece of cheesecloth.

2. Heat the butter and oil in a large saucepan over medium heat. Add the onion; sauté for 1 minute. Add the garlic and sauté for 1 minute more.

3. Stir in the fennel, carrot, and potato and cook for 5 minutes. Add the tomatoes, stock, and bouquet garni. Bring to a boil, then reduce the heat to a simmer. Cover and cook over low heat until the fennel is very soft, about 30 minutes.

4. Discard the bouquet garni. Let the mixture cool slightly and then purée it in batches in a food processor or blender. (If you are using tofu instead of cream, add it now and purée with the rest of the ingredients.)

5. Return the soup to the pot and stir in the Pernod and cream. Heat over medium-low heat to allow the soup to heat through, but do not boil. Season with salt and white pepper to taste. Garnish with parsley.

Fennel and Potato Gratin

This is a tasty variation of a traditional dish. This version is rich and flavorful and can be served in small portions. Replace the half-and-half with whole milk for a less rich dish. *Friend of the Farm.*

SERVES 4 TO 6

	butter for greasing the baking dish
1 medium	fennel bulb, cut crosswise into 1/8-inch slices (about 2 cups)
2 cups	thinly sliced Yukon gold potatoes (about 2 large potatoes)
	salt
	freshly ground black pepper
2 cups	half-and-half
2 tablespoons	butter

1. Preheat the oven to 350° F. Lightly coat a shallow 2-quart baking dish with butter.

2. Cover the bottom of the baking dish with a layer of fennel slices. Cover with half of the potato slices. Sprinkle with salt and pepper to taste. Repeat layers until you've used up all your slices.

3. Bring the half-and-half to a gentle boil in a medium pan over medium-high heat. Pour it over the fennel and potato.

4. Using a large spatula, press down on the top layer to submerge it. Dot with butter. Bake until potatoes are tender and the top is golden, about 1 hour.

A Shareholder

Our absolute favorite box so far was the one with the fennel. Since we got to the delivery site late, the swap box was loaded with fennel from the less experimental in our group. Their loss, since I now have three fabulous recipes for fennel dishes, including one of my daughter's all-time favorites.

Fennel Mayonnaise

If you don't already make your own mayonnaise, you might consider taking this bold step forward in your culinary life (see our recipe for Homemade Mayonnaise, page 332). It's easy to make, and once you try it, you won't go back. This recipe will certainly work with a store-bought version, but it really shines with your own homemade mayonnaise. Save a little piece of fennel bulb and the flavorful leaves when you make your next fennel dish, and use them to whip up this great recipe. This spread does wonders for a BLT or tuna fish sandwich, and it's great as a chip or vegetable dip. *Angelic Organics Kitchen* (adapted from *The Harrowsmith Salad Garden*).

MAKES ABOUT 1 CUP

2/3 cup	mayonnaise
2 tablespoons	orange or lemon juice
4 teaspoons	very finely chopped fennel bulb
4 teaspoons	finely chopped fennel leaves
1 small clove	garlic, minced (about 1/2 teaspoon) (optional)

1. Mix the mayonnaise and orange or lemon juice until the mixture reaches a smooth consistency.

2. Add the fennel bulb, fennel leaves, and garlic; mix thoroughly. Store tightly covered in the refrigerator for up to 1 week.

The Crop

HARVEST WEEK 10, 1997, NEWSLETTER

There is abundance in our fields thanks in part to some nice rains. Thanks also to a great crew that has managed to stay on top of the weeding, seeding, transplanting, and irrigating. We have a breathtaking crop of cauliflower, broccoli, cabbage, and Brussels sprouts in the making.

Fennel and Pepato (Pepper Asiago) Baguettes over Greens

This makes for excellent and elegant party fare. An eclectic cousin to tomato-basil bruschetta, the tantalizing combination of flavors in this recipe will have your guests clamoring for more. Pepato is a pepper Asiago cheese that you can find in cheese shops or specialty Italian stores. If you have trouble finding Pepato, you can use regular Asiago, but to capture that peppery taste be sure to sprinkle on ¹/₂ teaspoon pepper in step 7, when you top the baguettes with cheese. Or you can substitute a good quality Parmesan or firm sheep's milk cheese, with or without the pepper. *Friend of the Farm.*

SERVES 4

	juice of 2 lemons (about 6 tablespoons)
	zest of 2 lemons (about 2 tablespoons)
2 cloves	garlic, roughly chopped
1 teaspoon	prepared Dijon mustard
	salt
	freshly ground black pepper
¹/₃ cup	extra virgin olive oil
2	fennel bulbs, tops removed
1	baguette
1 tablespoon	olive oil combined with 1 small clove crushed garlic
4 ounces	Pepato cheese, finely grated or shaved with vegetable peeler
¹/₂ pound	seasonal salad mix

1. Combine the lemon juice, lemon zest, garlic, mustard, and a dash of salt and pepper in a food processor. While machine is running, drizzle in the olive oil until well combined. (Alternatively, combine the ingredients in a large jar. With the lid tightly screwed on, shake the jar vigorously until the oil and vinegar are fully combined.)

2. Preheat the broiler.

3. Cut the fennel bulb in half and then slice each half as thinly as possibly. (A mandoline or food processor with thin blade works best, but a very sharp knife will do.)

4. Combine fennel slices with two-thirds of the lemon dressing in a large bowl. Reserve remaining dressing.

5. Slice 8 long, thin, diagonal slices from the baguette and brush with the crushed garlic-olive oil. Arrange the slices on a baking sheet; broil until just golden and crisp, 3 to 5 minutes.

6. Arrange the fennel mixture over the toasted baguette pieces on the baking sheet, leaving excess dressing in the bowl. Top with the Pepato. Broil just until cheese is melted, 2 to 3 minutes.

7. Put the salad mix in the bowl with the remaining lemon dressing; toss well. Divide the salad among four individual plates and top with the fennel and cheese baguettes.

The Crop

Even though we selected the fennel we grow at Angelic Organics for its large, flattish bulbs, you'd still find our fennel flowering and producing seeds if we left it in the fields long enough. During harvest, the field crew passes over an occasional bulb of fennel that has some rot or another problem with quality. Left in the field on its own, that plant will flower and set seed. Finding a seedling in an unexpected place is a reminder that our vegetables live for something other than being eaten; they have their own agendas, including reproducing and completing a life cycle.

Garlic & Garlic Scapes

Garlic does not linger quietly on the back burner. Most people react to it adamantly, either with adoration or distaste. For the admirers out there, you've got plenty of company. Almost all cultures grow garlic and cook with it. In fact, it's been cultivated for so long that it's hardly found in the wild. As for cooking it, there are many exciting preparations to choose from: zesty raw garlic, mellow roasted garlic, pickled garlic, and the savory flavor of sautéed garlic that falls somewhere in between.

Angelic Organics also distributes garlic scapes, the curlicue flower stalks we snap off garlic plants in the spring. Not only will you get to enjoy garlic-flavored scapes while you wait for the bulbs to come on, you'll also get bigger bulbs of garlic later in the season as a result of our removing the flower stalks. Snapping off the flower redirects the plant's energy down toward the root, and some say this process increases the bulb size by 30 percent or more!

Storage

Like onions, garlic can be eaten fresh or dried. Dried garlic will keep for several months in a dark, dry, well-ventilated place at a cool room temperature. Fresh green garlic must be kept in a plastic bag in the refrigerator and should be used quickly, because any accumulated moisture in the bag will cause it to spoil. Store unwashed garlic scapes in a loosely wrapped plastic bag in the refrigerator for up to two weeks.

Handling

To separate the cloves, set the bulb, root end up, on a counter and press down on it with your palm. To peel an individual clove, trim off the root end and then press on the clove with the flat side of a knife. The skin should pop off nicely. If garlic is fresh—uncured—the skin will present more of a challenge.

Mincing garlic can be a bit of a trick, gradually perfected over time, but here is the basic idea. Lay the garlic clove on its flat side on a cutting board that you will never again use for fruit (unless you like garlic-apple pie). With a small, sharp paring knife, make thin lengthwise slices, using your fingers and thumb to keep the slices squeezed together. Then slice crosswise, making even more tiny slices. You'll still have to squeeze, so be careful to keep your fingers out of the way of the knife.

Or, an even simpler way to prepare garlic is to press it with a garlic press. These convenient tools are great, also, for those of us who don't want the aroma of garlic lingering on our fingers or in our cutting boards. Simply peel a clove, put it in the cavity of the press, and squeeze the handles together; the garlic will extrude out into wherever you'd like it to go. After use, promptly scoop out the garlic residue and clean the nooks and crannies of the press to prevent the garlic from sticking and plugging up the grate.

Sauté whole garlic cloves until they are soft and then crush them in the pan with a fork. Whole garlic cloves can be added to soups and stews, but you may want to fish them out before serving. If garlic is to be used raw, you can pound it into a paste with a mortar and pestle and a pinch of salt.

Garlic scapes can be minced, chopped, or sliced.

Culinary Uses

❖ Garlic is the base for many dishes, and it can also be used on its own as roasted garlic paste.
❖ For those who have reservations about eating completely raw garlic in salad dressings or other dishes, try boiling unpeeled garlic cloves in water for 3 to 5 minutes to make them milder.
❖ Use garlic scapes like fresh green garlic or like a garlic-flavored scallion. (See the chapter on onions and scallions for ideas.)

Mongolian Garlic

If you find yourself lucky enough to come upon a bounty of garlic, here is a wonderful recipe to use up some of it. These intensely flavorful little gems are great as a condiment, or, for an hors d'oeuvre, stick toothpicks in them and serve in a shallow plate in a pool of the sauce. Any leftover sauce is delicious over rice or egg noodles. *Friend of the Farm* (adapted from *The Modern Art of Chinese Cooking*).

MAKES ABOUT 2 CUPS

5 large, firm heads	garlic
2/3 cup	chicken or vegetable stock or water
1/4 cup	soy sauce
3 tablespoons	sake or Chinese rice wine
2 tablespoons	sugar
1 tablespoon	honey
1/2 teaspoon	hot chili oil (optional)

1. Separate the cloves of garlic from the head. Peel away all skins that fall away from the cloves, but leave the thin layer of skin that doesn't fall away on each clove. Use only large, firm cloves.

2. Combine the remaining ingredients in a medium saucepan and set over medium heat. When the liquid is just about to simmer, add the garlic, turn the heat to low, and partially cover.

3. Stew the garlic in the liquid until the garlic is very soft, 3 to 4 hours depending on the size of the cloves and the variety of garlic. It is very important that the liquid does not come to a boil; the garlic will turn bitter if boiled. Uncover the pot frequently to check that the liquid is just barely simmering and to stir the garlic. At the end of the cooking time, turn off the heat, cover the pot tightly, and let the cloves marinate in the liquid for 2 hours.

4. The cloves can be served at this point or refrigerated for up to a week. They are best served warm or at room temperature. The cloves are still in their skins. Pop them in your mouth this way and use your tongue to squeeze out the clove (it comes out easily), or squeeze it out with the flat side of a knife.

Garlic Scape and Fennel Spread

This spectacular spread enlivens any ordinary sandwich, works wonderfully with roasted meats, and is especially good with shrimp. Whether you stir it into your hummus or slather it over grilled vegetables, you can't go wrong. This recipe calls for four to five scapes, but if you have a few more, use them too; it'll be delicious. If you can't find mirin, a type of rice wine, you can use regular rice wine, available at any Asian market and many supermarkets. This spread will keep in your fridge for one week. *Angelic Organics Kitchen.*

MAKES 3/4 CUP

2 teaspoons	olive oil
1/2	fennel bulb, finely chopped (about 1 cup)
1/2 cup	water or chicken stock
2 teaspoons	mirin or other rice wine
1/4 teaspoon	salt plus more to taste
4 to 5	garlic scapes, quartered

1. Heat the oil in a medium skillet over medium heat. Add the fennel and cook until soft, about 5 minutes.

2. Add the water or stock and the mirin; bring to a boil. Add the salt. Cook until thick, 4 to 5 minutes. During the last 30 seconds of cooking, stir in the garlic scapes.

3. Transfer the mixture to a bowl. Cover and refrigerate for at least 5 hours to allow the flavors to develop. Season to taste with more salt.

Overheard

Whenever I want to eat something I shouldn't, I take my clothes off and look in the mirror. I just stand there looking at myself. Then I decide not to eat it.

A Shareholder

I want to express my total approval of this year's garlic—not just because of the flavor, but because the cloves are so big, and so easy to peel, that they take all the bother out of preparing garlic for the skillet. Thanks again!

Garlic Croutons

Many of the soups in this book call for a garnish of croutons. The great thing about making your own croutons is that you can make them at your leisure, when the inevitable stale half-loaf of bread appears in your kitchen. While store-bought croutons are adequate in a pinch, you'll find that the little extra time and effort it takes to make your own make this delicious homemade version an attractive option. Store the croutons in a bag in your pantry for later use. *Friend of the Farm.*

stale bread, any amount, sliced (white bread is best, but any kind works)
olive oil
salt
garlic cloves, peeled, top quarter sliced off

1. Preheat the oven to 450° F.

2. Brush both sides of the bread with a thin layer of olive oil. Place the bread on a baking sheet and sprinkle tops lightly with salt. Bake until lightly golden, 5 to 7 minutes, checking frequently to make sure bread doesn't burn.

3. Remove the bread from the oven and rub all over with the cut side of the garlic cloves.

4. Cut the bread into smaller pieces if desired. The bread is ready to be used or stored.

Roasted Whole Garlic

Eating whole cloves of creamy, roasted garlic fresh from their skins is undeniably sensuous. It's heady. It's extravagant. It can bring you to your knees. Spread it over warm bread, mix it into mashed potatoes, or make it the crowning touch for a pasta sauce. You can also mash it and add it to soups and mayonnaise. Roasted garlic keeps well in the refrigerator for several days, so while you're filling your entire kitchen and neighborhood with that distinctive smell, you might want to roast some extra heads to use in future recipes. Try roasting a few sprigs of your favorite herb along with the garlic for some extra flavor nuance. *Angelic Organics Kitchen.*

> 4 large heads   garlic, left whole
> 1/4 cup   olive oil

1. Preheat the oven to 350° F.

2. Cut the top one-third off each head of garlic to expose the cloves.

3. Place all 4 heads of garlic on a piece of aluminum foil; drizzle with olive oil. Tightly wrap up the garlic in the foil.

4. Roast until the cloves are soft and creamy, 45 minutes to 1 hour, depending on size.

The Crop

HARVEST WEEK 7, 1997, NEWSLETTER

We harvested the garlic crop at the right time, so the quality was high. There was considerable winter kill, which probably diminished your share by half. (Garlic is planted in the fall, then goes dormant in the winter.) This fall we will plant a lot more garlic, so you can expect more bulbs next year.

—**FARMER JOHN**

Honey-Garlic Tea
(Cold Remedy)

In many traditions and cultures garlic has been used to cure just about everything. It may or may not protect you from the evil eye, increase your sex appeal, or save you from passing vampires—but its undisputed anti-bacterial, antifungal properties can certainly help you to fight off illness and infection. Here's a simple remedy that combines fresh, potent garlic with soothing and healing honey. Prepare this fresh and take it twice daily when you have a sore throat or stuffy nose. If you are feeling nausea or other symptoms of stomach flu, add three slices of fresh ginger (each about the size of a quarter). This remedy is most effective at the earliest sign of cold or flu. *Angelic Organics Kitchen.*

SERVES 2

> 2 1/2 cups   vegetable stock or water
> 3 to 4 cloves   very fresh garlic, minced
>   (note: garlic growing green shoots
>   is not very fresh)
> 2 tablespoons   honey
> 1 teaspoon   miso

1. Bring the stock and garlic to a boil in a medium pot; reduce the heat and simmer for 10 minutes.

2. Turn off the heat and stir in the honey and miso (for optimal health benefits, do not boil). Drink hot.

The Crew

HARVEST WEEK 12, 1997, NEWSLETTER

Built tables for our new wash area. Installed four additional wash stations (new reels and hoses). Finished painting and caulking shade structure. Harvested and cleaned the whole onion crop. (Cleaning took about 5 percent as much effort as in previous years due to an onion cleaner we located last winter.) Weeded herbs, the last weeding of the season. Separated garlic cloves for their fall seeding. Completed a final cleaning of the greenhouse for the season. Harvested and packed 570 boxes.

Green Beans

Green beans, like all legumes, contribute to the health of our soil. They are also enthusiastically anticipated in the midst of summer by the Angelic Organics farm crew. However, since harvesting beans is too labor intensive for a CSA our size, we currently don't include them in our shares. If we did give them to everyone, we'd spend all day meticulously picking beans at the expense of harvesting melons and corn and other summer vegetables. Nevertheless, our crisp, tender green beans entice many shareholders and volunteers to the farm each season to pick their own. Our summer open house often is a perfect opportunity for shareholders and shareholding families to harvest them to their hearts' delight.

Storage

Store unwashed beans in a perforated plastic bag in the vegetable bin of your refrigerator for up to two weeks.

Handling

Rinse green beans under cold water. To preserve nutrients and flavor during cooking, trim or cut green beans after they have been cooked. Trim them by lining up the stems on a cutting board and slicing off the ends with a sharp knife. You can leave the beans whole or slice or julienne them.

Culinary Uses

- ❖ Enjoy green beans raw.
- ❖ Steam or blanch green beans to make the best of their bright color, firm texture, and fresh flavor. Baby beans blanch to tender-crisp in less than 1 minute. Five-inch-long beans blanch to tender-crisp in about 5 minutes.
- ❖ Add fresh or leftover beans to soups, stews, or stir-fries in the last minutes of cooking.

Partners for Green Beans*

- ❖ Basil, bay leaf, chives, cumin, dill, garlic, ginger, lemon balm, lovage, marjoram, oregano, parsley, rosemary, sage, savory, thyme;
- ❖ Dijon mustard, lemon juice, olive oil, soy sauce or tamari;
- ❖ Butter, cream, hard-cooked eggs, Parmesan cheese, yogurt;
- ❖ Almonds, pine nuts;
- ❖ Anchovies, black olives, carrots, corn, hot peppers, mushrooms, onions, potatoes, shallots, shell beans, tofu, tomatoes.

*See Louise Frazier's Complementary Herbs & Spices chart, page 345, for suggestions.

Overheard

SHANNON: The thing about not getting married is that you feel like you missed a big event.

MEAGAN: If I ever get married, I want a nice frying pan.

Green Bean Salad
with Walnuts and Shaved Parmesan in Lemon Dressing

This is one of those recipes that is stunningly good—both in spite of and because of its simplicity. The straightforward, summery freshness of green beans with lemon is offset perfectly by the deep, roasty flavor of freshly toasted walnuts and the distinctive tang of fresh Parmesan cheese. Use a cheese shaver or vegetable peeler to shave the cheese. *Friend of the Farm.*

SERVES 4 TO 6

1/4 cup	coarsely chopped walnuts
1 pound	green beans
1 teaspoon	salt plus more to taste
	freshly ground black pepper
1 1/2 tablespoon	freshly squeezed lemon juice (about 1/2 lemon)
3 tablespoons	extra virgin olive oil
4 ounces	Parmesan cheese, thinly shaved (about 1/2 cup)

1. Toast the walnuts in a dry, heavy skillet (preferably cast iron) over high heat until they start to brown in spots and become fragrant. (Be careful not to overtoast them, as they will burn very quickly once toasted.) Immediately transfer the nuts to a dish to cool.

2. Bring a large pot of water to a boil. Add the beans and salt; cook until tender but still firm, 3 to 5 minutes.

3. Transfer the beans to a colander in the sink and run cold water over them. Trim the beans if necessary.

4. Toss the beans and walnuts in a large bowl and season with salt and pepper to taste.

5. In a small bowl, whisk the lemon juice and olive oil until well combined. Pour this mixture over the beans and toss until well coated. Transfer the salad to a serving platter or to individual plates. Gently scatter the Parmesan shavings on top.

Farmer John Writes

HARVEST WEEK 5, 1998, NEWSLETTER

Our growing manager studies the spreadsheet to dozens of fields, hundreds of beds, thousands of rows, and dates and tillage strategies. What to do today, weed or transplant, seed in the greenhouse, trellis tomatoes, direct seed lettuce? Will the afternoon be hot, too hot to hoe? Will the clay soil be too crusted to weed? Is rain on its way? Do we have enough help lined up? How big should the bunch of beets be? Will the lettuce bolt? Is the sweet corn ready? The truck tire is flat again. The cooler is too cold, too warm. The pump blew a circuit breaker. She directs, prioritizes, makes hundreds of decisions every day, moves the farm steadily through the season.

The crew harvests almost four full days per week. They count bags, boxes, and rubber bands. They cut, bunch, and wash. They share stories as they whisk through the work. Water splashes their sleeves. Mud smears their knees. Dirt graces their hands. They send over 600 brimming boxes down the conveyors into our frigid truck. They weed; buttonweed, foxtail, nutsedge, pigweed fall as the crew sweeps through the leeks, chard, parsley, potatoes. They trellis tomatoes. They seed lettuce in the greenhouse, and set it out four weeks later, 2,500 at a time, sometimes 5,000. They seed the fall brassicas—broccoli, cauliflower, cabbage—and tend them in the greenhouse, hoping the fields will someday dry. They cover the mesclun, thwarting the ravenous flea beetles. They uncover the second planting of zucchini: their great leaves finally sway in the wind, bees swarm their big yellow flowers. They come in for a festive lunch, wash up. Their muscles gleam.

Green beans used to bore me. They come into season at the same time as more assertive vegetables like tomatoes and sweet corn. It was easy to overlook the mild-mannered beans on the side of my plate. Although I was an indifferent green bean eater as a youth, my sister has always loved them, especially when they are pickled. Ever since I can remember, she has been able to polish off a small jar of dilly beans in a day. A friend has since introduced me to her style of green bean preparation: fresh, steamed lightly, and dressed with toasted sesame oil and tamari sauce. Now I can't get enough.

The Crew

HARVEST WEEK 7, 1999, NEWSLETTER

Water on demand. We ordered a new traveling irrigation gun and some peripheral equipment yesterday. It was a great feeling to finally bring the irrigation system another huge step forward. This whole watering-at-will program is equivalent in financial scope to the acquisition of the delivery truck and the greenhouse. We're hoping that the pump will be installed by the time you read this and that within another week the whole irrigation system will be up and running.

Green Bean and Pasta Salad

with Artichoke Hearts

This salad is full of lusty Mediterranean flavors and is so satisfying that it easily serves as a complete meal—especially if you stir in a can of white tuna. It's a fantastic summer patio event. You might like to try this mixed in with, or alongside, a head of romaine lettuce torn into bite-sized pieces. *Friend of the Farm.*

SERVES 6

1/2 pound	green beans, cut into 1 1/2-inch lengths
1 jar (6 1/2 ounces)	marinated artichoke hearts, drained, quartered
2	hard-cooked eggs, peeled, halved, each half quartered
1	red bell pepper, sliced
1/2	red onion, thinly sliced
1/4 cup	black olives, pitted, halved
1/4 cup	chopped fresh parsley
3/4 cup	extra virgin olive oil
1/4 cup	wine vinegar
1 tablespoon	chopped fresh basil
1 teaspoon	prepared Dijon mustard
1 teaspoon	freshly ground black pepper
1 clove	garlic, minced (about 1/2 teaspoon)
2 1/2 cups	uncooked rotini or other pasta

1. Place the beans in a steamer basket set over 1 1/2 inches boiling water and cover. Steam until just tender, 3 to 5 minutes depending on freshness. Drain and immediately run under cold water. Transfer the beans to a clean, dry dish towel or to paper towels and pat dry.

2. Toss the green beans, artichoke hearts, eggs, bell pepper, onion, olives, and parsley in a large bowl.

3. In a small bowl, whisk the olive oil, wine vinegar, basil, mustard, black pepper, and garlic until dressing is thick and the oil and vinegar no longer separate.

4. Cook the pasta according to the package directions. Drain well.

5. Add the pasta to the bowl with the green beans. Pour the dressing over the salad and toss well.

Pungent Green Beans and Tomatoes
with Cumin, Garlic, and Ginger

If you love cumin, this dish will delight you. Like many recipes from India, this one pays a great deal of attention to details that bring out maximum flavor in the spices—so it contains both ground and whole cumin seeds, one dry-toasted and the other cooked in oil. The resulting full, rich, roasty-cumin flavor is intoxicatingly good, especially since it's mixed with lots of garlic and zingy ginger. You might try cooking this dish for less time at the end, so that it still has plenty of liquid left from the tomatoes; try serving it this way over couscous or quinoa, with the delicious juicy sauce sopped up by the grain. *Friend of the Farm.*

SERVES 4

10 cloves	garlic, smashed
1 piece	ginger (about 1 inch long), peeled, chopped
1½ cups	chicken or vegetable stock, divided
1 teaspoon	ground cumin
¼ cup	mild-flavored vegetable oil
2 teaspoons	whole cumin seeds
1 whole	dried red chile pepper (optional)
2–4	fresh tomatoes, stems removed, peeled (see page 92), finely chopped
2 teaspoons	ground coriander
1½ pounds	green beans, cut in half (about 8 cups)
1¼ teaspoons	salt
3 tablespoons	freshly squeezed lemon juice (about 1 lemon)
	freshly ground black pepper

1. Put the garlic, ginger, and ½ cup of the stock in a blender or a food processor; process until a smooth paste forms.

2. Place a large wok (or large pot) over medium heat. When the wok is hot, add the ground cumin and toast it just until it is fragrant. (This will take only a few seconds—be very careful not to overtoast it, as it can burn quickly). Immediately scrape the cumin onto a small dish and set aside.

3. Quickly wipe the wok with a damp cloth or paper towel to remove any remaining spice. Return the wok to the heat; add the oil, let it heat up for about 20 seconds and then add the whole cumin seeds. After 5 seconds, add the dried chile pepper. After another 25 seconds (30 seconds total for the seeds, with or without the chile), add the ginger-garlic paste. Cook and stir the ingredients for 2 minutes. Stir in the tomatoes and coriander. Cook, stirring, for 3 minutes.

4. Add the green beans, salt, and the remaining stock. Stir the ingredients until they come to a gentle boil. Reduce the heat to low and cover. Simmer, stirring once or twice, until the beans are tender, 6 to 8 minutes (or even less time for just-picked green beans).

5. Remove the cover from the wok. Stir in the lemon juice and the toasted ground cumin. Increase the heat and bring the mixture to a boil. Boil, stirring occasionally, until all the liquid has been cooked off. Remove the wok from the heat.

6. Remove the chile pepper. Season with plenty of freshly ground black pepper to taste.

The Crop

If we left our green beans growing on the vine long enough, they would go through three distinct stages of growth: snap, fresh shell, and dried. Snap beans are eaten raw or cooked, pods and all; shell beans are eaten raw or cooked without the pod; and dried beans must be soaked and cooked before being eaten.

Sweet corn, tomatoes, melons

Eggplant, hilling potatoes, watermelon

Kohlrabi, kohlrabis, leeks

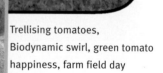

Trellising tomatoes,
Biodynamic swirl, green tomato
happiness, farm field day

Garlic harvest

Melon sharing, carrots and their harvesters

Goat love, barn raising, bucket

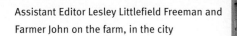

Assistant Editor Lesley Littlefield Freeman and
Farmer John on the farm, in the city

Kohlrabi

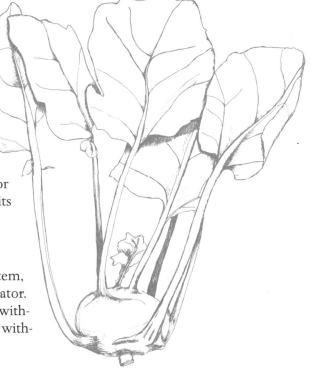

Midsummer we notice the fleet of alien spacecraft that has lined up in our fields—green and purple orbs growing lightly on the soil, antennas splayed in all directions. If we left them there long enough, they might actually levitate. These oddities are not in fact life forms from another planet but fellow earthlings and relatives of broccoli. Kohlrabi initiates know what a treasure these outlandish vegetables are in the kitchen. Their sweet crunch is excellent cooked or raw. After spending some time with kohlrabi, you might come to see its unusual mixture of attributes as appealing instead of alien.

Storage

If you plan to use it soon, wrap the whole unwashed kohlrabi—stem, stalks, leaves, and all—in a plastic bag and keep it in the refrigerator. Otherwise, remove the stalks and greens from the bulb and use them within a week. Store the bulb in another plastic bag in the fridge and use it within two weeks.

Handling

Rinse kohlrabi under cold running water just before use. Unless the skin seems particularly tough, kohlrabi does not have to be peeled. Just trim off the remains of the stalks and root. Grate, slice, or chop kohlrabi as desired.

Culinary Uses

❖ Cut raw kohlrabi into sticks for a refreshing addition to a raw vegetable tray, or grate it for salads and "kohlslaws."
❖ Lightly boil, steam, or bake it, or add it to stews and stir-fries.
❖ Substitute kohlrabi where recipes call for carrots, potatoes, or turnips (bearing in mind that kohlrabi has a milder flavor than turnips).
❖ Eat kohlrabi greens as you would kale.

Partners for Kohlrabi*

❖ Allspice, basil, celery leaves or seed, chervil, chives, cilantro, coriander, dill, fennel leaves or seed, garlic, lovage, mace, mustard seed, parsley, rosemary, turmeric;
❖ Lemon juice, red wine vinegar, soy sauce or tamari;
❖ Butter, cream, Parmesan cheese, Swiss cheese;
❖ Sesame seeds;
❖ Cabbage, carrots, celeriac, celery, leeks, onions, potatoes.

*See Louise Frazier's Complementary Herbs & Spices chart, page 345, for suggestions.

Our Cook

Alice B. Toklas described kohlrabi's taste as "having the pungency of a highborn radish born to a lowbrow cucumber."

Kohlrabi 'n' Carrot Slaw

Summer lunches on the farm often feature some variety of delicious and refreshing slaw. The cool, raw energy of the vegetables seems to bring new life into a tired crew after a morning of hoeing and harvesting. This recipe, a farm favorite, makes for a particularly attractive dish. *Angelic Organics Kitchen* (adapted from *Greene on Greens*).

SERVES 4 TO 6

1 pound	kohlrabi (about 4 medium bulbs), peeled, grated
2 medium-large	carrots, grated
1	red bell pepper, diced
1 small	red onion, chopped (about 1/2 cup)
2 teaspoons	chopped fresh thyme
1 large clove	garlic, minced (about 3/4 teaspoon)
1/2 cup	sour cream
1/3 cup	extra virgin olive oil
4 cups	wine vinegar
1 1/2 teaspoons	chili powder
1/2 teaspoon	salt
1/4 teaspoon	black pepper

1. Toss the kohlrabi, carrots, bell pepper, onion, thyme, and garlic in a large bowl.

2. Whisk the sour cream, oil, vinegar, chili powder, salt, and pepper in a medium bowl.

3. Pour the dressing over the vegetables and toss to coat. Cover and refrigerate for 2 hours before serving.

Simple Sautéed Kohlrabi

Quick, simple, and satisfying, this recipe celebrates the greatness of kohlrabi. Serve as is, as a salad on a bed of braising mix, or as a side to grilled or roasted meats. Braising mix is adolescent "mesclun mix," partly consisting of late season mustard greens that are too tough and too hot to eat raw. *Angelic Organics Kitchen*.

SERVES 2 TO 4

2 medium	kohlrabi bulbs, grated
1 teaspoon	salt
1/4 cup	butter or light oil
1 medium	onion, diced (about 1/2 cup)
1 clove	garlic, minced or pressed (about 1/2 teaspoon) (optional)
2 tablespoons	chopped fresh thyme, chives, or sage

A Shareholder

Until a week ago it had been about fifty years since I'd eaten a kohlrabi . . . and I was dubious. However, sautéed in a little oil and sprinkled with tarragon, it was delicious and a thousand times better than what I remembered as a kid. But the smell of it cooking is what brought back the childhood memories. There is no doubt that our memories are lodged in our olfactory glands!

Farmer John Writes

I glance across my fields as White Danube kohlrabi seed cascades into the powder of clay. The crops shimmer. They look crisp, rigid, shiny. Suddenly, the crops look frozen solid; it seems as though the heat has transformed into frigid cold.

—FROM JOHN'S ESSAY "HEAT," PAGE 152

1. Mix the kohlrabi and salt in a colander and let stand for 30 minutes to drain.

2. Melt the butter in a medium skillet over medium heat. Add the onion and sauté until translucent, about 3 minutes. Add the garlic and sauté for 1 minute more.

3. Stir in the kohlrabi. Reduce the heat to low, cover, and cook for 10 minutes.

4. Increase the heat to medium, uncover the skillet, and cook for 2 minutes. Remove from heat and stir in the fresh herbs. Let stand for a couple minutes to let the flavors develop.

Whipped Kohlrabi and Potatoes

You can't go wrong with this combination. It places your mashed potatoes in a different league than grandma's—but makes them just as great. The kohlrabi-potato mix is one of the great charms of root cooking. Make this for your next Thanksgiving feast, and you certainly won't have any left over. *Angelic Organics Kitchen* (adapted from *The Victory Garden Cookbook*).

SERVES 4

1 pound	baking or russet potatoes (about 4 potatoes)
2 pounds	kohlrabi (about 8 medium bulbs)
3 to 4 tablespoons	butter
1/4 – 1/2 cup	milk or cream, depending on how rich and creamy you like it
1/2 teaspoon	salt plus more to taste
	freshly ground black pepper

1. Boil the potatoes and kohlrabi separately (use two pots if needed) until tender, 20 to 35 minutes depending on size. Drain, reserving 1/2 cup of the liquid from either vegetable.

2. Peel the potatoes and kohlrabi. Mash them together in a large bowl. (Larger, more mature kohlrabi should be run through a food mill to remove fibers.)

3. Melt the butter in a small pot over medium heat. Add 1/4 cup of the milk or cream. Heat until almost simmering and remove from heat.

4. Pour the butter mixture over the potato mixture. Add 1/2 teaspoon salt and pepper to taste and beat until fully combined and smooth. Add another 1/4 cup of milk or cream for more rich creaminess, if desired. If you want a smoother texture, slowly stir in the reserved cooking water until it reaches the desired consistency. Season with more salt and pepper to taste.

The Crew

HARVEST WEEK 13, 1999, NEWSLETTER

Dug and picked up a few thousand pounds of potatoes. Removed remaining garlic from the greenhouse. Met with a local specialist in habitat restoration to develop plans for prairie plantings along the driveway and for revitalizing the woods. Transplanted a bed of lettuce. Lifted plastic in the summer squash and melon fields. Weeded and trimmed back the flower beds. Harvested and packed more than 700 boxes. Harvested more than 12,000 tomatoes—that's 1,500 per crew member. Do we have any volunteers for being the farm masseuse for a day or a week?

A Shareholder

An additional delight of being a shareholder is that I have gotten over my fear of the unknown. I have a mission each week—to make a wonderful something out of everything that I receive. I totally freaked out last year when I pulled a space ship (kohlrabi) out of the box. But it became the basis for some good eatin'. I've learned that cucumbers cook up well in a soup or stew, and nothing tastes as wonderful as an heirloom tomato.

The Farm Office

1998, Newsletter

Amazingly, it's been easier to grow more vegetables than it has been to handle the increasing flow of office activity. The reason is that we have invested vast amounts of money, time, and thought into upgrading field operations, while office operations have stayed basically the same. Now we will begin to bring the same attention to revamping our office that we have brought to revamping our field operations.

Kohlrabi Hash Browns

Shareholder Laura once told us that sometimes her box partner would forget to come over and pick up her share. Then one week she realized she had a whole shelf full of kohlrabi in the fridge—and, well, she says this recipe was a big hit with everyone who attended her kohlrabi feast. This makes a fabulous and unique bed for serving just about any meat, or try it with eggs instead of the traditional potato hash browns. It's great as a side dish with a dollop of sour cream or yogurt. Small, young kohlrabi usually don't need to be peeled, but most kohlrabi from Angelic Organics arrives a little more mature and, according to some shareholders, usually needs peeling. *Shareholder* (adapted from *The New Basics Cookbook*).

SERVES 4 TO 5

4 medium	kohlrabi bulbs, peeled (about 1 pound)
2	eggs, lightly beaten
1 small	onion, chopped (about 1/3 cup)
2 tablespoons	dried bread crumbs
1 teaspoon	salt
1/2 teaspoon	ground ginger
1/4 teaspoon	dried red pepper flakes
	freshly ground black pepper
2 tablespoons	olive oil
2 tablespoons	butter
	plain yogurt or sour cream

1. Grate the kohlrabi and wrap it in a dish towel. Squeeze out excess moisture.

2. Combine eggs, onion, bread crumbs, salt, ginger, red pepper in a large mixing bowl. Add black pepper to taste. Stir until well blended.

3. Heat the oil and butter in a large, heavy skillet. Add the kohlrabi and press down firmly with a sturdy spatula. Do not stir. Let the kohlrabi cook until brown, 5 to 7 minutes. Carefully flip the kohlrabi with the spatula, press down firmly with the spatula again, and brown for another 5 to 7 minutes. (If the kohlrabi is in a layer thicker than 1/4 inch, you may want to stir it up after the last 5 to 7 minutes to let the inner part cook and brown.) Serve with yogurt or sour cream.

Leeks

Our Cook

Leeks are fantastic when used like onions as a seasoning. They can also be specially prepared like vegetables—braised and grilled on their own. I like to add leeks to quiche, and the roots and green leaves are excellent in stocks.

Leeks, which look like large, flat-leaved scallions, can seem intimidating and exotic in their green headdresses. In the United States, leeks are usually eaten as a delicacy at high-class restaurants rather than prepared at home. However, it's worth the effort to learn to cook with leeks. Despite their majestic looks, they are easy to use, and their delicate, irreplaceable flavor makes a meal special. The subtle, buttery taste of leeks imparts elegance to many dishes, including old standbys that call for onions.

Storage

Loosely wrap unwashed leeks in a plastic bag and store them in the vegetable bin of your refrigerator. They will keep for at least a week.

Handling

Cut the leek about 1 inch above the white part, where the leaves begin changing from dark to light green. (Save the unused greens; they'll give great flavor to your next vegetable stock.) Slit the leek lengthwise and soak it in lukewarm water for up to 15 minutes. Fan the leaves under running water to dislodge any dirt collected there, then pat thoroughly dry. You can julienne a leek by cutting it lengthwise, or slice it crosswise.

If you want to clean a leek that you will be cooking whole, make a slit down one side to within an inch or two of the root end. Then spread the leaves under running lukewarm water to clean the leek. During cooking the leek will stay whole. When serving, arrange the leek with the cut side down.

Culinary Uses

* Use slimmer, younger leeks raw in salads.
* Grill, steam, or braise leeks.
* Sauté leeks for use in soups and stews.
* Add extravagance to any recipe by substituting leeks when onions are called for. However, because leeks don't caramelize well, check them often during cooking to make sure they don't burn.

Partners for Leeks*

❖ Bay leaf, caraway, chervil, chives, chile pepper, curry spices, dill, fennel, garlic, ginger, lovage, mustard, nutmeg, oregano, paprika, parsley, rosemary, saffron, sage, tarragon, thyme;

❖ Hazelnut oil, lemon, olive oil, peanut oil, soy sauce or tamari, wine;

❖ Butter, cheddar cheese, cream, crème fraîche, eggs, goat cheese, Gruyère cheese, Parmesan cheese;

❖ Capers, celery, barley, olives, onions, potatoes, scallions.

*See Louise Frazier's Complementary Herbs & Spices chart, page 345, for suggestions.

Over-read

Graffiti in a Whole Foods Men's Room: I like health food from chain stores.

A Shareholder

The produce continues to be beautiful and yummy and a pleasure to look forward to every week. This week we had delicious red sauces here, and the leek added a nice complexity to a mushroom risotto. Every once in a while my roommate and I mention how sad we will be with that last December delivery.

Greek Pasta and Leeks

This dish is always a crowd pleaser, great for picnics and potlucks, lunch or dinner. It's equally good hot or cold. If you don't have good fresh tomatoes, you can use one 28-ounce can of crushed tomatoes. To make fresh tomatoes virtually peel themselves, score a very shallow X on the bottom of each one, put them in a heatproof bowl or measuring cup, and pour boiling water over them. Leave them in the boiling water for a minute or so if necessary; the peel will loosen completely. *Angelic Organics Kitchen* (adapted from *Vegetarian Gourmet, Winter 1996*).

SERVES 4

12 ounces	uncooked spinach pasta (fusilli or penne is best)
2 tablespoons	olive oil
2	leeks thinly sliced
2 teaspoons	fennel seeds
6 cloves	garlic, minced (about 3 teaspoons)
1 pound	tomatoes, peeled and chopped (about 3 medium tomatoes)
1/2 cup	chopped kalamata olives
1 tablespoon	fresh oregano or 1 1/2 teaspoons dried oregano
1/2 teaspoon	salt
1 tablespoon	red wine vinegar
2–4 ounces	feta cheese, crumbled
	freshly ground black pepper

1. Cook the pasta according to the package directions. Drain well.

2. Heat the oil in a large skillet over medium heat. Add the leeks, fennel seeds, and garlic; sauté until the leeks are soft, about 20 minutes.

3. Stir in the tomatoes, olives, oregano, and salt; simmer, uncovered, until there is very little liquid left, about 20 minutes. Stir in the red wine vinegar.

4. Remove from heat. Add the feta cheese and black pepper to taste; toss.

Caramelized Leek Salad
with Pear, Cheese, and Toasted Walnuts

Sweet caramelized leeks together with ripe pears, toasted walnuts, and some good cheese conspire to make one of the best salads you will ever eat . . . ever. This is the ideal way to make a fantastic first impression at a dinner party—or simply to have lunch. *Angelic Organics Kitchen* (adapted from *Fields of Greens*).

SERVES 4

¹/₂ cup	walnut halves
1 tablespoon	unsalted butter
5 tablespoons	extra virgin olive oil, divided
2 large	leeks, white and green parts only, sliced (about 3 cups)
4 cups	mixed salad greens
¹/₄ teaspoon	salt
	freshly ground black pepper
1¹/₂ tablespoons	balsamic vinegar
2	pears, cored, sliced (you may want to sprinkle with lemon juice to keep from turning brown)

4 ounces cheese, crumbled or thinly sliced (chèvre, fresh pecorino, Parmesan, fontina, or smoked Gouda work well)

1. Toast the walnuts in a dry, heavy skillet (preferably cast iron) over high heat until they start to brown in spots and become fragrant. (Be careful not to overtoast them, as they will burn very quickly once toasted.) Immediately transfer the nuts to a dish to cool. Chop the nuts.

2. Heat the butter and 1 tablespoon of the oil in a large skillet over medium-low heat. Add the leeks; cook, stirring occasionally, until they are a deep golden color, about 45 minutes. Drain and cool.

3. In a large bowl, toss the salad greens with the salt and pepper to taste. Add the balsamic vinegar and toss; add the remaining olive oil and toss again. Divide the greens among four plates; sprinkle with the caramelized leeks and toasted walnuts. Arrange the pear slices on the leeks. Sprinkle with cheese.

The Crew

HARVEST WEEK 11, 1995, NEWSLETTER

Last Saturday morning the farm crew planted lettuce, spinach, and radicchio—more than 5,000 plants in all. They did it in a twinkle, because they also had to fit in picking melons and tomatoes, stirring and spraying Biodynamic Preparation 501, cultivating broccoli, hilling leeks, taking up irrigation lines, and discing weeds. Since there's not a lot of growing energy (heat and light) left in the season, we will probably transplant most of the seedlings from the Saturday planting directly into the greenhouse. That way you can be more assured of getting greens right into November.

The Crop

HARVEST WEEK 12, 1995, NEWSLETTER

I recently wrote an essay called "Heat" [page 152]. The extreme hot weather that day basically ended the onion crop. The leeks have made a feeble comeback since then, so you can count on a little more from the leeks than from the onions. You'll get some onions over the remaining season. They are small and few. This is a downside of being a CSA shareholder. When a crop is small, you get less.

—FARMER JOHN

Leek, Celeriac, and Beet Soup

We've noticed that the farm crew works with extra zeal after a lunch of this soup. It's rejuvenating and seems to lift the spirits. You need that when you have a 580-foot row of beets to hoe. *Angelic Organics Kitchen.*

SERVES 2 TO 4

3–4	medium beets
1 tablespoon	olive oil
2–3	leeks chopped
half	of 1 medium bulb celeriac, peeled, chopped
2 cloves	garlic, minced (about 1 teaspoon)
4 cups	vegetable or chicken stock
	juice of 1/2 lemon (about 11/2 teaspoons)
	salt
	freshly ground black pepper
1/4 cup	sour cream

1. Put the beets in a large pot and add enough water to cover them about halfway. Cover tightly and simmer until tender, 20 to 40 minutes depending on size.

2. Drain beets and let stand until cool enough to handle. Peel the beets and chop coarsely. Put them into a food processor and purée.

3. Heat the oil in a skillet over medium heat. Add the leeks, celeriac, and garlic; sauté until tender, about 20 minutes.

4. Combine the leek mixture and puréed beets in a large soup pot. Add the stock, lemon juice, and salt and pepper to taste. Simmer, partially covered, until the soup reaches the desired thickness, 15 to 30 minutes. Garnish each serving with a dollop of sour cream.

Leek and Mushroom Sauce with Thyme
over Pasta

Mushrooms and leeks work very well together. Although this is superb with wild mushrooms like chanterelles and morels, any more common kind, such as crimini or portabella, will do. *Angelic Organics Kitchen.*

SERVES 2 TO 4

1/2 pound	mushrooms
1/2 pound	fresh linguine or other thin pasta
2 tablespoons	unsalted butter
2/3 cup	chopped leeks (white and pale green parts only)
1/2 teaspoon	salt
1/8 teaspoon	black pepper
3 cloves	garlic, minced or pressed (about 11/2 teaspoons)
1/3 cup	dry white wine
2 teaspoons	chopped fresh thyme
	freshly grated Parmesan cheese

1. Brush or briefly wash the mushrooms and cut them into thick slices, including the stems.

2. Cook the pasta according to the package directions. Drain well.

3. Meanwhile, melt the butter in a large pan over medium heat. Add the leeks, salt, and pepper; sauté for 5 minutes. Stir in the garlic. Cover; cook until the leeks are tender, about 5 more minutes.

4. Add the mushrooms and wine; gently simmer, uncovered, for 10 minutes.

5. Add the pasta and thyme to the mushroom mixture; toss well. Top with grated Parmesan.

Leek and Mushroom Quiche

Quiche always draws a hungry crowd and is the perfect first course for a dinner party. It makes a fine lunch with a salad, and leftovers are simply wonderful the next day for breakfast. The two main ingredients in this recipe pair beautifully; however, if you are not a mushroom fan, you can substitute them with equal amounts of your favorite vegetable, or cooked shrimp, or baked ham—be creative. And be sure you wash your leeks well, as dirt can hide deep inside. *Friend of the Farm.*

SERVES 4 TO 6

Crust

	dough for 1 pie crust
1	egg
1 tablespoon	water

Leek and Mushroom Filling

5 tablespoons	butter, divided
1 1/2 pounds	leeks, quartered and thinly sliced, tough outer dark green parts discarded (about 2 cups)
3 tablespoons	water
1/2 pound	fresh mushrooms, any kind
3/4 teaspoon	salt, divided
3	eggs
1 1/2 cups	heavy cream or half-and-half
1/2 teaspoon	freshly ground white pepper
	pinch freshly grated nutmeg
1/3 cup	grated Gruyère or Swiss cheese
1 tablespoon	butter, cut into pea-size pieces

1. Preheat oven to 425°F.

2. Roll out the pie crust dough to fit into a 9-inch fluted quiche pan with a false (removable) bottom or a 9-inch pie pan. Place the crust in the pan and put it in the freezer for 10 minutes. Then prick the crust all over with the tines of a fork.

2. Line the crust with a large piece of aluminum foil and fill with pie weights or beans; bake for 12 minutes. Meanwhile, in a small bowl, beat the egg and then beat in the 1 tablespoon water to make an egg glaze.

3. Remove the foil and beans from the crust, brush on the egg glaze, and return the crust to the oven for 3 more minutes. (The crust will be only partially baked at this point.) Cool on a wire rack.

4. Reduce oven heat to 375° F.

5. Melt the butter in a large skillet over medium-high heat. Add the leeks and cook, stirring, for 3 minutes. Add the water, reduce the heat to low and cover; cook for 15 minutes more.

6. Remove the cover, increase the heat to medium-high, and add the mushrooms and 1/4 teaspoon of the salt. Cook until the mushrooms start to release their liquid, about 5 minutes. Using a slotted spoon, transfer the chunky pieces of the mixture to a bowl to cool; discard the liquid.

7. Beat the eggs, cream, white pepper, remaining 1/2 teaspoon salt, and nutmeg in a medium bowl. Stir in the leek-mushroom mixture.

8. Put the pie pan and crust on a baking sheet. Spread the grated cheese on the bottom of the crust.

9. Pour the filling into the crust (do not fill all the way to the top of the crust; the filling expands as it cooks. If you have a little extra, pour it into a custard cup and bake it along with the quiche.) Dot the top of the quiche with the pieces of butter.

10. Place the baking sheet in the oven and bake until a knife inserted in the center of the quiche comes out clean, about 30 minutes.

Grilled Vegetable Medley Pizza
with Grilled Leeks

Lacking that backyard brick oven? We recommend that you try grilling your pizzas. You'll need a covered grill: a kettle-type charcoal grill is preferred, but a gas grill works fine. This recipe works great in the oven, too. Oh, the flavors of grilled leeks, zucchini, tomatoes, and onions are simply divine! Have some fun experimenting with topping combinations and try adding your favorite fresh herbs—whatever you have, it will be delicious, with a wonderfully crisp, smoky-flavored crust. If you don't want to make your own pizza dough, prepared crusts are fine. This makes two 12-inch pizzas, and leftovers make a wonderful breakfast with a cup of coffee. *Friend of the Farm.*

MAKES 2 12-INCH PIZZAS

assortment of grilling vegetables (any of these in any combination and quantity):

> leeks
> zucchini or summer squash,
>   sliced lengthwise 1/4-inch thick
> red or green bell peppers, sliced
> fennel, roughly chopped
> red onion, sliced 1/2-inch thick
> large tomatoes, sliced 1/2-inch thick
> portabella mushrooms, sliced

1–2 tablespoons	olive oil
1 teaspoon	salt
1 batch	of your favorite pizza crust or prepared crusts (for two 12-inch pizzas)
3/4 cup	marinara or pesto sauce or your favorite pizza sauce
1/2 pound	sausage, cooked and crumbled, or 1/2 pound sliced pepperoni (optional)
4 cups	chopped spinach
1 pound	(or less) mozzarella or provolone, grated; or feta or goat cheese crumbled; or a blend of cheeses

1. Build a medium-hot hardwood charcoal fire, or set your gas grill to high. (You can also make this in your oven at 450° F; it won't be a grilled pizza, but a pizza nonetheless.)

2. To prepare the leeks for the grill, quarter them lengthwise, leaving them connected at the root. Fan out the strips of leek and clean under cold running water. Roughly reassemble the leek by tying it in two places with butcher's twine.

3. Brush all the vegetables with olive oil and sprinkle with salt.

4. When the coals are ready, spread them out on one side of the grill. Add the vegetables to the side with the coals. The vegetables will all require different cooking times; so turn them often until you see grill marks on both sides, and then remove them from the grill. If any vegetables start to burn, move them to the side without the coals. Add more coals to the fire while you prepare the pizza in the next steps.

5. Roll out the pizza dough and place it on a baking sheet. Spread half the sauce on the dough. Add half the meat and half the grilled vegetables.

6. Spread the coals in an even layer across the bottom of the grill. (If using a gas grill, turn one of the burners off and turn the other to medium.) Place the baking sheet on the grill rack. Cover the grill (be sure the vents are open). Uncover after 5 minutes; the crust will be firm. Mound the spinach onto the pizza; cover again and grill until spinach is wilted, about 5 minutes. At this point you can slide the pizza off the baking sheet right onto the grill to add crispiness and grill flavor to the crust—but take a peek at the underside of your crust first: if it's already deep brown in spots, leave it on the baking sheet. Top with half the cheese. Cover and grill until the cheese melts, 3 to 5 minutes.

7. Remove the pizza from the grill and set aside to cool slightly. Cut in pieces and serve hot, cold, or at room temperature. Repeat the process with the remaining crust and ingredients to make another pizza.

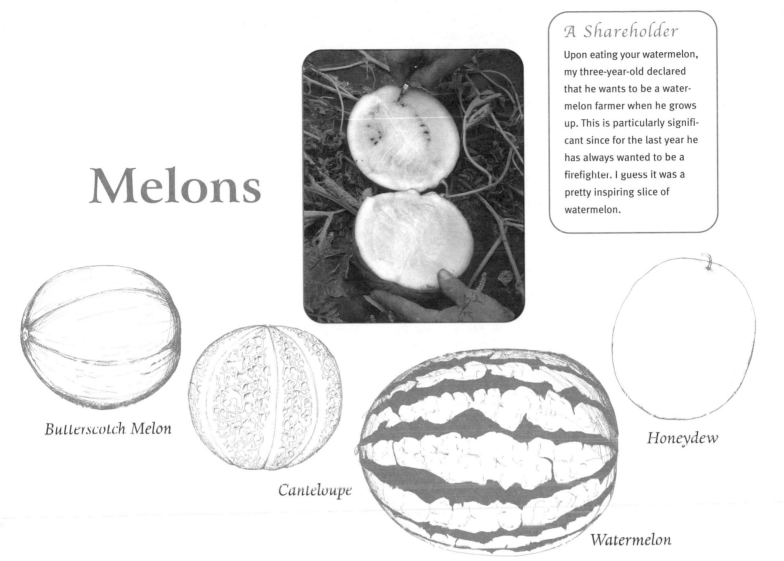

Melons

Butterscotch Melon

Canteloupe

Watermelon

Honeydew

At last—melons! A relative of cucumbers, melons are the only "fruit" we grow at Angelic Organics (though we grow plenty of vegetables that are botanically classified as fruits). The farm team loves to eat the sun-warmed, vine-ripened melons that come straight from our fields. And eat them they do! Under the pretense of research, the crew dives into a few melons at the beginning of every harvest, equipped with eager taste buds and a refractometer—a device used to measure the sweetness in fruits. They identify the sweetest and best melons of their sample, take note of ripeness cues—like coloration, size, stem slip, and "thump"—and harvest accordingly. Next to cutting into and tasting each melon, this is the best way to harvest the sweetest melons possible.

Melons Grown by Angelic Organic

Orange honeydew melon has ivory skin with a pale, salmon-color interior. The flesh is honey-sweet, tender, and crisp.

Butterscotch melon has sweet, fragrant, green and orange flesh. The sweetness extends all the way to the rind, and the flavor reminds some people of butterscotch.

Cantaloupe/Muskmelon has dense, netting-like skin with thick, juicy orange flesh and a sweet, musky flavor.

Watermelon has dark and light green stripes on the outside and on the inside is crisp, tender, sweet, and hydrating. We usually grow varieties with yellow and orange flesh in addition to conventional pink-red watermelons.

Passport melon is a galia, or "tropical," melon. A large melon, it averages 6 to 7 inches in diameter and 5 to 6 pounds. The flesh is very thick and darker green toward the outside and whitish green toward the seed cavity.

Storage

If your muskmelon, honeydew, or butterscotch melon seems a bit short of ripe, keep it at room temperature for a few days or until there is a sweet smell coming from the stem end. Once the melon ripens, store it in the refrigerator.

Handle watermelons carefully. When harvested at their peak ripeness, they can crack or split easily if bumped or roughly handled. Refrigerate watermelons right away. (Watermelons do not ripen off the vine and do not emanate a ripe smell.)

Cut melon should be covered in plastic wrap, chunks or slices should be kept in an airtight container, and both should be refrigerated. Eat all melons within a week.

Handling

A big knife and a large cutting surface are useful, especially for watermelons. Giving yourself plenty of room, cut the melon in half from stem to blossom end. Scoop out the seeds of muskmelons, butterscotch, or honeydews. If you'd like, you can cut the melon further into quarters or slices, or peel it and cut it into cubes for snacking.

Culinary Uses

❖ Jazz up melons with a pinch of salt or a squeeze of lime juice. Sprinkle on some chili powder as well, as is done in Mexico.
❖ Blend watermelon, water, and sugar or honey for a refreshing *agua de sandia*.
❖ Blend ice cold milk, cantaloupe chunks, vanilla, and sugar or honey for a *licuado de melón,* a Mexican-style fruit shake.
❖ Fill half a cantaloupe with plain or vanilla yogurt and top it with granola for a simple breakfast or dessert.

Partners for Melons

❖ Anise hyssop, chili powder, fennel leaves, lemon balm, mint, tarragon, vanilla,
❖ Chili sauce, honey, lemon juice, lime juice,
❖ Cream, milk, yogurt,
❖ Bee pollen, granola, sunflower seeds.

Cantaloupe and Tomato Salad
with Mint

This salad is best with sweet heirloom tomatoes or the low-acid yellow tomatoes, but any very ripe tomato will do. It's a superb accompaniment to any backyard barbeque. *Angelic Organics Kitchen.*

SERVES 4

1/2 small	cantaloupe, balled or cut in 1-inch pieces (about 1 cup)
2 small	tomatoes, cut into thin wedges (about 1 cup)
1/2	cucumber, peeled, diced (about 1 cup)
1 large	rib celery, diced (about 3/4 cup)
1 cup	plain yogurt
1/2 cup	chopped fresh mint plus more for garnish
1 tablespoon	sherry vinegar
2 teaspoons	honey
2 teaspoons	lemon juice
	salt
	freshly ground black pepper

1. Combine the cantaloupe, tomatoes, cucumber, and celery in a large salad bowl.

2. Whisk the yogurt, mint, sherry vinegar, honey, and lemon juice in a small bowl.

3. Pour the dressing over the melon salad and toss until will combined. Season with salt and pepper to taste; garnish with mint leaves.

VegVeyor

HARVEST WEEK 9, 2001

A new exciting piece of equipment has arrived on the farm—the VegVeyor. The VegVeyor is quite a procession—our 826 tractor, the bright yellow conveyor, and then a hay wagon with large wooden bins on top. The conveyor pivots out to float perpendicularly across several beds. Now, instead of throwing each melon to someone waiting at the edge of the field, the harvester sets their melon on the conveyor belt right in front of them, which brings it up to the wagon and drops it into a bin. It's fun and amazing. It saved us at least 1 to 1.5 hours in the corn harvest.

Watermelon Soup

This soup was inspired by a dish created by acclaimed chef Nora Pouillon. It is served as a first course at her establishment Restaurant Nora in Washington, D.C. Far removed from such a fine eatery, the farm crew ravenously slurps down this soup to the exclusion of any other food on those steamy hot summer days when watermelon is the only sensible thing to eat. *Shareholder*

SERVES 4 TO 6

9 to 10 cups	watermelon, cut into chunks (about 6 pounds, or 1 small watermelon)
1/2 cup	diced fennel
1/2 cup	chopped fresh mint plus sprigs for garnish
2	bell peppers (yellow, orange, or red), diced
1	red chile pepper or jalapeño pepper, minced
2 tablespoons	freshly squeezed lime juice (about 1 lime)
2 tablespoons	freshly squeezed lemon juice (about 1 small lemon)
1 1/2 teaspoons	grated ginger
	salt
	freshly ground black pepper
2/3 cup	fresh blueberries or frozen blueberries, thawed

1. Run the watermelon through a food mill to remove all the seeds, or pick them out by hand. If not using a food mill, purée the watermelon in batches in a food processor or blender.

2. Put the watermelon in a large bowl. Add the fennel, mint, bell peppers, chile pepper, lime and lemon juices, ginger, and salt and pepper to taste.

3. Refrigerate for at least 2 hours. Garnish with blueberries and mint sprigs just before serving.

The Crop

HARVEST WEEK 10, 1996, NEWSLETTER

A most extraordinary event has occurred at the farm. Our watermelons, which had been rapidly shriveling up and apparently dying from some extreme fungal condition, are staging a marked recovery. In the sections of the field where the leaves were almost totally black, there is now lush new growth. It remains to be seen whether watermelons will actually form in these areas, but in the more marginal areas that we had written off, there are definitely nice watermelons scattered about. Every major wilt we have ever seen in a melon or squash crop has been fatal, and now we have a big turnaround that reminds us we don't know everything.

The Crop

HARVEST WEEK 9, 1995, NEWSLETTER

Your melons have sweetened up a lot in the last week! The muskmelons have risen from 5.5 brix to about 9 brix. Butterscotch averages 10 to 11 brix. (The brix scale measures the percentage by weight of sugar in solutions.) Our cooler smells like perfume from all the ripening melons. We are having a yummy week on the farm. We still don't know what the problem was with the low brix. Maybe it was heat related. By the way, make sure to wait until your melon is ripe before eating it. Wait until the muskmelon smells "perfumey" and feels a little bit soft. The butterscotch melon will show a little patch of yellow as it approaches its peak moment.

Ginger Melon Sorbet

This is the perfect celebration of the cantaloupe—sweet and gingery, wholly refreshing, and a great palate cleanser after a heavy meal. Don't skip the ginger; it makes this recipe shine. Sorbet from the store will never taste the same again! *Angelic Organics Kitchen*.

SERVES 4

1 medium	cantaloupe (3 to 3½ pounds), cut into 1-inch cubes (about 4 cups)
½ cup	sugar
1½ tablespoons	freshly squeezed lemon juice (about ½ lemon)
2 tablespoons	freshly grated ginger
	fresh mint leaves (optional)

1. Combine the melon, sugar, and lemon juice in a blender or food processor and purée just until smooth. Add the ginger and pulse briefly to combine.

2. Transfer the mixture to an ice cream maker and freeze according to the manufacturer's directions. (If you don't have an ice cream maker, pour the mixture into a tray or zip-top bag and freeze it on a flat surface in your freezer. Remove the frozen mixture from the freezer and let it thaw out, then return it to the blender or food processor and process again until smooth. Repeat this process at least once more (two times total does the trick) or until the mixture is very smooth and blended with no separation.

3. Spoon into individual glasses or serving dishes and garnish with mint leaves.

Overheard

I cut up the melon. It was yellow. It was the most fun I have had in a long time. I love cutting melons.

Over-read

In the September 1995 issue of *Wired*: Speaking of Government Action: Just in time for the summer, Iran banned the sale of seedless watermelons. Why? Well, seems those godless melons, bereft as they are of reproductive mechanisms, "promote homosexuality and asexuality."

Cantaloupe and Cardamom

This is the height of refreshment and just the thing you need when the temperatures are soaring. Cardamom brings to cantaloupe a certain sophistication that will dazzle you. It's preferable to grind the cardamom fresh using a mortar and pestle, but any ground cardamom will do. Make an elegant dessert by serving it over vanilla ice cream. For a sweeter version, add 1 teaspoon maple syrup. *Angelic Organics Kitchen*.

SERVES 4 TO 6

1 medium	cantaloupe (3–3½ pounds), cut into 1-inch cubes (about 4 cups)
¼ teaspoon	ground cardamom
1–2 tablespoons	freshly squeezed lime juice (about 1 medium lime)
	freshly ground black pepper
¼ cup	chopped fresh cilantro

Toss all the ingredients in a large bowl and refrigerate for at least 1 hour.

The Crew

HARVEST WEEK 12, 1996, NEWSLETTER

Cleaned one ton of onions, harvested and cleaned one ton of melons, and harvested and removed the tops from 1 1/2 tons of carrots with the assistance of twenty volunteers from Beloit College. Tilled and prepared potato and onion ground for winter sleep. Weeded. Substantial repairs of tractor and carrot lifter due to harvesting carrots in hard ground. Future Farmers of the World Meeting. Topic: Farm Infrastructure—how to develop the built environment of Angelic Organics in a way that takes care of the long-term residents, seasonal helpers, volunteers, and other guests. Documentary filming of Farmer John. Intern's twenty-first birthday party.

A Shareholder

My husband and I just ate one of your butterscotch melons for the first time this morning for breakfast. What a treat! It was wonderful. I just made fresh juice with the rest of it. Thanks for allowing us to try new things and enjoy the fruits of your labor.

Peppers

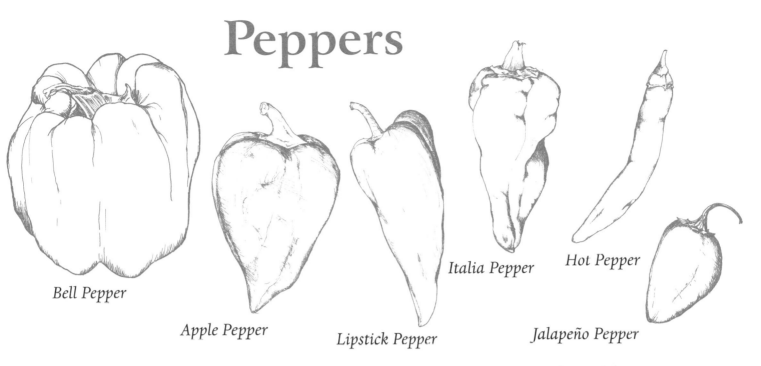

Bell Pepper

Apple Pepper

Lipstick Pepper

Italia Pepper

Hot Pepper

Jalapeño Pepper

Banana, corona, italia, Anaheim, cherry, Fresno, Mexi-bell, peperoncini, cubanelle, chilaca, and Scotch bonnet are but a few of the hundreds of peppers grown throughout the world. From black to purple to scarlet, from pointed to round to twisted, from tangy to hot to fruity, peppers display a stunning array of characteristics. All this can seem rather overwhelming, but among peppers you'll basically need to make only one fundamental distinction: is it sweet or is it hot? At Angelic Organic, we help you by dividing the sweet and hot peppers into separate bags during packing, so you won't get them mixed up.

Whether sweet or hot, a pepper will spark up almost any dish. If you don't like hot peppers but don't want to forgo them altogether, read the "Handling" section below for ways to make hot peppers more palatable.

Peppers Grown by Angelic Organic

Sweet peppers, also called **bell peppers,** have a sweet, crisp, slightly piquant flavor. Almost all bell peppers are sweet, not hot. We give you sweet bell peppers that are green, red, yellow, orange, purple, and chocolate-colored.

On an aesthetic note, purple peppers may turn an odd shade of gray if cooked, so it's more artful to use them raw. (We often harvest bell peppers that have begun changing hue, but are not yet fully colored. The

longer we wait for peppers to change color, the more they are likely to succumb to rot, disease, or other spoilage. This helps explain why colored peppers are usually sold for higher prices: the farmer sacrifices quantity of peppers to achieve the prized coloring.)

Italias are specialty sweet peppers that are long and red—not to be confused with the skinnier, long, hot peppers we also distribute—and small, round red peppers called **apples** and **lipsticks.**

Hot peppers, also known as chiles, are usually smaller than sweet peppers. We distribute green and red **jalapeños** and long, red-hot peppers called **hot Portugals** (not to be mistaken for the sweet, red italia variety).

Storage

Place whole, unwashed peppers in a plastic bag, seal, and refrigerate for a week or more. Beware of any excess moisture in the bag that could cause peppers to spoil. Red, orange, and yellow peppers are fully ripe and need to be eaten sooner.

Handling

Gently rinse peppers under cold running water just before use. For sweet peppers, cut around the stem with a small knife and lift out the core. Slice down the side to open it up and then cut out the inner membranes. Since the shiny outer skin tends to repel knives, slice or dice the pepper from the inside.

When handling hot peppers, be sure not to touch your eyes or nose. Wash your hands well afterward, and if you have sensitive skin, consider wearing gloves. Slice off the top of the hot pepper, including the stem. Since the heat in chile peppers is concentrated in the seeds, you can use the whole pepper for a spicy dish, or if you prefer, cut out the heat-filled seeds and inner membranes and use just the flesh of the hot pepper for cooking. That way you get the chile flavor without the bite. Dry hot peppers by hanging a string of them in a dark, warm, nonhumid corner (not over the stove).

Culinary Uses

❖ Add bits of fresh raw sweet pepper to any salad or other fresh vegetable arrangement.

❖ Combine peppers with tomato and eggplant; Mediterranean cuisine contains nearly infinite variations of these three, along with ever-popular fresh basil.

❖ Sauté a pepper at the beginning of a recipe; as with sautéed garlic and onions, this substantially enhances the flavor of the final product.

❖ Steam peppers for ten minutes and then stuff with your favorite stuffing. (Try a sausage stuffing; or rice with pine nuts and herbs; or the classic ground beef with rice, tomato, and corn.)

❖ Roast peppers (see our two related recipes, pages 217 and 218).

❖ Add hot peppers to many dishes (as long as you're prepared for the consequences). Chiles are great in sauces, soups, stews, and raw salsas. Larger hot peppers can even be stuffed, fried, and served whole.

Partners for Peppers*

❖ Anise, basil, cayenne, cilantro, curry, fennel, garlic, ginger, lovage, marjoram, mustard, oregano, parsley, rosemary, saffron, thyme;

❖ Balsamic vinegar, olive oil, sherry vinegar;

❖ Butter, cream, eggs, Fontina cheese, goat cheese, mozzarella cheese, Parmesan cheese;

❖ Corn, eggplant, onions, summer squash, tomatoes;

❖ Capers, olives, rice.

*See Louise Frazier's Complementary Herbs & Spices chart, page 345, for suggestions.

Farmer John Writes

I was mesmerized by these shortcuts. I've never minded make-up, never thought it was something people weren't supposed to do. But as I navigated this labyrinth of images, aromas, and colors, I kept imagining customers buying engorged, glossy peppers in a produce department. The organic section in this imaginary store did not have a customer.

—FROM JOHN'S ESSAY "BLOOMINGDALE'S AND PRODUCE," PAGE 237

Marinated Roasted Peppers

About the only place you would not want to put these fantastic little flavor bombs is on ice cream. They truly add excellence to just about anything, and depending on how you cut them, you have a lot of opportunity: dice them small for a garnish in soups, or slice them thin and make attractive garnishes on meats, croquettes, and salads, or leave them whole for a killer sandwich all on their own or with cheese and sliced meat. And of course, you can vary the marinade ingredients to suit any accompanying dish; you can leave out the honey, use peanut oil, or mix in some soy sauce. Whatever you do, it will be fantastic. *Angelic Organics Kitchen* (adapted from *The Harrowsmith Salad Garden*).

SERVES 6 TO 8

6	bell peppers (red, orange, yellow, or green)
1/3 cup	extra virgin olive oil
1 tablespoon	sherry or red wine vinegar
2 teaspoons	minced scallions
2 teaspoons	minced fresh parsley
2 teaspoons	minced fresh marjoram or oregano
2 teaspoons	honey (optional)
1 clove	garlic, crushed
1 teaspoon	prepared Dijon mustard
1/2 teaspoon	salt

1. Roast the peppers (see Roasted Bell Peppers, below) and let cool. Peel and seed the peppers. Cut them into thin strips and place them in a bowl or container.

2. Combine the remaining ingredients in a large jar. With the lid tightly screwed on, shake the jar vigorously until the oil and vinegar have combined and thickened.

3. Pour the marinade over the peppers and let stand at room temperature for 2 hours or more, turning the peppers occasionally.

Roasted Bell Peppers

Roasted bell peppers have a mysterious and irresistible smoky flavor and are very versatile. They are great on sandwiches of all kinds, perfect on pizzas, and wonderful chopped up and mixed in mayonnaise or hummus. They're a delicious addition to your favorite pasta dishes, and they'll make any omelette supreme. After roasting and removal of the skins, the peppers (especially red peppers) are noticeably sweeter and their texture is tender. You might like to always have some ready in a jar in your refrigerator; they will keep for weeks if totally covered in oil (save the oil when the peppers are gone—it makes a great vinaigrette!). If not covered in oil, roasted peppers will keep for about a week. *Shareholder.*

4	bell peppers (red, orange, yellow, or green)
	olive oil

1. Turn your gas burner on high (an electric stove will work too, but a gas flame produces better results) and place the peppers directly on the flame. Use any number of available burners to accommodate the peppers, or if the peppers are small you can place two on one burner.

2. Using tongs, turn the peppers as their skins blacken; you want to end up with a pepper that is completely black (the amount of time for this depends on the size of the pepper, how hot the flame is, and how often you turn the peppers). Once they're blackened, place the peppers in a paper bag and seal the bag tightly. Let them sit for about 10 minutes.

3. Remove the peppers from the bag, cut them in half, remove the stem and seeds, and flatten each half on your cutting board. Use a knife or your fingers to scrape away the skin. The peppers are now ready for use.

4. To store your roasted peppers, place them in a container, cover with olive oil, and seal tightly. Store peppers in the refrigerator for 6 to 7 days.

Bell Peppers Lemonly Dressed and Cumin-esque

This versatile recipe will add just the right amount of color to any dish in need of some visual pizzazz. What's more, the lemony cumin in the peppers will pizzazzify the flavors on your plate. You can use these as a sprightly bed for grilled fish or meats or just as a color and flavor enhancement to rice pilafs or pasta salads. They're great in sandwiches, on a bed of greens, or all by themselves. *Angelic Organics Kitchen* (adapted from *Recipes from a Kitchen Garden*).

SERVES 4

1/2 cup plus 1 tablespoon	extra virgin olive oil, divided
2	red or purple bell peppers, thinly sliced
2	green or yellow bell peppers, thinly sliced
1/4 cup	freshly squeezed lemon juice (about 1 large lemon)
2 tablespoons	minced parsley
1 teaspoon	ground cumin
1 teaspoon	honey (optional)
1 clove	garlic, minced (about 1/2 teaspoon) (optional)
1/4 cup	finely chopped scallions or red onion
1/2 teaspoon	salt
	freshly ground black pepper

1. Heat 1 tablespoon of the oil in a large skillet over medium-high heat. Add the peppers; sauté, stirring until slightly soft, about 3 minutes. Let cool.

2. Combine the remaining oil, lemon juice, parsley, cumin, honey, and garlic in a large jar. With the lid tightly screwed on, shake the jar vigorously until the oil and vinegar have combined and thickened.

3. Toss the peppers and scallions or red onion with the vinaigrette in a large bowl; add the salt and season with pepper to taste. Cover; refrigerate for 1 hour.

Roasted Red Pepper Soup

Here is a rustic pepper soup recipe that warms the heart and whets the appetite. It's an ideal start to a pizza or pasta dinner and great on its own as a lunch with garlic bread. Served hot or cold, this soup is packed with a savory-sweet roasted pepper flavor that might have you skipping the main course and opting for a second bowl of soup instead. It's preferable to use homemade roasted red bell peppers in this soup; to make your own, see the recipe for Roasted Bell Peppers on page 217. *Shareholder.*

SERVES 4 TO 6

3 tablespoons	butter
1 medium	onion, chopped (about 1/2 cup)
1 small	potato, quartered
2 to 3 cloves	garlic, minced (1 to 1 1/2 teaspoons)
1	bay leaf
1 tablespoon	fresh oregano or thyme, or 1/2 tablespoon dried, plus more for garnish
1 tablespoon	tomato paste
4 large	red bell peppers, roasted, skinned, chopped
2 teaspoons	paprika
1 teaspoon	salt
4 cups	vegetable or chicken stock or water
1 tablespoon	balsamic vinegar or more to taste
	freshly ground black pepper
	salt
	freshly grated Parmesan cheese
	croutons (see Garlic Croutons, page 187) (optional)

1. Melt the butter in a soup pot over medium-high heat. Add the onion, potato, garlic, bay leaf, and herbs; sauté until potato and onion begin to brown, 8 to 10 minutes. Add the tomato paste and cook for 1 minute. Add the roasted peppers, paprika, and 1 teaspoon salt; cook for 30 seconds.

2. Pour in stock or water and scrape up any of the flavorful caramelized pieces stuck to the bottom of the pot. Bring the soup to a boil, then lower heat to a gentle simmer; cook, partially covered, for 30 minutes.

3. Purée soup in a blender or food processor or run it through a food mill. Return it to the pot and heat until warmed through. Add the balsamic vinegar and a few grindings of fresh black pepper. Taste; add salt if desired.

4. Garnish each serving with some Parmesan, a little fresh herb, and croutons if desired.

AN INTERN'S DREAM

Lemus and I were going to harvest peppers. They were under the water. We had to pay an old woman a dollar before diving in. We swam into an underwater tunnel where the peppers were.

Pepper and Cheese Casserole
with Bulgur and Mushrooms

This comfort-food casserole is just what you need on a cool, rainy night. You can increase the comfort by using 1 cup of cooked sausage in place of 1 cup of the bell peppers. Makes for great leftovers, too. *Angelic Organics Kitchen* (adapted from *The Moosewood Cookbook*).

SERVES 6 TO 8

	butter for greasing the baking dish
1¹/₂ cups	uncooked bulgur
1¹/₂ cups	boiling water
2 tablespoons	butter
1¹/₂ cups	chopped onion (about 3 small onions)
4 cups	minced green peppers (about 4 peppers)
1¹/₂ cups	sliced mushrooms, any kind
1¹/₂ tablespoons	tamari
1¹/₂ tablespoons	dry sherry
1 teaspoon	crushed dried marjoram or
3 teaspoons	minced fresh marjoram
¹/₂ teaspoon	salt
	freshly ground black pepper
1¹/₂ cups	cottage cheese
³/₄ cup	crumbled feta cheese
4	eggs, beaten, lightly salted
	paprika

1. Preheat the oven to 350° F. Coat a 2-quart casserole dish with butter.

2. Put the bulgur into a sauté pan and pour the boiling water over it. Cover and let stand for at least 15 minutes.

3. Melt the butter in a medium skillet. Add the onions; sauté until translucent, about 5 minutes. Add the peppers and mushrooms; continue to cook until peppers are just becoming tender and the mushrooms have released their water, 5 to 7 minutes. Remove from heat and stir in the tamari, sherry, marjoram, salt, and pepper to taste; mix well.

4. In a small bowl, combine the cottage cheese and feta cheese.

5. Spread the bulgur in the prepared baking dish. Cover it with the vegetables and then the mixed cheeses. Pour the beaten eggs over everything; let the eggs seep through the ingredients by tapping the casserole dish on the counter a few times. Sprinkle with paprika. Bake, uncovered, for 45 minutes. Let stand for 10 minutes before serving.

Our Cook

The warmer climates of the world have given us many delicacies: peppers, tomatoes, eggplant, melons. Up here in the Midwest, we love those foods all the more because they are with us so briefly. Last summer I was so enraptured by peppers and afraid of their eminent demise that I put up several jars of relish—a mixture of red, yellow, orange, and green peppers. The jars were beautiful but did not capture the real thing. This year I tell myself that I will cook every day during this Mediterranean vegetable spell and will stuff myself with enough sunny flavors to last through the winter.

Mushroom-and-Spinach-Stuffed Peppers
with Parmesan

This vegetarian take on the meat-and-rice-stuffed classic is every bit as delicious and comforting. It's loaded with goodness and lends itself to substitutions and additions, as any extra stuffing just gets spread around the peppers in the final cooking. Blanching the peppers produces better results than steaming and lets you cook your rice in the flavored water. *Angelic Organics Kitchen* (adapted from *Laurel's Kitchen: A Handbook for Vegetarian Cooking and Nutrition*).

SERVES 4

4 quarts	water
4	bell peppers (any color), tops sliced off, seeds removed (reserve and chop the flesh around the stems)
1 tablespoon	salt plus more to taste
1/4 cup	butter, divided
1	large onion, minced (about 1 cup), divided
1 1/2 cups	uncooked long-grain white rice
1/2 pound	mushrooms, chopped
1 cup	finely diced celery (about 2 ribs)
1/4 cup	finely diced carrots (about 1 small carrot)
1/4 cup	fresh or frozen corn
1	large handful spinach, chopped
1 teaspoon	minced fresh ginger (optional)
2 cloves	garlic, minced (about 1 teaspoon) dash cayenne pepper
1 large	tomato, peeled (see page 92), seeded, diced
1/2 cup	freshly grated Parmesan cheese, divided, plus more to taste freshly ground black pepper

1. Preheat the oven to 350° F.

2. Bring 4 quarts of water to a boil in a large soup pot; add the peppers and 1 tablespoon salt. Cook the peppers until they are almost soft, 3 to 4 minutes. Using tongs or a slotted spoon, remove the peppers from the water and set in a colander to drain (reserve the cooking water in the pot). Transfer the peppers to a rack, cut-sides up, and let cool.

3. Heat 2 tablespoons of the butter in a medium skillet over medium heat. Add half of the onions; sauté until translucent and soft, about 5 minutes. Add the rice and continue cooking, stirring frequently, until the rice begins to turn golden, about 10 minutes. Add 3 cups of the peppers' cooking water and bring to a boil. Reduce the heat to low, cover, and cook until the liquid is completely absorbed, 12 to 15 minutes.

4. Melt the remaining butter in a large skillet over medium heat. Add the chopped pepper tops, the remaining onions, mushrooms, celery, corn, spinach, ginger, garlic, and cayenne; sauté until vegetables are tender, about 10 minutes. Add salt to taste.

5. Combine the rice and sautéed vegetables in a large bowl. Stir in the tomato and half the Parmesan cheese. Season with pepper to taste.

6. Fill each pepper case with the filling and arrange them in a 9-inch-square baking dish. Garnish with the remaining cheese; add more cheese if desired. Spread any extra filling around the peppers. Bake until heated through, about 20 minutes.

The Crew

HARVEST WEEK 15, 1996, NEWSLETTER

Harvested about 6,000 pounds of peppers and 1,000 pounds of tomatoes just prior to the frost. That was a huge day for the crew. Completed the pumpkin harvest—about eight tons worth—with lively assistance from Beloit College student volunteers. Harvested thousands of jack-be-littles and gourds. Removed the remaining irrigation line from the fields. Harvested about 1,000 pounds of carrots. Purchased a used carrot harvester—which also harvests beets, rutabaga, and celeriac. Purchased a soil mixer and conveyor for our greenhouse. Estimated labor saved due to these two devices is about 1,000 hours per season. Also purchased a subsoiler for occasional deep tillage.

Chiles Rellenos

This is special-occasion food, a dinner for someone you want to impress or to ring in a celebration. There's great anticipation when biting into a stuffed pepper delicately coated in a soufflélike batter—there's always that surprise over what's inside. In this recipe you stuff the peppers with cheese, tomato, and scallion, but you can add chorizo or make the traditional picadillo stuffing, too. If you can't find poblano peppers, try using Anaheims, or for a fun little twist—and if you like it really hot—use jalapeños. Traditionally, chiles rellenos are served in a light tomato broth, but when tomatoes are plentiful, we like them best served with a fresh tomato salsa. *Friend of the Farm.*

SERVES 4 TO 6

	oil for frying
6	large poblano chile peppers, stems left on
1/2 pound	Mexican Chihuahua cheese or Monterey Jack cheese, grated (about 2 cups)
2	medium tomatoes, chopped
1/2 cup	thinly sliced scallion (about 3 scallions)
1/2 cup	pine nuts
1 clove	garlic, minced (about 1/2 teaspoon)
4 large	eggs, separated
1/4 teaspoon	salt plus a pinch of salt, divided
1 cup	plus 2 tablespoons all-purpose flour, divided
1/2 teaspoon	baking soda

1. Pour 1 to 1 1/2 inches of oil into a deep, heavy skillet and heat over medium-high heat until it reaches 350° F (if you do not have a deep-fry thermometer, the best way to tell when the oil is ready is to dip the tip of one of the peppers into the oil; if the oil is ready the pepper will sizzle vigorously. Do not allow the oil to smoke, as this will impart an unpleasant flavor to your dish). Add the peppers to the oil and turn continually until they are well blistered. Drain and let cool on a paper towel. Remove the pan of oil from the heat and set aside.

2. When the peppers are cool enough to enough to handle, gently scrape off the skins with a paring knife. Make an incision along the side of the chile roughly 1/2 inch from the stem to 1/2 inch to the tip. With a small spoon or your finger, scrape out the seeds. (Don't worry about getting every one.)

3. Mix the cheese, tomatoes, scallions, pine nuts, and garlic in a large bowl.

4. Stuff the peppers with the cheese mixture (each pepper will hold about 1/2 cup of filling, depending on the size). Insert a toothpick or two to secure the peppers closed. Refrigerate until firm, at least 2 hours.

5. Beat the egg whites and a pinch of salt in a large mixing bowl until they form stiff peaks, 3 to 5 minutes.

6. Beat the egg yolks in a separate bowl until thickened, about 1 minute. Fold half of the beaten egg yolks into the egg whites and combine well; then fold in the remaining egg yolks. Beat in 2 tablespoons of the flour and the baking soda.

7. Line a plate with several layers of paper towel. Heat the oven to 200° F.

8. Heat the oil again in the skillet or in a deep-fryer until about 350° F.

9. Place the remaining 1 cup of flour in a shallow bowl. Holding the peppers by the stems, dip them into the flour, shaking off the excess, then dip them directly into the batter, and immediately place them gently into the hot oil. Fry until they are lightly golden all around, 3 to 4 minutes per side. Drain them on the paper towel to lined plate and keep them warm the oven until all are fried. Serve hot.

A Shareholder

Thank you all at Angelic Organics for the boxes of bright energy that we have received each Saturday for the past umpteen weeks.

Hot Pepper Sauce

Where do you put your hot sauce? Eggs? Pasta? Green beans? Steak? On everything you eat? When you see how easy it is to make your own scorchin' hot sauce, you'll soon become a hot-sauce-over-everything person. And then you'll start improvising, adding maybe a few garlic gloves, or some tomato paste, or rosemary sprigs. Different people have different secrets to a great hot sauce, but here we give you the basics. You can make this in a quart-size mason jar, or you can do it like they do in the South: in a big old rum bottle. Measurements are approximate; you do what you need to fill your container completely. *Friend of the Farm.*

MAKES ABOUT I I/2 CUPS

about 1 pound	jalapeño or Serrano peppers or other hot peppers, or a combination, washed, stems removed
10 whole	black peppercorns
about 1½ cups	apple cider vinegar
½ teaspoon	salt

1. Stuff as many peppers as you can in the bottle or jar, dropping in a few peppercorns between peppers.

2. Bring the vinegar to a boil in a medium pot. Stir in the salt and remove from the heat. Let it cool for about a minute. Pour the vinegar over the peppers until they are fully covered. (You might not use all of the vinegar.)

3. Pound a cork into the jar or bottle (an old clean wine cork works fine) or screw the lid on tightly. Put the peppers in a cool closet for 1 week; then transfer to the refrigerator. The sauce will be ready to use after 1 week, but it will get even better and hotter with time. Once the sauce has reached a heat to your liking you can transfer it to a smaller clean container and store it in the refrigerator; at this point it will keep indefinitely.

Chile Con Queso

This is essentially a fondue. It's great party fare, one of those addictive dishes that everyone hovers over, holding a chip, nudging their way in closer to the pot. You'd better double this recipe to have enough for the crowd. Have an array of sliced dipping vegetables at the ready, too. *Angelic Organics Kitchen* (adapted from *Judy Gorman's Vegetable Cookbook*).

SERVES 4

3 tablespoons	unsalted butter
3	green hot peppers, seeded, thinly sliced
1 clove	garlic, minced (about ½ teaspoon)
1 tablespoon	all-purpose flour
½ teaspoon	salt
1 cup	half-and-half
1 pound	Monterey Jack cheese, grated (about 4 cups)
1	tomato, skinned (see page 92), seeded, finely chopped
1 tablespoon	ancho chili powder or regular chili powder
1 tablespoon	tequila (optional) freshly ground black pepper milk

1. Melt the butter in a large saucepan over medium heat. Add the hot peppers and garlic; cook, stirring, over medium heat for 30 seconds. Add the flour and salt; cook, stirring, until the mixture foams.

2. Remove from the heat and stir in the half-and-half. Return to the heat; cook, stirring, until the mixture thickens slightly. Add the cheese a little at a time, stirring after each addition, until melted. Stir in the tomato, chili powder, tequila, and black pepper to taste.

3. Transfer the mixture to a fondue pot and keep warm over an alcohol burner. You may need to thin with a little milk as the cheese thickens.

Sweet Corn

Eating sweet corn is one of the great joys of summer. Native to the Americas, sweet corn has become an icon of American picnics and barbecues. For many people, corn on the cob is a testament to summer's arrival, to a time of abundance and celebration. At Angelic Organics we aim to pick our sweet corn at its very height of sweetness, before the sugars convert to starch. While new hybrids stay sweet longer than old-fashioned varieties we still recommend that you eat sweet corn within a day or two of harvest. Considering the number of ears most people can eat in one sitting, it probably won't be a problem to use what you have right away.

Storage

Eat it now! But if you must put off eating corn, leave the husks on and refrigerate the ears in a plastic bag for as little time as possible After about four days the corn's sweetness diminishes. Though it's still perfectly edible and tasty, corn at this stage is more suited for use in recipes than for eating right off the cob.

Handling

Corn is a low-maintenance vegetable. No handling is necessary if you eat raw corn on the cob—yes, it's delicious—or plan to cook it in the husks. Otherwise,

Our Cook

These, my friends, are the days of salsa and spaghetti, the days of pesto and sweet corn. The peak of the season is upon us and the eating is so fine. Here at the farm, the payback for long hours of harvesting is found at the kitchen table, part and parcel of my definition of quality country living. I hope that your vegetable boxes bring you the same taste of the country and the same sense of abundance we enjoy here at the farm.

Overheard

A Former Intern: There's a woman here I've been working with who is totally letting loose lately. Today she made her hair all woozy and talked about doing donuts in the corn and cutting off mens' ponytails. It made me so happy to see her like that.

shuck the cob by pulling the husks down the ear and snapping off the stem. Those little yellow brushes sold in grocery stores this time of year really do make removing the silks easier (but silks practically fall off on their own if you cook the corn in its husk). Rinse the shucked cob under cold running water and remember that worm damage is not cause to throw away a whole ear; just cut out the damaged section. To cut the kernels off the cob, stand the cob upright on its base and run a sharp knife from the tip of the ear down to the base.

Culinary Uses

❖ Enjoy the freshest-picked sweet corn raw.
❖ Steam or boil corn on the cob and season with butter and salt.
❖ Bake or grill the whole ears, husks and all, while preparing the rest of your meal.
❖ If fresh corn loses its sweetness after a few days, cut it off the cob and add it to chowders, chutneys, soups, salsas, breads, puddings, or casseroles.

Partners for Sweet Corn*

❖ Basil, chile, cilantro, cumin, dill, garlic, mustard, oregano, parsley, rosemary, sage, thyme;
❖ Butter, cheddar cheese, Colby cheese, cream, feta cheese, Monterey Jack cheese;
❖ Beans, lime, onions, peppers, squash, tomatoes.

*See Louise Frazier's Complementary Herbs & Spices chart, page 345, for suggestions.

A Shareholder

Thanks for nourishing our family with wonderful produce. Our four-year-old began asking about "that cob-corn box" around April or May, and now we're eagerly awaiting Brussels sprouts, a newly discovered family favorite after last year's supply. We cook and eat both sweet corn and Brussels sprouts on Saturday as soon as the box comes in the door. No point in letting the best flavors of summer and autumn waste away in the refrigerator.

Sweet Corn Salsa

There is something almost spiritual about harvesting sweet corn, walking down the dew-covered rows in the early morning hours, the towering stalks blocking your view from all sides. You walk the rows feeling each ear of corn; this one's too small, this one will be ready tomorrow, this one is perfect. And with a swift downward pull you release the stalk. Every harvester has the joy of taking a quick break to shuck a particularly perfect ear and indulge in that divine, dreamy sweetness of just-picked corn. Fortunately, that sweetness can lend itself to this salsa. Here we combine indigenous foods of the Americas into a most flavorful salsa. The combination of sweet, hot, and sour makes a wonderful pairing with grilled foods or, really, with just about anything. If you have a grill going, you can add a nice flavor to the salsa if, instead of sautéing, you rub the ears of corn lightly with oil and grill them over a low fire; roll the ears around with a pair of tongs so they cook evenly. A little charring is okay. Homemade salsa is best if used up the day it is made—and leftovers probably won't be an issue! *Friend of the Farm.*

MAKES ABOUT 2 1/2 CUPS

3 ears	sweet corn
1 tablespoon	extra virgin olive oil
3 medium	tomatoes, diced
1/2	red onion, finely chopped, rinsed
1/2 cup	loosely packed chopped cilantro leaves
	freshly squeezed juice of 2 limes (about 1/4 cup)
1	jalapeño pepper, seeded and chopped
1 small clove	garlic, minced (about 1/2 teaspoon) (optional)
1/4 teaspoon	salt

1. Cut the corn kernels off the cobs. Heat the oil in a large skillet over medium heat; add the corn kernels and sauté for 3 minutes.

2. Combine the corn and all remaining ingredients in a medium bowl and mix well. Serve warm or chilled.

Savory Comforting Corn Pudding

This old-fashioned New England recipe is pure comfort food. You can vary the dish by adding a little chopped fresh herb such as tarragon, sage, or thyme. This is a good recipe to use with any corn that's been in the refrigerator for a few days that you may not have had a chance to get to yet. Consider serving as a side to roasted chicken or lamb chops or burgers. For a sweeter, more dessertlike corn pudding, add 1 1/2 teaspoons sugar in step 2. *Friend of the Farm.*

SERVES 4

	butter for greasing the baking dish
8 ears	sweet corn
1/2 cup	heavy cream
1/2 cup	milk
2 tablespoons	all-purpose flour
3/4 teaspoon	salt
	freshly ground white pepper, to taste
1 tablespoon	butter

1. Preheat the oven to 325° F. Butter a 1-quart baking dish.

2. Cut the corn kernels off the cobs into the baking dish, and scrape in any remaining corn juice from the cobs. Add the cream, milk, flour, salt, and pepper; mix gently but thoroughly. Dot with butter.

3. Bake until golden brown on top and creamy inside, about 1 hour.

The Crew

HARVEST WEEK 3, 1998

Hilled the potatoes and the sweet corn, mechanically eliminating 90 percent of the weeds. This made the crew smile. Applied Biodynamic preparations to the fields. Hoed three fields of winter squash. Seeded fall beets and fall broccoli in the greenhouse. Hand weeded late summer carrots. Celebrated Ari the Cook's birthday with an amazing farm talent show. Harvested and packed more than 600 boxes.

WEATHER

HARVEST WEEK 9, 2002, NEWSLETTER

I was driving on I-90 yesterday, looking at the shriveled corn fields—a tragic sight. In July, our farm received .65 inches of rain; the average rainfall for July is 3.90 inches. And July temperatures were much higher than average. We felt a year might come when, if we didn't have irrigation, your boxes would be half full, week after week. Three years ago, we spent money we didn't have, $40,000, on an irrigation system, because we didn't want to ever face such a performance on this farm. Your full boxes reflect that scary decision.

—FARMER JOHN

Cajun Corn and Kale Salad

This is simple summer cooking. The bright, clean flavors of this dish will put a smile on anyone's face. The farm staff once exclaimed that this was one of the best kale dishes they'd ever had! If you don't have a Cajun seasoning mix, you can make your own by combining 1/4 teaspoon salt and a big pinch of each of the following: cayenne pepper, freshly ground black pepper, dry mustard, crushed fennel seeds, and dried thyme. You can serve this dish over couscous or with chunks of boiled or steamed potato mixed in. If you use frozen corn, simply thaw it and skip step 1 (you'll use about 1 1/2 cups corn kernels). *Angelic Organics Kitchen.*

SERVES 4 TO 6

2 quarts	water
4 ears	sweet corn
1 large bunch	kale, stems removed (about 1 pound)
2 teaspoons	salt plus more to taste
1 large	red bell pepper, diced
1	green bell pepper, diced
1 large	tomato, diced
1 small	sweet onion, minced
1 clove	garlic, minced (about 1/2 teaspoon)
1/4 cup	extra virgin olive oil
2 tablespoons	fresh lemon juice
1 1/2 teaspoons	Cajun Spice Seasoning

1. Bring 2 quarts of water to a boil in a large pot; add the ears of corn. Turn off the heat and let the corn cook in the hot water for 5 minutes. Set the ears aside and reserve the cooking water. When the corn is cool, slice the kernels from the cobs.

2. Return the corn water to a boil and add the kale and 2 teaspoons salt; cook until kale is just tender and still bright green, about 5 minutes. Transfer the kale to a colander to drain and cool. When the kale is cool enough to handle, squeeze out the excess liquid with your hands and then finely chop.

3. Toss the kale with the remaining ingredients in a large bowl until well combined. Season with salt to taste.

Fresh Sweet Corn Bread

The succulent texture of fresh corn kernels, the smooth richness of cheese, and the aroma of rosemary all conspire to make this corn bread truly irresistible. It is a must with any chili and makes a wonderful next-morning breakfast with some good honey and a cup of tea. You can use this corn bread for a Thanksgiving turkey stuffing base, too. *Friend of the Farm.*

SERVES 4 TO 6

	butter and flour for preparing the baking pan
1 cup	cornmeal
1 cup	unbleached all-purpose flour
2 tablespoons	brown sugar
1 teaspoon	sea salt
1 teaspoon	baking soda
1 teaspoon	baking powder
3	eggs, beaten
1 cup	buttermilk
2/3 cup	grated pepperjack cheese
1 cup	fresh corn kernels
1/4 cup	unsalted butter, melted
1 teaspoon	chopped fresh rosemary

1. Preheat the oven to 400° F. Butter and flour a 9-inch-square baking pan.

2. Combine the cornmeal, flour, brown sugar, salt, baking soda, and baking powder in a large bowl.

3. In another bowl, combine the eggs, buttermilk, and cheese. Mix well.

4. Make a well in the center of the dry ingredients and pour in the liquid mixture; beat together lightly. Fold in the corn, butter, and rosemary. Pour the mixture into the baking pan and bake until a toothpick inserted into the center comes out clean, 35 to 40 minutes.

Golden Corncakes

Serve these delightful little cakes as an hors d'oeuvre or a side dish. They're fantastic topped with avocado, salsa, cheese, smoked salmon, or a spicy curry. Or, if you want the cakes as a flavorful accompaniment to other dishes, try adding about 1½ teaspoons of your favorite herbs or spices to the batter. You can cut last night's leftover corn off the cob and use it here, and you can also make this batter several hours ahead of time and refrigerate it for later use. *Friend of the Farm.*

MAKES ABOUT 20 MEDIUM PANCAKES

1½ cups	fresh sweet corn kernels (about 4 ears)
¼ cup	thinly sliced scallions (about 2 small scallions)
1	egg, lightly beaten
¼ cup	coconut milk, soy milk, or milk
½ cup	all-purpose flour
1 teaspoon	salt
½ teaspoon	baking powder
½ teaspoon	freshly ground black pepper
	corn oil

1. Mix the corn and scallions in a large bowl. Add the egg and coconut milk and mix well. Stir in the flour, salt, baking powder, and pepper.

2. Heat a large, heavy skillet over medium heat. Add enough oil to coat the bottom of the pan. Test the oil by dropping a small amount of batter in the pan. If the oil immediately bubbles up around the batter, it has reached the proper temperature. Be careful not to let the oil overheat and smoke.

3. Drop the batter by heaping tablespoonfuls into the hot oil and lightly press each into a pancake shape with a spatula. Cook until the bottoms are golden brown, about 2 minutes. Flip the pancakes and cook until the bottom is brown, 2 to 4 minutes. Transfer the pancakes to paper towels to drain. Add oil between batches as needed. Serve immediately or keep the pancakes warm in the oven.

Farmer John Writes

I thought of hospitalized farmers I'd known over the years, some chained to their beds, screaming to go home and grind feed or pick corn before they were "well."

—FROM JOHN'S BOOK *FARMER JOHN ON GLITTER & GREASE*

HEAT ROCKS

HARVEST WEEK 5, 1995, NEWSLETTER
Corn will grow 6 inches a day in this hot, humid weather. Again, corn will grow 6 inches a day in this weather. Weeds will grow 4 inches a day, and their roots descend, shooting tentacles into the clay.

The Crop

HARVEST WEEK 10, 1999, NEWSLETTER
Sweet corn is a very difficult crop to raise organically. Corn rootworm beetles love to eat the silks, ruining pollination. You can't fool them by rotating your crops. These beetles fly in from miles away and still find the corn. Also, deer want to eat it; so do raccoons. This was our best year yet for sweet corn. The ears filled out well and they were sweet. We thwarted the beetles, the deer, and the raccoons.

Tomatoes

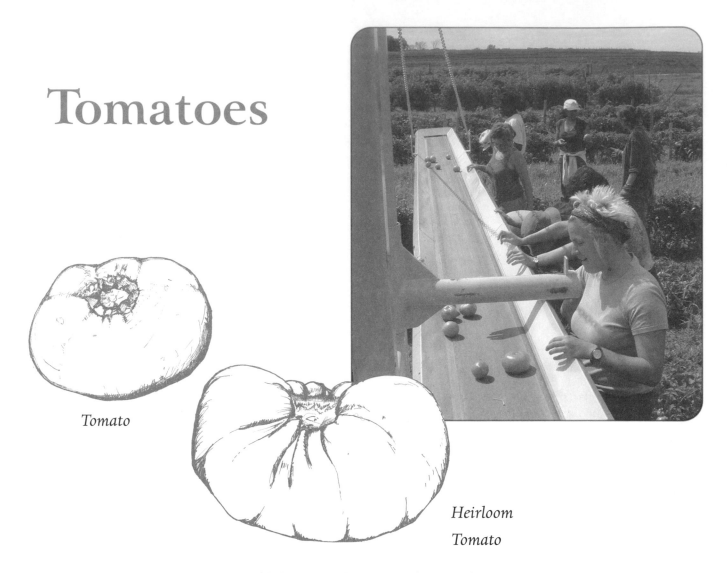

Tomato

Heirloom
Tomato

Tomatoes are the homecoming queen of the vegetable world. They win the vegetable popularity contest by a long shot, despite the fact that so many tomatoes sold in this country are of dubious taste and texture. So, shareholders, count yourselves lucky, because the tomatoes coming your way are the best to be found: they're truly vine-ripened, juicy, sweet, and flavorful. Try eating a few out of hand just to savor every luscious drop; then check out our tomato recipes and get busy.

Since tomatoes are such a key ingredient, they appear in abundance throughout this book. This tomato section contains many lovely recipes, but there are also salsas, salads, soups, stews, sauces, bruschettas, and lots more great recipes elsewhere. Check the index for a complete listing of recipes containing tomatoes.

Near the end of the growing season you may receive a bag or two of green tomatoes that were harvested to save them from frost. You will find here a couple of recipes to make use of these intriguing and tasty green tomatoes. (You may also find it helpful to learn that green tomatoes can be used in place of about one-quarter of the eggplant in any recipe.)

Tomatoes Grown by Angelic Organics

We usually grow many types of tomatoes, both hybrid varieties and heirlooms. The heirlooms are particularly special. They come in a range of beautiful colors and shapes representative of a time when diversity flourished in farms and gardens. (Heirlooms have smaller yields than hybrids, so we don't include as many in our boxes.)

Our heirloom varieties include the following:

Antique roma is a large, red, tapered roma tomato. With dense flesh and few seeds, it is a favorite for thick, rich tomato sauce.

Brandywine is a luscious, slightly spicy tomato with deep-pink skin and red flesh.

Cherokee purple has dusky pink to burgundy skin and full-flavored flesh that ranges from purple to green to brown.

German is a large, heart-shaped, deep red tomato.

Persimmon is a flatter, globe-shaped tomato with a vibrant, creamy orange color similar to the persimmon fruit. For a non-red tomato it has a very rich flavor.

Pineapple is a large tomato that is uniquely yellow with a red sunburst on the bottom. Cut in half, its interior looks like that of a pineapple except with yellow and red marbling. The flesh has a mild, low-acid fruity sweetness. This tomato gets the most raves from shareholders and crew members.

Pruden's purple is a large to very large tomato that is flattened and smooth, with occasional shoulder ribbing. Its skin is dark and vividly pink; the flesh is crimson.

Viva Lindsey's Kentucky Wedding is a pale yellow (bordering on ivory) tomato with a mellow flavor.

Storage

If your tomatoes smell fragrant and yield slightly when squeezed, they are ready to use. If not, store them for a few days at room temperature until they are ripe. Putting dry tomatoes in a brown paper bag may accelerate the ripening process; a sun-free spot on your counter will also work. You can dry tomatoes for long-term storage or can or freeze them in sauces or salsas. Unless you have some very ripe tomatoes near to spoiling, avoid refrigerating them; cold temperatures diminish their flavor and texture.

Handling

If serving tomatoes raw or lightly cooked, give them a quick rinse and slice, chop, or cut them into chunks as desired. If you'll be cooking them for a substantial length of time, consider removing the skins, so they don't float around in your dish. To remove the skin, score a small X in the bottom of each tomato and place them into a pot of boiling water (or, put them in a heatproof bowl or measuring cup, and pour boiling water over the X's). Leave them in the boiling water for a few seconds (or for a minute or so if necessary); the skin will loosen and peel back slightly. Remove the tomatoes from the boiling water and peel them under cool running water.

Some cooks recommend removing tomato seeds because they can distract visually from a dish. To remove seeds, slice your tomato in half horizontally and squeeze it gently over a strainer into a bowl. Reserve the juice for cooking; it's full of vitamin C.

Considering the amount of tomatoes you might be cutting, it's worth investing in the proper tomato knife. An inexpensive serrated knife with a 6- to 8-inch blade is perfect. Guaranteed, it will greatly expedite tomato slicing.

Avoid cooking them in aluminum or iron pots because tomatoes react with those substances, giving the dish a metallic taste. Tomatoes will also assume the "seasoning" of your cast-iron cookware, so use stainless steel.

A Shareholder

I just ate the year's most perfect tomato. It was a huge sucker—one of those habañero-orange heirloom varieties. When I say "huge," I mean at least a pound. And it was so ripe it was starting to burst. One day on my counter and it began to melt. I ate it tonight. I had just turned off the burner on some tofu I was cooking and took up the tomato. I was going to slice it and have it with dinner. I rinsed it, cut away some mushy parts, and then cut my first to-keep slice. I picked it up and tried a part. I paused a second at that first bite. It was . . . awesome. I paused just that brief second and then started eating it right there at the cutting board. Knife, then salt shaker, then back to knife—all the time eating tomato. Every time I took a bite, the world faded. The flavor was amazing, indescribable. Full, rich, the perfect amount of acidity, the perfect amount of that resinous tomato flavor. I finished it quickly—not quickly enough while I still held the huge tomato in my hand—but too quickly now that it is gone. I sit here in tomato afterglow. The summer has been consummated.

Culinary Uses

❖ Enjoy the rich, unique flavors of heirloom tomatoes raw in sandwiches or salads or in almost any mixed vegetable dish.

❖ Embellish summer meals with a platter of fresh sliced tomatoes sprinkled with salt and pepper.

❖ Try broiled, open-faced sandwiches with fresh tomato, basil, and cheese.

❖ Roast, grill, or broil tomatoes.

Partners for Tomatoes*

❖ Basil, chives, cilantro, cinnamon, coriander, cumin, curry, dill, garlic, ginger, lemon balm, lovage, mint, mustard, oregano, paprika, parsley, pepper, rosemary, tarragon, thyme;

❖ Lemon juice, lime juice, olive oil, orange juice, vinegar;

❖ Butter, cheddar cheese, cottage cheese, cream, cream cheese, feta cheese, goat cheese, Mozzarella cheese, Parmesan cheese, yogurt;

❖ Anchovies, broccoli, capers, carrots, coconut milk, corn, cucumber, eggplant, legumes, olives, peppers, squash, shallots.

*See Louise Frazier's Complementary Herbs & Spices chart, page 345, for suggestions

---

Overheard

I hate feeling fat. I feel like I'm taking up space that doesn't belong to me. I guess it's the same reason I sometimes don't share; I don't want to take up space that doesn't seem like mine.

A Shareholder

What is the name of this stupendous yellow tomato with red veins inside that you don't see till you cut it open? It is really beautiful and delicious. I want to keep looking at it, but I want to eat more. Another amazing work of art from Angelic Organics. Note: The heirloom tomato this shareholder raves about is called "Pineapple."

Tomato Basil Salad

with Shaved Parmesan and Balsamic Reduction

It's no secret that the distinct tangy-crunch of Parmesan cheese is an exceptional partner for tomato. But this recipe forgoes the broiler and the pasta pot—forgoes the grater, even—letting the two shine side-by-side in a simple salad presentation. Delicate shavings of Parmesan look beautiful and taste marvelous on top of fresh tomato slices and lacy strands of basil, all glistening with a drizzle of olive oil. You can even try garnishing this with a few toasted pine nuts. It's important to use a high-quality balsamic vinegar to make your reduction, as the cheaper varieties produce an unpleasant, bitter tang. *Friend of the Farm.*

SERVES 4

1 cup	balsamic vinegar
2 teaspoons	honey
1/4 teaspoon	minced garlic
1/4 teaspoon	minced shallot
1 small sprig	fresh rosemary
4 medium	tomatoes, cored, cut crosswise into 1/2-inch slices
8 large	fresh basil leaves, sliced very finely salt
	freshly ground black pepper
	red onion, to taste, sliced as thinly as possible
1–2 ounces	Parmesan cheese, very thinly sliced
1/4 cup	extra virgin olive oil or more to taste

1. Put the balsamic vinegar in a stainless steel or ceramic-coated pot over medium-high heat. Add the honey, garlic, shallot, and rosemary sprig. Bring the ingredients to a boil, then reduce to a simmer. Gently simmer the mixture, uncovered, until it has reduced to about 1/3 cup and is the consistency of syrup, about 20

minutes. Remove the pot from the stove and set it aside to cool. Strain if desired.

2. Arrange the tomato slices on individual plates. Scatter the basil evenly over the tomatoes. Season with salt and pepper to taste. Sprinkle with onion to taste.

3. Drizzle 1½ teaspoons of the balsamic reduction over each serving. (Don't drench the plates; the reduction is concentrated and very flavorful—a little goes a long way.) Top each serving with Parmesan slices and drizzle with about 1 tablespoon oil, or more if you desire. Serve immediately.

OUR COOK ON GREEN TOMATOES

I love green tomatoes. I mean I love, love, love them. One of my cooking missions is to reveal to northerners what they are missing out on by looking only to the showy, bright red expression of tomato-hood. Green tomatoes have an intriguing, unequaled flavor and a firm texture that stands up to stewing and frying. Although fried green tomatoes are heavenly, I most often use green tomatoes as a regular vegetable, adding them to soups, stews, and stir-fries. I especially like them combined with eggplant. Just don't get carried away—one small green tomato per dish is enough to tickle your tongue, while more is mouth-puckering. If puckering is what you're after, make a green tomato pickle or conserve, and let your guests determine their tolerance level.

A Classic Tomato Sauce

Doesn't every grandmother have her own "classic" sauce? Your neighbor probably does, too. It's something cooks take most seriously, and it's often the first thing cooks experiment with. Tomato sauce is one of those things you never seem to make the same way twice: you're missing celery, or you have only sherry instead of red wine, or you don't have any basil. Each time you change it—often by mistake—you can be very pleasantly surprised, and thus a new "classic" is born, and you stick with it. And this is a recipe you might stick to as well! Cooking the tomatoes first concentrates their flavor a little, the wine adds a nice zip, and the vegetables round it all out. Be sure to slice and add the basil at the end to preserve its delicate flavor (heat isn't good for basil). If using canned tomatoes, you'll need about 2 cups, and you can skip the first step. To make fresh tomatoes virtually peel themselves, score a very shallow X on the bottom of each one, put them in a heatproof bowl or measuring cup, and pour boiling water over them. Leave them in the boiling water for a minute or so if necessary; the peel will loosen completely. This recipe makes enough sauce for 1 pound of pasta. *Angelic Organics Kitchen* (adapted from *Greene on Greens*).

MAKES 2 CUPS

2 pounds	large ripe tomatoes, peeled, chopped (about 6 medium tomatoes)
5 tablespoons	unsalted butter
1 medium	onion, minced
1 stalk	celery, chopped
1 medium	carrot, chopped
2 cloves	garlic, minced (about 1 teaspoon)
¼ cup	dry red wine
¾ teaspoon	salt
½ teaspoon	dried thyme
	freshly ground black pepper
2 tablespoons	thinly sliced fresh basil

1. Put the tomatoes in a large saucepan over low heat; cook, partially covered, for 45 minutes, stirring occasionally and breaking up the tomatoes with the back of a wooden spoon. Transfer the tomatoes and their juices to a bowl.

2. Melt the butter in a large skillet over medium heat. Add the onion; cook until soft, about 5 minutes. Add the celery and carrot; cook for 3 minutes. Stir in the garlic and cook for 1 minute more.

3. Add the wine, bring to a simmer, and cook for 2 minutes. Stir in the tomatoes, salt, thyme, and pepper to taste. Continue to cook at a very light simmer, stirring occasionally, until it becomes a thick sauce, about 45 minutes. Remove from heat and stir in the fresh basil.

Roasted Tomato Basil Pesto

This variation on pesto is so delightful it's amazing that it's not more common. The roasted tomato flavor is superbly highlighted by the sweet aromatic basil—but a very ripe regular tomato will work well too. Don't limit this pesto to just pasta; try it on pizzas and roasted potatoes, in an omelette, or over grilled vegetables. You can make an equally delicious variation by using cilantro instead of basil. *Shareholder* (adapted from the *Seed Savers Calendar, 1998*).

SERVES 2

2	pre-roasted tomatoes or 1 large fresh tomato
2–3 cloves	garlic, peeled, halved
3 tablespoons	pine nuts
2 tablespoons	extra virgin olive oil
1 cup	fresh whole basil leaves
¹/₂ cup	freshly grated Parmesan cheese
2 tablespoons	butter, softened
	salt
	freshly ground black pepper

1. Combine the tomatoes, garlic, pine nuts, and oil in a blender and process until just combined. Add a handful of basil and process again briefly; continue adding the basil in small amounts until all is combined.

2. Stir in the Parmesan cheese and butter and season with salt and pepper to taste.

Grilled Tomatoes
Marinated in Basil Vinaigrette

Grilling or broiling will enhance the flavor and concentrate the sweetness of almost any vegetable, and tomatoes are no exception. The natural sugars are caramelized in the process, creating a rich complement to the tomatoes' acidity. Marinating the grilled tomatoes is a beautiful finishing touch. These tomatoes can stand as an elegant side dish all on their own, but they are also terrific on a bed of lettuce, on slices of crispy toasted bread with or without a creamy cheese, or over rice or pesto-tossed pasta. *Angelic Organics Kitchen.*

SERVES 4 TO 6

¹/₄ cup	extra virgin olive oil
2 tablespoons	red wine vinegar or sherry vinegar
1 tablespoon	finely chopped fresh basil
3	bay leaves
2 cloves	garlic, minced (about 1 teaspoon)
¹/₄ teaspoon	salt
	oil for greasing the pan
6	tomatoes, halved horizontally, seeds squeezed out

1. Preheat the broiler or the grill.

2. Combine the olive oil, vinegar, basil, bay leaves, garlic, and salt in a medium bowl; stir until well combined.

3. If you are using the broiler: Lightly oil a baking pan or broiling pan. Place the tomato halves cut-sides down in the pan. If you are using the grill: Lightly oil the grill. Place the tomato halves cut-side down directly on the grill.

4. Broil or grill the tomatoes until they start to char and blister (or shrivel and show good grill marks if on the grill), about 4 minutes. Using tongs or a spatula and spoon, carefully turn the tomatoes over and broil or grill them for 2 minutes more.

5. Remove the cooked tomatoes from the heat and place them cut-sides up in the dish with the oil and vinegar mixture. Spoon some of the mixture over the tomatoes. Set the tomatoes aside to marinate for at least 1 hour, or cover them and keep them in the refrigerator for up to 5 days. Serve at room temperature.

Creamy Tomato Soup

This familiar soup is exquisitely delicate and fresh-tasting when made without the help of a can opener. It enlivens the soul, brightens the spirit, and brings people together. Serve it with some homemade Garlic Croutons (page 187). If it's raining and it's tomato season, the farm kitchen smells like Creamy Tomato Soup—they seem to go hand-in-hand. But don't wait for it to rain to make this soup; it's equally good when the sun is shining. *Angelic Organics Kitchen.*

SERVES 6

3 tablespoons	butter
1 medium	onion, coarsely chopped
2 tablespoons	flour
2 cups	water or vegetable or chicken stock
4 pounds	tomatoes (about 12 medium tomatoes)
2 tablespoons	light brown sugar
6 whole	cloves
1 cup	half-and-half or cream
1/2 teaspoon	salt
	freshly ground black pepper
1/3 cup	sliced basil (optional)

1. Melt the butter in a large stainless steel or enamelware pot over medium-high heat. Add the onion; cook, stirring constantly, until tender, 5 to 7 minutes. Reduce the heat to medium. Sprinkle the flour over the onions and cook, stirring constantly, until the mixture foams. Pour the water or stock into the mixture and bring to a boil.

2. Peel the tomatoes (see page 92) and remove the stems. Cut them in half, squeeze out the seeds, and chop. Set aside 3/4 cup of the chopped tomatoes.

3. Add the remaining tomatoes, brown sugar, and cloves to the pot. Leave uncovered and reduce the heat so that the mixture continues at a gentle simmer. Cook, uncovered, stirring occasionally, for 30 minutes.

4. Remove the pot from the heat and set it aside to cool slightly. Remove and discard the cloves.

5. Transfer the soup to a blender or a food processor and process to a smooth purée.

6. Return the soup to the pot, place over low heat, and add the reserved chopped tomato. Stir in the half-and-half or cream and add the salt and pepper to taste. Heat the soup, stirring constantly, until very warm (but avoid boiling it, as this will curdle the cream). Turn off the heat; stir in the basil if desired.

A Shareholder

The following poem has long been a family favorite that I felt you would appreciate. A note about this poem that gives it special significance is that the book we found it in was first published in 1954. It is curious to think that people were so dissatisfied with "commercially" available food over fifty years ago.

And Another Thing . . .

BY ROBERT PAUL SMITH

The tomato sat on the plate
And it looked like a tomato, like
　a real tomato
Not like a picture in a magazine
It was red, mostly
But also it was yellow, somewhat
And, in places, orange
And, at the stem end, green.
The kitchen knife sat on the
　plate
And the tomato cut like a
　tomato
Resistant, to a degree
Soft, up to a point;
And some of the seeds stayed in
And some fell on the white
　plate.
The tomato tasted like a tomato,
And I said to the kids, who
　know tomatoes
As pure red, perfectly round,
　perfectly tasteless
Absolutely uniform wet globes
　that come in a cardboard
And cellophane package all year
　round
"Kids, time for you to taste a real
　tomato."
They did. And one of them
　looked at me
And said, "Is that what a tomato
　tastes like?"
Yes, my children, that is what a
　tomato tastes like.

The Crop

HEIRLOOM TOMATOES? DETERMINANT TOMATOES?

Heirloom tomatoes are varieties often grown from seeds that have been passed down through generations. Heirloom tomatoes are grown for flavor—their strong point. Our fragile heirloom tomatoes often have distinctive shapes, tastes, and colors. However, they sometimes look just like hybrid tomatoes. Heirloom tomatoes on our farm enjoy such names as Cherokee purple, persimmon, pineapple, brandywine, and Viva Lindsey's Kentucky Wedding.

A Shareholder

When I received one of my boxes this summer and discovered this huge orange round tomato in it, I decided to serve it as a side dish to my guests. These two guests are world travelers and present a cooking challenge. I cut the tomato in thick slices, gently fanned them out on a beautiful green glass plate, topped them with some balsamic and garlic vinegar, and garnished them with chopped chives. When my friends were eating, they heartily helped themselves to my orange tomato, which turned out to be as sweet as watermelon with practically no seeds in it whatsoever. Afterwards, rather sheepishly, they said, "Hey, Mi, this orange stuff is really great, but what is it?"

FORCES IN FOOD

Tomatoes have a significant effect on everything that tends to separate itself from the organism and develop an independent organization within the body. Two things follow from this. On the one hand, it confirms the statement of an American researcher, namely, that under certain circumstances, adding tomatoes to the diet can have a beneficial effect on an unhealthy human liver. Because the liver is the organ that works most independently in the human body, when the liver is diseased, especially in animals, it could also be treated in general with tomatoes. Here we gain insight into the relationship between plants and animals. On the other hand, therefore—let me say this in parenthesis—people diagnosed as having cancer should immediately be forbidden to eat tomatoes, because cancer from its very inception makes a certain part of the human or animal body independent of the rest of the organism.

—RUDOLF STEINER, *AGRICULTURE COURSE*

Fried Green Tomatoes
with Crispy Cornmeal Crust

If you've never tried green tomatoes, please do! They're surprisingly wonderful but very different from ripe tomatoes. As winter weather approaches, Angelic Organics harvests green tomatoes before a killing frost can get to them. You'll also see them at farmers markets, and of course they're in backyard gardens, too. Bacon drippings were traditionally used to fry green tomatoes, but now only the most diehard Southerners—and a few inspired cooks—do it that way. *Angelic Organics Kitchen.*

SERVES 4 TO 6

1/2 cup	milk, or 1 egg beaten with 1/4 cup water
1/2 cup	cornmeal or flour, or a combination
1 1/4 teaspoons	salt plus more to taste
1/4 teaspoon	freshly ground black pepper plus more to taste
	mild-flavored vegetable oil
4 large	firm green tomatoes, cored, cut into 1/4-inch slices

1. Line a plate with paper towels.

2. Put the milk or the egg-water mixture in a shallow bowl; set aside. Put the cornmeal or flour in another small, shallow bowl and stir in the salt and pepper.

3. Fill a large skillet 1/4-inch deep with oil. Heat over high heat until the oil just begins to smoke, about 3 minutes.

4. Dip each tomato slice into the liquid, then into the cornmeal or flour. Carefully place the tomato slices in the oil and cook until golden and soft (but not mushy), 3 to 4 minutes on each side (working in batches as necessary). Adjust the heat as necessary to prevent burning.

5. Transfer the fried tomatoes to the paper towel–lined plate to drain. Season with more salt to taste. Serve immediately.

Provençal Tomato and Cheese Tart

This is wonderful picnic fare. Have a glass of Cotes du Rhone and perhaps a nice bean salad on the side, and you'll be living large. You don't want the cheese to cover the tomatoes completely—they should be peeking through. Don't worry about the anchovies overpowering this dish; they mellow in the cooking and marry nicely with the other ingredients. You can use a pre-made, refrigerated piecrust, or make your own. *Angelic Organics Kitchen* (adapted from *From Asparagus to Zucchini*).

SERVES 8

Crust

	dough for 1 pie crust
1	egg
1 tablespoon	water

Tomato Filling

8	plum tomatoes, stems and seeds removed, cut into 1/4-inch slices
	salt
3 tablespoons	olive oil
1 1/2 cups	sliced onions (about 2 medium onions)
4	garlic cloves, minced (about 2 teaspoons)
6–8	anchovies, mashed to a paste with a little anchovy oil from the jar (optional)
1 1/2 cups	grated Swiss cheese, divided
3 tablespoons	chopped fresh oregano or 1 tablespoon dried oregano
12	kalamata olives, pitted and halved, divided
1/2 teaspoon	freshly ground black pepper

1. Preheat the oven to 425° F.

2. Roll out the pie crust dough to fit into a 9-inch fluted quiche pan with a false (removable) bottom or a 9-inch pie pan. Place the crust in the pan and put it in the freezer for about 10 minutes. Then prick the crust all over with the tines of a fork.

3. Line the crust with a large piece of aluminum foil and fill with pie weights or beans; bake for 12 minutes. Meanwhile, beat the egg with the 1 tablespoon water to make an egg glaze.

4. Remove the foil and beans from the crust, brush on the egg glaze, and return the crust to the oven for 3 more minutes. (The crust will be only partially baked at this point.) Cool on a wire rack.

5. Reduce oven heat to 375° F.

6. Line a baking sheet with several layers of clean dish towels or paper towels. Arrange the tomatoes in a single layer on the towels. Sprinkle the tomatoes generously with salt and set aside to drain for 30 minutes.

7. Heat the oil in a large skillet over medium-high heat. Add the onions; sauté until tender and golden, about 15 minutes. Add the garlic and cook for 2 more minutes.

8. Spread the anchovy paste over the bottom of the cooled pie crust. Sprinkle with half the cheese. Add the onion-garlic mixture in an even layer. Arrange the tomatoes evenly over the onions. Sprinkle with oregano and the remainder of the cheese. Add the olives in an attractive pattern over the cheese and sprinkle with the pepper.

9. Bake until the tart has a nice golden crust, 30 to 35 minutes. Transfer the pan to a wire rack and let cool for 10 minutes before slicing. Serve hot or at room temperature.

A Shareholder

I wanted to tell you that never in my life have I liked tomatoes. In my first box I gave almost all of them away. It wasn't until someone offered me a slice of one of the tomatoes I had given her that I realized how much I love tomatoes. I almost wept! Never have I tasted such wonderful, heavenly tomatoes! Now I rarely give them away; I want them myself. Besides, there usually aren't any left to give to anyone!

LATE SEASON

AN EMPHASIS ON ROOTING
MID-SEPTEMBER to EARLY OCTOBER

> "Life and good health will be destroyed within us if we think of nutrition as merely a matter of calories, proteins, carbohydrates, etc., regardless of their life content. Life is a spiritual-physical phenomenon. Dead food can only make of us the walking dead. Only knowledge of what constitutes true nutrition will help us to appreciate and understand the necessity of life-giving natural foods. "
>
> —J. HERBERT FILL, M.D.,
> ANTHROPOSOPHIST

Overheard

My mom is a Coke fiend and always tried to get me to drink the stuff when I was little. I cried and cried. I tried once to drink a Coke. I had just given blood, and someone handed me a Coke. They popped the top. That dewy, refreshing-seeming fizz sprayed out, then I forced myself to take the first sip, thinking it would have to be refreshing from the sound of the can being opened. I took the first sugary, syrupy, acidic sip. It burned my mouth. I held it there, trying to swallow it. I almost spat it on the floor, but I forced myself to swallow it. Then I thought about how huge those cans are, how much liquid is in one of those cans, how I could never drink one. I always want a bottle of water to be bigger, but I could never drink a can of pop.

Bloomingdale's and Produce

by John Peterson

(FARM NEWS, 1994)

I was in Bloomingdale's New York this weekend. I was in New York for reasons I'm not quite sure of. Perhaps it had to do with a hundred days straight in the fields of Angelic Organics. Maybe I needed a break from dry weather, hot weather, cold weather, workers quitting, weeds flourishing, scorched clutches. Maybe I was just in terror of the stampede of vegetables coming our way—twice the crop we've ever raised, the daunting, exhilarating problem of a dream come true. Perhaps I needed a reminder that the throb of Angelic Organics produce was not the only commotion in the world. Anyway, I found myself in New York City—at the Lexington and 59th subway station. As I ascended the steps, I noticed the entrance to Bloomingdale's. I was wearing a shabby straw hat. Perhaps this marvel of consumerism would have a suitable replacement.

Dozens of groomed women greeted me with spritzers as I made my way through the enormous cosmetics department.

"Would you like to try our Jaipur by Boucheron?" The poised, uniformed clerk, her features impeccably shaded and toned, misted my wrist with a luxurious, fruity haze of eau de toilette Jaipur. "It's made exclusively for Bloomingdale's of New York. You can't get it anywhere else in the world."

Does this mean it's indigenous? I wondered to myself.

I wandered the aisles of glamour. Chanel, Lancaster, Orlane Paris, Sheisido, Studio Gear, Clarins, Clinique. Scrubbed, coifed clerks offered exotic aromas. Teeth gleamed. Eyes glistened. The Lancôme display implored, "Choose your two colors: Personal Eyes." Bien Fait enticed with "Total Well-Being for Your Skin. Total Hydration. Total Radiance."

Something in this is familiar, I mused. There is an impulse here that is similar to an impulse in the produce business.

Alexander de Markoff offered "Eye Shapers—the nonsurgical eye lift" and "Face Shapers—the secret weapon that's easier than a face lift."

> Was the crop really grown on well-mineralized, biologically active soil? Was it really harvested recently? Is that reflective skin an expression of inner glow or just the right wax?

In produce, I thought, quality is usually associated with exterior qualities: sheen, uniformity, and the absence of blotches, insect damage, or worm damage. A certain look is regarded as identical to wholesomeness, freshness, quality. But was the crop really grown on well-mineralized, biologically active soil? Was it really harvested recently? Is that reflective skin an expression of inner glow or just the right wax?

"Lasting, luxury lipstick gives a smooth, moist youthening glow."

This is the image era. The image becomes confused with the real thing. Photographs are marketed as memories. Intense personal moments are like something in the movies. The image becomes the real thing. The wax on the apple becomes the message of health. The blush applied to the woman's face becomes her vitality. That celebrity who celebrated the beauty of pregnancy by offering her naked body to the front cover of a national magazine—the image went back to the studio again and again for manipulation, once for a smaller neck.

"Why are you picking up all those brochures?" the Gale Hayman saleswoman asked me.

"I'm a farmer, and this cosmetics floor is making me think about vegetables." She looked bewildered.

"It's about looks," I offered. "Cosmetics and vegetables. Do any of these companies offer health programs, spas, food seminars? Anything Ayurvedic?"

"Ayurvedic?"

"It's an Indian approach to well-being. It's a little more comprehensive than this." I gestured towards the counters.

"Oh, you mean from the inside out," she chirped. "No, on Fifth Avenue there's a company that does that. I don't think it's Indian, though. This is all from the outside in. Just looks. I grew up in Vermont," she added. "Everyone had gardens. No one worried about what they were eating there, 'cause they just went out in their backyard and grabbed it."

She interrupted her memory to answer the question of a more promising customer than this farmer in the tattered straw hat.

She then continued, "You know what I'm really worried about, though. I don't want pig genes in my potatoes. They're starting to do that, you know, and it's terrifying."

"It won't even be labeled," I mentioned. "The FDA will pull supplements off the shelves of health food stores, but they won't protect you from animal vegetables."

I proceeded through the plume of fragrances. Estee Lauder beckoned with lotions—Youth Dew, Knowing, Beautiful. I was mesmerized by these shortcuts. I've never minded makeup, never thought it was something people weren't supposed to do. But as I navigated this labyrinth of images, aromas, and colors, I kept imagining customers buying engorged, glossy peppers in a produce department. The organic section in this imaginary store did not have a customer.

"What are you doing?" I asked the lanky, redheaded Tuscany clerk.

She quickly covered a drawing.

"Nothing," she answered.

"You're doodling," I challenged.

"That guy over there," she nodded towards a handsome young man in a white jacket at the Aramis booth. He was flanked by Plexiglas display columns of Tuscany fragrances. "He keeps making drawings of me. He puts them in my drawer. I want to get back at him."

She reached into a drawer and handed me a flattering sketch of her done with a slight Art Nouveau flourish.

"He wants a date," I said.

She giggled.

"Show me your drawing," I requested.

She reluctantly revealed a primitive sketch of round eyes, a triangular nose, a line mouth—the beginnings of a stick person. Behind the clerk loomed a giant illuminated-from-behind black and white photograph of a couple-in-love, reveling in the fragrance of Joop.

"Did you hear that?" she asked.

"What?"

"The bird noise. You'll hear it."

A tropical warble floated through the Bloomingdale's din.

"It's that guy who draws me," she offered. "All day he makes those bird noises. He doesn't even open his mouth."

I watched him polish bottles of Devin cologne. His mouth seemed closed.

Another beautiful bird sound floated through the hubbub.

"I have to get back to work," she said.

She flitted behind the booth, tucked herself behind a tall display case, rested her chin on the top of the wooden molding, and stared at the bird caller.

I departed amidst the wild noises of Bloomingdale's. The next day I found the right hat. I'll model it at our next field day. And don't forget to smell my wrist.

> "I'm a farmer, and this cosmetics floor is making me think about vegetables."

Farmer John Writes

I remembered a shareholder's description of snorkeling — the coral in its many fantastic colors and shapes and textures, the appearance of different kinds of fish at different times of the day, the colors changing rapturously with the passage of the sun from morning to night. It must be like that in our soils, I thought — if we could just see it — vibrant, ever changing, a great dancing picture of harmony and life.

—FROM JOHN'S BOOK *FARMER JOHN ON GLITTER & GREASE*

Anthroposophical Nutrition

Food is more than a collection of vitamins and minerals; food is a potential carrier for forces that build up our thinking, feeling, and willing. Anthroposophy maintains that food imbued with these forces (which are especially enhanced by Biodynamic practices) can contribute immensely to the task of bringing healthy social impulses to humanity.

Childhood Nourishment

by Louise Frazier

REPRINTED FROM *BIODYNAMICS* JANUARY/FEBRUARY 1996 AND ANGELIC ORGANICS' HARVEST WEEK 18, 1999 NEWSLETTER WITH PERMISSION AND EDITING OF THE AUTHOR.

When we think of nourishing a child, more is implied than "what will we have for supper tonight" or "let's have healthy snacks." The well-being of the whole individual is progressing every day through each stage of a child's development. Far-reaching effects of daily nutrition will determine to what extent his or her potential capacities—be it of body, soul or spirit—are able to ripen for fulfillment throughout life. Whether they languish or flourish is the awesome responsibility of the child's care-giving adults. Time pressures and timidity must be overcome when it comes to food choices to support the relentless pursuit of the child to develop its own unique self.

Delight in good food can be a most important heritage for one to bestow on a child. In affirmation of this, a woman recently shared an example from her childhood, when her then five-year-old brother inquired hesitantly about a serving of green vegetable on his plate: "Mother, do I like this?" Mother immediately replied with gusto: "Of course dear, you love it!" Brightening, the little boy said "oh" and ate it up, enjoying it for years to come. The whining child expressing many a dislike may in fact be crying for such a loving response to bring zest into its life. We are reminded of Rudolf Steiner's reply to Ehrenfried Pfeiffer's question of why people today seem unable to develop and act according to all they learn and seem to know: "This is a problem of nutrition" (see page 18). Dr. Steiner later noted how undernourished people will become as a result of the poor quality food often served in restaurants.* Imagine what comes to children today through fast-foods, packaged snacks and other "square" food.

If, in each stage of a child's life, attention is given to appropriate nutrition, the fabric of its developing sheaths will become strong and colorful—like Joseph's

coat of many colors. Even when seemingly stripped and sold into the "slavery" of materialism's path later on, deep in their sheaths they will still have the ability to interpret the dream of life and rise up to meet the challenges of their times.

On the other hand, if left undernourished, their coat of sheaths will be drab and thin, leaving them with weakened forces. Lackluster and unable to envision, attitudes of cynicism, surliness, or smart-aleckness become prominent and they can easily be caught in the currents of the times. Patterns are imprinted in childhood sheaths and many an adult rues the poor diet and no regular mealtimes observed by their family in their growing years. It is indeed difficult to try to enjoy vegetables after thirty years of shunning them. One often hears laments of elders regarding attitudes and lack of will evidenced in the younger generations, overlooking the fact that in their own childhood they may have had the advantage of more life-giving foods from garden and farm. Often in an effort to give their children "advantages" they didn't have, affluence and ease ruled choices while shunning food from family farms, which bore the stigma of poverty.

It is time to again ponder what it is that truly nourishes the human being. In the first stage of life, from birth to age seven, a child is busy developing its physical "Earth self." A sense of the goodness of life should come to children from their immediate environment. The sweetness of food helps to assure them of this goodness, beginning with Mother's milk. They are open to all that they see and hear, and without the ability to reason yet, imitation prevails. First foods are introduced—cereal grains, fruits, then vegetables. Millet is alkaline and easily digested, bringing grounding qualities; oats have a natural sweetness, bringing a sense of goodness through warmth while aiding the spiritual qualities of mid-brain; barley as a gruel strengthens stomach, colon and lungs, spawning the qualities of will to activity—essential for crawling, walking, talking, and use of the hands; brown rice regulates the fluid system and is high in the energy-giving life forces. Fruit with all its blossoming qualities helps the child to flower as an individual. A variety of vegetables beginning with the sweet roots carrots and beets, on to squash, peas and green beans, then the leafy greens, strengthen their life forces. There is protein enough in these foods and milk, so the introduction of other protein foods of the family are best left aside until later interest is expressed by the child.

All food is sensed as foreign by the human organism and certainly baby makes that evident, spitting out what is introduced until it becomes accustomed to it and senses satisfaction of hunger. Every time we take in food, our metabolic system must break it down, overcome the foreign qualities, and build anew the human being. If through timidity, the adult care-giver assumes dislike and doesn't offer again the foods that are met with shudder, spitting or head turning, the child may be cheated of the opportunity to strengthen itself and overcome tendencies to idiosyncrasies.

> Every time we take in food, our metabolic system must break it down, overcome the foreign qualities, and build anew the human being.

Dietary allergies, such as wheat or dairy intolerance, are evidenced with much stronger metabolic effects after ingestion and are best diagnosed by a physician. Wheat products are not recommended in the first year as they are not readily broken down by the early metabolic system. Will and imitation serve together in this physical development stage, and even though the small child eats all kinds of good foods, when fed, it will soon begin to pattern itself after older siblings and parents at the family table. If Dad doesn't eat his vegetables or has different food at breakfast, it is his choices, and those of the others the small child sees, that will be imprinted in its sheath. Such contradictions are soon noticeable when the child expresses its desire for the food of others, in preference over its previous favorites.

As the child enters the second stage of life—ages seven to fourteen—the ability to reason begins. For this age group, beauty is important and often comes through the sense of order in life. The rhythms of the seasons and foods thereof, regular meal-times, and even observing a pattern of serving the same foods at the same time are desirable, not boring, to the child. Serving the suggested grains of the day (Sunday, wheat/spelt; Monday, rice; Tuesday, barley; Wednesday, millet; Thursday, rye—more metabolically acceptable in bread or morning breakfast at this age; Friday, oats; Saturday, corn) can bring a nice sense of order. One need not be surprised at the enthusiasm with which children may greet the daily grain: "Today's millet day, isn't it?" At this age, children look for loving authority, and in spite of vocal expressions to the contrary, can feel quite insecure with adult queries of what they would like. Protestation is part of healthy childhood development and not really meant to sway the caring adult. At age nine, a critical awareness of one's separateness enters, and the child is best supported through the knowledge of surrounding adults. The best educational years are from age nine through twelve, and participation in cooking can be an important means of heightening interest in foods and nutrition.

In the late stage of childhood, the teen years, all that has been brought to bear must be questioned as this age group seeks to develop a sense for truth. One can hardly

Overheard

At a restaurant, I like to eat my dessert first. I order pie, then I order my dinner, and then I order pie again. If I order two pieces of pie at the end, everyone notices, but if I order a piece first, by the time I am done with my dinner, everyone forgot I ordered pie already, and no one thinks anything about me ordering my second piece.

Overheard

YOUNG WOMAN: I was having trouble with my roommate in college—communication problems. I kept eyeing a dead tree outside my dorm. After a week I brought the dead tree into our room and set it up between our beds. Every day I hung another dirty sock on a branch.

ACQUAINTANCE: What did she say about that?

YOUNG WOMAN: Nothing. She never said a thing.

ACQUAINTANCE: Did she know it was there?

YOUNG WOMAN: Yeah, she knew. A couple of the branches went right into her closet.

bring much influence to a teen at this point, and if good food habits have not been brought earlier, there will be little to draw upon and scant chance for improvement. While strong authority may be rejected, respectful guidance is of utmost importance. Teens need foods that their metabolic systems can struggle with in order to strengthen them as they meet the outside world.

Rye is a grain that serves them well, as it grows through all the seasons and carries the fullness of the Cosmos with it. Rye in bread, morning cereal, whole grain pizza, or served cooked whole with rice can be of interest to teens if encouraged. Foods in popular form—julienne root vegetables instead of french fries, whole grain patties/veggie burgers—are often met with their enthusiasm. Fresh fruits and fruit desserts can be welcomed too. When presented with the understanding that eating millet helps against acne, as well as fresh vegetable salads of all kinds, teens are known to listen. Regular family meals, especially breakfast and supper, if everyone is dispersed, will go a long way in support of youth and provide them an opportunity to submit to good sense and participation within the privacy of home, away from peer pressure. Continuous snacking has a damaging effect on liver and spleen, so planned tasty good-food snacks for after school and gatherings are valuable contributions for teens. For truth to will out, it must be supported by the values and patterns of caring adults; thus will the young sapling be able to withstand the winds and weather of its times and grow strong in adulthood. Childhood patterns will resonate over and over in the various stages of adulthood, serving or hindering activity.

Around age thirty the wisdom of the ancient saying of "train up a child in the way s/he should go and when s/he is older s/he will not depart from it" begins to show forth. The earlier adult in the ego developing years of twenty-one to twenty-eight may seem to swerve in exploring the world with its myriad choices, but in due time, the strong sheaths of childhood will resonate multifariously to color life.

*from the Preface to *Agriculture* by Rudolf Steiner, Ph.D.
Louise Frazier's biography appears in the Appendix, page 360.

Welcome to the Late Season

An Emphasis on Rooting
Mid-September to Late October
Harvest Weeks 14 to 20

> ❝The root primarily nourishes the head [the nervous system].
>
> The middle of the plant, stem and leaves, primarily nourishes the chest [the rhythmic system—heart and lungs].
>
> Fruit [including fruiting vegetables, such as squash and cucumbers] nourishes the lower body [the metabolic system—digestive organs].❞
>
> **—RUDOLF STEINER, PARAPHRASED FROM HIS LECTURE *THE EVOLUTION OF EARTH AND MAN AND INFLUENCE OF THE STARS***

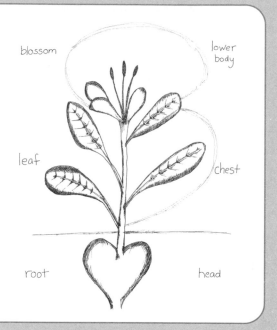

Forces in Food

If I want to work upon my head, I have roots or stems for dinner.
—LECTURE BY RUDOLF STEINER, *THE EVOLUTION OF EARTH AND MAN AND INFLUENCE OF THE STARS*

Overheard

This morning I made coffee and wanted to put sugar in it, so I put flour in the sugar bowl, thinking the flour was sugar, and then put the flour in my coffee. I realized what I had done, so I dumped out the flour from the sugar bowl and the coffee from my cup and put sugar in the sugar bowl and sugar in my coffee, but the sugar I thought I had put in the sugar bowl was really salt, which meant I had salt in my coffee. I then dumped out the coffee, but I did not dump out the salt from the sugar bowl. Next I poured more coffee and put sugar right from the sugar bag into the coffee. How could I go wrong? Then I was going to put milk into my coffee, but I saw the sugar bowl and decided, out of habit, that I needed to put something from the sugar bowl into my coffee. I spooned the salt from the sugar bowl into my coffee. Now I am making a new pot of coffee. *Note from Farmer John:* Perhaps this fellow needs a carrot in his coffee.

Late Season Vegetables

The contents of a vegetable box will vary from week to week and from year to year with changes in the weather, among other factors. Some of the vegetables listed below are also harvested at other times of the year. (See Vegetable & Herb Availability from Angelic Organics, page 334, and the Illustrated Vegetable Identification Guide, page 336.)

(See Vegetable & Herb Availability from Angelic Organics, page 334, and the Illustrated Vegetable Identification Guide, page 336.)

Broccoli

Brussels Sprouts

Cabbage

Cauliflower

Celeriac

Daikon Radishes

Parsnips

Potatoes

Rutabagas

Sunchokes (Jerusalem Artichokes)

Sweet Potatoes

Winter Squash

FARM NEWS

HARVEST WEEK 14, 1998, NEWSLETTER

This kind of farming, with all the handwork (in spite of the many ways we have automated) is quite an anomaly within the general framework of today's well-capitalized, highly mechanized, intensively chemicalized commercial agriculture. Our shareholders support a hands on, in-the-dirt relationship to the land among those who plant and harvest their crops. If people ever want an intimate perspective on it, we tell them to come volunteer for a day.

A Diary of Late Season Weather

Notice the variability from year to year.

Mid-September	Early October	Late October
HARVEST WEEK 14, 1997, NEWSLETTER Five inches of rain in two storms. Warm.	**HARVEST WEEK 17, 1997, NEWSLETTER** Hot. Some days in the low 90s. Windy. Dry.	**HARVEST WEEK 19, 1997, NEWSLETTER** Freezing at night. High 20s. Chilly days. A few snow flurries. Drizzle.
HARVEST WEEK 14, 1998, NEWSLETTER Beautiful. Breezy, cool, and sunny.	**HARVEST WEEK 17, 1998, NEWSLETTER** Sunny and mild turning to cold (low in mid 30s). Cold rain Friday and Saturday.	**HARVEST WEEK 19, 1998, NEWSLETTER** A true frost Tuesday night. Balmy (70s) on Thursday and Friday. A few inches of rain and strong winds on Saturday.
HARVEST WEEK 14, 1999, NEWSLETTER Very dry and cool.	**HARVEST WEEK 17, 1999, NEWSLETTER** Almost five inches of rain fell on Monday and Tuesday. Blustery, sunny weather followed. Frost covered the ground Friday morning.	**HARVEST WEEK 19, 1999, NEWSLETTER** Warm early and late in the week. Heavy frost Wednesday night.

DILIGENCE

FARM NEWS, 1997

It takes a conscientious, cooperative crew to effectively respond to the capricious weather. It takes a fleet of ready machines to go back into the fields on quick notice to remedy a loss. It takes a certain spirit not to cave in, to deal with the weather like it's a tough mentor and not a vindictive god. We're not bigger than the weather at Angelic Organics, but so far this season, we're a match for it.

Late Season Eating

As summer draws to a close, our shareholders find more and more cool-weather crops filling the weekly vegetable boxes. Like a cornucopia, the boxes spill forth an abundance of colorful roots—beets, potatoes, carrots, celeriac, daikon radishes, and rutabagas—along with winter squash, a late-fruiting crop. These vegetables are full of vitality and energy, having gathered the heat, light, and rains of the whole season. After months of maturing under the care of the Angelic Organics crew, they are finally ready to release their treasures. Heavy and hearty, they are the perfect foods to eat as the air turns crisp and cool. (Of course the greens, cauliflower, and broccoli keep coming too, all of which get sweeter and sweeter in the cool fall air.)

Late Season Farming

The days shorten. The mornings carry a chill. There is a sense of urgency to get the remaining crops in before the weather turns really bad. Many of the fields are already harvested and tilled and seeded to cover crops like oats and peas, or vetch. Irrigation lines are dismantled. Members of the field crew wear warm sweaters and long johns and eat hot cereal for breakfast. Interns start to think about their good-byes.

FARM NEWS
MUD

HARVEST WEEK 14, 1998, NEWSLETTER

This is Monday evening of week fourteen. All day, from the break of dawn, the crew has been harvesting in the rain. Mud prevails. One truck got stuck early in the morning. The four-wheel-drive truck that was going to muscle out the stuck truck had a flat tire. The lug nuts on the flat tire were rusted on tight; Primo bent the tire wrench trying to free the lug nuts. Then he broke a socket. This is farming some days—rain, flat tires, rusted bolts, broken wrenches. The crew was in remarkably good spirits at lunch and had actually managed to stay fairly close to the harvest schedule. The choreography required for getting 6,000 to 7,000 pounds of vegetables out of the fields, through the wash lines, and into your boxes twice each week is truly bewildering. And no one here ever doubts that the boxes will be packed and delivered to you on time.

Farmer John Writes

Mom said, "It was 75 degrees that afternoon. . . . The next morning it was 25 below. All those chickens froze, right there on that stump in a clump."

—FROM JOHN'S BOOK *FARMER JOHN ON GLITTER & GREASE*

Broccoli

Broccoli typically doesn't arrive with the same fanfare as sweet corn, tomatoes, or melons. Even so, it is an exotic crop, when you think about it. Unlike a pinch of saffron or sip of chamomile tea, broccoli is a flower that can really fill you up. Yes, it's true: broccoli is a flower—a bunch of flowers, to be exact. All those tiny little buds just haven't opened up yet. If we were to let our broccoli plants keep growing in the fields without harvesting them, they would overdevelop or "bolt." Each plant would erupt into a bouquet of tiny yellow flowers. Now if that's not a glamour crop, what is?

Storage

Wrap broccoli loosely in a plastic bag and keep it in the vegetable bin of your refrigerator. Don't use an airtight bag, because broccoli continues to respire after being harvested and needs some room to breathe. It keeps for over a week but is firmest and tastiest if used within a few days.

Handling

Part of eating organically involves tolerating a few bugs on your produce. (Think: If it's organic enough for the bugs, it's organic enough for me.) Broccoli in particular sometimes comes with innocuous friends tagging along in its depths. Immediately before cooking, soak your broccoli, head down, in cold, salted water (1 teaspoon salt to a 8 cups of water) for 5 minutes. Any critters will float to the top where you can rescue them or allow them to suffer a salty death. (Note: If you soak your broccoli in salt water and then store it, it will become too rubbery and wilted to enjoy. So wait until the last minute to salt and soak it.)

After cutting or breaking off the florets, don't discard the stem. Sliced stems are juicy, crunchy, and perfectly edible wherever the florets are called for. If the skin on the stem is particularly thick, you can remove it with a paring knife or vegetable peeler before adding the stem to your dish.

Culinary Uses

* For salads and vegetable platters, you may first want to blanch broccoli in boiling water for 1 to 2 minutes and then chill it instead of serving it completely raw (raw broccoli can be hard for some people to digest).
* Steam and stir-fry broccoli.
* Use chopped broccoli as a pizza topping or in any combination with tomatoes. Broccoli's tiny flower buds delightfully soak up luscious sauces and juices.

* To preserve its crunch, add broccoli to soups or stews in the last 10 to 15 of total cooking time. (If you overcook broccoli it will become sulfurous, mushy, and limp.)

Partners for Broccoli*

* Basil, caraway, cilantro, curry, dill, fennel leaves and seeds, garlic, ginger, lemon balm, marjoram, mint, mustard, olives, oregano, parsley, red pepper flakes, thyme;
* Lemon juice, olive oil, peanut oil, toasted sesame oil, wine;
* Butter, cheddar cheese, cream, feta cheese, mozzarella cheese, Parmesan cheese, Swiss cheese,
* Almonds, pine nuts;
* Cauliflower, carrots, hot peppers, onions.

*See Louise Frazier's Complementary Herbs & Spices chart, page 345, for suggestions.

Farmer John Writes

Several of them are missing toes and fingers from machinery accidents. The last finger the family lost didn't even stop the haying.

—FROM JOHN'S BOOK *FARMER JOHN ON GLITTER & GREASE*

A Shareholder

Just wanted to let you know that your hard work is very appreciated. We've been CSA shareholders for four years, the last two with Angelic Organics, and we have never seen an early box so full! Our kids remarked, "Now that's a green dinner, Mom!" Those three heads of broccoli in our box will be used for a village-wide potluck on the Fourth of July. Your green thumbs are amazing!

Our Cook

Broccoli is one vegetable I eat whenever I can get my grubby little hands on it. Raw broccoli florets are a great addition to salads or veggie platters. Steamed broccoli is wonderful alone or cooked into many dishes. The stalks can be sautéed or added to soups and casseroles. But don't overcook broccoli.

HARVEST WEEK 15, 2002, NEWSLETTER

Our open house last weekend was perhaps the biggest ever. Somewhere between 250 and 300 people attended. There were many shareholders here who have been members for five years and longer, who have stayed with the farm through tough times and good times. The consensus among these veterans was that, from a box quality and quantity standpoint, this is the best year so far.

There was a tremendous outpouring of appreciation toward Angelic Organics—for the crew, for the vegetables, for the managers. Many shareholders expressed their gratitude for having a farm they feel a part of—a healthy place their children can experience, a place where life flourishes.

Overheard

Last fall when I was at the hot springs I was so sick. I had double pneumonia and chills. I have such good memories of being there, even though I was sick. And it's so good I went, because otherwise I wouldn't even remember that I'd been sick.

Broccoli and Tofu
with Peanut Sauce

Served over brown rice, this dazzling, nutty dish makes for a wonderfully tasteful, healthful, and complete meal. To drain tofu, place it on a towel, place a baking sheet on top of it, and weight the baking sheet down with a heavy pot or pan. *Angelic Organics Kitchen* (adapted from *From Asparagus to Zucchini*).

SERVES 4

1/4 cup	unsalted cashews
3 tablespoons	peanut oil, divided
1 large	onion, chopped (about 1 cup)
1	red or yellow bell pepper, chopped
1–2	cloves garlic, minced (1/2–1 teaspoon)
1/2 teaspoon	dried red pepper flakes
1 pound	herbed firm tofu, well drained, cubed
3 tablespoons	tamari or soy sauce, divided, plus more to taste
1/2 cup	peanut butter (preferably chunky)
1/2 cup	vegetable or chicken stock or water
2 teaspoons	rice wine vinegar
1 teaspoon	toasted sesame oil
4 cups	chopped broccoli, including peeled stalks

1. Toast the cashews in a dry, heavy skillet (preferably cast iron) over high heat until they start to brown in spots and become fragrant. (Be careful not to overtoast them, as they burn very quickly once toasted.) Let cool and then roughly chop.

2. Heat 2 tablespoons of the peanut oil in a large skillet over medium-high heat. Add the onion, bell pepper, garlic to taste, and pepper flakes; sauté until soft, about 5 minutes. Transfer the mixture to a bowl.

3. In the same pan, heat the remaining 1 tablespoon peanut oil over medium-high heat. Add the tofu and 1 tablespoon of the tamari; sauté until the tofu starts to brown in spots, 8 to 10 minutes. Transfer the tofu to the bowl with the onion and bell pepper mixture.

4. In the same pan, mix the peanut butter, stock, rice vinegar, and remaining 2 tablespoons tamari. Heat over medium heat, stirring, until the mixture reaches a gravy-like texture and comes to a boil. Immediately turn off the heat and stir in the tofu mixture and sesame oil. Season to taste with more tamari.

5. Place the broccoli in a steamer basket set over 1 1/2 inches boiling water and cover. Steam for 5 minutes. Transfer the broccoli to the pan with the peanut butter mixture and mix well. If necessary, heat through before serving. Garnish with toasted cashews.

Broccoli and Potato Frittata

This is a good recipe to make the next morning if you have any broccoli left over from dinner. The amount of broccoli can vary, so if you have only 1 cup, it will still be delicious—and even if your broccoli has been seasoned in a certain way, as in Broccoli with Asian-Style Dressing (below), throw it in; it will add a unique character to the frittata. Frittatas make a wonderful room-temperature snack or lunch, so wrap any leftovers and leave them on your counter—they'll be gone by dinner. *Angelic Organics Kitchen* (adapted from *Greene on Greens*).

SERVES 4 TO 6

6 tablespoons	unsalted butter, divided
2 tablespoons	olive oil
3/4 cup	1/4-inch diced potato, any kind
1/2 cup	chopped onion or leek
1/2 teaspoon	red pepper flakes
1 clove	garlic, minced (about 1/2 teaspoon)
2 cups	chopped broccoli florets
2 1/2 teaspoons	salt, divided
6	large eggs
1/2 cup	freshly grated Parmesan cheese, divided
1/2 teaspoon	freshly ground black pepper

1. Fill a large pot with water and bring to a boil.

2. Combine 1/4 cup (4 tablespoons) of the butter and the olive oil over medium heat in a heavy, 10-inch, non-stick skillet with an ovenproof handle. Heat over medium heat until the butter is melted. Add the potatoes, onion, and red pepper flakes; sauté until the potatoes are soft and brown and the onions are golden, 12 to 15 minutes. Add the garlic; cook, stirring, for 2 minutes. Transfer to a plate to cool.

3. Add the broccoli and 2 teaspoons of the salt to the pot of boiling water. Cook until the broccoli is barely tender, 3 to 5 minutes. Drain and let cool.

4. Beat the eggs in a large bowl. Add the cooled potato mixture, broccoli, 6 tablespoons of the Parmesan cheese, the remaining 1/2 teaspoon salt, and pepper. Stir to combine.

5. Preheat the broiler.

6. Melt the remaining 2 tablespoons of butter in the same skillet over medium heat. Pour in the egg mixture and immediately reduce the heat to low. Cook, without stirring, until the edges of the eggs are well set, about 10 minutes. The top will still look eggy and undone. Sprinkle on the remaining Parmesan cheese and transfer the frittata to the broiler. Broil until puffy and slightly browned, checking every 30 seconds. The cooking time will depend on how cooked the egg already is and how hot your broiler gets.

7. Let stand a few minutes before serving.

Broccoli with Asian-Style Dressing

Be careful—this can be addictive. You may not want your broccoli any other way after trying this recipe. For variety, try adding matchstick-size strips of steamed carrots or daikon. *Angelic Organics Kitchen*.

SERVES 2 TO 4

1 medium head	broccoli
1/2 cup	rice wine vinegar
3 tablespoons	peanut oil
2 tablespoons	soy sauce
1 teaspoon	grated fresh ginger
1/2 teaspoon	minced garlic
1/2 teaspoon	toasted sesame oil
1/2 teaspoon	hot chili oil (optional)

1. Separate the florets from the stalk; break into smaller florets. Cut the stalk into 1-inch lengths and then into matchstick-size strips.

2. Place the broccoli in a steamer basket set over 1 1/2 inches boiling water and cover. Steam for 5 minutes. Transfer the broccoli to a bowl.

3. Combine the remaining ingredients in a small bowl; stir until well combined. Pour the dressing over the broccoli and mix well.

Flaky Broccoli Pockets

For a really nice touch serve these with a warm hollandaise sauce on top. These broccoli pockets also make a fantastic lunch, so it's a good idea to make a double batch if you're making them for dinner. They'll keep for a week in the refrigerator. If you want to use broccoli stalks in this recipe, simply peel and finely chop them, and cook them with the florets in step 2. *Angelic Organics Kitchen* (adapted from *The New Moosewood Cookbook*).

SERVES 4 TO 6

	oil for greasing the baking sheet
1 tablespoon	butter
1 cup	minced onion (about 1 medium onion)
1 medium	head broccoli florets, finely chopped
1/2 teaspoon	salt plus more to taste
1/2 teaspoon	freshly ground black pepper plus more to taste
2 cloves	garlic, minced (about 1 teaspoon)
2 cups	crumbled feta cheese
1 1/4 cups	fresh bread crumbs
1/3 cup	chopped kalamata olives
2 tablespoons	freshly squeezed lemon juice (about 1 small lemon)
10 sheets	thawed phyllo pastry (about 1/2 pound) oil or melted butter for preparing the phyllo

1. Preheat the oven to 375° F. Lightly coat a baking sheet with olive oil.

2. Melt the butter in a large skillet over medium-high heat. Add the onion; sauté for 5 minutes. Add broccoli, 1/2 teaspoon salt, and 1/2 teaspoon pepper; cook, stirring, for 5 minutes. Add the garlic and cook until the broccoli is just tender, 2 to 3 minutes longer. Remove from heat.

3. Stir in the feta, bread crumbs, olives, and lemon juice. Add salt and pepper to taste.

4. Lay a single sheet of phyllo dough on a clean, dry counter or large cutting board. Lightly brush the top side only with oil or melted butter, then top with another sheet and brush with oil or butter. Continue this process until you have 5 sheets layered on top of one another (do not butter or oil the top layer at this point). Repeat this procedure with the remaining 5 sheets of phyllo to make a second stack.

5. Working with the first stack of 5 phyllo sheets, place half the filling at one short end of the dough, leaving about a 1-inch border of dough. Fold in the sides and gently roll the pastry to make a log. Carefully transfer the pastry to the oiled baking sheet. Brush the top of the log with more oil or melted butter. Repeat this procedure to make a second roll with the remaining phyllo stack and filling and place it on the pan.

6. Bake until pastry is golden and crisp, 25 to 30 minutes. Cut with a serrated knife and serve hot or at room temperature.

The Crop

1995, NEWSLETTER

You know how some wine connoisseurs can take a sip and say, "The grapes must have experienced a dry summer along the Rhine . . . "? While picking broccoli yesterday, I mused that you shareholders have the opportunity to develop a similar weather-reading ability when you gaze at your broccoli. Now that we've picked many of the main heads from our broccoli plants, little side shoots have begun to form. These shoots grow so quickly that each shoot describes the weather in the single week that it developed. Broccoli forms tight beads in cool weather, loose beads in warm weather.

Besides temperature, variety is a factor that affects tightness or looseness of beads. Old-fashioned, open-pollinated varieties of broccoli have looser, more "open" beads than modern hybrid varieties. The loose beads of open-pollinated varieties are even looser in warm weather.

Brussels Sprouts

"Eat your Brussels sprouts. They're good for you." After hearing those words, how many children have poked at loathsome canned sprouts already pushed to the sides of their plates? For half a century, processed Brussels sprouts have plagued children, many of whom are now adults. For you shareholders, eating our sweet, firm, nutty Brussels sprouts can actually be a treat instead of drudgery. These enchanting miniature cabbages are nutritious, delectable little morsels. If Brussels sprouts aren't yet part of your cooking repertoire, give our version a try. You and your family just might start eating them with enthusiasm.

Storage

Brussels sprouts keep longest if they are left attached to the stalk, and Angelic Organics distributes them this way. If you're short on refrigerator space, snap off the sprouts and store them unwashed in a closed plastic bag in the veggie bin. Even when they are left on the stalk, Brussels sprouts should be wrapped in plastic to prevent wilting. Their flavor is sweetest right after harvest, so try to use them within a few days.

Handling

If you haven't done so already, snap Brussels sprouts off the stalk and remove any loose or discolored leaves.

Our Cook

The best thing about Brussels sprouts from a kid's point of view (or at least mine and my brother's when we were young) is that when you eat them you can pretend that you are a giant eating whole heads of cabbage in one bite. You can pretend broccoli spears are trees too, but the green trunk kind of messes up that illusion.

Trim the base of each sprout and cut a shallow X in the stem end to speed cooking. Rinse the sprouts in cool water. It can take a while to prepare Brussels sprouts, so be sure to give yourself some extra time, especially if company is coming.

Culinary Uses

The key to using Brussels sprouts is cooking them enough—but not too much. As with full-size cabbage, overcooking Brussels sprouts evokes an unpleasant, sulfurous smell that makes people run for cover. Ideally, sprouts should be tender enough to yield when pierced with a fork but not so soft that the fork sinks right in.

* Roast Brussels sprouts: first boil the sprouts until just tender, 5 to 10 minutes depending on size. Drain, then coat lightly in olive oil, place in a roasting pan and roast in a 375° F oven until lightly browned, 15 to 20 minutes.
* Steam and boil Brussels sprouts, but maintain an eagle eye and a handy fork.
* Slice Brussels sprouts to about 1/3 inch thick and stir-fry them with onions and ginger.

Partners for Brussels Sprouts*

* Basil, bay leaf, borage, caraway, curry spices, dill, garlic, juniper, mustard, nutmeg, oregano, paprika, parsley, sage, thyme;
* Béchamel sauce, lemon, mustard oil, olive oil, vinegar;
* Blue cheese, butter, cheddar cheese, cream, goat cheese, hard-cooked egg, provolone cheese, ricotta cheese, Swiss cheese;
* Capers, celeriac, celery, onions, shallots, sunchokes, water chestnuts.

*See Louise Frazier's Complementary Herbs & Spices chart, page 345, for suggestions.

Brussels Sprouts Polonaise

Polonaise is simply the French way of saying "in the manner of Poland." This dish has a wonderful play of textures and tastes, all conspiring for a fantastic and simple way to serve the underappreciated Brussels sprout. *Angelic Organics Kitchen* (adapted from *The Victory Garden Cookbook*).

SERVES 4

1 pound	Brussels sprouts (about 4 cups)
6 tablespoons	unsalted butter, divided
	juice of 1/2 lemon (about 1 1/2 tablespoons)
	salt
	freshly ground black pepper
1/4 cup	fresh bread crumbs
1/2 cup	chopped hard-cooked egg (about 1 1/2 eggs)
2 tablespoons	chopped fresh parsley
2 tablespoons	chopped fresh dill

1. Cut an X into the stem end of the sprouts to promote even cooking. Place them in a steamer basket set over 1 1/2 inches boiling water; cover. Steam until tender-crisp, 5 to 10 minutes depending on size. Be sure to check at 5 minutes; overcooked Brussels sprouts have an unpleasant flavor and texture. Drain.

2. Heat 2 tablespoons of the butter in large skillet. Add the Brussels sprouts; stir until well coated. Add the lemon juice and season with salt and pepper to taste; stir well. Transfer to a serving dish.

3. Melt the remaining 1/4 cup butter in a medium skillet over medium-high heat until it is nutty brown. Add the bread crumbs; cook, stirring, until toasted and golden. Immediately remove from heat.

4. Sprinkle the chopped egg, parsley, dill, and browned bread crumbs over the Brussels sprouts.

Brussels Sprouts Slaw
with Dates

Brussels sprouts are essentially little cabbages, so why not treat them like we often treat cabbage, and make a slaw out of them? You will be pleasantly surprised and happy to find a new use for your Brussels sprouts. Here the sweetness and chewy texture of chopped dates combine beautifully with shredded sprouts to produce a unique and most healthful slaw. *Friend of the Farm* (adapted from *The Food Pharmacy Guide to Good Eating*).

SERVES 4

1/2 pound	Brussels sprouts (about 2 cups), shredded
1 cup	grated carrot
1 cup	chopped dried dates
2 tablespoons	olive oil
2 tablespoons	apple juice
1 tablespoon	balsamic vinegar
1 tablespoon	red wine vinegar
	salt
	freshly ground black pepper

Combine the Brussels sprouts, carrot, dates, oil, apple juice, balsamic vinegar, and red wine vinegar in a large bowl and mix well. Season with salt and pepper to taste. Refrigerate for 2 hours before serving.

Roasted Brussels Sprouts
with Maple-Mustard Vinaigrette

There is nothing more delicious than roasted vegetables, especially Brussels sprouts. The maple syrup and balsamic vinegar make a perfect marriage with the slightly crisp sprouts. *Angelic Organics Kitchen*.

SERVES 4

1 pound	Brussels sprouts (about 4 cups)
3 tablespoons	olive oil
3 tablespoons	balsamic vinegar
2 tablespoons	maple syrup
2 tablespoons	red wine vinegar
1 clove	garlic, minced (about 1/2 teaspoon)
1/2 teaspoon	prepared Dijon mustard
1/4 cup	water

1. Preheat the oven to 400° F.

2. Soak the Brussels sprouts in a large bowl of water for 10 minutes; drain. Spread the Brussels sprouts in a large baking dish and drizzle them with the olive oil.

3. In a large bowl combine the balsamic vinegar, maple syrup, red wine vinegar, garlic, and mustard; mix well. Pour the vinaigrette over the sprouts.

4. Add the water to the bottom of the baking dish. Bake until the Brussels sprouts are tender-firm, 30 to 45 minutes.

> ### A Shareholder
>
> My husband Steve thinks he doesn't like Brussels sprouts. When he wants to tease our daughter he tells her that we're having them for dinner. He makes fun of them on a regular basis. I serve them anyway. I love Brussels sprouts, and we eat whatever the box brings us. Last week I steamed the fresh-from-the-box Brussels sprouts. As I was clearing the table, Steve sheepishly asked if there were any Brussels sprouts left in the pot. He finished them off happily. I haven't heard any Brussels sprouts jokes this week.

> ### A Shareholder
>
> I just wanted to tell you how much I enjoyed the boxes this year. I am a first-time member, and I especially liked the heirloom tomatoes and the wonderful garlic. But the most outstanding item is the Brussels sprouts. They are the best I ever tasted. I took some with me to Iowa for Thanksgiving, and my sister had bought some at the grocery store to be sure we had enough. As I was preparing them, I smelled the cut end of mine and then of hers, and they smelled very different. So I said I wanted to cook them separately but the same way, so we could taste-test them. Everybody—nine of us—sampled first one and then the other, and everybody immediately said, "These [the Angelic Organics ones] do taste a lot better." In fact, even though my sister and I did all the cooking together, she kept the leftovers aside for herself!

Brussels Sprouts with Portabella
and Sunflower Seeds

Served over quinoa, this makes a delicious, complete meal. It's great all on its own too. You will whip this up in no time and impress your family and guests with your culinary acumen. *Friend of the Farm.*

SERVES 4 TO 6

1 pound	Brussels sprouts (about 4 cups)
2 tablespoons	butter
1/2 cup	minced onion
1 clove	garlic, minced (about 1/2 teaspoon)
1 large	portabella mushroom, roughly chopped
1/2 cup	unsalted sunflower seeds
1 teaspoon	lemon juice
1 teaspoon	fresh oregano
	salt
	freshly ground black pepper
1/4 cup	freshly grated Parmesan or Asiago cheese or more to taste (optional)

1. Place the Brussels sprouts in a steamer basket set over 1 1/2 inches boiling water and cover. Steam until tender-crisp, 5 to 10 minutes depending on size. Be sure to check at 5 minutes; overcooked Brussels sprouts have an unpleasant flavor and texture. Transfer the Brussels sprouts to a serving platter.

2. Melt the butter in a large skillet over medium heat. Add the onion; sauté until translucent, 5 to 7 minutes. Add the garlic; cook for 1 minute more. Add the mushroom, sunflower seeds, lemon juice, oregano, salt, and pepper to taste; cook, stirring, until the mushroom has reduced in size and released most of its liquid, 8 to 10 minutes.

3. Pour the mushroom mixture over the sprouts. Top with cheese.

Browned Brussels Sprouts
in Parmesan Cru~~st~~

This is a most delightful way to p~~repare~~ sprouts: fried in oil, tucked inside a pe~~rfect~~ "crust," and coated with cheese. Eac~~h~~ This goes great with roasted or grilled ~~meat. Make~~ your own seasoned bread crumbs, m~~ixing bread crumbs~~ with 1 teaspoon dried oregano or thy~~me, 1/4 teaspoon~~ salt, and 1/4 teaspoon freshly groun~~d black pepper.~~ *Angelic Organics Kitchen.*

SERVES 2 TO 4

1/2 pound	Brussels sprouts (
	salt
1/2 cup	olive oil
1 cup	seasoned dry bre~~ad crumbs~~
1/4 cup	freshly grated Parmesan cheese
	freshly ground black pepper

1. Bring 2 cups of water to a boil in a large skillet. Add the Brussels sprouts and a large pinch of salt; cook until bright green and just tender-crisp, 5 to 7 minutes depending on size. Drain; briefly rinse under cold water to stop the cooking.

2. Heat the oil in a large skillet over medium-high heat until hot but not smoking. Add the Brussels sprouts; cook, stirring occasionally, until they begin to brown, 10 to 12 minutes. Add the bread crumbs and slowly roll the sprouts around until they are completely covered. Continue cooking until the bread crumbs are brown, 3 to 4 minutes.

3. Using a slotted spoon, transfer the sprouts to a serving platter and immediately sprinkle with Parmesan. Season with salt and pepper to taste. Serve immediately.

Cabbage

With its sweet, refreshing flavor and crisp texture, cabbage is worthy of much higher status than it is usually accorded. The key to tasty cabbage lies in the preparation. Many a cabbage novice has boiled it too long, turning out unappetizing, slimy piles. If you want to love cabbage, eat it raw or cook it—but don't cook it for long. Today's tender varieties don't need the long cooking that old-fashioned varieties required.

Farm shareholders will likely have lots of cabbage to use for cooking experimentation, because a fall cabbage, having spent late summer soaking up sun and soil, can reach outlandish proportions. One head may occupy a large corner of your family-sized refrigerator, prompting you to ask, "What are we going to do with this brute?" A great solution is to learn a few ways to cook it. Don't piddle around adding a few slivers here and there. Make dishes that are loaded with cabbage to share with friends and family at picnics and potlucks.

Cabbage Grown by Angelic Organics

Savoy cabbage has a fine flavor, tender texture, and thin, green crinkly leaves that can easily be damaged in transport (which is probably why you don't see them in grocery stores very often).

The Crop

HARVEST WEEK 22, 1998, NEWSLETTER

Some crops love frost. Your Brussels sprouts, cabbage, and kale have gone through some hard frosts in the last couple weeks. This should sweeten them up nicely. The sweet quality induced by frost is seldom experienced in grocery store brassicas (cole crops), because they are raised mostly along the West Coast where the temperatures do not get that cold. Even locally, farmers harvest their brassicas before the threat of frost can damage their crops. Stores just don't have personal relationships with farmers that would allow them to grow and harvest optimally for taste.

Red cabbage has thick, crisp leaves. The color will run into other ingredients when cooked.

Green cabbage is the standard for cooking and eating raw. We also grow one or two varieties of winter-storage green cabbage for November and December harvests. Their thicker leaves and smaller heads withstand cold weather in the fields and keep longer once harvested. Cooking brings out the sweetness in these sturdier leaves.

Storage

Cabbage is cleverly self-packaged. Just stick dry, unwashed cabbage in the refrigerator, preferably in the vegetable bin. The outer leaves may eventually get floppy or yellowish, but you can remove and discard them to reveal fresh inner leaves. Cabbage can keep for more than a month. Once it's cut, seal it in a plastic bag and continue to refrigerate; it will keep for several weeks.

Handling

Rinse the cabbage under cold running water just before use. You'll need a big, sharp knife and plenty of elbow room. Peel away a few of the outer leaves, then cut the cabbage in half through the stem end. Lay it flat and quarter it, again through the stem end. Then balance each section upright and slice away the triangular core that is exposed at the base. From there you can chop, sliver, or grate the quarters.

Culinary Uses

* Make raw cabbage into coleslaw or sauerkraut.
* Substitute finely slivered raw cabbage for bean sprouts.
* Briefly steam slivered and rinsed cabbage with the wash water still clinging to its leaves.
* For the best of cabbage, stir-fry or braise it until slightly browned.
* Wrap savory grain, rice, or meat fillings in large, boiled cabbage leaves.

Partners for Cabbage*

* Basil, caraway, celery salt or celery leaves, coriander, cilantro, curry, dill, fennel leaves or seeds, ginger, horseradish, juniper, marjoram, mint, mustard, poppy seeds, sage, savory, thyme;
* Apple cider, Dijon mustard, lemon juice, mayonnaise, mustard oil, olive oil, peanut oil, sesame oil, sour cream, vinegar;
* Butter, cream, cheddar cheese, Telaggio cheese, Teleme cheese, Parmesan cheese, Swiss cheese;
* Chestnuts, pine nuts;
* Apples, carrots, Chinese mushrooms, onions, peppers, potatoes, spinach;
* Buckwheat, pasta, rice.

*See Louise Frazier's Complementary Herbs & Spices chart, page 345, for suggestions.

Cabbage
with Indian Spices

This is wonderful served with any Indian curry dish or with basmati rice. *Friend of the Farm* (adapted from *The Great Curries of India*).

SERVES 4

3 tablespoons	vegetable oil or ghee
2 cups	minced onion (about 4 medium onions)
1½ teaspoons	minced ginger
1	green hot chile pepper, cut in half lengthwise
1 pound	cabbage (about 1 small head), shredded
1 teaspoon	ground coriander
¼ teaspoon	cayenne pepper
	pinch turmeric
3 tablespoons	water
1	large fresh tomato, peeled (see page 92), chopped (about 1½ cups)
½ teaspoon	salt

1. Heat the oil or ghee in a large skillet over medium high heat. Add the onions, ginger, and chile pepper; sauté, stirring often, until the onion is browned, 15 to 20 minutes.

2. Stir in the cabbage. Add the coriander, cayenne, and turmeric and mix well. Add the water, reduce the heat to a simmer, cover, and cook for 10 minutes.

3. Add the tomato and salt; stir to combine. Cover and cook until tender, 5 to 10 minutes. Remove the hot chile pepper before serving.

Asian Cabbage Slaw

You don't have to be cooking an all-Asian meal to make this flavorful slaw; it goes perfectly with typical backyard barbeque fare, too. It works well with additional vegetables—some julienned cucumber is nice—and it makes a wonderful bed for grilled food, such as Thai-style grilled shrimp. *Angelic Organics Kitchen*.

SERVES 2 TO 4

2 cups	shredded cabbage (about ½ small head)
⅓ cup	grated carrot
½ cup	minced red onion
2 tablespoons	minced fresh mint
2 tablespoons	minced fresh cilantro
2 tablespoons	rice vinegar
2 tablespoons	peanut oil
1 tablespoon	rice wine (such as mirin or sake)
2 teaspoons	honey
1 teaspoon	toasted sesame oil plus more to taste
	salt
	freshly ground black pepper

1. Combine the cabbage, carrot, onion, mint, and cilantro in a large bowl. Toss well.

2. Mix the vinegar, peanut oil, rice wine, honey, and sesame oil in a small bowl until well combined. Pour the dressing over the cabbage mixture; toss. Season with salt and pepper to taste.

3. Refrigerate for 1 hour before serving.

IN THE CABBAGE FIELD

Cabbages are quite an amazing feat of nature. Cabbage plants produce normal-looking leaves for quite some time before reaching a threshold, then they suddenly start curling in, layering one leaf on top of the other until they create a tight sphere. These tight spheres are quite fun to work with. They make a satisfying sound when you cut them; they bob in the tank when you wash them; and when loading them up during harvest, they can seem like a large softball or shot-put when you toss them to the cabbage catcher. I accidentally nailed Evan, a one-month visitor, in the head with a cabbage on his first day of work a couple of years ago. What could I say, as he reeled a bit and picked up the pieces of his broken sunglasses, except, "Hi, I'm Meagan. Nice to meet you."

Easy Coleslaw

This quick and easy recipe will be even more convenient if you use a food processor to shred the cabbage. This is a great standby when you're in a pinch for time. Recipe-editor Matt relates that caraway seeds help in digestion of raw cabbage, so they are included in this recipe. Homemade Mayonnaise, page 332, will do wonders for this recipe. *Shareholder* (adapted from *Fast Vegetarian Feasts*).

SERVES 4 TO 6

5 cups	shredded green or red cabbage (about 2 medium heads)
2 large	carrots, grated
3/4 cup	mayonnaise
1/3 cup	apple cider vinegar
2 tablespoons	honey
1 teaspoon	caraway seeds
3/4 teaspoon	salt or more to taste

1. Toss the cabbage and carrots in a large bowl.

2. Mix the mayonnaise, vinegar, honey, and caraway seeds in a small bowl. Pour the dressing over the cabbage; toss to combine. Stir in salt to taste. Chill until ready to serve.

Coleslaw
with Cilantro and Chives

It might be that some people dread coleslaw because so often it's made from months-old cabbage; while cabbage does keep well, the older heads should be cooked. There is almost nothing better to do with a fresh head of cabbage than to make it into a slaw. It's refreshing on a hot summer's day and pairs nicely with all kinds of fresh raw vegetables. Here we simply accent the cabbage with cilantro and chives, but you can add julienned carrots, bell peppers, celery, or whatever crunchy fresh vegetable you like. *Shareholder*.

SERVES 8 TO 10

4 to 6 cups	shredded cabbage (green, red, or a combination) (2 to 3 small heads)
1/4 cup	minced cilantro
1/4 cup	chopped chives
3 tablespoons	extra virgin olive oil
3 tablespoons	white wine vinegar
2 tablespoons	sugar
1 teaspoon	salt

1. Toss the cabbage, cilantro, and chives in a large bowl or container; refrigerate, covered, for at least 1 hour or overnight.

2. When ready to serve, mix the oil, vinegar, sugar, and salt in a small bowl until well combined. Pour the dressing over the chilled cabbage mixture. Mix well just before serving.

The Crop

FARM NEWS, 1996

The cabbage is snowballing! The cabbage is delayed again! There are just too many things to fit into your box this week. The basil was getting so bushy; we had to harvest it, or it would have flowered. The lettuces are in great abundance. Lettuce has a fairly narrow window when it must be harvested—too early and you don't get a salad's worth, too late and it gets bitter. The cilantro won't wait another week. The beets are relentless. We found one as big as a fast-pitch softball last week. If we don't harvest them, they'll split. The chard is looking a bit prehistoric in its gargantuousness. If we don't cut it this week it will flower or explode or cast a giant shadow over the rest of the farm. We love this logistical problem, but we had to do considerable figuring to arrive at the right thing to leave out of your box: cabbage. We'll try again next week. If you don't hear from us, it's because we cut a cabbage and it started rolling faster and faster and finally flattened us.

Holmski Borshcht

We bring this lusciously red, thick, and gratifying soup to you all the way from the small, charming town of Holm, Russia. During her stay in Holm one summer, cookbook staff writer Lesley got this recipe from a local fellow who always wowed even the most unmovable of Russians with his rendition of this traditional soup. He suggests serving this with some ryumochki (shot glasses) of vodka on the side. He also says to make sure the beets go in only after the potatoes are tender—otherwise the apple cider vinegar (a secret ingredient!) keeps potatoes a bit hard. For an even more traditional taste, you can use unrefined sunflower oil that still has its toasty sunflower aroma, sometimes available in health food stores. And try making this with real pieces of chicken and its stock—the flavors will be richer yet. *Friend of the Farm.*

SERVES 6 TO 8

1 medium	beet, peeled, grated (1½ to 2 cups)
2 tablespoons	apple cider vinegar
5 tablespoons	vegetable oil, divided
1 medium	onion, chopped (about 1 cup)
2 large	carrots, chopped (about 1½ cups)
½ medium head	cabbage, cut in slivers (4 cups)
20 whole	peppercorns
2½ teaspoons	salt, divided
1 to 1½ pounds	boiling potatoes, peeled, cut in 1-inch chunks (about 4 cups)
2 medium	tomatoes, chopped (about 1 cup) (optional)
4 large	bay leaves
⅓ cup	chopped fresh dill plus more for garnish
⅓ cup	chopped fresh parsley minced or chopped fresh garlic, to taste, plus some for garnish sour cream

1. Bring a large pot of water to a boil over high heat.

2. Meanwhile, put the beets in a medium skillet over medium-high heat. Add the apple cider vinegar and 2 tablespoons of the oil. Cover and sauté stirring occasionally, until beets redden and are tender, about 10 minutes. Remove from heat and set aside.

4. In a large skillet, heat the remaining 3 tablespoons of oil over medium-high heat. Add the onions and carrots; cook, uncovered, stirring occasionally, until carrots are tender and onions are beginning to brown, 12 to 14 minutes. Remove from heat and set aside.

3. When the water in the pot boils, add the cabbage, reduce heat to medium-high, and add the peppercorns and 2 teaspoons of the salt. Cook until cabbage is just tender, 8 to 10 minutes.

4. Add the potatoes; cook until just tender, 15 to 20 minutes.

5. Add the beet mixture. When the soup returns to a boil, add the carrot-onion mixture, tomatoes (if using them), bay leaves, and the remaining ½ teaspoon salt. Cook until tomato is soft, 7 to 8 more minutes (or if not using fresh tomato, cook until soup is piping hot, 4 to 5 more minutes). Remove from heat

6. Stir in the dill, parsley, and garlic to taste. Let the soup stand for at least 15 to 20 minutes to let the flavors develop.

7. Garnish each serving with a dollop of sour cream, sprinkles of dill, and some chopped raw garlic.

German Sauerkraut
and Lacto-Fermented Sauerkraut

After the ubiquitous coleslaw, the next most famous preparation of cabbage is sauerkraut (although the Germans might take issue with the word *next*). While there certainly are some good canned or bagged krauts on the market, making your own is easy, and the results are by far superior. You've probably been subjected to some pretty horrible kraut in your life; it's often not done right: either it's overcooked to a mushy mass, or worse, it's served straight from some dusty old can . . . hardly appetizing fare. There are many preparations for sauerkraut; here we give you two. One is a typical, hearty German version (the potato adds contrast in taste and texture); the other is the age-old lacto-fermented version.* Lacto-fermented fruits and vegetables have elevated vitamin content and digestibility, helpful enzymes, and immune system boosters. Lactic acid, the main by-product of this process, keeps the food perfectly preserved and also promotes growth of beneficial flora in the intestines. Whey can be used to help start up the lacto-fermentation process; it has lots of lactobacilli and it's great for the digestive tract. If you can get fresh whey (not the powdered kind), use 2 tablespoons of whey with 2 teaspoons of salt. Both versions of sauerkraut are fantastic. We can't imagine bratwurst without one of them. *Friend of the Farm.*

German Sauerkraut

SERVES 4

¹/₄ cup	butter
2 pounds	cabbage (about 2 small heads), finely shredded
1¹/₂ cups	water
1 cup	minced onion (about 1 medium onion)
1 large	tart apple, cored, peeled, roughly chopped (Granny Smith or greening are best)
1 teaspoon	salt
¹/₂ teaspoon	freshly ground black pepper
¹/₂ cup	fruity white wine (a German variety would be perfect)
1 small	russet potato, grated (optional)

1. Melt the butter in a large soup pot. Add the cabbage; cook for 5 minutes, stirring frequently. Add the water, onion, apple, salt, and pepper. Partially cover the pot; cook, stirring occasionally, until cabbage is tender, about 15 minutes.

2. Add the wine and the potato if desired; cook, uncovered, for 5 minutes. Serve warm or at room temperature.

Lacto-Fermented Sauerkraut
(Adapted from *Nourishing Traditions*)

MAKES 2 QUARTS

1 pound	cabbage (about 1 small head), shredded
2 tablespoons	sea salt
1 tablespoon	caraway seeds

1. Put all of the ingredients in a large wood or stainless steel mixing bowl. Using a pounder or meat hammer or a can from the pantry, pound the cabbage in the bowl for a full 10 minutes so that the cabbage starts to release its juices.

2. Transfer the cabbage to 2 clean 1-quart jars, leaving a good inch of head space below the rim of the jar. Screw on the lids. Let stand on the counter for 3 days. By about the second day you'll notice the lacto-fermentation process taking place—you'll see bubbles in the jars and the jars will hiss—this is good.

3. The sauerkraut will be ready and will have a wonderful sour, tangy taste after 3 days. The flavor will only get better with age. After the first 3 days, store the jars in a cool, dark cellar or in your refrigerator. This will keep for at least 6 months.

*For more, see Louise Frazier's article on lactic acid fermentation of vegetables at www.AngelicOrganics.com/vegetableguide, and click on Outtakes.

Farmer's Cabbage and Mushroom Pie

This is a farmer's pie—rustic, a little rude, and downright delicious. Traditionally, the pie was set in the middle of the table and everyone, fork in hand, had at it. But you can serve it in slices to avoid fights over the last bits. Try crumbling a few slices of crispy bacon into the pie for even more flavor. *Angelic Organics Kitchen.*

SERVES 6 TO 8

2	unbaked 9-inch pie crusts
2 tablespoons	olive oil
1/2 cup	chopped onion (about 1 medium onion)
1 1/2 cups	chopped mushrooms
1 teaspoon	fresh thyme or 1/2 teaspoon dried thyme
1/2 teaspoon	lemon juice
2 cups	chopped cabbage (about 1/2 head)
4 ounces	farmer's cheese or cream cheese, softened
	salt
	freshly ground black pepper
3	hard-cooked eggs, sliced

A Shareholder

Last night I cut into your cabbage and it felt springier than a store cabbage. I had planned to steam it, but when I tasted some raw leaf, it was flavorful and juicy. I couldn't bear to subject it to further processing, so I made a peanut sauce and enjoyed it. Thanks!

Our Cook

Leaves around leaves around leaves, together they form a beautiful deep purple or pale green layered globe. Cabbage turns sweet when steamed or gently boiled. I slice it super-thin and use it instead of bean sprouts in stir-fries.

1. Place one of the pie crusts into the bottom of a pie pan, making sure to leave at least 1/2 inch of dough hanging over the edge. Refrigerate both top and bottom crust until you are ready to use.

2. Preheat the oven to 375° F.

3. Heat the oil in a large skillet. Add the onion; sauté until tender, about 5 minutes. Stir in the mushrooms, thyme, and lemon juice. Add the cabbage; cook until tender, 15 to 20 minutes. Stir in the cheese and add salt and pepper to taste.

4. Layer half of the cabbage mixture in the piecrust. Add a layer of sliced eggs. Top with remaining cabbage mixture.

5. Moisten the overhanging edge of pie crust with water. Cover the pie with the top crust, sealing the edges with your fingers. Bake until crust is browned on top, 30 to 40 minutes.

Cauliflower

Cauliflower is the mildest member of the brassica family. Like its cousin broccoli, cauliflower is actually a mass of unopened flower buds that will burst into edible yellow flowers if allowed to mature. Hiding its head demurely within a bonnet of furled leaves, cauliflower stays tender and maintains a white or creamy color. In spots where the leaves uncurl a little early, the sun turns the cauliflower slightly yellow or brown (we usually mitigate this coloration by rubber-banding the tops of the leaves over the head of the cauliflower). Easy to enjoy as a snack or as a meal, cauliflower contrasts artfully with dark greens in salads and in colorful mixed vegetable dishes.

Storage

Wrap dry, unwashed cauliflower loosely in plastic and store it in the refrigerator. It will keep for up to a week but will taste sweetest if used within a few days.

Handling

Trim off the leaves and any brown spots caused by sun exposure. Rinse the cauliflower and cut out the cone-shaped core at the base using a small paring knife. Stop there if you plan to cook it whole. Otherwise, proceed to break it into florets. You can also chop cauliflower rather than break it apart by hand. This method is much quicker, but the results will be more suitable for stew or curry than they will be for a vegetable platter.

Culinary Uses

❖ Serve cauliflower raw on vegetable trays with a thick dip or dressing.
❖ Use cauliflower in soups, curries, or salads.
❖ Enjoy simple steamed cauliflower as an unpretentious and tasty addition to a meal.
❖ Cook the whole head of cauliflower for an interesting table presentation—sort of a vegetable rendition of a turkey. Cut out the core and set the cauliflower, stem-side down, in a pot with an inch or so of boiling water or stock, then cover and steam until barely tender. Jazz up this method by adding herbs and spices to the cooking water. After cooking, drizzle the head with sauce, or butter and lemon juice.

Partners for Cauliflower*

❖ Basil, caraway, cilantro, curry, dill, fennel leaves or seeds, garlic, ginger, lemon balm, nutmeg, paprika, parsley, red pepper flakes, saffron, tarragon, thyme;
❖ Hollandaise sauce, lemon juice, mustard oil, olive oil, red or white wine vinegar, soy sauce or tamari;

- ❖ Butter, blue cheese, cheddar cheese, cream, Gruyère cheese, Parmesan cheese, Swiss cheese;
- ❖ Almonds, pistachio nuts, walnuts;
- ❖ Broccoli, Brussels sprouts, carrots, cooking greens, peppers, potatoes, tomatoes;
- ❖ Black or green olives, capers, sun-dried tomatoes.

*See Louise Frazier's Complementary Herbs & Spices chart, page 344, for suggestions.

Our Cook

Cauliflower is one of my favorite crops to harvest: we wade through a knee-deep field of brassicas in rubber boots, pressing apart fresh green-and-white-ribbed leaves that encircle a bright white convex flower. We take our blue-handled harvesting knives and, wrestling with the leaves, reach to the stem to make a diagonal cut. I love the moment between separating the cauliflower from the plant and tossing it to the cauliflower catcher, who stands near the perfect forms of luminescent white piled in the bed of the orange truck. It's a very good way to spend the time between sunrise and breakfast.

Cauliflower Saffron Dill Risotto

It's a good idea to always have some Arborio rice in the kitchen and some good light soup stock (meat, chicken, or veggie) in the freezer so you can whip up a hearty, delicious risotto in no time. Risotto is commonly served as a first course, but served with a salad it's a great meal on its own. The possibilities are endless: vegetables, meats, seafood, cheese, or a combination of any of these. You have only to master the simple, basic technique of preparing risotto, and you will always be less than an hour away from a fantastic, satisfying meal. Here we use cauliflower, not a common ingredient in risotto, but one that produces outstanding results nonetheless. *Angelic Organics Kitchen.*

SERVES 4 TO 6

5 cups	light vegetable, chicken, or beef stock
1/2 teaspoon	chopped saffron threads
3 tablespoons	butter, divided
2 tablespoons	olive oil
1/2 cup	minced onion
1 pound	cauliflower (about 1/2 head), finely chopped
2 cups	uncooked Arborio rice
	salt
1/3 cup	freshly grated Parmesan cheese
1 tablespoon	chopped fresh dill

1. In a large pot, heat the stock to just below a simmer. Stir in the saffron.

2. Meanwhile, combine 2 tablespoons of the butter and the oil in a heavy, preferably enamel-coated cast-iron pot. Heat over medium-high until butter is melted. Add the onion; cook over medium-high heat until onion is slightly golden, about 10 minutes.

3. Set some water to heat in a tea kettle or saucepan in case you need it in the next steps.

4. Add the cauliflower to the onions in the pot and cook for 5 minutes, stirring occasionally. Stir in the rice and add salt to taste; cook, stirring constantly, until the rice is lightly brown, 3 minutes.

5. Add 1/2 cup of the hot stock; cook, stirring constantly, until all the stock is absorbed by the rice, 4 to 5 minutes.

6. Continue as described above, adding another 1/2 cup of stock after each addition is fully absorbed. This will take between 25 and 30 minutes total. The rice should not be mushy and should have a little bite in the center. If you have run out of stock, and the rice is still not tender enough, continue with hot water.

7. Remove from heat and stir in the remaining butter and the Parmesan cheese and dill.

Cauliflower Pasta
with Tomato, Cheeses, and Herbs

Cauliflower adds nice texture to a pasta dish. Combined with tomatoes, plenty of garlic, and a mix of cheddar and Parmesan cheeses (yes, an unlikely combination), cauliflower makes an ideal sauce. Spaghetti is a good pasta choice here, but penne or fusilli work just as well. *Angelic Organics Kitchen* (adapted from *The Moosewood Cookbook*).

SERVES 4 TO 6

1/4 cup	olive oil, divided
3 cloves	garlic, minced (about 1 1/2 teaspoons)
1 medium	head cauliflower, broken into bite-sized florets
1 teaspoon	salt
3 tablespoons	water
2 cups	tomato purée (see page 333 for Tomato Purée recipe)
2 teaspoons	finely chopped fresh parsley
1 teaspoon	finely chopped fresh thyme or 1/2 teaspoon dried thyme
	freshly ground black pepper
1 pound	uncooked pasta
2 tablespoons	butter
1 1/2 cups	grated cheddar cheese
1/2 cup	freshly grated Parmesan cheese plus more to taste
2 teaspoons	finely sliced basil

1. Heat 2 tablespoons of the oil in a large skillet over low heat. Add the garlic; sauté for 1 minute.

2. Add the cauliflower and sprinkle with 1 scant teaspoon of salt. Turn up the heat to medium-high and sauté for 5 minutes. Add 3 tablespoons of water to the skillet, cover, and cook for 5 minutes more.

3. Stir in the tomato purée, parsley, and thyme; bring to a simmer, and cook for 15 minutes, stirring occasionally. Season with pepper to taste.

4. Cook the pasta according to the package directions. Drain. Transfer the pasta to a large bowl. Pour the cauliflower sauce over the pasta and toss to coat. Stir in the remaining oil and the butter, cheeses, and basil; toss until everything is well combined. Garnish with more Parmesan cheese if you desire. Serve hot.

Cauliflower Pie
with Potatoes, Spinach, and Basil

Here's one for true cauliflower lovers. This hearty pie is another of those ultimate comfort food dishes. Recipe-tester Pamela says this is a very hearty, filling, and warming dish. It's good for your soul and just the thing for a cool fall night. *Angelic Organics Kitchen* (adapted from *From Asparagus to Zucchini*).

SERVES 6 TO 8

	butter for greasing the pan
3–4 medium	boiling potatoes (about 1 pound)
1/4 cup	minced scallions (about 1 large scallion)
1 tablespoon plus 1/4 teaspoon	salt, divided
	freshly ground black pepper
1 large head	cauliflower, chopped
	juice of 1 lemon (about 3 tablespoons)
3 tablespoons	butter
1 cup	chopped onion (about 1 medium onion)
3 cloves	garlic, minced (about 1 1/2 teaspoons)
1	jalapeño pepper, seeded and finely chopped
12 ounces	fresh spinach leaves, rinsed (about 3 cups)
1 tablespoon	finely sliced fresh basil
1	egg, lightly beaten
6 ounces	Gruyère cheese, grated

1. Preheat the oven to 375° F. Lightly butter a 9-inch pie pan.

2. Put the potatoes in a small pot, cover with water, and bring to a boil. Boil until tender, about 10 minutes; drain. Mash the potatoes with a potato masher. Stir in the scallions and add 1/4 teaspoon salt and pepper to taste. Press the potato mixture into the pie pan and bake for 30 minutes.

3. Bring a large pot of water to a boil. Add the cauliflower, the remaining 1 tablespoon of salt, and lemon juice; boil, uncovered, until very tender but not mushy, 5 to 7 minutes. Drain. Transfer the cauliflower to a large bowl. Roughly mash with a potato masher.

4. Heat the butter in the same large pot over medium-high heat. Add the onion, garlic, and jalapeño; sauté for 5 minutes. Add the spinach (with the water still clinging to it from its washing), and cover; cook until wilted, 3 to 5 minutes. Uncover and boil away any excess water (if there's too much, just carefully spoon or drain it out—you want very little liquid left in the pan). Mix in the mashed cauliflower, basil, and more salt and pepper to taste. Cook for 1 more minute.

5. Remove from heat and stir in the egg. Spread this mixture into the potato crust. Sprinkle Gruyère over the cauliflower mixture. Bake until cheese is lightly golden on top, 30 to 35 minutes.

Cauliflower Quiche

Make this for a special Sunday brunch. It's easy to prepare and still very impressive—in looks and taste! *Angelic Organics Kitchen.*

SERVES 4 TO 6

Crust

	dough for 1 piecrust
1	egg
1 tablespoon	water

Cauliflower Filling

1/4 cup	butter, divided
1 small	onion, sliced
2 cups	chopped cauliflower (about 1 small head)
1 teaspoon	salt, divided
3 tablespoons	water
3	eggs
1 1/2 cups	heavy cream
pinch	freshly ground nutmeg
3/4 cup	grated Fontina or Swiss cheese
	salt
	freshly ground black pepper

1. Preheat oven to 425° F.

2. Roll out the piecrust dough to fit into a 9-inch fluted quiche pan with a false (removable) bottom or a 9-inch pie pan. Place the crust in the pan and put it in the freezer for about 10 minutes. Then prick the crust all over with the tines of a fork.

3. Line the crust with a large piece of aluminum foil and fill with pie weights or beans; bake for 12 minutes. Meanwhile, beat the egg with the 1 tablespoon water to make an egg glaze.

4. Remove the foil and beans from the crust, brush on the egg glaze, and return the crust to the oven for 3 more minutes. (The crust will be only partially baked at this point.) Cool on a wire rack.

5. Reduce oven heat to 375° F.

6. Melt 2 tablespoons of the butter in a medium skillet. Add the onion and sauté until translucent, 5 to 7 minutes. Add the cauliflower, 1/2 teaspoon of the salt, and 3 tablespoons water; cover and cook for 10 minutes, shaking the pan occasionally. The cauliflower should be just barely tender, as it will cook more in the oven. Remove from heat and let cool.

7. Whisk the eggs in a medium bowl. Stir in the cream, remaining 1/2 teaspoon salt, and nutmeg.

8. Sprinkle half the cheese on the bottom of the crust. Add the cauliflower mixture in an even layer. Pour the egg/cream mixture over the top, being careful not to add so much that it goes all the way to the top of the crust, as it will rise during baking. Sprinkle with salt and pepper. (If you have some left over, you can pour it in a custard cup and bake it separately.) Sprinkle on the remaining cheese and dot with the remaining butter.

9. Bake until quiche is lightly browned in spots, 25 to 35 minutes.

Curried Cauliflower

For a satisfying, complete meal serve this with saffron basmati rice and dal. You can add green peas or small bits of broccoli for some attractive color on your plate. *Angelic Organics Kitchen* (adapted from *The Ayurvedic Cookbook*).

SERVES 4 TO 5

1 tablespoon	ghee or vegetable oil
1/2 teaspoon	mustard seeds
1 teaspoon	turmeric
1/2 teaspoon	sea salt
1 medium	head cauliflower, cut into bite-sized pieces
1/2 cup	water
2 teaspoons	crushed coriander seeds
1/2 teaspoon	curry powder

1. Heat the ghee or oil in a medium skillet over medium-high heat. Add the mustard seeds. As soon as they start to pop, stir in the turmeric and salt. Add the cauliflower; mix well. Cover and cook for 5 minutes.

2. Stir in the water, coriander, and curry. Adjust the heat to low and cook, covered, for 5 minutes.

FALL FERTILITY

HARVEST WEEK 15, 1998, NEWSLETTER

Late September is usually our last chance to get the fields ready for next year. Primo is spreading compost pretty much every day. If we don't get rained out, we'll soon sow winter rye on about half our fields. This will make an excellent contribution to next year's soil health. Getting the compost on in the fall, and then getting a cover crop established, will stimulate the soil microbial life, add nutrients, and reduce erosion.

In addition, we will apply the Biodynamic Preparation 500 and Pfeiffer Field Spray. The 500 works on an "energetic" level. Pfeiffer Field Spray, which has its origins in Rudolf Steiner's agricultural recommendations, contains many types of microbes that stimulate soil life, encourage earthworm activity, and help to build humus. Many people today view soil from the standpoint of its nutrient composition, but the microbial life in the soil is also a key to its health. There is a most intricate organismic community that inhabits the soil, working synergistically to support plant life.

Celeriac

Imagine walking through a modern grocery store, its produce section brimming with beauty-queen vegetables: colorful, shiny, perfect. Then imagine a celeriac in their midst. It doesn't quite fit, does it? In the days before vegetables' looks outweighed their other qualities, celeriac—also known as celery root—enjoyed much more popularity than it does today. The wizened roots store for months in a root cellar; this was a distinct advantage if you lived in a sod house on the prairie.

Celeriac is a vegetable that cleans up well. Once you peel away its gnarled outer layer, you find a sparkling-white interior with a clean, refreshing taste that has wide appeal. Once prepared, it shows no signs of its humble past. Celeriac served with wild rice, celery, and parsley is as sophisticated an autumn dish as one could ask for.

Storage

Store unwashed celeriac in a plastic bag in the refrigerator, where it will keep for several weeks.

Handling

Soak celeriac briefly in warm water and then scrub it with a stiff brush. Take a thin slice off the top and bottom and peel it with a sharp paring knife or a sturdy vegetable peeler. A few deep crevices will remain; leave them, or slice them out if you prefer. You may need to remove the core if it seems pithy or hollow. Like apples, celeriac will darken if exposed to the air for too long. If you don't plan to cook it immediately, submerge the celeriac in a bowl of water with the juice of one lemon squeezed in.

Culinary Uses

❖ Add raw celeriac in grated beet, carrot, or apple salads. Or serve plain, raw celeriac with a creamy dipping sauce.

❖ Use celeriac as a seasoning or a vegetable: it has the flavor of celery and the texture of a turnip. Substitute celeriac where recipes call for celery.

❖ Combine celeriac with other winter roots in stews and gratins, and warm yourself through the worst of blizzards.

❖ Add cooked celeriac to mashed potatoes: peel and quarter celeriac, then boil until soft, 20 to 30 minutes depending on the size of the chunks.

❖ Introduce french-fry-cut celeriac strips to your friends, as former Angelic Organics field manager Meagan did with the farm crew. Pan-fry or roast them with a little oil and salt.

❖ Try making sandwiches out of the "hairy" root parts, rinsed in a strainer.

Partners for Celeriac*

❖ Allspice, basil, coriander, dill, fennel leaves or seeds, garlic, lovage, marjoram, mustard, nutmeg, oregano, paprika, parsley, sage, tarragon, thyme;

❖ Dijon mustard, olive oil, peanut oil, sesame oil, sunflower oil, walnut oil, wine vinegar;

❖ Butter, cream, Gruyère cheese, Parmesan cheese, Swiss cheese;

❖ Hazelnuts, walnuts;

❖ Apples, lemon;

❖ Beets, carrots, celery, leeks, mushrooms, onions, parsnips, potatoes, rutabagas, turnips, watercress;

❖ Capers, wild rice.

*See Louise Frazier's Complementary Herbs & Spices chart, page 345, for suggestions.

Scalloped Celeriac and Potatoes

Here's a variation on a classic that just might be better than the original. Traditionally, scalloped potatoes are cooked in milk or cream; here, however, we cook them in stock, and the result is a more flavorful and delightfully lighter dish. The celeriac adds a brightness here that assertively sets the dish apart from its classic cousin. *Friend of the Farm.*

SERVES 6

	butter for greasing the baking dish
1 pound	celeriac, peeled, halved, sliced about 1/8 inch thick
1 pound	baking potatoes, peeled, sliced about 1/8 inch thick
	salt
	freshly ground black pepper
1 cup	grated Gruyère or domestic Swiss cheese, divided
1/2 teaspoon	dried thyme
2 cups	chicken, beef, or vegetable stock
2 tablespoons	butter

1. Preheat the oven to 350° F. Grease a 2-quart baking dish with butter.

2. Place the celeriac and potatoes in alternating layers in the baking dish, seasoning every few layers with salt and pepper. At about the halfway point, add 1/3 cup cheese in an even layer; sprinkle with the thyme. Continue with the celeriac and potatoes, until you have used all of your slices (don't go all the way to the top edge; leave a little room to allow the liquid to boil).

3. Pour the stock over the celeriac and potatoes. Dot with butter. Cover with foil and bake for 45 minutes. Remove the foil and bake for 15 minutes more. Sprinkle the remaining 2/3 cup cheese over the top layer, add several grindings of fresh pepper, and bake until the cheese turns golden, about 15 minutes.

4. Let stand for 10 minutes before serving.

A Shareholder

Every week I come home with the box and put all of the vegetables onto the kitchen table to marvel at their beauty. Then I call my husband in to check out their beauty. Then I say to him, very gravely, "I love that farm," and he says back, "I know you do."

Our Cook

One author stated that celeriac, quite homely in appearance, would fit well into a tale told by the Bothers Grimm. Do not be deterred by appearances: good things can come in ugly packaging.

Our Cook

Back in the days of summer, the crew did some tasting of different melon varieties. As I marveled over the lovely array of flavors, the question came to me, "How does one properly describe the fine distinctions of flavor, for example, between kinds of melons or winter squash varieties? How, for that matter, does one describe to a neophyte something entirely new, such as rutabaga?"

Among meat-eaters I have noticed a tendency to compare any new meat to chicken. "Tastes like chicken," is the old refrain. My mom just loves butter, and the other day—when Angie described the luscious leeks as tasting "buttery"—I knew exactly what she was talking about. Or at least I could relate and heartily agree. Last week Farmer John surprised us by pinpointing the unique flavor in a soup I served containing leeks, potatoes, and celeriac. To me, the soup tasted warm, rich, delicious—but I couldn't have said "celeriac-y."

It seems too great a challenge for me to capture flavors with words. I would rather encourage you to see for yourself while I stick to dependable generalities. A few months back, dazzling summer flavors graced our table. Today, warm, mellow fall flavors reign. Tastes like . . . a journey, a cycle nearly completed.

Creamy Celeriac Soup

When celeriac is in season, the farm cook inevitably makes a huge batch of Creamy Celeriac Soup, and the crew wants it, loves it, devours it. Of all the "cream-of" soups, this is, undeservedly, the most underrated and undercelebrated. Including it here is our effort to bring it out of the closet, as it were, to awaken the public to its greatness and to garner it some respect. Try it, and you'll see what we mean. *Angelic Organics Kitchen.*

SERVES 6 TO 8

3 tablespoons	butter
3 large	leeks, quartered, sliced
1 large	celeriac, peeled, roughly chopped (about 3 1/2 cups)
1 large	potato, any kind, peeled, roughly chopped
4 cups	vegetable or chicken stock
1/2 cup	coarsely chopped blanched almonds
1/4 teaspoon	mace or nutmeg
1/2 cup	cream or half-and-half
1 teaspoon	salt
	freshly ground black pepper

1. Melt the butter in a large soup pot over medium-high heat. Add the leeks; cook until soft, 5 to 7 minutes. Add the celeriac, potato, stock, and almonds; bring to a boil. Reduce heat, cover, and simmer 25 minutes.

2. Let the soup cool slightly and then purée it in a food processor or blender. Return the soup to the pot; stir in the cream, salt, and pepper to taste and heat on low until heated through.

Celeriac and Apple Salad
with Tarragon and Roasted Walnuts

It probably isn't often that you think ooooh, celariac, and your mouth waters. But this recipe could change all that. Crisp celeriac is combined with sliced apple and roasted walnuts, producing delightful results in both texture and taste. The key here is to be sure to cut the celeriac to matchstick-size, no bigger; it will hold the sauce better. Also, don't be tempted to skimp on the pepper, as pepper and apples have a certain unexplored appeal that will surprise you. *Angelic Organics Kitchen.*

SERVES 4 TO 6

4 cups	water
	juice of 1 lemon (about 3 tablespoons)
2 tart	apples, peeled, cored, sliced into 1/4-inch strips
1 large	celeriac, peeled, cut into match stick-sized strips
1/2 cup	chopped walnuts
1 1/2 tablespoons	white wine vinegar
2 1/2 tablespoons	mayonnaise
1 tablespoon	heavy cream
2 teaspoons	prepared Dijon mustard
1/2 teaspoon	dried tarragon
1/2 teaspoon	freshly ground black pepper
	salt

1. Combine water and lemon juice in a large bowl. Add the apple slices and celeriac strips and let stand for 15 minutes (this acidified water will keep the celeriac and apple from turning brown).

2. Toast the walnuts in a dry skillet over high heat, stirring frequently, until they begin to darken in spots, 3 to 5 minutes. Let cool.

3. Drain the celeriac and apple mixture; return to the bowl, add the vinegar, and toss.

4. Combine the mayonnaise, cream, mustard, tarragon, pepper, and salt to taste in a small bowl. Pour the dressing over the celeriac and apple mixture; toss to coat. Add the walnuts and toss again. Chill for at least 1 hour before serving (2 or 3 hours is even better).

Celeriac Sauce

Although this rich, velvety sauce has become a part of farm cook Lora's Thanksgiving dinner, it's wonderful on a summer dinner plate as well. It's very versatile; it complements a wide range of vegetables, grains, fish, and poultry. *Angelic Organics Kitchen* (adapted from *Cooking with Grains*).

SERVES 2 TO 3

2 cups	vegetable stock
1 medium	celeriac, diced
	(about 2 cups)
1	leek, quartered and sliced
1/3 cup	cream
1/4 cup	butter
1 teaspoon	lemon juice
	salt
	white pepper

1. Bring the vegetable stock to a rolling boil in a small pot over high heat. Add the celeriac and leek; reduce heat to medium and cook until celeriac is tender, about 15 minutes. Let cool slightly and then purée it in a blender or food processor.

2. Return the celeriac mixture to the pot and bring to barely a simmer. Add the cream, butter, and lemon juice and stir well; continue to heat until soup is steaming and a few bubbles just barely start to break the surface. Season with salt and white pepper to taste; remove from heat. Serve hot.

The Crop

HARVEST WEEK 15, 1996, NEWSLETTER

We are working hard to bring in the crops during this spell of warm, dry weather. We still have a huge amount of vegetables in the fields—broccoli, cauliflower, cabbage, sunchokes, leeks, celeriac, celery, lettuce, beets, kale, chard, carrots, rutabaga. Of these, the crops that we can bring in and store for the cold, rainy weeks ahead are rutabaga, celeriac, sunchokes, carrots, and topped beets. And we already have vast quantities of the storage crops in our coolers and sheds—squash, onions, carrots, potatoes, peppers. (We had to suddenly classify peppers as a storage crop due to the frost. They will hold up well for two to three weeks. Beware the pepper cascade!)

Celeriac Rémoulade

Walk into a French bistro in the fall, and you'll likely fine a celeriac rémoulade on the menu. If you order it with the goose confit, the garçon will nod approvingly. This dish combines earthy celeriac with the classic French ingredients of mayonnaise, Dijon mustard, capers, and cornichons. Take a look at our recipe for Homemade Mayonnaise on page 332—it will do wonders for this dish! *Friend of the Farm*.

SERVES 4 TO 6

1 large	celeriac, peeled and cut into matchstick-sized strips
2 tablespoons	lemon juice
1/2 cup	mayonnaise (preferably homemade)
2 tablespoons	prepared Dijon mustard
2 tablespoons	chopped cornichons
1 1/2 tablespoons	capers, drained
1/2 teaspoon	herbes de Provence
1/2 teaspoon	salt plus more to taste
1/4 teaspoon	freshly ground black pepper

1. Toss the celeriac and lemon juice in a large bowl.

2. Add the remaining ingredients; toss well to combine. Add more salt if desired. Let stand for half an hour before serving.

The Crew

HARVEST WEEK 17, 1999, NEWSLETTER

Experimented harvesting mesclun and weeding spinach with the Drängen tractor. Inventoried the remaining 1999 seeds in preparation for next season's seed ordering. Began harvesting storage crops, such as celeriac. Cleared out the remaining peppers, eggplant, and tomatoes from the fields as the first frost arrived. Picked up the last of the squash. Harvested and packed more than 700 boxes.

Daikon Radishes

Storage

If the greens are still attached, remove and refrigerate them in a plastic bag and use them within a week. Wrap the unwashed root in a separate plastic bag and place it in the refrigerator, where it will keep for up to two weeks.

Handling

There usually is no need to peel daikon radishes. Wash them thoroughly in cold running water to remove any lingering dirt. Slice, dice, chop, or grate the daikon according to the directions of your recipe.

Culinary Uses

* Make a colorful winter salad using a mixture of grated raw daikon, beets, carrots, and apples.
* Serve daikon greens raw if they are still small and tender.
* Serve daikon raw as a condiment with a heavy meal, as they are said to aid digestion and cleanse the palate.
* Use daikon much as you would carrots or turnips in soups, stews, and stir-fries. They are a classic addition to miso soup.
* Add more mature daikon greens to vegetable soups if they are large.

Partners for Daikon Radishes*

* Basil, borage, chives, curry powder, dill, ginger, lovage, marjoram, mint, oregano, parsley, thyme;
* Honey, lemon juice, miso, orange juice, sesame oil, soy sauce or tamari, vinegar;
* Butter, cream, cream cheese, feta cheese, sour cream;
* Cabbage, carrots, cucumbers, onions, scallions, sugar snap peas.

*See Louise Frazier's Complementary Herbs & Spices chart, page 345, for suggestions.

Although daikon radishes are actually members of the far-flung cabbage family, they look like overgrown white carrots and taste like mild radishes. Unchecked, daikon radishes have been known to weigh in at 50 pounds. We don't let our daikon get that big, but sometimes we do need to cut them in half just to fit them into your vegetable boxes.

Most of us think of radishes as salad fixings, but in Japanese and Indian cuisine daikon radishes are a common cooking vegetable. Besides adding crunch and zip to a meal, daikon radishes are well known for their medicinal properties. Macrobiotic and Ayurvedic traditions rate them highly as a health-promoting food. Since daikon radishes are milder in flavor than regular radishes, they can be used like any other root vegetable in cooking.

Daikon in Plum Sauce

This fast and delightful recipe makes for a great introduction to the daikon. It's sweet and savory with a pleasing texture, and the daikon's distinct flavor shines through. *Angelic Organics Kitchen.*

SERVES 3 TO 4

3 tablespoons	soy sauce
2 tablespoons	rice vinegar
1 teaspoon	cornstarch
2 tablespoons	plum sauce
1 tablespoon	minced scallion
3 tablespoons	peanut oil
1	daikon, peeled, cut into matchstick-sized strips
2 tablespoons	water

1. Combine the soy sauce, vinegar, and cornstarch in a small bowl; stir until cornstarch dissolves. Stir in the plum sauce and scallions.

2. Heat the oil in a wok or large skillet over high heat. Swirl the oil around the wok so that it covers the cooking area, then add the daikon; cook, stirring constantly, for 30 seconds.

3. Add the water and cover. Cook until the daikon is tender, 1 to 2 minutes.

4. Add the soy sauce mixture and continue cooking, stirring vigorously, until the sauce has thickened, 2 to 3 minutes.

A Shareholder

When I was growing up in the Bay Area, my Uncle George used to go out salmon fishing. Quite often during the season, he'd stop by unannounced on his way home, and as soon as I saw his truck pull into the driveway, I'd start grating the daikon root. We would drop our dinner plans and put the fish right into the broiler. Gorgeous fresh salmon with lemon juice, soy sauce, grated ginger, and loads of daikon. It was my favorite meal then, and still is now.

Ginger Miso Soup
with Daikon, Kale, and Carrots

Not your traditional miso soup, this exceptional variation is loaded with vegetables and distinction (traditionally it's served with tofu, scallions, and seaweed). The brightness of daikon and the sweetness of carrots balance the earthy undertones of the kale, and it's all punctuated by a prominence of ginger. Be careful not to bring the broth to a boil, as it will ruin the miso's healthful properties and tends to alter the flavor. *Angelic Organics Kitchen* (adapted from *Friendly Foods*).

SERVES 2 TO 4

2 cups	water, divided
1/4 cup	white miso
1 tablespoon	lemon juice (optional)
1 1/2 teaspoons	grated fresh ginger
2 packed cups	finely chopped kale leaves
1 cup	diced daikon (about 6 ounces)
1 cup	diced carrots

1. Put 1/2 cup of water and the miso in a medium pot. Mix the miso with the water until it is diluted to a thin paste. Stir in the remaining 1 1/2 cups water, lemon juice, and ginger. Place over medium-low heat and bring to a very light simmer, reducing heat as necessary to prevent boiling.

2. Add the kale; continue to simmer, stirring occasionally, until the kale is nearly tender, about 10 minutes.

3. Stir in the daikon and carrots and cook until the vegetables are just tender, 5 to 7 minutes more. Serve immediately.

Our Cook

Nuts! Here I am just warming up in the kitchen and the season has come to a close! Such is farming. One must accept the parameters that nature imposes and do one's best to live in sync with the seasons. I hope that you will enjoy your last box of the year and think of us here at the farm. We'll be back as soon as we can.

Stir-Fried Daikon

Simple, satisfying, and whipped up in minutes, this makes a great meal with teriyaki salmon and a bowl of rice. *Angelic Organics Kitchen* (adapted from *From Asparagus to Zucchini*).

SERVES 4

2 tablespoons	peanut oil
1/4 cup	sliced scallions
1 medium	daikon, thinly sliced (about 3 cups)
10–12	red radishes, thinly sliced
2 tablespoons	water
2 tablespoons	soy sauce
1 teaspoon	sugar
1/4 teaspoon	hot chili oil or more to taste (optional)

1. Heat the peanut oil in a wok over high heat. Add the scallions; stir-fry for 30 seconds. Add the daikon and red radishes; stir-fry for 1 minute. Add the water and continue stir-frying until all the water has all evaporated.

2. Add the soy sauce, sugar, and chili oil, mixing everything together vigorously and cooking for 30 seconds more. Immediately transfer to a serving platter. Serve hot.

The Crop

HARVEST WEEK 13, 1997, NEWSLETTER

Beets look great. The late-planted spinach germinated thanks to irrigation line we just laid out. It might make a crop; it might not. Great daikon radishes. Beautiful stands of many other types of radishes for early October. Winter squash is taking its time maturing. Squash vines are usually dead by now. Oh, the crew took 600 melons out of the field last Wednesday, and there are still more muskmelons to ripen!

Daikon with Tahini Dressing

This is an attention-getting dish: it's unique, it's attractive, and it tastes wonderful. It goes well wherever you might see coleslaw. It's fantastic on a bed of lettuce served with fish, and it makes a great light sandwich when stuffed into pita bread. Mix in some cooked shredded chicken and an extra 1/4 cup tahini, and you have a delicious, unique chicken salad. *Angelic Organics Kitchen* (adapted from *Recipes from a Kitchen Garden*).

SERVES 4

4 inches	daikon, cut into matchstick-sized strips
3/4 cup	thinly sliced red radishes
1 medium	carrot, grated (about 1/2 cup)
1/4 cup	tahini
4	scallions, thinly sliced
1 1/2 tablespoons	freshly squeezed lemon juice (about 1/2 lemon)
1 tablespoon	dry sherry or vermouth
	dash salt
	sugar
1/4 cup	chopped almonds (optional)

1. Combine daikon, red radish, and carrots in a medium bowl.

2. Whisk the tahini, scallions, lemon juice, sherry, salt, and sugar to taste in a small bowl until well combined. Thin the dressing with a few tablespoons of water until the mixture is a smooth paste.

3. Toss the dressing with radishes until well combined. Garnish with almonds if desired.

Our Soil

HARVEST WEEK 20, 1998, NEWSLETTER

Most of the farm is now lush with winter rye. It is reassuring to walk the fields knowing that these millions of little seedlings are converting sun, rain, and minerals into living soil. They aerate our silty clay soil, feed the beneficial soil microbes, and hold the fields in place against pounding fall and spring rains.

Parsnips

Brussels sprouts harvest, red cabbage and
Brussels sprouts growing

Daikon growing,
daikon unearthed,
beet harvest,
spreading compost

Potatoes

Fordson,
spinach harvest

Squash and
pumpkin harvest

Sunchokes

the
real dirt
on farmer john

THE REAL DIRT ON FARMER JOHN
narrated and written by FARMER JOHN PETERSON
editor GREG SNIDER director of photography TAGGART SIEGEL
original music score MARK ORTON & music by DIRTY THREE
producer TERI LANG directed and produced by TAGGART SIEGEL

Parsnips

Contrary to appearances, parsnips are not pale versions of carrots. In fact, they have a nutty-sweet taste and a tender-hearty texture that is entirely distinct from carrots and uniquely their own. The first-century Roman emperor Tiberius was reportedly so fond of parsnips that he imported them from the Rhineland, ordering his cooks to boil them gently and serve them in honey nectar. (Check out Steamed Parsnips with Sweet Butter Sauce, page 287, for a version of this "classic" recipe.) Although in recent years parsnips seem to have fallen out of mainstream favor, they were for centuries a more common staple than the potato—and deservedly so. Satisfying, versatile, and highly nutritious, these delicious roots make a terrific base to any meal.

If you haven't had parsnips for a while, tasting them again is bound to be a rediscovery. This is what happens on the farm; year after year, parsnips have proven to be a favorite vegetable of our farm team. One intern was even known to eat a plate of them for a hearty breakfast! But if you don't want to give up your favorite breakfast cereal just yet, you'll find some great recipes in this chapter to help you enjoy parsnips for lunch, dinner, and even for dessert.

Storage

Refrigerate unwashed parsnips in a loosely wrapped or perforated plastic bag. Stored in the vegetable bin of your refrigerator, they can keep up to two weeks.

Handling

Young parsnips don't need to be peeled. Simply scrub them under cold running water with a vegetable brush. Larger parsnips should be peeled, and you can cut out the core if it seems woody. However you slice or chop parsnips, be sure to make all the pieces relatively the same size. With their tapered shape this can be a challenge, but your efforts will ensure an evenly cooked dish.

Culinary Uses

❖ Grate raw young parsnips into salads, or cut them into sticks as part of a raw vegetable tray.
❖ Steam or boil parsnips and season with butter or oil, salt, and pepper for a simple, delectable side dish.
❖ Bake them in a cake or quick bread.
❖ Sauté them with butter and parsley, roast with whole cloves of unpeeled garlic, or purée well-boiled parsnips. Cook them in soups and stews.

❖ Substitute parsnips for some or all of the potato or carrot in a favorite recipe to give it a delicious twist.

> ### Our Cook
>
> I haven't done as much cooking with parsnips as I have with carrots, but it's always exciting to have a new ingredient. I added some parsnips to the split pea soup I made for the crew a couple of weeks ago, and it was delicious. I remember cooking a curried vegetable pie with parsnips for some of my housemates when I was a freshman in college. All seven of us approached it somewhat warily, but it was tasty.

Partners for Parsnips*

❖ Anise hyssop, basil, chervil, chile, chives, cinnamon, coriander, cumin, curry, dill, fennel leaves or seeds, garlic, ginger, lovage, mace, mint, mustard, nutmeg, parsley, sage, rosemary, thyme;

❖ Butter, cream, nut butters, sharp and creamy cheeses, yogurt;

❖ Lemon juice, mirin, olive oil, roasted peanut oil, soy sauce, toasted sesame oil;

❖ All root vegetables, apples, black beans, cooking greens, green beans, lentils, onions, oranges, prunes, raisins, tofu;

❖ Brown sugar, honey, maple syrup.

*See Louise Frazier's Complementary Herbs & Spices chart, page 345, for suggestions.

Spiced Parsnip Cake with Pecans

Move over, carrot cake! The parsnip has arrived and wants some of the action. Good, fresh, firm parsnips have a wonderful, natural sweetness that makes them ideal in baked desserts. This cake is delicious with a traditional glaze or frosting, but if you're running short on time, serve it with a warm fruit compote or applesauce. This recipe calls for mace, which is the dried and powdered outer surface of nutmeg. Mace has a wonderful, nutty flavor like nutmeg—and it has a brighter, zestier edge that won't fade during baking. A touch of mace adds complexity to the warm, familiar spiciness of cinnamon. If you cannot find mace, you can substitute 1/8 teaspoon nutmeg. *Friend of the Farm.*

SERVES 6 TO 8

	butter for greasing the baking pan
2 cups	flour
1 tablespoon	baking powder
1 tablespoon	baking soda
2 teaspoons	ground cinnamon
1/4 teaspoon	salt
1/8 teaspoon	ground mace
1 1/4 cups	sugar
3/4 cup	butter, softened
1/2 cup	mild-flavored vegetable oil
4	eggs, at room temperature
3 cups	peeled and grated raw parsnips (about 3 large parsnips)
1 1/2 cups	finely chopped pecans

1. Preheat the oven to 325° F. Lightly coat a 10-inch Bundt pan or tube pan with butter.

2. Sift the flour into a large bowl. Stir in the baking powder, baking soda, cinnamon, salt, and mace.

3. In another large bowl, combine the sugar, butter, and oil; beat with an electric mixer until fluffy. Add 1 egg and beat well. Add about a quarter of the flour mixture and beat well. Repeat the process until all of the eggs and flour mixture are used and well combined.

4. Stir in the parsnips and pecans.

5. Pour the batter into the pan and bake until a toothpick inserted near the center comes out clean, about 1 hour.

6. Remove the pan from the oven and set it aside to cool on a wire rack for 10 minutes. Carefully remove the cake from the pan. Serve warm or at room temperature.

Parsnip and Apple Slaw
with Creamy Parsley Dressing

It rarely comes to mind to eat parsnips raw, but perhaps this is simply because we rarely have the pleasure of working with them when they are fresh and tender-crisp. What a delightful, delicate slaw they make! *Friend of the Farm.*

SERVES 2 TO 4

1/2 cup	sour cream
2 tablespoons	minced onion
2 tablespoons	minced fresh parsley
1 tablespoon	freshly squeezed lemon juice
1 teaspoon	sugar
1/2 teaspoon	salt plus more to taste
	freshly ground black pepper
4 medium	parsnips, peeled, coarsely grated
2 medium	apples (unpeeled), cored, finely diced
3 tablespoons	pine nuts or slivered almonds (optional)

1. In a large bowl, combine the sour cream, onion, parsley, lemon juice, sugar, 1/2 teaspoon salt, and pepper to taste. Stir until well combined.

2. Mix in the parsnips and apples. Cover and refrigerate for at least 2 hours.

3. If you are using the nuts, toast them in a dry, heavy skillet (preferably cast iron) over high heat until they start to brown in spots and become fragrant. (Be careful not to overtoast them, as they will burn very quickly once they are toasted.) Immediately transfer the nuts to a dish to cool.

4. When you are ready to serve, taste the salad and season with additional salt and pepper if desired. Sprinkle on the nuts. Serve chilled.

Steamed Parsnips
with Sweet Butter Sauce

The parsnip's humble appearance conceals its luscious taste; it needs very little fuss in order to be sweet and delicious. Simply steamed and topped with just a touch of maple syrup or honey, parsnips are irresistibly good. The tender strips in this recipe can be served whole, sliced, or even mashed. *Friend of the Farm.*

SERVES 3 TO 4

3 large	parsnips, sliced lengthwise into 1/2-inch-thick strips
1/4 cup	butter
1 tablespoon	maple syrup or honey
	salt
	freshly ground black pepper

1. Place the parsnips in a steamer basket set over 1 1/2 inches boiling water and cover. Steam for 10 to 15 minutes depending on size. Transfer to a serving bowl.

2. Melt the butter in a small pot over medium heat. Remove the pot from heat and stir in the maple syrup or honey.

3. Pour the butter mixture over the parsnips. Season with salt and pepper to taste.

Farmer John Writes

HARVEST WEEK 13, 1997, NEWSLETTER

A 4 1/2-inch rain slammed down one night. That's the normal rainfall for the whole month of June. It carved ditches in the newly tilled ground, broke off carrot and parsnip seedlings, swept away variety-identification stakes. The deluge also compacted the soil, causing the germination of a fantastic amount of grass. Fields where grass has not been a problem for years have sprouted grassy carpets. Mesclun beds, normally free of weeds, are inundated with lanky grasses that quadruple harvest time. Lettuces repose in a sea of downy foxtail.

Sweet-and-Sour Glazed Parsnips

The natural sweetness in parsnips is offset by an earthy, almost bitter note that gives interest and depth to their flavor. Here we use sweet and sour ingredients to accentuate this wonderfully complex quality. It's an easy, pretty, and delicious side dish. *Friend of the Farm.*

SERVES 2 TO 4

4 medium	parsnips, cut diagonally into 1/4-inch slices
1/4 cup	butter, divided
1 teaspoon	sugar
3 tablespoons	orange marmalade
	salt
	freshly ground black pepper
	freshly squeezed lemon juice
	freshly grated nutmeg

1. Put the parsnips into a large skillet along with enough water to cover by 1 inch. Add 2 tablespoons of the butter and the sugar; set over medium-high heat. Bring to a simmer; cook, uncovered, until the parsnips are tender, 10 to 12 minutes.

2. Add the marmalade and remaining 2 tablespoons butter. Increase the heat to medium-high and continue cooking, stirring constantly, until all the liquid has evaporated and the parsnips are coated with a shiny glaze, about 6 minutes. Remove from heat.

3. Season with salt, pepper, and fresh lemon juice to taste. Top each serving with a dash of nutmeg.

A Shareholder

I picked up my last box yesterday and felt so sad to see the season end that I went home and reread some old farm newsletters! My niece was a shareholder also, and she split the box with me. Every time we went to pick it up, she'd open the box and say, "Oh, this was such a good idea!" Getting the box and splitting it with her was like getting a double present: a share of incredible vegetables and another opportunity to get to know her better.

Cinnamon Apple Parsnip Soup

The combination of apples and parsnips with a hint of cinnamon is truly fantastic. This sweet, silky, luscious soup makes for a great start to an autumn meal. *Friend of the Farm.*

SERVES 4 TO 6

3 tablespoons	butter
1 large	onion, chopped (about 1 cup)
4 medium	parsnips, peeled, roughly chopped
2 baking	apples (Granny Smith or greening), peeled, cored, roughly chopped
1/2 teaspoon	ground cinnamon
1/2 cup	dry white wine
4 cups	chicken or vegetable stock
1/2 cup	100% pure apple juice (unsweetened, not from concentrate)
1	bay leaf
1/2 teaspoon	salt
1/2 teaspoon	freshly ground black pepper
	freshly grated nutmeg for garnish

1. Heat the butter in a soup pot over medium heat. Add the onion; cook, stirring occasionally, until nicely golden, 10 to 12 minutes. Add the parsnips, apples, and cinnamon; toss to coat. Stir in the wine and simmer for 5 minutes.

2. Add the stock, apple juice, and bay leaf; partially cover the pot and gently simmer until the parsnips are tender, 20 to 30 minutes.

3. Remove and discard the bay leaf. Transfer the soup to a blender of food processor; purée. (Alternatively, run the soup through a food mill.) Return the soup to the pot and add the salt and pepper; simmer 10 to 15 minutes to let the soup thicken a little more. Garnish each serving with a sprinkle of freshly grated nutmeg.

"People like potatoes," Farmer John's mom used to say. A plain baked potato will please even the most finicky child or conscientious dieter, while more elaborate creations delight gourmets worldwide. Potatoes are the most widely grown and eaten vegetable. Although you may meet the average of eating one potato per person per day, the potatoes we grow at Angelic Organics are anything but average. Our heirloom potatoes come in a range of shapes, sizes, and colors.

Potatoes Grown by Angelic Organics

Boiling potatoes have a firm, waxy texture. Because they hold their shape when boiled or steamed, these low-starch potatoes are good choices for salads, soups, stews, or au gratin dishes. (Tip: if, after slicing a raw potato, the knife comes out clean, chances are it is more suited to boiling than to baking.)

New potatoes, the smallest and smoothest of the potatoes we grow, are harvested while the skins are still tender. To keep from damaging these fragile young potatoes, we don't always thoroughly wash them; we leave it to our shareholders to clean them gently. New potatoes, which are young potatoes of many different varieties, are always considered boilers, since they haven't had time to develop the high starch of bakers.

Cranberry red potatoes have bright red skin and an unusual moist, pink interior.

Langlade potatoes are handsome, round, white, and versatile.

Norland Dark Red potatoes have an almost burgundy colored skin with white flesh.

Viking Purple potatoes have a true purple skin with bright pink splashes and pure white flesh.

Baking potatoes have a drier, starchier flesh and cook up with a fluffy texture. They are best baked, mashed, or deep-fried. (Tip: if, after slicing a raw potato, the knife is coated with white, foamy starch, chances are it is more suited to baking than to boiling.)

Potatoes

Russet Sebago potatoes are high-starch bakers with an outstanding flavor.

Butte potatoes are oval-shaped, white-fleshed, and delicious.

All-Purpose potatoes have qualities that fall in between those of boiling potatoes and baking potatoes.

All-blue potatoes have deep blue-purple skin and moist blue flesh.

Caribé potatoes have lustrous purple skin covering smooth, white flesh.

Rose gold potatoes have rosy-red skin and deep-yellow flesh.

Yukon Gold potatoes are medium-large and have yellowish brown skin and cream-colored flesh.

Kennebec potatoes have buff skin and white flesh.

Storage

Keep unwashed potatoes in a cool, dark, dry place—such as a loosely closed paper bag in a cupboard. They will keep for weeks at room temperature, longer if you can provide their ideal temperature of 40 to 50 degrees. Beware: If your refrigerator is set at the normal refrigerator temperature, somewhere in the 30s, the low temperature will convert the starch to sugars. However, new potatoes—which are young and thin-skinned—may be refrigerated if you don't plan to eat them within a few days. Try to use new potatoes soon, because their delicate flavor wanes with time. Moisture causes potatoes to spoil, light turns them green, and proximity to onions causes them to sprout. (You can still use a potato that has sprouted, however; simply cut off the "eyes" before use.)

Handling

Scrub potatoes well and cut off any sprouts or green skin. (Delicate new potatoes should be cleaned gently.) Peeling is a matter of preference. In soups and stews, the skins may separate from the flesh and float in the broth, but when baked, pan-fried, or roasted, the skins acquire a wonderful crisp, crunchy texture. Cut potatoes according to the specifications given in your recipe. If baking a whole potato, be sure to prick the skin in at least two places to allow steam to escape.

Culinary Uses

❖ Boil, mash, and fry potatoes.
❖ Use potatoes (peeled or unpeeled) in soups, hash browns, and salads.
❖ Roast sliced (or whole small) potatoes with fresh herbs, salt, and olive oil at 400°F until tender.
❖ Bake small, whole potatoes plain or covered with kosher or sea salt.
❖ Boil whole potatoes in salted water or spicy crab boil (available in most supermarkets) until slightly tender, then slice and grill them.
❖ Angelic Organics shareholders can have fun with the colored heirloom potatoes we provide: make red and blue french fries, or serve a colorful root vegetable roast that combines several varieties of cubed potatoes with julienned beets and carrots.

Partners for Potatoes*

❖ Basil, chervil, chives, curry spices, garlic, lovage, mace, marjoram, mustard, oregano, paprika, parsley, pepper, rosemary, saffron, sage, sorrel, thyme;
❖ Olive oil;
❖ Butter, Cantel cheese, cheddar cheese, cream, Fontina cheese, goat cheese, Gruyère cheese, sour cream;
❖ Carrots, cooking greens, green beans, leeks, onions, peppers, root vegetables, tomatoes.

*See Louise Frazier's Complementary Herbs & Spices chart, page 345, for suggestions.

Colcannon

You'll find this classic dish on the menu at any real Irish restaurant. It's a recipe that takes two staples of the island, potatoes and kale (or sometimes cabbage), and transforms them into a dish truly worthy of the word classic. One Irish grandmother we know, Mrs. Nesbit, has implored us to cook the potatoes and kale separately. Convenience and economy tell us to do it in one pot, since they take around the same time to cook. But if you had tasted Mrs. Nesbit's food and seen her grace in the kitchen, you'd do exactly as she says. She'd be most disappointed if you didn't. *Angelic Organics Kitchen.*

SERVES 6

1½ pounds	medium boiling potatoes (about 3 medium potatoes)
2 teaspoons	salt, divided, plus more to taste
1½–2 pounds	kale (15–20 large leaves)
1 cup	chopped leeks or scallions
1 cup	half-and-half or milk
½ teaspoon	freshly ground black pepper
½ cup	butter, melted

1. Put the whole potatoes in a large pot, cover with water, and bring to boil. Add 1 teaspoon of the salt and boil until the potatoes are tender, 15 to 20 minutes. Drain the potatoes and mash. Put in a heatproof dish and keep warm in a 200° oven.

2. Meanwhile, put the kale in a pot, cover with water, and bring to boil. Add the remaining 1 teaspoon salt and cook until the kale is tender, 15 to 20 minutes. (There you go Mrs. Nesbit, it's in the directions. Don't worry, everyone will do it this way now that it's spelled out exactly.) Drain and finely chop the kale.

3. Place the leeks or scallions in a small pot, cover with the half-and-half, and cook over low heat until very soft, 15 to 20 minutes.

4. Add the kale to the warm potatoes and mix well. Add the half-and-half with leeks or scallions. Add the pepper; season with salt to taste.

5. Spoon a little of the melted butter over each serving and serve hot.

Potato, Onion, and Roquefort Soup

This soup is not quite for dieters—it will dazzle you with its rich, deep flavors. It's very filling, so if you're serving it as a first course, a small cup is plenty. If you're not a fan of Roquefort cheese, you can substitute Gruyère. *Angelic Organics Kitchen.*

SERVES 4 TO 6

3 tablespoons	unsalted butter
2 medium	onions, thinly sliced
1 teaspoon	minced garlic (about 2 cloves)
3 medium	boiling potatoes (about 1½ pounds), peeled, cut into 1-inch chunks
2 cups	chicken or vegetable stock plus more if needed to thin the soup
1 cup	half-and-half
⅓ cup	cream
½ cup	crumbled Roquefort cheese plus more to taste
	salt
	freshly ground white pepper

1. Melt the butter in a large saucepan over medium-high heat. Add the onions; cook, stirring, until the onions are limp but not brown, about 15 minutes. Add the garlic; cook for 30 seconds more.

2. Add the potatoes and stir until well coated with butter; cook for 5 minutes, stirring them up a few times.

3. Add 2 cups stock and bring to a boil. Reduce the heat, cover, and simmer until the potatoes are tender, 20 to 30 minutes. Remove from heat and let cool.

4. Add the half-and-half and the cream; gently reheat the soup, but do not boil. Stir in ½ cup Roquefort cheese.

5. Transfer the soup to a blender or food processor in batches and purée until smooth. Thin with additional stock if necessary. Season with salt and pepper to taste. Garnish with additional cheese if desired and serve hot or cold.

The Crop

HARVEST WEEK 18, 1999, NEWSLETTER

We have a lousy potato crop, which we usually have, except that last year was an amazingly huge potato crop, so we thought maybe we had learned something about raising potatoes. We did pretty much the same thing as last year on really similar ground, but the yield was dismal. We even bought a two-row potato harvester this year, figuring we'd have a big crop to harvest. We always look for reasons when a crop isn't good, and we think it might be that we had such a drought and heat wave during flowering (but then again this might not be the reason at all).

The Crop

HARVEST WEEK 20, 1998, NEWSLETTER

Thank you, Angelic Organics shareholders. You were with us during a pretty wild year. I think our crew did a good job smoothing out the torrential weather edges, but you still had a personal experience of the pervasive dampness that caused a squash and tomato shortfall. But just look at all the potatoes! The potato windfall was probably caused by the same conditions that caused the squash and tomato shortage. And the beautiful fall weather let us give you delicious spinach, lettuce, and mesclun right into the final weeks. The weather giveth and the weather taketh away. We hope it all evened out for you.

FORCES IN FOOD

People who eat lots of potatoes do not get strong thoughts, but they get heavy dreams. If somebody has to eat potatoes all the time, he will be actually a bit tired all the time, and will always be wanting to sleep and dream. Therefore the food that man actually receives has an important bearing on the history of civilization.

—RUDOLF STEINER, *NUTRITION AND STIMULANTS*

Skillet Potato
and Cabbage Pancakes

This is not your ordinary potato pancake; this recipe adds the subtle tang of cabbage. It makes for a fine breakfast topped with fried eggs or the perfect side dish to pork chops. Top your pancakes with sour cream or applesauce or just enjoy them as they are. *Angelic Organics Kitchen.*

SERVES 4

1 cup	shredded cabbage
2 1/2 cups	grated potatoes, any kind
1/4 cup	sliced scallions
1 clove	garlic, minced (about 1/2 teaspoon) (optional)
1	egg, beaten
1 1/2 teaspoons	salt
1/2 teaspoon	freshly ground black pepper
1/4 cup	butter
2 tablespoons	oil
	sour cream or applesauce (optional)

1. Place the cabbage in a steamer basket set over 1 1/2 inches boiling water. Cover; steam until tender, 15 to 20 minutes.

2. Place the grated potatoes in a clean dish towel. Gather up the edges, twist the towel tight, and hold the bundle over the sink. Squeeze out as much moisture as you can. (While this step helps you get nicely browned and crisp pancakes, it is not absolutely necessary).

3. Combine the potatoes, cabbage, scallions, garlic, egg, salt, and pepper in a bowl. Mix well and then use your hands to form thin, loose patties of the size you prefer.

4. Combine the butter and oil in a large skillet over medium-high heat; heat until butter melts. Add as many patties as will fit in your skillet without overcrowding; press down on them firmly with the back of a spatula. Cook until the pancakes are brown to your liking, 7 to 10 minutes. Flip the pancakes, press down firmly, and cook until bottoms are brown, 7 to 10 minutes.

5. Top with sour cream or applesauce if desired. Serve hot.

Potato Croquettes
Stuffed with Spicy Beets

These croquettes are crispily perfect, with the soft and buttery potatoes giving way to tender, spicy beets—what an impressive first course. Try them with Homemade Mayonnaise, page 332, or sour cream or yogurt. Of course, they're perfectly delicious all on their own. They also make an impressive bed for a filet mignon or tuna steak. *Angelic Organics Kitchen.*

SERVES 3 TO 4

Potato Patties

4 medium	boiling potatoes (about 2 pounds)
3 tablespoons	very finely minced onion
3 tablespoons	butter, melted
3/4 teaspoon	salt
pinch	cayenne pepper
	freshly ground black pepper

Stuffing

1 medium	beet, peeled, cut into 1/4-inch dice (about 3/4 cup)
1 tablespoon	chopped fresh cilantro
1 teaspoon	lemon juice
1/4 teaspoon	salt
1/4 teaspoon	ground cumin
1/4 teaspoon	ground coriander
big pinch	cayenne pepper
	freshly ground black pepper

Crust

1 cup	all-purpose flour
2 large	eggs
1 1/2 cups	dried bread crumbs
1/2 cup	freshly grated Parmesan cheese
1 teaspoon	fresh thyme or 1/2 teaspoon dried thyme
1/2 teaspoon	salt
	freshly ground black pepper
	vegetable oil for frying

1. Put the whole potatoes in a pot, cover with water, and boil until tender when pierced with a fork, 15 to 20 minutes depending on size. Use a slotted spoon to transfer the potatoes to a large bowl; reserve the potato cooking water in the pan.

2. Mash the potatoes with a potato masher or the back of a fork. Add the onion, butter, salt, cayenne, and black pepper to taste and stir until well combined. With your hands, form roughly 10 patties (about 4 inches in diameter).

3. Return the potato water to a rapid boil. Drop in the beets and boil until tender, about 5 minutes. Drain. In a large bowl combine the beets, cilantro, lemon juice, salt, cumin, coriander, cayenne, and black pepper to taste.

4. Put 1 tablespoon of the beet stuffing in the center of each of the patties (you may need to adjust this measurement according to the size of your patties.) Fold the potato mixture over the stuffing to form a rough half-circle, and then flatten gently to form a neat patty about 2 1/2 inches in diameter.

5. Line a plate with several layers of paper towel. Put the flour in a shallow bowl. Lightly beat the eggs in a second shallow bowl. Combine the bread crumbs, Parmesan, thyme, salt, and pepper in a third shallow bowl.

6. Drop one patty in the flour to coat it all over, including the edges. Gently shake off the excess flour by passing it between your hands. Dip the coated patty in the egg, allowing the excess to drip off, and then drop it into the bread crumb mixture, turning it to coat well. Set aside on a plate and continue the process with the remaining patties.

7. Pour oil into a large skillet to a 1/4-inch depth and heat over medium-high heat until hot but not smoking. To tell if the oil is ready, drop a pinch of flour into it; if it sizzles, it's ready. Working in batches, add the patties to the hot oil (don't overcrowd) and fry until the bottoms are a nice golden brown, about 5 minutes. Flip the patties and fry until bottoms are golden brown, 5 minutes more. Drain the fried patties on the paper towel to lined plate.

Overheard

BANK TELLER: Up until a couple years ago, I never even knew what a potato plant looked like. I thought potatoes grew on trees.

FARMER: Did you think the potatoes got heavier and heavier on the tree until the tree fell over and then the farmer could harvest the crop?

BANK TELLER: I thought they just fell off the tree when they got big. I thought that's why they were so dirty—because they hit the ground so hard.

Overheard

Today we dug more potatoes and I felt melancholy for most of the day. I played some Irish airs on my fiddle at lunch and took a nap on some burlap sacks and when I woke up it was quiet and the wind was blowing through the trees and I imagined having a baby right there without anyone knowing it and then going back to work.

Farmer John Writes

1996, NEWSLETTER

My walk changed a little the other day. If you had been watching me, you might not have noticed anything different. It was just a slight change in gait. I felt it especially in my shoulder blades and upper arms. It felt like a yearning, like something was suddenly incomplete. This walk, I thought to myself, is an it's-time-to-get-the-potatoes-out walk. The time to dig potatoes showed up in my stride before it even showed up in my thoughts.

Potato Dumplings
(Gekochte Kartoffelklöße)

This is a creative and delicious alternative to mashed potatoes. The potato dumpling is happy when accompanied by lots of sauce, for it is most suited to sop it all up. It's thrilled when served in a thin soup in need of some girth, and it simply loves a bed of sauerkraut. *Friend of the Farm.*

SERVES 4

2 pounds	potatoes, any kind (about 4 medium potatoes)
2 cups	flour
2	eggs, beaten
1 teaspoon	plus 1 tablespoon salt, divided
1/4 teaspoon	nutmeg
1 tablespoon	butter
1 cup	cubed, day-old bread

1. The day before you are going to make this dish, boil the potatoes in their skins until tender. Store in the refrigerator overnight.

2. The next day, peel and mash the potatoes. Mix in the flour, eggs, 1 teaspoon of the salt, and nutmeg. Knead the mixture into a dough.

3. Bring a large pot of water to a boil and add 1 tablespoon salt.

4. Melt the butter in a medium skillet over high heat. Add the bread cubes; fry until nicely toasted, 3 to 5 minutes.

5. Shape the potato mixture into dumplings that are a size appropriate for your dish, usually about the size of a golf ball or little larger.

6. Use your finger to press a hole into each dumpling. Put a few pieces of the fried bread cubes into each hole and then seal it closed.

7. Drop the dumplings into the water and cook until firm, 10 to 15 minutes.

Rutabaga

Rutabaga, whose name in Old Nordic means "baggy root," is an old-fashioned vegetable you may have unknowingly eaten at some point in your life. Sometimes grandmothers serve it with butter and pass it off as mashed potatoes to reluctant grandchildren. Closely related to winter turnips, rutabagas differ only in their deeper color and slightly sweeter taste. Rutabagas and winter turnips can be used interchangeably in most recipes. Since rutabagas hold up for months in cold storage, seasonal eaters can appreciate them for the variety they add to the Midwestern winter table. More than an imported tomato, these roots will sustain you through winter—especially when you eat them blanketed in milk- and butter-laden sauce!

Storage

Rutabagas store exceptionally well. Keep unwashed rutabagas in a plastic bag in the refrigerator for a month or longer.

Handling

Scrub rutabagas well to remove any lingering dirt. Take a thin slice off the top and bottom. Whether peeling is necessary is debatable. Some people claim that peeling off the skin reduces nutrients, while others peel rutabagas to avoid eating the thick skin of larger roots. If you decide to peel the rutabaga, use a small knife or sturdy vegetable peeler.

Culinary Uses

❖ Grate or julienne small, raw rutabagas straight from the field into salads. (Unless you are a bona fide rutabaga fan, the storage variety will probably be a bit too pungent to be eaten raw.)
❖ Mash cooked rutabaga with carrots and/or potatoes (and other root vegetables).
❖ Cook rutabaga into stews or gratins as part of medley of winter roots.
❖ Roast or braise rutabaga.

Partners for Rutabagas*

❖ Allspice, basil, bay leaf, borage, caraway, cinnamon, cumin, dill, garlic, mustard, oregano, parsley, pepper, rosemary, savory, tarragon, thyme;
❖ Blue cheese, butter, cream, cream cheese, Gruyère cheese, Parmesan cheese;
❖ Lemon juice, olive oil;
❖ Beets, broccoli, carrots, celeriac, celery, cooking greens, leeks, parsnips, potatoes, roasted garlic, scallions, turnips, watercress;
❖ Honey, raisins.

*See Louise Frazier's Complementary Herbs & Spices chart, page 344, for suggestions.

Farmer John Writes

"You Dwyer guys like this farming, don't you?"

"What else is there? There ain't nothing else."

—FROM JOHN'S BOOK *FARMER JOHN ON GLITTER & GREASE*

Rutabaga Waldorf Salad

Here's a clever take on the classic Waldorf Salad, named after the Waldorf-Astoria Hotel in New York. Bring it to your next picnic instead of the same old coleslaw or potato salad. This recipe is the perfect home for the often neglected rutabaga. It pairs up nicely with the cabbage and apple, and since there is no cooking involved, you can whip up this dish in no time. If you like, grapes and walnuts are more traditional than raisins and peanuts. *Angelic Organics Kitchen.*

SERVES 4

1/2 cup	mayonnaise
1 tablespoon	lemon juice
1 cup	shredded cabbage
1 cup	peeled, diced apple
1/2 cup	coarsely grated peeled rutabaga
1/4 cup	raisins
1/4 cup	chopped toasted peanuts
	salt
	freshly ground black pepper

1. Put the mayonnaise in a small bowl. Add the lemon juice, a little at a time, stirring until smooth.

2. In a large bowl, combine the cabbage, apple, rutabaga, raisins, and peanuts. Add the mayonnaise mixture and toss to coat well. Season with salt and pepper to taste. Chill before serving.

Farmer John Writes

Hollywood, in its very early days, was determined not to make stars out of its actors for fear that the talent would get too much power and would then demand big salaries. Actors were not even identified in the credits. Movies were not about stars, but about scripts and technology. Most vegetables today are at the level where those movie actors and actresses were in the early Hollywood days: generic. Vegetables do not have individuality in the minds of most consumers. However, Angelic Organics offers fresh, organic, Biodynamic produce that people can come and visit. We at Angelic Organics think of our vegetables as stars that you can eat.

Rutabaga and Pear Purée

This is a nice fall recipe. Pear adds a subtle, fruity sweetness to the rutabaga and makes this dish irresistible. Serve this as you would mashed potatoes or, as recipe-editor Matt suggests, as a side to meat dishes such as pork or lamb chops. It's best eaten the day it's made. *Shareholder.*

SERVES 2 TO 4

1 small	rutabaga, peeled, cubed
1 large,	ripe pear, peeled, cored, cut into chunks
1/4 cup	sour cream or plain yogurt
1 tablespoon	butter
	pinch nutmeg
	salt
	freshly ground black pepper

1. Place the rutabaga in a steamer basket set over 1 1/2 inches boiling water, cover and steam until almost tender, 15 minutes depending on thickness. Add the pear; continue to steam until rutabaga is tender, 5 to 10 more minutes. Drain well.

2. Purée the rutabaga mixture in a blender or food processor until smooth. (Alternatively, use a food mill or mash the mixture by hand.)

3. Add the sour cream, butter, nutmeg, salt, and pepper to taste; process until just combined.

4. Reheat in saucepan over medium-low heat until heated through.

Over-read

Immediately guilt swooped at me like a bat or a swallow. I wonder of this guilt, is it a lifetime companion? A friend from Minnesota once said to me, "This is Midwestern guilt; see if you don't notice that only people from the Midwest say 'I'm sorry' instead of 'Pardon me' when bumping into someone."

Savory-Sweet Rutabaga Pudding

Somewhere between a fluffy ricotta dessert and mashed potatoes, this delectable rutabaga pudding has all the qualities needed to become a standard in your culinary repertoire. This dish will surprise you in many ways: in taste, in texture, in ease of preparing, and in the compliments it will bring to your table. It pairs exceptionally well with lamb. *Friend of the Farm* (adapted from *Nika Hazelton's Way with Vegetables*).

SERVES 6 TO 8

1 large	rutabaga (about 2 pounds), peeled, cut into 2-inch dice
1 1/2 teaspoons	salt, divided
	butter for greasing the baking dish
2	eggs plus 1 egg yolk, beaten
1/4 cup	heavy cream
1/4 cup	dried bread crumbs
1 tablespoon	maple syrup
pinch	freshly grated nutmeg
1/3 cup	raisins, plumped in hot water for 15 minutes and drained (optional)
	freshly ground black pepper
2 tablespoons	butter

1. Bring a large pot of water to boil. Add the rutabaga and 1 teaspoon salt, partially cover, and cook until the rutabaga is very soft, 30 to 45 minutes. (You will need to reserve 1/2 cup of the cooking water.)

2. Preheat the oven to 350° F. Coat a 2-quart baking dish with butter.

3. Beat the eggs and egg yolk in a medium bowl. Stir in the cream, bread crumbs, maple syrup, and nutmeg.

4. Drain the rutabaga, reserving 1/2 cup of the cooking water. Mash the rutabaga thoroughly with a potato masher or run it through a food mill. If the mixture seems dry, add a little of the reserved rutabaga water as you mash. Add the egg mixture, raisins, remaining 1/2 teaspoon salt, and a few grindings of pepper; stir to combine.

5. Transfer the rutabaga pudding to the prepared baking dish. Smooth the top and dot with butter.

6. Bake until lightly golden on top, about 45 minutes. Serve hot.

A Shareholder

I've been a vegan for fifteen years, so I know my vegetables. Whenever someone asks, I tell them the rutabaga is the most underrated vegetable of all. Most of the time when I check out at the grocery store, the checker doesn't even know what it is. If you like white potatoes, sweet potatoes, or winter squash, you'll like rutabaga too—and get more nutrition for less calories. Of course the rutabaga from the farm are the best. I only wish there were more of them! My favorite way to eat rutabaga is to cut it up in little chunks (I don't even peel it) and bake it in a clay pot with red cabbage at 400 degrees for 70 minutes. It's the best!

Our Cook

Rutabagas are roots that develop just below the surface of the earth. They store for at least a month in the refrigerator, longer packed in sawdust in a cool, dry, dark cellar. Rutabagas are really good roasted whole in the oven for up to an hour, depending on the size. (I think "Rutabaga" makes a very good pet name for children.)

A Shareholder

This is our second year of participating in the twenty-week share. I take the veggies out of the box and set them on the counter just to admire the variety and colors before storing them for the week. (It would make a beautiful photograph!) Using the selection of veggies has at times been challenging (since I didn't even know what some of them were), but I have had fun experimenting with new foods and recipes. The experience has certainly kept me out of a veggie rut!

Mashed Rutabaga Potato Supreme

Mashed potatoes are good, but rutabaga mashed potatoes are supreme. The carrot gives this purée some color and a nice hint of sweetness. If you don't want to use milk in this recipe, you can substitute ¼ cup of the cooking water from the rutabaga and potato pot. *Angelic Organics Kitchen* (adapted from *Greene on Greens*).

SERVES 4

few pinches	salt
½ large	rutabaga (about 1 pound) peeled, cut into ½-inch chunks
½ pound	potatoes, any kind, peeled, cut into ½-inch chunks
1 medium	carrot, chopped
¼ cup	milk
3 tablespoons	unsalted butter, melted
¾ teaspoon	salt
¼ teaspoon	freshly grated nutmeg freshly ground black pepper

1. Bring a large pot of water to a boil. Add a few pinches of salt and then drop in the rutabaga; cook for 10 minutes. Add the potato and carrot; cook until everything is tender, 15 to 20 more minutes. Drain.

2. Heat the milk in a small saucepan, but do not boil.

3. Mash the rutabaga and potato with the butter until smooth, adding a little of the warm milk at a time until the mixture reaches the consistency you like. Stir in the salt, nutmeg, and pepper to taste. Serve hot.

The Crop

HARVEST WEEK 17, 1998, NEWSLETTER

The year 1998 has been a season of rain. An impact of rain was that, with all the mud, we had to hold some crops in the greenhouse way past the optimum transplanting time. This had various ramifications: seedlings became leggy and rootbound, thus more prone to transplant shock; some seedlings became so advanced that we simply had to discard them; and root crops, such as beets (to a minor degree) and rutabaga (to a great degree), matured in unusual shapes due to their early prolonged confinement. Some of you will see flagrant evidence of this phenomenon when you receive your rutabaga in the next week or two.

Sunchokes
(Jerusalem Artichokes)

Jerusalem artichokes, more aptly called sunchokes, aren't from Jerusalem and are not artichokes. These vegetables, native to the United States, look a lot like ginger root and not at all like artichokes. Harvested in the fall, or over-wintered and harvested in the spring, sunchokes are the knobby tubers that are sliced or broken from the extensive root system of a tall, perennial sunflower. Eaten raw, they are crisp and refreshing like water chestnuts. Cooked, they are moist, sweet, and starchy. Their nutty flavor reminds some people of globe artichokes and reminds others of asparagus.

Storage

Although sunchokes can overwinter in the ground, they store poorly after they've been harvested because of their delicate skins. If you can't eat them right away, keep unwashed tubers in a perforated plastic bag in your refrigerator crisper drawer for up to two weeks. If the skin looks shriveled after you take sunchokes out of storage, rehydrate them in a bowl of cold water.

Handling

Rinse sunchokes under cold water, scrubbing gently with a brush if dirt fills the cracks in the skin. Whether you eat them raw or cooked, you may want to leave the skin on. The skin is thin and nutritious and, during cooking, retains nutrients and holds the tuber together. If you want to remove the skin, you'll find it relatively easy to slip off after cooking. Remember that contact with the air causes the flesh of raw sunchokes to discolor, so soak sliced or skinned raw tubers briefly in a mixture of 2 tablespoons lemon juice and 1 quart water.

Culinary Uses

Be careful not to leave sunchokes unattended when cooking, because they can abruptly go from firm and tender to mushy. Also, don't cook cut or peeled sunchokes in aluminum or iron cookware, as it can discolor the flesh. Like potatoes, sunchokes complement many other flavors.

- ❖ Use raw, sliced, or julienned sunchokes in salads or on a tray with other raw vegetables.
- ❖ Steam, boil, bake, or mash sunchokes with butter or olive oil and lemon

Our Cook

HARVEST WEEK 19, 1994, NEWSLETTER

I notice that the spring-dug sunchokes hold up better to boiling than the more tender fall sunchokes, which tend to dissolve. With the spring crop, my favorite preparation method is to boil them, with the skins on, until they're tender with no crunch left. Serve them with ghee or olive oil and a little salt. With the fall crop, I opt for roasting, which really enhances the sweetness of sunchokes.

juice as you would potatoes. Disguise them by mashing them and using to thicken soups or stews.

❖ Make sunchoke french fries.

❖ Slice sunchokes 1/4 inch thick and sauté in oil with salt until lightly browned, or stir-fry them.

❖ Roast whole sunchokes alone or with other root vegetables in a 425° F oven until tender, 30 to 40 minutes.

Partners for Sunchokes*

❖ Anise, bay leaf, chervil, chives, coriander, dill, fennel leaves or seeds, garlic, ginger, mace, mint, parsley, rosemary, sage, tarragon, thyme;

❖ Lemon, sunflower oil, olive oil, vinegar;

❖ Butter, cream;

❖ Celery, leeks, onions, potatoes.

*See Louise Frazier's Complementary Herbs & Spices chart, page 345, for suggestions.

Garlicky Sunchoke Salad
with Dill and Feta

This refreshing salad is the perfect side to a heavy meal, and with some good bread it makes a great lunch. Topped with an attractive and flavorful garnish of sliced radish and crumbled feta cheese, it's just the sort of dish that gets people talking: "What is this crisp, delicious veggie?" *Angelic Organics Kitchen* (adapted from *Madison Herb Society Cookbook*).

SERVES 4

2 1/2 cups	thinly sliced sunchokes (about 8 sunchokes)
1/2 cup	chopped onion (about 1/2 medium onion)
2–3 teaspoons	minced garlic (about 1 large clove)

1/4 cup	olive oil
1/3 cup	cider vinegar
3 tablespoons	chopped fresh dill or 1 1/2 tablespoons dried dill
1 1/2 teaspoons	chopped fresh tarragon or 1 teaspoon dried tarragon
1/2 teaspoon	salt
	freshly ground black pepper
	sliced radish
	crumbled feta cheese

1. Combine the sunchokes, onion, and garlic in a bowl. Add the oil, vinegar, dill, tarragon, and salt and pepper to taste. Toss well.

2. Marinate in the refrigerator for 8 to 12 hours, stirring occasionally.

3. When ready to serve, garnish with sliced radish and crumbled feta cheese.

The Crop

FARM NEWS, 1994

Sunchokes are often dug in the early spring instead of the fall. Farmers give two reasons for a spring sunchoke harvest. First, these crops can survive the winter, so why not let them take care of themselves for a while and give farmers a break? Second, the winter freeze converts the starch to sugar in the sunchokes, making for a tastier crop. But since we don't make early spring deliveries, we opt for the fall flavor compromise.

The Crop

Jerusalem artichokes. What are they? Their Latin name gives a clue about what's going on. *Helianthus tuberosa* literally means a sunflower that forms a tuber. A couple of alternative names for the Jerusalem artichoke, sunchoke and sunroot, achieve more accuracy. Here's one guess as to the origin of the weird name: Girasole, the Italian word for sunflower, was spoken slowly and deliberately by an Italian gardener showing off this tuber to a non-Italian-speaking gardener who misheard the word as "Jerusalem." The artichoke bit is harder to figure, except that this vegetable—when boiled or steamed until tender—does have a vaguely "artichoke-y" flavor.

Sunchoke Salad
with Alfalfa, Carrot, and Tarragon

The most common comments you'll receive when you serve this salad are "how wonderfully refreshing!," and "this is so delightfully different!" At least that's what we hear when we serve this dish. It's the perfect salad to accompany a quiche. You can of course include more salad greens—regular red leaf or romaine are fine. Just be sure to double the dressing; if you don't use it all, it's good to have extra around. *Angelic Organics Kitchen* (adapted from *The Harrowsmith Salad Garden*).

SERVES 4 TO 6

1 cup	thinly sliced sunchoke (about 3 medium sunchokes)
	juice of 1 lemon (about 3 tablespoons)
1 1/2 cups	young chicory or dandelion greens plus more to taste
1/2 cup	grated carrot
1/2 cup	alfalfa sprouts
1/4 cup	extra virgin olive oil
2 tablespoons	white wine vinegar
3 tablespoons	finely chopped scallions
2 tablespoons	finely chopped fresh tarragon
1 tablespoon	freshly ground horseradish root
1 small	clove garlic, minced (about 1/2 teaspoon)
	salt
	freshly ground black pepper

1. Place the sunchokes in a bowl; add the lemon juice and enough water to cover (this will prevent the sunchokes from turning brown while you prepare the remaining ingredients).

2. Toss the greens, carrots, and sprouts in a large bowl. Set aside.

3. Whisk the remaining ingredients in a small bowl, adding salt and pepper to taste.

4. Drain the sunchokes and add them to the other vegetables; toss. Pour the dressing over the top and toss until everything is well combined.

Sautéed Sunchokes

An easy yet absolutely delicious way to cook up some sunchokes is to sauté them in butter. This is a great alternative to potatoes on the dinner plate, and just as versatile. You'll surely be asked, "What do you do to your potatoes? They're so good." *Angelic Organics Kitchen* (adapted from *The Victory Garden Cookbook*).

SERVES 4

3 tablespoons	butter
1 1/2 teaspoons	vegetable oil
1 pound	sunchokes (about 8 sunchokes), sliced into 1/-inch rounds
2 tablespoons	minced fresh parsley, divided
	salt
	freshly ground black pepper

1. Heat the butter and oil in a skillet over medium-high heat. Add the sunchokes and 1 tablespoon of the parsley; cook, turning frequently, until the sunchokes are lightly browned on the outside and tender inside, 4 to 6 minutes.

2. Season with salt and pepper to taste and garnish with the remaining parsley.

Overheard

FARMER #1: You always milked?

BOONE COUNTY FARMER: I went to college, then I taught for two years. I've been milking ever since. About twenty years now.

FARMER #1: Which do you prefer, milking or teaching?

BOONE COUNTY FARMER: You kidding? Who would teach when they can milk?

Sweet Potatoes

The sweet potato is a member of the morning glory family and has its origins in the American West Indies. These lush, vining plants spend the summer collecting and funneling energy into their roots, culminating in a fall crop of beautiful, bronze tubers. The sweet potato's rich and creamy orange flesh and earthy, sweet flavor is incredibly versatile, lending itself to both sweet and savory dishes. It also ranks as one of the most nutritionally complete vegetables, proving that it is more than just a pretty potato.

Storage

Keep unwashed sweet potatoes in a cool, dark place, such as a loosely closed paper bag in a cupboard or cool basement, and use them within a few months. Do not store sweet potatoes in the refrigerator; cold temperatures can darken the potatoes and will adversely affect their taste. While rugged in appearance, sweet potatoes do not keep as long as regular potatoes because their fairly thin skins make them subject to spoilage. At room temperature, sweet potatoes should be used within two months.

Handling

Scrub sweet potatoes gently before cooking. Peel them if you will be eating them raw; otherwise, leave the skins on, as they are a great source of flavor, texture, and nutrients. If you will be puréeing or mashing them, bake or boil them whole and then remove the skins.

Culinary Uses

Because of their natural sweetness, sweet potatoes are well complemented by savory or spicy ingredients. On the other hand, their sweetness can be accented by sweet spices and used as a wonderful base for desserts, such as pies, cookies, puddings, and quick breads.
❖ Try raw sweet potatoes cut into sticks for dipping, or grate them into salads.

Our Cook

Sweet potatoes are a wonderful and versatile vegetable. I remember that as a child we would roast whole sweet potatoes, slice them in half crossways, and top them with a little pat of butter. I would eat the sweet potato out of my hand like it was an ice cream cone. In college, I started treating myself to a Friday night dinner of sweet potato oven fries, sliced into thin shoestrings and broiled on a pan with a little oil and salt. I could easily fill up on nothing but those tasty fries.

Sweet potato plants love hot weather, so they flourish in Kansas, where I was born and raised. The lovely vines are heart shaped and trail beautifully—a sweet potato patch is a gorgeous mass of green valentines.

- Bake whole sweet potatoes (pierce them with a knife in a few places) at 400°F until soft in the center, 45 to 60 minutes depending on size.
- Boil whole sweet potatoes in salted water until very tender, 25 to 40 minutes.
- Add 1/2-inch-cubed potatoes to stews for the final 20 minutes of cooking
- Sauté or fry 1/2-inch slices of sweet potatoes in oil until nicely browned on both sides and fork-tender.
- Use sweet potatoes to add special sweetness and texture to recipes in the same way as sliced carrots.
- Substitute puréed sweet potatoes for pumpkin in many recipes.

Partners for Sweet Potatoes*

- Allspice, basil, chile, cinnamon, coriander, cumin, curry powder, dill, ginger, mustard, nutmeg, parsley, sage, tarragon, thyme, vanilla;
- Apple cider vinegar, balsamic vinegar, lemon juice, lime juice, nut oils, olive oil, toasted sesame oil;
- Butter, sharp or tangy or pungent cheeses;
- Beans, cooking greens, garlic, hot and sweet peppers, leeks, onions;
- Apples, coconut, fruit juices, pineapple;
- Hazelnuts, pecans, sesame seeds, sunflower seeds, toasted pumpkin seeds, walnuts;
- Brown sugar, honey, maple syrup, molasses.

*See Louise Frazier's Complementary Herbs & Spices chart, page 345, for suggestions.

Oven Sweet Potato Chips

This is a very simple and satisfying way to prepare sweet potatoes. You'll want to have plenty of these chips on hand for your next party or road trip or . . . well, you'll just want to have them around all the time. They are addictive and utterly irresistible. *Friend of the Farm.*

SERVES 3 TO 4

2 large	sweet potatoes, scrubbed well
1/4 cup	olive oil
1–2 teaspoons	dried red pepper flakes (optional)
1/2 teaspoon	salt

1. Preheat the oven to 400°F. Line a baking sheet with parchment paper or waxed paper.

2. Slice the sweet potatoes into rounds as thin as you can get them (a mandoline works best if you have one).

3. Place the sweet potatoes in a bowl. Add the oil, pepper flakes, and salt. Toss until the sweet potatoes are well coated.

4. Spread the rounds on the baking sheet and bake until they are browned, crispy chips, about 20 minutes.

Sweet Potato Enchiladas

Irresistible and comforting, these enchiladas are also easy to make. This is a weekday meal you can throw together after work and be completely satisfied. Prepare the sauce while the potatoes are cooking, and the rest comes together quickly. Sweet potatoes make a unique yet fabulous filling. If you'd like, add a cup of cooked chorizo at the end of step 4. We provide a recipe for Enchilada Sauce below, but you can use your favorite recipe or brand. *Friend of the Farm*.

SERVES 4 TO 6

3 medium	sweet potatoes (about 1 pound)
3 tablespoons	butter
2 medium	onions, diced
3 cloves	garlic, minced (about 1½ teaspoons)
2 teaspoons	ground cumin
2 teaspoons	fresh oregano or 1 teaspoon dried oregano
1 teaspoon	ground coriander
1 teaspoon	salt
12	corn tortillas
1 recipe	Enchilada Sauce or 4 cups prepared enchilada sauce
1 cup	grated sharp cheddar cheese

1. Preheat the oven to 350° F. Lightly grease a 9 x 13-inch baking dish.

2. Bake the sweet potatoes on a baking sheet until soft, 40 to 50 minutes. Let cool, and then peel and mash.

3. Melt the butter in a medium skillet over medium-high heat. Add the onions; sauté until translucent, 5 to 7 minutes. Stir in the garlic and cook for 1 more minute.

4. Stir in the cumin, oregano, coriander, and salt; cook, stirring constantly, for 2 minutes. Add the mashed sweet potatoes and cook for 2 minutes longer. Remove from heat.

5. Wrap the tortillas in a dish towel and place in a steamer basket over boiling water for about 10 minutes.

6. Fill each tortilla with about ⅓ cup of the sweet potato filling and roll up. Place the filled tortillas in the prepared baking dish. Pour the sauce over the top and sprinkle with the cheese. Bake until the sauce is bubbling and the cheese is melted, 20 to 25 minutes.

Enchilada Sauce

MAKES ABOUT 4 CUPS

1 tablespoon	vegetable oil
1 medium	onion, minced
1 tablespoon	chili powder
2 teaspoons	ground cumin
2 teaspoons	fresh oregano or 1 teaspoon dried oregano
8 cloves	garlic, minced (about 1 tablespoon)
4 cups	puréed tomatoes
	salt

1. Heat the oil in a medium skillet over medium heat. Add the onion, chili powder, cumin, and oregano; cook, stirring, for 5 minutes. Stir in the garlic and continue to sauté until the onion is soft, 2 to 3 more minutes.

2. Add the tomatoes and a pinch of salt. Cook over low heat until flavors are fully developed, 30 to 45 minutes. Season with more salt to taste.

Our Cook

When I was still in grammar school my dad was something of a backyard vegetable gardener. Just barely. One year he'd put in a few carrots, another year some zucchini. One year tomatoes volunteered, magically rising from our compost pile. That compost pile, Dad's project, was quite a provider. One year baby bunnies emerged from a hole dug into it. (But I guess in that case credit goes to our escaped and expecting rabbit, not my dad.)

Sweet Potato Samosas

Samosas are East Indian savory stuffed pastries that are traditionally fried and served by street vendors as snacks. This version uses a rich cream cheese pastry and is baked instead of fried. In India, samosas are most often filled with potatoes and peas or sometimes with meat. But in this recipe, you'll bite through the little half-moon-shaped pastry into a luscious sweet potato filling. These samosas are delicious either as a snack or as an hors d'oeuvre, and they can also be made ahead of time and frozen—just make sure to freeze them before baking. The dipping sauce is optional, but we highly recommend it! *Friend of the Farm.*

MAKES ABOUT 40 SAMOSAS

Cream Cheese Pastry

8 ounces	cream cheese, softened
1 cup	butter, softened
2 cups	all-purpose flour
1/4 teaspoon	kosher salt or sea salt

Sweet Potato Filling

1/4 cup	olive oil
1 large	onion, chopped
	juice of 1 lime (about 2 tablespoons)
1 teaspoon	grated fresh ginger
1 clove	garlic, minced (about 1/2 teaspoon)
1/2 teaspoon	salt
1/4 teaspoon	ground cardamom
4 medium	sweet potatoes, baked, peeled, and mashed

Green Dipping Sauce (optional)

1 cup	whole-milk yogurt
1/2 cup	loosely packed cilantro leaves
1/2 cup	fresh mint leaves
1	jalapeño pepper, seeded, chopped
2 cloves	garlic
dash	salt

1. To prepare the pastry, beat the cream cheese and butter together in a mixing bowl until smooth and creamy. Gradually work in the flour and salt until the mixture comes together in a ball. Wrap in plastic, flatten, and refrigerate for at least 1 hour. (You can make this dough up to 3 days ahead of time and refrigerate or freeze it for up to a month.)

2. To prepare the filling, heat the oil in a large skillet over medium heat. Add the onion; sauté until golden, 15 to 20 minutes. Add the lime juice, ginger, garlic, salt, and cardamom; continue cooking until onions are soft and translucent, 2 more minutes.

3. Transfer the onion mixture to a bowl. Add the mashed sweet potato and combine well. Set aside to cool (if the filling is too warm, the dough won't hold up well).

4. Preheat the oven to 375° F. Line a baking sheet with parchment paper or waxed paper.

5. Roll the dough on a floured surface to about 1/8 inch thick. Using about a 3-inch round cookie cutter or biscuit cutter, cut circles in the dough as close together as possible. Set the dough circles aside as you make more. Refrigerate the dough scraps, re-roll when chilled, and cut more circles. If the rounds soften too much, chill them before filling.

6. Place a scant tablespoon of the sweet potato filling in the center of a dough circle. Fold the circle in half to form a half-moon shape. Tightly seal the edges and place on the parchment-lined baking sheet. Repeat with remaining filling and dough. Bake until the edges are lightly golden, about 20 minutes.

7. While the samosas are baking, make the dipping sauce: combine all sauce ingredients in a food processor or blender and process until smooth.

8. Serve the samosas warm or at room temperature.

Sweet Potato, Broccoli, and Tomato Stew

Make this tasty, one-pot vegetable stew and you'll have dinner on the table in no time and with little mess. Put your kids or even your dog on this simple project and go relax—dinner will be served within the hour no matter what. This stew will go well with your favorite corn bread. *Angelic Organics Kitchen.*

SERVES 4

2 tablespoons	olive oil
1 large	onion, sliced
4 cloves	garlic, thinly sliced
1 28-ounce can	stewed tomatoes
2 cups	cooked or canned garbanzo beans, drained
1½ cups	chicken or vegetable stock or water
3 medium	sweet potatoes (about 1 pound), cubed
1 medium	head broccoli, cut into large chunks (about 2 cups)
	salt
	freshly ground black pepper

1. Heat the oil in a soup pot over medium heat. Add the onion; cook until soft, about 5 minutes. Stir in the garlic and cook for 1 more minute.

2. Add the tomatoes, garbanzo beans, stock, and sweet potatoes. Simmer, partially covered, for 15 minutes. Add the broccoli, cover, and simmer until the sweet potatoes and broccoli are tender, about 5 minutes. Season with salt and pepper to taste.

The Crop

HARVEST WEEK 15, 1997, NEWSLETTER
Here we are in Week 15, the three-quarter mark, with tomatoes almost behind us and peppers and eggplant not far behind the tomatoes.. Now the winter squash, roots, and fall greens will dominate your box.

Sweet Potato Pancakes

Serve these for breakfast or as a side dish. Small, even tiny, pancakes, topped with spicy pineapple salsa or something creative of your choosing, make ideal hors d'oeuvres. *Friend of the Farm.*

MAKES ABOUT 20 3½- TO 4-INCH PANCAKES

6 medium	sweet potatoes (about 2 pounds), peeled and grated
1 medium	red onion, thinly sliced or finely chopped
1 cup	all-purpose flour
3 large	0eggs, lightly beaten
3 tablespoons	olive oil
½ cup	milk
½ teaspoon	salt
¼ teaspoon	freshly ground black pepper
½ cup	vegetable oil

1. Combine the sweet potatoes and onion in a large bowl. Add the flour, eggs, and olive oil; mix well. Stir in the milk, salt, and pepper.

2. Heat the vegetable oil in a heavy skillet over medium heat. Test the heat by dropping a small amount of batter in the pan—if the oil immediately bubbles up around the batter, it has reached the proper temperature. Be careful not to let the oil overheat and smoke.

3. Using a ladle, ½ cup measuring cup, or large spoon, drop the pancake batter into the hot oil and then lightly press it into a pancake shape with a spatula. Cook until pancakes are golden brown on the bottom, about 5 minutes, then flip them and cook until brown on the other side, 5 minutes. Remove pancakes and drain on paper towels. Serve immediately or keep them warm in the oven.

The Crew

HARVEST WEEK 18, 1997, NEWSLETTER
Harvested and washed thousands and thousands of pounds of roots and squash. Your vegetables will be snug in storage when the rains, winds, and frosts arrive. Packed 570 boxes.

Sweet Dumpling Squash

Delicata

Acorn Squash

Winter Squash

Pie Pumpkin

Red Kuri

Spaghetti Squash

Butternut

After arriving home on a cold, snowy night, nothing beats a dinner of winter squash, baked until crusty and caramelized, filled with butter and maple syrup. Winter squash is a cousin of the ubiquitous zucchini, but their growing patterns are different. Summer squash swell from blossom to fruit in a matter of days, while winter varieties absorb energy from the sun and soil for months on their way to harvest—no wonder they are such a good comfort food. The dense, sweet flesh of winter squash brings the light and warmth of a whole summer to your winter table.

Winter Squash Grown by Angelic Organics

Acorn squash are mildly sweet and have orange flesh with green-black skin. They are acorn-shaped with distinctive heavy ribbing.

Sweet dumpling squash are small and teacup-shaped with very sweet and tender orange flesh. The skin is ivory with dark green stripes. These are good squash to stuff.

Delicata squash are oblong and cream-colored with

dark green stripes and flecks along their length. Their highly sweet flavor makes them good for baking and also for stuffing. The thin skin of delicata is often tender enough to eat.

Butternut squash have tan skin and a shape reminiscent of a peanut. They have bright orange flesh and are sweet and moist. Without anyone knowing the difference, butternut squash can be substituted for part or all of the pumpkin in pumpkin pie.

Spaghetti squash have pale yellow skin and an oblong shape. The flesh of this squash is stringy like spaghetti. They are often baked or boiled and then the mildly sweet flesh is scooped out and topped with sauce.

Buttercup squash, also known as kabocha squash, have a square or rounded shape and are dark green. The deep-orange, fiberless flesh is quite sweet. Buttercup squash have a gray "button" on the blossom end.

Red kuri squash, a type of hubbard squash, are medium-size, teardrop-shaped red squashes that are especially good for pies and purées.

Pie pumpkins are about the size and shape of an under-inflated volleyball and have a thick stem and deep-orange flesh and skin.

Cha-Cha squash are medium-size, dark green squash with a slightly flat-round shape and a very sweet and nutty flavor.

Storage

Store winter squash in a cool, dry, dark place with good ventilation. (A porch or garage can work well as long as you don't let them freeze.) They should keep for up to a month or more, depending on the variety. (Delicata, pie pumpkins, buttercup, and red kuri have a shorter storage life than acorn, sweet dumpling, and butternut squash.) You can also incorporate winter squash into a beautiful arrangement for your table. They won't keep quite as long at room temperature, but if they're already on your table, you might be inspired to eat them more quickly. Once squash has been cut, you can wrap the pieces in plastic and store them in the refrigerator for five to seven days.

Handling

Do be careful when preparing winter squash, especially when the cutting requires a particularly large knife. The amount of force you must exert to cut these gentle giants means that any slippage could cause a bad, bad accident. So be slow and cautious and be sure that you have a stable working surface.

Depending on your recipe, you may need to have peeled, uncooked chunks. It can

A Shareholder

Last night a woman called the farm and said, "I had some of your squash at the home of one of your shareholders, and I've never had anything like it in my life. I just couldn't believe it. I had a sense of well-being afterwards that I have never gotten from food before."
I said, "Yeah, some of our stuff is like that this year. I don't quite understand it either. Maybe it's the Biodynamic influence. It has kind of startled me, too."

—FARMER JOHN

be difficult to do this with most winter squash, but butternut is the easiest variety to process raw. Cut the butternut into quarters, then peel and chop. If you don't have a butternut squash but must have chunks, use the pre-baking method: first, pierce the squash to allow heat to escape while it is in the oven, then bake the squash whole at 350° F until it is just barely tender to the poke of the finger, 20 to 30 minutes. This softens the shell and makes cutting and peeling much easier.

You can very easily make a purée from any type of squash. Mash the cooked squash with a fork or potato masher, or for the smoothest of purées run the cooked flesh through a food mill or food processor.

Culinary Uses

* To bake winter squash: cut squash in half, scoop out the seeds and pulp, and place the halves, cut-side down, on a glass baking dish filled with about a half inch of water. Bake at 350° F until the halves are completely soft and just starting to collapse (45 minutes to 1 hour or more, depending on size). Remove them from the oven, fill with butter, seasonings, or fillings, and serve them in the shell.
* Top baked squash halves with butter, maple syrup, and nuts.
* Or, stuff them with a savory grain filling.
* Harness the soul-warming qualities of winter squash by cooking it into stews and soups.
* Don't forget to try winter squash in pies and baked goods. It can be substituted for pumpkin or sweet potatoes in dessert recipes with wonderful results.

Partners for Winter Squash*

* Allspice, celery leaves, chile, cloves, coriander, cumin, curry, garlic, ginger, marjoram, oregano, parsley, red pepper flakes, rosemary, sage, thyme;
* Olive oil, sunflower seed oil;
* Butter, cream, Fontina cheese, Gruyère cheese, Parmesan cheese, Pecorino cheese, Romano cheese;
* Leeks, onions, quince, radicchio;
* Apple, lime, pear;
* Toasted squash seeds, pecans, walnuts;
* Brown sugar, coconut milk, lemongrass, wild rice.

*See Louise Frazier's Complementary Herbs & Spices chart, page 345, for suggestions.

Our Cook

Being a Southerner and all, I used to think of winter squash as an oddly shaped sweet potato. Several long winters have taught me the value of its more traditional uses in casseroles, stews, and stuffings. Squash seem to crave pairings with other substantial foods like grains, and the results will certainly get you through an hours-long outdoor farm auction in mid-January. (Yes, this happened to me.) Even though I've come to appreciate winter squash in its own right, I still secretly substitute delicata squash in my favorite sweet potato recipes.

Farmer John Writes

The soil under the sweet clover twinkled. The soil was pulsing with light, rejoicing in a sort of operatic celebration of life . . . I remember something like joy. Whether it was my joy, or the soil's joy, or a shared joy, I really don't know. But there was a great joy down there.

—FROM JOHN'S BOOK *FARMER JOHN ON GLITTER & GREASE*

Nice fields! As we approach season's end, the bug pressure and heat have let up and the remaining crops are looking the best they have all season. There are beautiful scallions, kale, arugula, daikon, carrots, radishes, dill, celeriac, Brussels sprouts, kohlrabi, rutabaga, parsley, sage, thyme, and young romaine lettuce. Broccoli will be a close call. It will depend on the weather. You'll receive at least small cabbage, maybe dandelion greens, and probably spinach. There are still leeks, a few potatoes, a little garlic, a few dry onions, and ample squash. And we have lots of greens in the greenhouse.

This crop report makes me feel good. You know what they said in King Arthur: "As the king goes, so goes the land." (I think this was from King Arthur, and I think that's what they said.) I personally have always been more conscious of the opposite influence: "As the land goes, so goes the king."

—FARMER JOHN

A Shareholder

We had a splendid time at the open house. Our two boys had a blast seeing the draft horses, goats, and ducks. 'Twas a delight to view the fields of veggie dreams. We've named our pumpkins Sparky and Spunky. Thanks again for doing all that you do.

Spicy Coconut Pumpkin

Pumpkin and curry powder are ideal mates. Combined with ginger, coconut milk, and a hint of cardamom, this dish is loaded with flavor and will bring praise to your table. For a hearty meal, enjoy this over basmati rice accompanied by kale and chutney. *Angelic Organics Kitchen* (adapted from *The World in Your Kitchen*).

SERVES 3 TO 4

3 tablespoons	butter
1 tablespoon	vegetable oil
1 zarge	onion, thinly sliced (about 2 cups)
1 tablespoon	minced fresh ginger
2 to 3 teaspoons	curry powder
1 teaspoon	finely chopped jalapeño or Serrano pepper
1/2 teaspoon	ground cloves
1/4 teaspoon	ground cardamom
1 1/2 pounds	pie pumpkin (about 1/2 medium or 1 small pie pumpkin), peeled, seeded, cut into 1-inch pieces
1 1/2 cups	coconut milk
1 tablespoon	raisins
1 teaspoon	maple syrup or brown sugar
	salt
	freshly ground black pepper

1. Heat the butter and oil in a heavy pan over medium heat. Add the onion; sauté until lightly browned, about 20 minutes. Add the ginger; cook for 3 more minutes.

2. Stir in the curry powder, jalapeño, cloves, and cardamom; cook for 2 minutes, stirring constantly.

3. Add the pumpkin chunks, coconut milk, raisins, and maple syrup. Cover; cook over low heat until the pumpkin is tender, about 30 minutes. Uncover, and if the sauce is thin, let the coconut milk boil away until the mixture thickens to your liking. Season with salt and pepper to taste.

Our Cook

My first cooking experience was making stuffed acorn squash in the kitchen of my freshman dorm. I had randomly selected the recipe from the *Moosewood Cookbook,* which all my college friends raved about. I had never actually eaten winter squash and only vaguely knew what it was, so the pre-meal shopping trip was a bit mystifying. Nevertheless, I charged bravely ahead, working with a shoddy assortment of pots and utensils left behind by former students who had moved on to better things. It turned out awful. I wasn't even offended when my boyfriend at the time refused to eat it. The friend who had recommended the cookbook from whence it came was a bit more polite (subdued?), but she did not polish off her portion—not by a long shot. My, how everything grows and changes.

Indian Squash and Split Peas

The winter squash is far more versatile than the standard halved-and-baked-and-sweetened version (good as that is) would have you believe. Here is an excellent savory way to use up some butternut, acorn, or red kuri squash. Served with basmati rice and your favorite greens, this makes the perfect winter meal. *Angelic Organics Kitchen* (adapted from *The New Laurel's Kitchen*).

SERVES 4 TO 6

1/3 cup	shredded unsweetened coconut
1 1/2 teaspoons	ground cumin
1/2 cup	very hot water
1/2 cup	yellow split peas
1 teaspoon	fennel seeds
2 cups	water, divided
1 teaspoon	salt, divided
2 pounds	winter squash (1 large butternut, 2 medium acorn, or 4 to 5 delicata or buttercup), peeled, seeded, cut into 3/4-inch cubes, about 6 cups)
1/2 teaspoon	turmeric
1 tablespoon	ghee or oil
1 teaspoon	black mustard seeds
1/2 teaspoon	dried red pepper flakes

1. Stir the coconut and cumin into the hot water; set aside.

2. Combine the split peas and fennel seeds in a saucepan. Add 1 cup of water. Partially cover and boil until peas are soft, about 30 minutes. (The peas will absorb most but not all of the water.) Remove from heat. If necessary, add more water to reach the consistency of oatmeal. Add 1/2 teaspoon of the salt to the cooked peas and stir well.

3. Place the squash in a large skillet. Add the remaining 1 cup of water and the turmeric. Bring to a boil, reduce heat, and cover. Simmer for 10 minutes, then uncover and simmer until most of the water has evaporated and the squash is soft, 10 to 20 minutes. Stir in the remaining 1/2 teaspoon salt.

4. Purée the coconut and its soaking water in a blender or food processor until very smooth.

5. Combine the peas, coconut, and squash in a saucepan over medium-high heat; simmer until mixture is heated through, about 3 minutes.

6. In a small, heavy pan, heat the ghee or oil over medium-high heat; add the mustard seeds and red pepper flakes. When the seeds start popping, turn off the heat; cover and let stand until the popping stops. Add the seeds to the squash mixture; stir well.

The Crop

HARVEST WEEK 17, 1998, NEWSLETTER

Our subsoil is clay. Because it retains moisture in dry years, this is usually a blessing. However, in the rare years when there is excess moisture, it becomes like wet putty. Roots cannot flourish in this environment. Our winter squash crop, which usually does extremely well, yielded about one-third as much squash as normal this year. Furthermore, a considerable portion of the squash we did harvest was prone to spoilage.

A remedy for waterlogged soil is to grow deep rooting legumes—such as clover and alfalfa—and let their tap roots become firmly and deeply established over three to four years. These roots will create channels through the subsoil, enhancing drainage, providing a little oxygen, and adding some microbial activity.

Acorn Squash Salad
with Cilantro, Ginger, and Maple Syrup

Here is a unique way to prepare and serve acorn squash. Mixed with this somewhat eclectic dressing, which perfectly complements and enhances the squash, and then served on bed of lightly dressed salad greens, this main course dish will result in many ooohs and aaahs at the table. If you can't find candied ginger, you can use 1 tablespoon of minced fresh ginger. *Angelic Organics Kitchen*.

SERVES 4 TO 6

2 medium	acorn squash
1/2 cup	olive oil
1/3 cup	minced fresh cilantro
6 tablespoons	orange or tangerine juice
3 tablespoons	maple syrup
2 tablespoons	minced candied ginger
1/2 teaspoon	salt
1/8 teaspoon	cayenne pepper

salad greens (one handful per serving), washed, dried, lightly dressed in extra virgin olive oil

1. Preheat the oven to 375° F.

2. Cut the squash in half and scoop out the seeds. Place the squash halves cut-sides down on a baking sheet. Bake until tender, 30 to 45 minutes depending on size. Cool completely, scoop out the soft flesh, and roughly chop. Place the squash in a bowl and set aside.

3. Combine the olive oil, cilantro, orange juice, maple syrup, ginger, salt, and cayenne in a blender or food processor. Blend well.

4. Pour the dressing over the squash and toss gently. Chill for at least 1 hour to allow the flavors to combine.

5. Serve on a bed of lightly dressed greens.

Pumpkin Cheesepie

Is it a pie, or is it a cheesecake? Well, it's a little of both, and consequently it's exponentially delicious. You can see the commercial now: at the left, a man with pumpkin pie in hand; at the right, a woman with cheesecake in hand. They are walking toward each other, their eyes on their own desserts, lips smacking, and WOOPS! They collide and the pie falls on the cheesecake. Light bulbs appear above their heads and they dig in, smiling, happy, and then they fall in love. You will fall in love with this Pumpkin Cheesepie. *Angelic Organics Kitchen*.

SERVES 6 TO 8

1 1/2 cups	pumpkin purée (canned or fresh)
1 1/2 cups	vanilla wafer or graham cracker crumbs (about 45 wafers or 22 crackers)
6 tablespoons	butter, melted, divided
3/4 cup plus 1 tablespoon	sugar, divided
3	eggs
8 ounces	cream cheese, softened
2 teaspoons	ground cinnamon, divided
1 teaspoon	vanilla
1 teaspoon	ground ginger
1/2 teaspoon	freshly grated nutmeg
1/4 teaspoon	ground cloves
1 cup	sour cream

1. Preheat the oven to 350° F.

2. To prepare fresh pumpkin: cut the pumpkin in half and scoop out the seeds. Cut each half in half and lightly brush with oil. Place on a rimmed baking sheet and bake for 45 minutes, or until very tender when pierced with a butter knife. Scoop and scrape the flesh from the skin, and mash it as you would when making mashed potatoes.

3. Reduce the oven temperature to 325° F.

4. Combine the crumbs, 5 tablespoons of the butter, and 1 tablespoon sugar in a small mixing bowl. Mix well.

5. Grease the bottom of a 9-inch springform pan with the remaining 1 tablespoon butter. Press the buttered crumbs into the bottom of the pan to form a crust. Press on the crumb mixture with the bottom of a glass to form a solid, tightly packed crust.

6. Bake the crust until lightly brown, about 10 minutes. Remove from the oven and let cool. Increase the oven temperature to 450° F.

7. Reserve 2 tablespoons of the sugar. Beat the eggs

with the remaining sugar. Stir in the pumpkin purée, cream cheese, 1 teaspoon of the cinnamon, vanilla, ginger, nutmeg, and cloves. Pour the mixture into the crust; bake until the top is browned and the center is still a little jiggly, about 40 minutes.

8. Remove from oven; let stand on a rack for 5 minutes.

9. Combine the sour cream, the reserved 2 tablespoons sugar, and the remaining 1 teaspoon cinnamon. Spoon the mixture on top of the pie. Bake until browned and bubbly, about 5 minutes. Let cool; then chill before serving.

Squash and Kale
with White Bean Stew

A very hearty fall meal that only gets better the next day, this stew will fill you with warmth and energy. Note from the farm cook: a lot of people go back for seconds on this one. *Shareholder* (adapted from *Leafy Greens*).

SERVES 6

1 pound	white beans (cannellini or Great Northern), soaked overnight and drained
¼ cup	olive oil, divided
1 whole head	garlic (stem and roots removed)
1	bay leaf
1 large	onion, diced (about 1 cup)
4 cloves	garlic, thinly sliced
1 tablespoon	minced fresh sage
1 teaspoon	cumin
pinch	dried red pepper flakes
1 large	butternut squash (3 to 4 pounds), peeled, seeded, cut into 2-inch cubes
3 cups	vegetable or chicken stock or water (or more as needed)
1 pound	kale (about 10 large leaves), thick stems removed, chopped or coarsely torn
	salt
	freshly ground black pepper

1. Place the beans in a large soup pot. Add enough water to cover the beans by 2 inches. Add 2 tablespoons of the olive oil, the head of garlic, and the bay leaf; bring to a boil, partially cover, and reduce to a simmer. Simmer until the beans are very tender, 1 to 3 hours (see the bean package for cooking times; all beans differ). Drain, rinse, and drain again. Remove the garlic head (it's a great snack as you continue making your meal).

2. Heat the remaining 2 tablespoons of oil in a deep baking dish or Dutch oven. Add the onion; sauté until translucent, about 5 minutes. Stir in the sliced garlic, sage, cumin, and red pepper flakes; sauté for 1 minute more.

3. Add the squash; stir to combine. Add the stock or water (if it does not cover the squash, add a little more to cover). Bring to a simmer. Add the kale; cook until the squash and kale are tender, about 20 minutes. Season with salt and pepper to taste.

4. Stir in the beans; simmer until the beans are heated through.

Curried Winter Squash Soup

This is one of our favorite squash soups. Late in the season, when the sun seems never to shine, and the winds come, and it's cold, the farm kitchen smells of this soup. It's filling, and it warms the soul on days when the last thing you want to do is to be outside prepping the fields for next year. You can add a ham hock with the squash in step 2 for some extra flavor; just be sure to cook it for a good hour until the hock is very tender. And remember to take it out before step 3! *Angelic Organics Kitchen* (adapted from *Greene on Greens*).

SERVES 6 TO 8

3 tablespoons	unsalted butter
1 cup	chopped scallions (about 6 scallions)
1/4 cup	chopped fresh parsley
1	jalapeño pepper, seeded, finely chopped (about 1 tablespoon)
2 cloves	garlic, minced (about 1 teaspoon)
2 pounds	butternut squash (about 1/2 large squash), peeled, seeded, cubed
4 cups	chicken or vegetable stock
1 14-ounce can	whole tomatoes, chopped, or 2 cups peeled (see page 92), chopped fresh tomatoes
12 whole	fresh curry leaves (optional)
1/2 teaspoon	ground allspice
1/4 teaspoon	ground mace
pinch	freshly grated nutmeg
2 teaspoons	curry powder
	salt
	freshly ground black pepper
1/4 cup	chopped fresh parsley

1. Melt the butter in a large saucepan over medium heat. Add the scallions; sauté until soft and wilted, about 3 minutes. Stir in the parsley, jalapeño, and garlic; cook, stirring occasionally, for 5 minutes.

2. Add the squash and toss to coat it with the scallion mixture. Add the stock, tomatoes, curry leaves, allspice, mace, and nutmeg. Bring to a boil; reduce the heat and simmer, covered, until the squash is very tender, about 45 minutes. Let cool slightly.

3. Transfer the soup in batches to a blender or food processor; purée.

4. Transfer the soup back to the pot. Stir in the curry powder and add salt and pepper to taste. Return the soup to a simmer to heat through. Garnish with parsley just before serving.

Baked Squash with Kale and Pear

The pear really makes this dish shine—its unique sweetness balances the kale's earthy overtones. You can add some cooked sweet Italian sausage in step 4 if you like. This dish is also good made with apple instead of pear. *Shareholder* (adapted from *McCall's*, November 1996).

SERVES 6

	butter or oil for greasing the pan
3	acorn squash
1/2 cup	grated Parmesan cheese, divided
1/2 teaspoon	salt, divided
1/2 teaspoon	freshly ground black pepper, divided
1 1/2 tablespoons	olive oil
1 large	leek, chopped (about 2 cups)
4 cups	coarsely chopped kale
1 cup	vegetable or chicken stock
1/2	red bell pepper, cored, seeded, diced
1 teaspoon	minced garlic (about 2 cloves)
1 tablespoon	butter
1	pear, firm-ripe, peeled, halved, cored, cut in 1/2-inch pieces (about 1 cup)

1. Preheat the oven to 375° F. Lightly grease a 13 x 9-inch pan with butter or oil.

2. Cut the squash in half and scoop out the seeds. Place the squash halves cut-side down on a baking sheet; bake until tender, 30 to 45 minutes. Turn the squash halves over and sprinkle with 1/4 cup Parmesan, 1/4 teaspoon salt, and 1/4 teaspoon pepper. Bake for an additional 5 minutes.

3. Heat the oil in a large skillet over medium-high heat. Add the leeks; sauté until soft, about 5 minutes. Add the kale, stock, bell pepper, garlic, and remaining 1/4 teaspoon salt and 1/4 teaspoon pepper. Bring to boil, cover, and cook for 5 minutes. Remove the cover and increase the heat to medium-high; cook, stirring frequently, until kale is tender and the liquid evaporates, 8 to 10 minutes. Transfer the mixture to a bowl and set aside.

4. Melt the butter in a large skillet over medium-high heat. Add the pear; sauté until lightly browned and tender but not mushy, 2 to 3 minutes. Add the pear to the kale mixture and stir well. Spoon the kale and pear filling into the squash halves. Top with the remaining 1/4 cup Parmesan cheese. Bake for 10 minutes.

Pumpkin Sage Soup

Pumpkin is not just for pies. This flavorful soup is just the thing on a cool October night when the leaves are falling, the wind is blowing, and your soul needs a little boost. Sweet pumpkin and savory sage commingle, producing delightful results. This soup is superb as a meal all on its own, sprinkled with a little grated Parmesan or Swiss cheese and served with a good hunk of crusty bread. It's also the ideal start to just about any fall menu. This recipe makes a lot, but don't worry, it only gets better over the next couple days. And it freezes well. *Friend of the Farm.*

SERVES 5 TO 6

2 medium	pie pumpkins (4 to 5 pounds)
1/3 cup	olive oil
1/3 cup whole	sage leaves
1 large	onion, minced (about 1 1/2 cups)
2 cloves	garlic, minced (about 1 teaspoon)
2 1/2 quarts	vegetable or chicken stock or water
1/4 cup	minced fresh parsley
1 teaspoon	thyme or 1/2 teaspoon dried thyme
1/4 teaspoon	ground cinnamon
2 teaspoons	salt
	freshly ground black pepper

1. Preheat the oven to 375°F. Line a plate with paper towels.

2. Cut the pumpkin in half, scoop out the seeds, and place the halves cut-side down on a baking sheet. Bake until soft, 30 to 40 minutes. Let cool.

3. Meanwhile, heat the olive oil in a soup pot over medium heat. Holding one sage leaf by its stem, dip it in the oil. If it sizzles, the oil is ready; add all the sage leaves. Cook the sage leaves until they are speckled and beginning to turn a very dark green. Scoop them out and transfer them to the paper towel–lined plate.

4. Add the onions to the sage oil and sauté, stirring frequently, until lightly golden, 10 to 15 minutes. Stir in the garlic and cook for 2 additional minutes.

5. When the pumpkin is cool enough to handle, scoop out all of the flesh and chop it roughly. Add it to the soup pot; stir well. Add the stock or water, parsley, thyme, and cinnamon. Bring to a boil. Add the salt; add pepper to taste. Reduce the heat and simmer for 30 minutes.

6. Serve the soup chunky, or if you prefer a smooth soup, run it through a food mill or purée it in a blender or food processor. Garnish with the fried sage leaves.

EXTENDED SEASON

AN EMPHASIS ON PROLONGING
LATE OCTOBER to MID-DECEMBER

“This brings us to something about which I can only speak on a soul level; for Anthroposophy should never come forward to agitate for anything, should never advocate either one thing or another, but should only put forward the truth. The conclusions which a person draws with regard to his manner of living are his personal affair. Anthroposophy does not give rules, but puts forward truths. For this reason I shall never, even for fanatics, lay down any kind of law based on what an animal produces from its plant food. No dogmatic rulings shall be given in regard to vegetarianism, meat-eating and so on, for these things must entirely be a matter of personal judgment and it is really only in the sphere of individual experience that they have value. I mention this in order to avoid giving rise to the opinion that Anthroposophy entails standing for this or that kind of diet, whereas what it actually does is to enable people to understand any form of diet.”

—RUDOLPH STEINER,
FROM *MAN AS SYMPHONY OF THE CREATIVE WORD*

Overheard

ATTRACTIVE DUTCH WOMAN IN MEXICO: I can't believe I'm having such a hooker breakfast.

FARMER: Hooker breakfast? What's a hooker breakfast?

DUTCH WOMAN: Coffee and a cigarette.

Pig Newtons Did Not Save the Farm

by John Peterson

Farmer John Writes

Maybe I should live in New York, I thought. There is life here; it's the way my farm used to be. An old man passed, licking an ice cream cone. I could sell ice cream.

—FROM JOHN'S BOOK *FARMER JOHN DIDN'T KILL ANYONE UP HERE: AN UNEASY AUTOBIOGRAPHY*

(In the early '80s, my farm was hopelessly in debt. The following describes one of many ideas that my partner, Isa, and I came up with to solve the money problem.)

Isa invented Pig Newtons in her magic kitchen. We consulted mold makers and cookie bakers, box factories and trademark attorneys, the Pig Alphabet and the American Institute of Baking, gourmet cookie shops and Pig American Magazine. We scrutinized the strengths and weaknesses of the Nabisco Corporation. To save the farm, we sent Nabisco a Pig Newton in a glass case and the following letter:

October 8, 1980
Research and Development Division
Nabisco, Inc.
River Road, Deforest Avenue
Hanover, New Jersey 07936

To Whom It May Concern:

We own and operate a farm, which celebrates art and agriculture. Raising pigs is one of the main enterprises. Consequently, we are the recipients of a variety of pig paraphernalia. Upon the receipt of a pig-shaped cookie cutter, Isa Jacoby, a renowned gourmet pastry chef, proceeded to create a crisp butter cookie with a naturally sweet fig, date, and raisin filling. "Have a Pig Newton!" she said. Pig Newtons quickly became the snacktime rage of friends and family from coast to coast.

The motif of this cookie is a most exciting feature. The American public has embraced the adorable pig in countless ways, almost ensuring the success of Pig Newtons. Enclosed are two cover stories regarding the phenomenon of the pig in our culture.

The cookie presentation can fully exploit the pig theme. The package design has myriad graphic possibilities. The blister tray can be shaped to individually accommodate the cookies, affording them protection and creating a collectible item. A pig alphabet card, included in each package, would provide continuous enthusiasm for the product.

We believe that Nabisco could successfully modify this cookie for mass production and longevity. Please contact us for further consultation on this opportunity.

Sincerely,
Mr. John Peterson
Ms. Isa Jacoby

The bank, Isa, and I awaited Nabisco's reply.

October 22, 1980
Mr. John Peterson
Ms. Isa Jacoby
The Midwest Coast

Re> C-1095
Pig Newton Cookies
Dear Mr. Peterson and Ms. Jacoby:

Your submission has been reviewed by our marketing people. Unfortunately, they do not share your enthusiasm for this product.

We understand that in certain sections of the country, pigs are a treasured resource and are viewed with fondness. However, despite Miss Piggy's recent fame, in our opinion a "Pig Newton" cookie would not be a viable national product. We feel that in many parts of the country pigs still have a definite image problem.

To be frank, we believe that marketing of a "Pig Newton" cookie could adversely affect the sales of our FIG NEWTON product by creating an association between that product and the unappetizing sights and odors which are evoked in many by the depiction of a pig.

The term FIG NEWTON is a registered trademark of Nabisco. It is internationally famous and there is enormous goodwill associated with the mark. We take great pains to maintain that goodwill. Should you consider marketing your cookies regionally or having it marketed by another, we would insist that you select a name which is not confusingly similar to the trademark FIG NEWTON, a name which would not evoke an association with our product in the mind of the public or in any way damage the goodwill associated with our famous mark.

We are returning your samples and the magazines you forwarded to us under separate cover. Although we are unable to use your idea, we appreciate the opportunity of reviewing it.

Very truly yours,

(signed, a man from the Nabisco Legal Department)

To be frank, we believe that marketing of a "Pig Newton" cookie could adversely affect the sales of our Fig Newton product by creating an association between that product and the unappetizing sights and odors which are evoked in many by the depiction of a pig.

(**Note from Farmer John:** In April 2002 I spotted Fig Newmans in a health food store—a fig cookie delight developed by Paul Newman. Is Paul Newman trying to save his farm?)

Anthroposophical Nutrition

The Etheric Divide

In the nineteenth century, the practice arose of observing only the sequence of events on earth and ignoring the consequences of cosmic activity on earthly events. The scientific view remained therefore: first simpler forms, then less simple, and finally, the human being.

This is what natural science—which does not admit the etheric—gave (and gives) us as the evolution of organisms. It could not have been any other than it was and still is. Once one accepts its hypotheses—and the etheric is inadmissible—then the question is posed in such a way that earthly existence includes only what is visible. Then there is no choice but to accept the stream of evolution as exclusively physical.

This is what Darwinians do. This is what Haeckel did. And, on their assumptions, it is madness to demand more or argue about the way the science of evolution has developed. Only by adding knowledge of the etheric world can one begin to perceive what truly belongs to it. You can see then why it makes no sense to argue. Clearly, if a person wishes to remain within the parameters of natural science, he or she can do so. And they can always turn to those who speak on the basis of a different view and tell them they are talking nonsense. Having become used to a purely earthly point of view, they will say that what you speak of is not there.

If one wants to speak differently, one must first gain knowledge of the etheric world. There is no other choice then for a valid, reasonable polemic with contemporary science than to say: In your domain, you are entirely right: things can't be at all different, and there is no other conclusion. But if you want to speak with us about the things we have in mind, then you must first acquaint yourselves with the elementary processes in the cosmic ether. Then we can talk. Otherwise, we shall have no common ground of reality to stand on.

—RUDOLF STEINER, FROM *NUTRITION AND STIMULANTS*

❝The cow lying in the meadow is in actual fact spiritual substance that takes up earthly matter, absorbs it and makes it similar to itself.

When the cow dies the spiritual substance which it bears within it can be taken up by the earth together with the earthly matter to benefit the life of the whole earth. And man is right when he feels in regard to the cow: you are the true beast of sacrifice, for essentially you continually give to the earth what it needs, without which it could not continue to exist and would harden and dry up. You continually give spiritual substance to the earth and renew the inner mobility, the inner living quality of the earth.❞

—RUDOLF STEINER, *MAN AS SYMPHONY OF THE CREATIVE WORD*

Farmer John Writes

What if we get a cow? What if we get a bunch of cows? I looked over the edge of the trench again. I sort of saw a cow. I sort of saw a herd of cows. I sort of heard the hooves of cows clomping towards the waterer. The phantom cows mooed softly.

—FROM JOHN'S BOOK *FARMER JOHN ON GLITTER & GREASE*

Milk, Meat, and Plants

by Rudolf Steiner

FROM *NUTRITION AND STIMULANTS*

It is interesting to compare three kinds of food with regard to their cosmic significance: (1) milk and milk products, (2) the plant world and all that is made from it, and (3) meat. We can compare milk, plants and animals as foods when, through esoteric development, we have become more sensitive to the effects of these foods. It will then be easier to evaluate what is confirmed by a rational observation of the outer world. . . .

Now let us consider how we experience milk as a food. To occult vision milk is, for the human body, (we will limit ourselves to man) that element which binds him to the earth, to our planet. It connects him with the human race on the earth, as a member of the common species of mankind. Mankind, as regards the physical system of sheaths, forms one whole; partly owing to the production of nourishment by living beings for living beings of the same species. What is given to the human organism in milk prepares him to be a human creature of the earth, unites him with the conditions of the earth, but does not really fetter him to the earth. It makes him a citizen of the earth, but does not hinder him from being a citizen of the whole solar system.

It is different with meat. Meat is taken from that kingdom which is specifically earthly, it is not like milk taken from the actual life-process of the human or ani-

---

> Through meat diet he binds himself
> very strongly to the planet earth.

---

mal being, but it is taken from that part of the animal substance which is prepared ready for the animal. This meat really fetters man to the earth. It makes him into a creature of the earth, so that we must say that to the extent that man permeates his organism with the effects of meat in his food, he deprives himself of the forces which would enable him to free himself from the earth. Through meat diet he binds himself very strongly to the planet earth. Whilst milk enables him to belong to the earth as a transitory stage in his development, meat condemns him—unless he is raised up by something else—to make his sojourn on earth like a permanent one to which he adapts himself completely. If I decide to take milk it means: "I will sojourn on the earth so that I may fulfill my mission there but I will not exist exclusively for the earth." The will to eat meat means: "I like the earthly existence so well that I renounce all heaven and prefer to be wholly absorbed in the conditions of earthly existence."

Vegetarian diet stimulates those forces in the organism which bring man into a kind of cosmic connection with the whole of the planetary system. What man has to accomplish when he further transforms vegetarian food in his organism stimulates forces which are contained in the whole solar system, so that man in his physical sheath participates in the forces of the whole solar system; he does not become alien to them, he does not tear himself away from them. This is something which the soul in the course of its anthroposophical or esoteric development can experience, for it takes in with the plant something not pertaining to the heaviness of the earth, but to the sun, i.e., the central body of the entire planetary system. The lightness of the organism which results from a vegetarian diet lifts one out of the heaviness of the earth, and gradually one develops a capacity

> Vegetarian diet stimulates those forces in the organism which bring man into a kind of cosmic connection with the whole of the planetary system

of experience that can develop by degrees into something like a perception of taste in the human organism. It feels—this organism—as though it shared with the plants the very sunlight which accomplishes so much in them.

From what has been said you will gather that in occult, esoteric development it is of tremendous importance not to fetter oneself, as it were, to the earth, not to encumber oneself with the heaviness of the earth through the consumption of meat if it can be dispensed with in view of individual and hereditary circumstances. The ultimate decision must depend upon the personal circumstances of the individual. It will facilitate the whole development of man's life if he can refrain from eating meat. On the other hand certain difficulties will arise if a person becomes a fanatical vegetarian in the sense of rejecting milk and all milk products. In the development of the soul towards the spiritual this brings certain dangers, simply because, in avoiding milk and all milk products, a person may easily develop a love solely for that which detaches him from the earth and he may thus lose the threads which connect him with all human activities on the earth. Therefore the striving Anthroposophist should be warned not to allow himself to become a fanatical spiritual dreamer by creating the difficulty in his physical sheath which will separate it from all relationship to what is earthly and human.

> In the development of the soul towards the spiritual this brings certain dangers, simply because, in avoiding milk and all milk products, a person may easily develop a love solely for that which detaches him from the earth and he may thus lose the threads which connect him with all human activities on the earth.

Farmer John Writes

Buildings and cars seemed like fluff.

—FROM JOHN'S BOOK *FARMER JOHN ON GLITTER & GREASE*

In order that we may not become too eccentric when striving for soul development, in order that we may not become estranged from human feeling and human doings, it is well for us as pilgrims on earth to take on "ballast" through consumption of milk and milk products. And it may even be a really systematic

training for a person who is not in a position, so to speak, to live perpetually in the spiritual world and thereby become a stranger on earth, but who besides this has to fulfill his duties on earth; it can be a systematic training not to be a strict vegetarian but to take milk and milk products as well. He will thereby relate his organism, his physical sheath, to the earth and to humanity, but not fetter it to the earth and weigh it down as would be the case with eating meat.

Thus it is interesting in every way to see how these things are connected with cosmic secrets, and how through the knowledge of these cosmic secrets we can follow the actual effect of food substances in the human organism.

Rudolf Steiner's biography appears on page 360.

(Note from Farmer John: There is much controversy today about the consumption of dairy products. To take a closer look, see Dr. Thomas Cowan's article "Raw Milk" at www.AngelicOrganics.com/vegetableguide, and click on Outtakes.)

I f Steiner had been nothing but a philosopher, or theologian, or educator, or authority on Goethe, or agricultural expert, or architect, or [knower of] medicinal plants, or dramatist, or gifted artistic innovator, or inventor of eurythmy, an age that respects specialization would have reserved a special niche for him. But Steiner was all these things at the same time.

—STEWART C. EASTON IN HILMAR MOORE'S *RUDOLF STEINER'S CONTRIBUTION TO THE HISTORY AND PRACTICE OF AGRICULTURAL EDUCATION*

Welcome to the Extended Season

Late October to Mid-December

Harvest Weeks 21 to 24

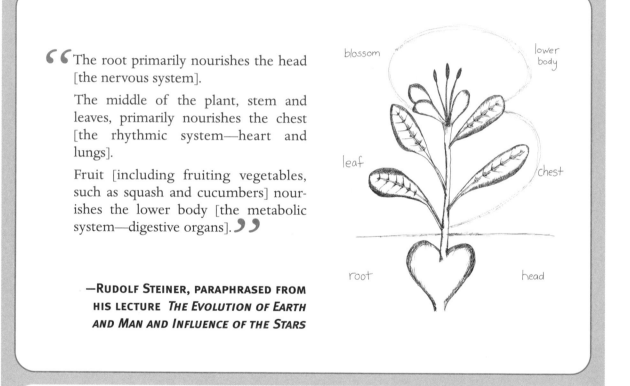

"The root primarily nourishes the head [the nervous system].

The middle of the plant, stem and leaves, primarily nourishes the chest [the rhythmic system—heart and lungs].

Fruit [including fruiting vegetables, such as squash and cucumbers] nourishes the lower body [the metabolic system—digestive organs]."

—RUDOLF STEINER, PARAPHRASED FROM HIS LECTURE *THE EVOLUTION OF EARTH AND MAN AND INFLUENCE OF THE STARS*

Forces in Food

When I eat bread, the bread works upon my head because the root elements of a plant work up into the stem. The stem, even though it is stem and grows above the ground in the air, still has root forces in it. The question is not whether something is above in the air, but whether it has any root forces. Now the leaf, the green leaf, does not have root forces. No green leaf ever appears down in the earth. In late summer and autumn, when the sun forces are no longer working so strongly, the stem can mature. But the leaf needs the strongest sun forces for it to unfold; it grows towards the sun. So we can say, the green part of the plant works particularly on heart and lungs, while the root strengthens the head.

—LECTURE BY RUDOLF STEINER, *THE EVOLUTION OF EARTH AND MAN AND INFLUENCE OF THE STARS*

Extended Season Vegetables

The contents of a vegetable box will vary from week to week and from year to year with changes in the weather, among other factors. All of the vegetables listed below are also harvested at other times of the year. (See Vegetable & Herb Availability from Angelic Organics, page 334, and the Illustrated Vegetable Identification Guide, page 336.)

Beets

Broccoli

Brussels Sprouts

Cabbage

Cauliflower

Carrots

Celeriac

Cooking Greens (Kale, Collards, Chard, Spinach, Beet Greens)

Garlic

Herbs (Sage, Thyme)

Kohlrabi

Onions

Parsnips

Potatoes

Rutabagas

Sunchokes (Jerusalem Artichokes)

Sweet Potatoes

Winter Squash

EARLY FROSTS

The two low temperatures on the autumnal equinoxes of 1974 and 1995 are the two earliest recorded frosts. I am privileged that I have experienced these two humbling events from the vantage point of the same location— this farm—and (in many ways) the same career—farming. I feel strangely honored that my fate is tied so closely to these two extreme events of weather.

Farm News

HARVEST WEEK 23, 1998, NEWSLETTER

Thoroughly cleaned all work spaces and the farmyard. Cleaned all the machinery. Moved tractors and machinery into the barns. Inventoried last season's seeds and moved seeds inside. Finished installing the heating system in the coolers, so they can handle winter storage of vegetables. Attended meetings and meetings about the winter's projects and activities.

A Diary of Extended Season Weather

Notice the variability from year to year.

Mid-November

HARVEST WEEK 22, 1997, NEWSLETTER
Fall weather. Snow, too.

HARVEST WEEK 22, 1998, NEWSLETTER
Blasting 60 m.p.h. winds and about two inches of rain caused relatively little significant damage. Buckets blew across one field, across the driveway, and across the next field. Bits of shingles peppered the farmyard. Otherwise it has been relatively mild with lows around freezing and highs in the 40s.

HARVEST WEEK 22, 2001, NEWSLETTER
We had fairly calm, pleasant weather for most of the week. There was a significant frost on Thursday night, but we caught wind of it in time to harvest plenty of that beautiful chard.

Early December

HARVEST WEEK 23, 1998, NEWSLETTER
Incredibly mild and dry with lows in the 40s and highs in the 50s or 60s.

HARVEST WEEK 23, 1999, NEWSLETTER
Rain finally fell and temperatures returned to normal with lows in the 20s and highs in the 40s.

HARVEST WEEK 23, 2000, NEWSLETTER
The cold nights of last week were just too much for those little broccoli side shoots; some of the spinach and kale even felt a nip. Last week's snow melted but we're expecting more this Wednesday or Friday. Thankfully, it warmed up a little (into the low 40s) this week, making outdoor work more pleasant.

Mid-December

HARVEST WEEK 24, 1998, NEWSLETTER
Winter finally started to arrive, dropping a trace of icy snow. Temperatures are still above normal with lows in the 20s and highs in the 40s.

HARVEST WEEK 24, 1999, NEWSLETTER
A beautiful blizzard flitted through on Sunday leaving two inches of snow. The snow then melted and the mud season arrived.

HARVEST WEEK 24, 2000, NEWSLETTER
Near zero temperatures, a foot of snow, drifts to three feet, and the coldest packing day in Angelic Organics history. But it was fun—even shoveling. We hope you picked up your vegetables before they froze.

The Crop

HARVEST WEEK 23, 1999, NEWSLETTER
Due to the unseasonably warm temperatures over the past month, many fall crops that are normally done growing by the end of October have continued to grow through the end of November. We have more broccoli, cabbage, Brussels sprouts, spinach, collards, kale, and herbs than will fit in your boxes!

Overheard

The sky is so great. All you do is look at it and go, "huh." Because you can't have an opinion about it except that it's pretty. Sure, there's bad weather, but that's not the same as the sky itself being ugly.

Extended Season Eating

We have noticed that, over the years, some of our shareholders become less inclined to pick up their vegetables as the season winds down. Maybe they are too busy with kids and school by this time, or maybe the fall crops aren't quite as enticing to them as the summer crops. At Angelic Organics, we like to give people a choice to continue. We'd much rather bring boxes to the third who really want their fall vegetables. Besides, after November 1, we have very little crew left, so we can't handle packing one thousand shareholder boxes into December.

Angelic Organics shareholders who opt to receive an Extended Season share will primarily receive storage vegetables in the boxes: potatoes, garlic, onions, winter squash, carrots, cabbage, Brussels sprouts, sweet potatoes, celeriac, sunchokes and rutabagas. Depending on how late and how hard the frosts are, they might get a nice sampling of greens as well. And we try to hold some broccoli and cauliflower for at least the first couple deliveries—the arrival of late fall weather at our farm doesn't mean that we don't have plenty of delicious produce to give!

Extended Season Farming

After a few heavy frosts, many of the crops that remain in the field wither and die. Our fields soon look barren. During a warm winter, kale and spinach may thrive late into the season, but for the most part the crops that once flourished now complete their life cycles and are incorporated back into the soil. Some plants, like beets, potatoes, celeriac, and winter squash leave their legacies in roots and fruits that we are able to store and enjoy throughout cold winter months.

Farm News

HARVEST WEEK 18, 2001, NEWSLETTER

It froze!

What froze?

It rained!

What rained?

It's warm out!

What's warm out?

What is this it, anyway, that people are talking about when they talk about the weather? What could someone substitute for it? Could someone say the weather froze?

Uh-uh.

The sky rained?

Nope.

The clouds rained?

Nah.

So it froze several nights back. I don't know what froze—other than just about everything—but it just got cold and froze.

—FARMER JOHN

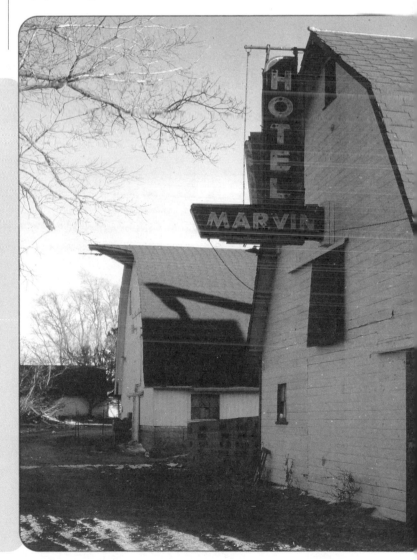

WINTER

AN EMPHASIS ON PLANNING
LATE DECEMBER to MID-MARCH

"I had a friend in my youth with whom I ate meals very often. We were fairly sensible about our food and would order what we were in the habit of thinking was good for us. Later, as it happens in life, we lost track of each other, and after some years I came to the city where he was living, and was invited to have dinner with him. And what did I see? Scales beside his plate! I said, 'What are you doing with those scales?' I knew, of course, but I wanted to hear what he would say. He said, 'I weigh the meat they bring me, to eat the right amount — the salad too.' There he was, weighing everything he should put on his plate, because science told him to. And what had happened to him? He had weaned himself completely from a healthy instinct for what he should eat and finally no longer knew! And you remember? It used to be in the book: 'a person needs from one hundred and twenty to one hundred and fifty grams of protein'; that, he had conscientiously weighed out. Later, the proper amount was estimated to be fifty grams. . . . "

—RUDOLF STEINER, FROM *NUTRITION AND HEALTH*

Farmer John Writes

As shareholders, you are part of this rejuvenation of agriculture that is occurring at Angelic Organics. You are, in a sense, members of this extended farm village that has emerged out of the ashes of my failed conventional farm. It is a very important role you play: you are participating in the very early phase of a renewal of culture at its most basic source—the farm organism. During the winter months, when our vegetables serve you as both a memory of the past and an anticipation of the future, I invite you to reflect on this contribution you are making to Angelic Organics, to the earth, and to the evolution of humanity.

Winter Farming

Members of the farm crew who remain at Angelic Organics during the winter turn their attention to devising the next year's field plans, revamping field and office procedures, marketing and selling shares, maintaining infrastructure, recruiting and hiring interns and workers, and conducting myriad other tasks that go into keeping the farm running. True, we are able to wake up a little later and enjoy a bit more free time, but activity at Angelic Organics doesn't stop in the cold weather.

Farmer John Writes

On one of my winter sojourns to Mexico, I thought a lot about the equipment back on the farm. I sent emails home on a regular basis, like the following:

❖ fix cooling system on delivery truck (call McGilvra Electric in Beloit, and make an appointment to bring the truck in and see if the three-phase motor on the cooling unit works);

❖ clean and organize each tractor toolbox: equip with heavy hammer, large and small crescent wrench, 2 phillips head and 2 regular screwdrivers, pliers, vice grips, 1/2, 9/16, 5/8, and 3/4 inch wrenches, and any specialized tools that go with that tractor's functions;

❖ Pallet Jacks: check bearings and oil level in hydraulic jacks (Primo might have rebuilt these recently).

I emailed pages of this kind of stuff to the farm...

—FROM JOHN'S BOOK
FARMER JOHN ON GLITTER & GREASE

A Shareholder

Thank you once again for bringing our household a bounty of healthy and delicious vegetables during the past season. We appreciate the planning, the plowing, the seeding, the weeding, the harvesting, the washing, the packing, the delivery, the composting, the building, the repairing, not to mention the nurturing of both the food you grow and us shareholders as you help us to see the wonder in the whole incredible process that sustains us.

A Shareholder

As I finish this wonderful baked red potato, I find myself wishing for more. How will I wait a whole year for more?! Until this fall, I had never experienced such a sweet-tasting red potato; they are incredibly comforting on these cold winter days.

A Shareholder

Thanks for a wonderful vegetable year. Our family is so happy to have the veggies and we miss them so much when the year is out.

A Shareholder

In midwinter we still remember vividly the pleasure we got from eating your produce all summer.

Winter Eating

During the winter, you may be appreciating foods from the farm that you canned, froze, or dried during the growing season. You may also be enjoying storage crops from the fall, such as squash, potatoes, onions, garlic, carrots, and rutabagas. As these disappear from your pantry, basement, or refrigerator, you might be anticipating a visit to the produce section of your grocery store. Perhaps this is a gloomy prospect for you, to sort through the mounds of vegetables from all over the world, wondering how and where they were grown, and by whom. Or, perhaps it's just a sign to you that spring, and a summer's worth of fresh vegetables, is just around the corner.

THE WOODS

FARM NEWS, 2000

One of our farm projects this past winter was the clearing of brush out of the woods. The woods had become quite overgrown and mangy during the last twenty years, and some of last year's crew stayed on during the winter and worked in the woods. Soon the woods will be the perfect place for shareholders to picnic and camp.

Basic Recipes

Mixed Herb Tomato Sauce
with Dried Fancy Mushrooms

Just because you're too busy to babysit a stewpot of slow cooking tomatoes for half a day doesn't mean you can't concoct your own stunningly good pasta sauce. If you add some good-quality ingredients and scads of fresh herbs to a can of whole tomatoes, you can easily come up with a batch of great tomato sauce. This recipe makes enough thick, classic spaghetti sauce for 1 pound of pasta. For a seasonal variation, try serving this over spaghetti squash, with either grated Parmesan or cubes of chèvre that will melt and ooze over the strands of squash and mingle with the sauce. Dried fancy mushrooms of all kinds are widely available in grocery stores and specialty stores. If you prefer, you can use fresh mushrooms (fancy or plain); add them to the skillet a few minutes before the herbs. *Friend of the Farm.*

MAKES ABOUT 4 CUPS

2 cups	hot vegetable or chicken stock
1/2 cup	dried fancy mushrooms, porcini or any kind
6 tablespoons	extra virgin olive oil
1 clove	garlic, minced (about 1/2 teaspoon)
1 cup	chopped fresh parsley
1 cup	chopped mixed fresh herbs (such as basil, thyme, marjoram, oregano, tarragon, dill, fennel fronds)
1/2 cup	dry white wine or sherry
1 can (15 ounces)	whole tomatoes in juice, chopped
1/2 cup	diced onion (about 1 medium onion)
1/2 teaspoon	salt
	freshly ground black pepper

1. Pour the hot stock over the mushrooms in a medium bowl.

2. Heat the oil in a large skillet over medium heat. Add the garlic; sauté until it starts to turn golden, 3 to 5 minutes. Stir in the parsley and mixed herbs (if you're using basil, add it at the end of the total cooking time). Pour in the wine or sherry and adjust the temperature so that the ingredients simmer. Cook for 10 minutes, stirring occasionally.

3. Meanwhile, remove the soaked mushrooms from the stock (reserve the liquid). Chop the mushrooms, removing and discarding any tough stems.

4. Transfer the mushrooms to the skillet with the simmering wine and herbs. Add the mushroom-soaking stock, tomatoes (undrained), onions, salt, and pepper to taste. Reduce the heat to very low and cook, stirring occasionally, until it is rich and thick and intensely flavorful, 50 to 60 minutes. (You can cook it longer to develop the flavors more. Just add more stock or water if it starts to dry out.)

Homemade Mayonnaise

Every dish that calls for mayonnaise—be it potato salad, tuna salad, a BLT, or any mayo-using recipe in this book—becomes a superstar dish when made with your own mayonnaise. Sure, the jarred version will work in a pinch, but for the best flavor and optimal results, homemade mayo delivers. There are three basic rules of thumb for making mayo. Follow these rules, and your mayo will come out perfect every time. Store homemade mayo in the refrigerator for not longer than one week. *Friend of the Farm.*

❖ Everything must be at room temperature.

❖ Each egg yolk can absorb no more than $3/4$ cup oil.

❖ *When making it by hand:* Don't stop whisking the oil into the egg yolk until half the oil is incorporated. If your forearm gets tired, switch hands and get right back at it. Once the mixture starts to resemble mayonnaise, it's safe to take a *brief* pause. This method may be tiring, but it's rewarding.

When using a food processor: This method works marvelously as well, and you don't have to worry about your forearms getting tired.

Usually you don't want to use an oil with lots of flavor because the mayonnaise will taste too much like the oil and not like mayonnaise. Therefore, extra virgin olive oil is not usually a good choice, unless you cut it in half with vegetable oil. Blends of oils work great and produce different results; for example, you can add a nice flavor to your mayonnaise by using $1/4$ cup peanut or walnut oil with $3/4$ cup vegetable oil.

Note: You are undoubtedly aware of the controversy over eating raw eggs. Study the pros and cons; then decide for yourself if making this recipe is worth the health risk. The author and publisher bear no responsibility for the consequences that may result from ingesting raw eggs.

MAKES ABOUT 1 CUP

2	egg yolks
1½ tablespoons	white wine vinegar or lemon juice plus more to thin the mayonnaise
½ teaspoon	prepared Dijon mustard
	pinch salt
½ cup	olive oil
½ cup	vegetable oil
¼ teaspoon	freshly ground white pepper
1 tablespoon	boiling water

1. Using a large whisk, beat the egg yolks, 1½ tablespoons vinegar or lemon juice, mustard, and salt in a large bowl for 30 seconds. *Or, if using a food processor, process for 30 seconds.*

2. *By hand:* beat in the oil 1 teaspoon at a time, incorporating each addition completely into the egg yolk before adding the next teaspoon. Do this until *half* the oil is in the mixture. Then you can add the remaining oil in greater quantities (2–3 tablespoons at a time). Toward the end the mixture will get very thick; you can thin it with a little extra vinegar or lemon juice if it becomes too tough to manage.

Using a food processor: turn on the processor and pour in the oil through the feeder tube in a very thin stream, or if your model comes with a food pusher (usually a hollow white tool that fits perfectly in the feeder tube), check to see if it has a small hole on the bottom. If so, place the pusher in the feeder tube, turn the processor on, and fill the hollow pusher with as much oil as will fit; the oil will drain into the processor in a thin stream. Repeat until you have added all of the oil.

3. When all the oil is incorporated, stir in the white pepper. Whisk in 1 tablespoon boiling water to temper the mayo. At this point you can stir in any herbs or additional spices.

Basic Vegetable Stock

A basic vegetable stock is an essential part of the vegetable-lover's cooking repertoire. In addition to using it to add flavor to soups and sauces, you can use it in place of water when making rice or other grains. Making vegetable stock lends itself to improvisation, so feel free to use what you have in the kitchen. Vegetables to avoid, however, are cabbage, eggplant, or greens (although kale is sometimes used). Fennel adds a nice element, but its characteristic anise flavor might overpower more delicate soups and sauces. Dried mushrooms add great depth to your stock, and roasting your vegetables first gives the stock a whole new dimension and complexity. Here we give you a basic, all-purpose, flavorful stock recipe—and don't worry, the garlic will mellow nicely. Do not put salt in the stock until you are ready to use it in a recipe. *Angelic Organics Kitchen.*

MAKES ABOUT 7 CUPS

2 quarts	water
3 large	carrots, cut in 1-inch pieces
2 large	onions, quartered (if skins and roots are clean, leave them on the onion)
1–2	leeks, white parts only, or 4–5 scallions, including half of the green part, sliced
2 large	ribs celery, including some of the leaves, cut in 1-inch pieces
1 medium	turnip, cut in 1-inch pieces
10	cloves garlic, skins on, flattened slightly with the side of a knife
5–10 whole	cloves
12	parsley stems, no leaves attached
3	bay leaves
8 sprigs	fresh thyme or 3/4 teaspoon dried thyme
1 tablespoon	soy sauce

1. Place all the ingredients in a large pot and bring to a gentle simmer. Partially cover the pot and simmer until the water is nicely flavored, 45–60 minutes.

2. Set a mesh strainer over a large bowl or container. Strain the stock once through the strainer and discard any solid pieces of vegetable or herb. Rinse the strainer, line it with a couple layers of cheesecloth, and strain the stock again. Refrigerate for up to 1 week or freeze for up to 5 months—any longer, though, and it might start to take on the flavor of your freezer.

Preparing Tomatoes for Sauce (Tomato Purée)

This is a great alternative to canned tomatoes that will allow you to enjoy great, fresh-tasting tomato sauce all winter long. Make it fresh throughout the summer, or stock up on tomatoes in September and make multiple batches to freeze in zip-top bags. You can use this sauce as the base for a wide variety of classic tomato sauces, such as those found in this cookbook. This basic technique, common in Italian cooking, requires use of a food mill to easily separate the skins and most of the seeds from the tomatoes and to purée them perfectly. If you don't have a food mill, drain the tomatoes in a colander, reserving all the liquid. Once the tomatoes are cool enough to handle, peel and finely chop them. *Friend of the Farm.*

MAKES ABOUT 2 CUPS

2 pounds	fresh tomatoes, quartered (about 6 medium tomatoes)

1. Place the tomatoes in a large pan over medium heat. Cover and cook, shaking the pan occasionally, for 10 minutes.

2. Set a food mill over a medium bowl. Remove the pan from the heat and pour the tomatoes with all their juices into the food mill. Run the tomatoes through the mill.

3. Use immediately, or refrigerate and use within a week, or freeze.

Vegetable & Herb Availability from Angelic Organics

These times approximate when each crop is available. Shareholders do not receive every crop that is in season every week—it would never fit in the box! We offer the more popular crops (tomatoes, melons, etc.) most weeks they're in season, and provide more unusual crops like fennel and rutabagas a few times each season. Our boxes contain a balanced selection of about twelve to sixteen different items each week.

Fruiting Crops	June	July	Aug	Sept	Oct	Nov	Dec
Cucumbers**		▓▓▓▓▓					
Eggplant**			▓▓▓▓▓▓▓▓▓				
Green Beans**			▓▓▓▓▓▓				
Melons**			▓▓▓▓				
Peppers (Hot & Sweet)**			▓▓▓▓▓▓▓				
Sugar Snap Peas (late spring; not available from Angelic Organics)							
Sweet Corn**			▓▓▓▓				
Tomatoes**			▓▓▓▓▓▓▓				
Winter Squash					▓▓▓▓▓▓▓▓		▓
Zucchini & Summer Squash**	▓▓▓▓▓▓▓						

Leafs and Stems	June	July	Aug	Sept	Oct	Nov	Dec
Asparagus (mid- to late spring; not available from Angelic Organics)							
Salad Greens	▓▓▓▓▓▓▓▓▓▓▓▓▓▓						
Celery			▓▓▓▓				
Chicories (Endive, Escarole, Radicchio)*	▓▓▓▓▓			▓▓▓▓			
Cooking Greens (Beet Greens, Chard, Collards, Kale)*	▓▓▓▓▓▓▓▓▓▓▓▓▓▓▓▓						
Spinach*	▓▓▓			▓▓▓▓▓▓			
Tetragonia			▓▓▓				
Choi*	▓▓						
Fennel			▓▓▓				

* Sweetens with frost   ** Cannot survive frost

Early November begins Extended Season

Herbs

Herbs	June	July	Aug	Sept	Oct	Nov	Dec
Anise Hyssop		▓	▓	▓	▓		
Basil**		▓	▓	▓	▓		
Cilantro			▓	▓	▓		
Dill			▓	▓	▓		
Lemon Balm			▓	▓	▓		
Oregano	▓	▓	▓	▓	▓	▓	
Parsley*	▓	▓	▓	▓	▓	▓	
Rosemary (mid-July to late fall; not available from Angelic Organics)							
Sage	▓	▓	▓	▓	▓	▓	▓
Summer Savory		▓	▓	▓	▓	▓	▓
Tarragon		▓	▓	▓	▓	▓	▓
Thyme		▓	▓	▓	▓	▓	▓

Brassicas (Cole Crops)

Brassicas (Cole Crops)	June	July	Aug	Sept	Oct	Nov	Dec
Broccoli*		▓		▓	▓	▓	
Brussels Sprouts*					▓	▓	▓
Cabbage*		▓			▓	▓	▓
Cauliflower*		▓			▓	▓	
Kohlrabi*					▓	▓	▓

Onion Crops

Onion Crops	June	July	Aug	Sept	Oct	Nov	Dec
Garlic			▓	▓	▓	▓	▓
Garlic Scapes		▓					
Leeks				▓	▓	▓	▓
Onions			▓	▓	▓	▓	▓
Scallions		▓					

Root Crops

Root Crops	June	July	Aug	Sept	Oct	Nov	Dec
Beets		▓		▓	▓	▓	▓
Carrots			▓	▓	▓	▓	▓
Celeriac					▓	▓	▓
Daikon Radish					▓	▓	
Fall Potatoes				▓	▓	▓	▓
New Potatoes			▓				
Parsnips*						▓	▓
Radishes		▓			▓	▓	
Rutabagas					▓	▓	▓
Sunchokes (Jerusalem Artichokes)*					▓	▓	▓
Sweet Potatoes**				▓	▓	▓	▓
Turnips*		▓					

*Sweetens with frost **Cannot survive frost

Early November begins Extended Season

Illustrated Vegetable Identification Guide

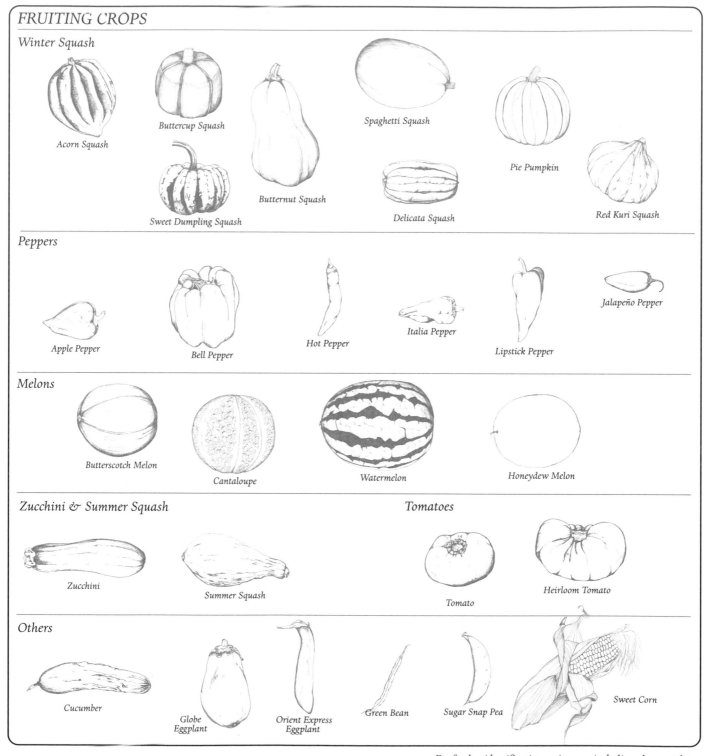

FRUITING CROPS

Winter Squash

Acorn Squash · Buttercup Squash · Spaghetti Squash · Pie Pumpkin · Sweet Dumpling Squash · Butternut Squash · Delicata Squash · Red Kuri Squash

Peppers

Apple Pepper · Bell Pepper · Hot Pepper · Italia Pepper · Lipstick Pepper · Jalapeño Pepper

Melons

Butterscotch Melon · Cantaloupe · Watermelon · Honeydew Melon

Zucchini & Summer Squash

Zucchini · Summer Squash

Tomatoes

Tomato · Heirloom Tomato

Others

Cucumber · Globe Eggplant · Orient Express Eggplant · Green Bean · Sugar Snap Pea · Sweet Corn

For further identification assistance, including photographs, visit www.AngelicOrganics.com/vegetableguide.

LEAFS & STEMS

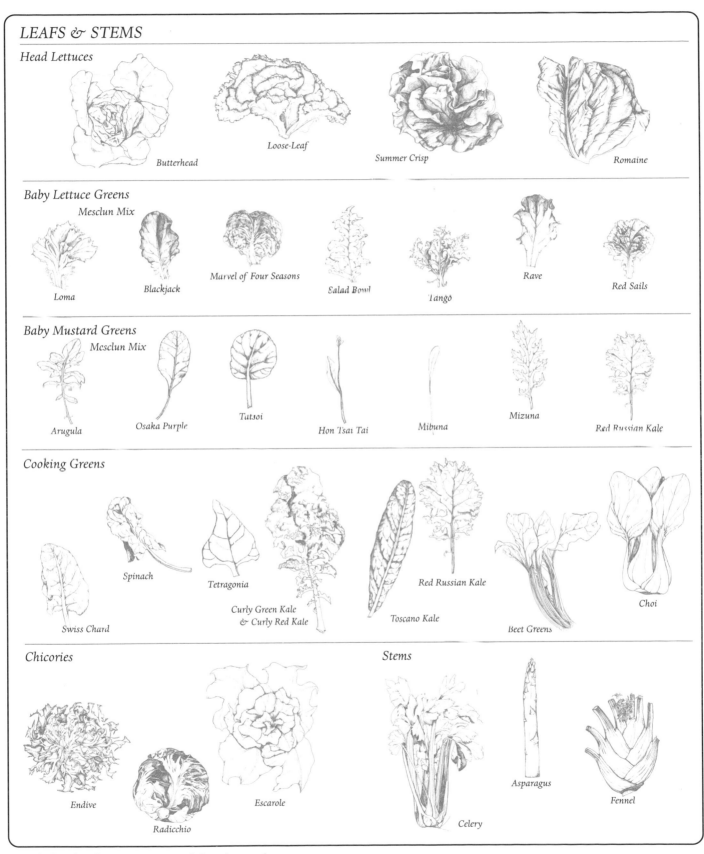

Head Lettuces

Butterhead

Loose-Leaf

Summer Crisp

Romaine

Baby Lettuce Greens

Mesclun Mix

Loma

Blackjack

Marvel of Four Seasons

Salad Bowl

Tango

Rave

Red Sails

Baby Mustard Greens

Mesclun Mix

Arugula

Osaka Purple

Tatsoi

Hon Tsai Tai

Mibuna

Mizuna

Red Russian Kale

Cooking Greens

Swiss Chard

Spinach

Tetragonia

Curly Green Kale
& Curly Red Kale

Toscano Kale

Red Russian Kale

Beet Greens

Choi

Chicories

Endive

Radicchio

Escarole

Stems

Celery

Asparagus

Fennel

For further identification assistance, including photographs,
visit www.AngelicOrganics.com/vegetableguide.

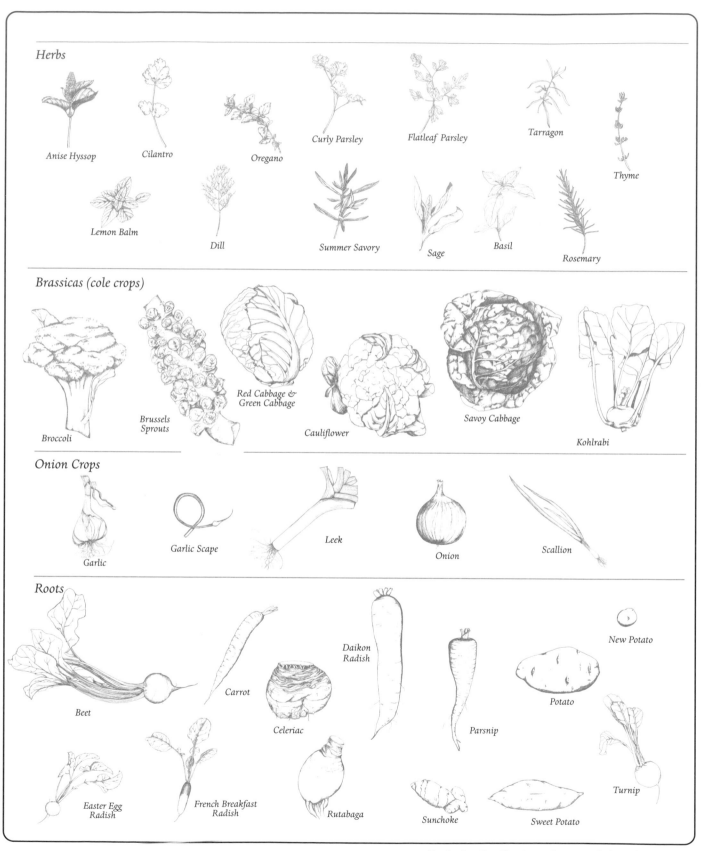

Herbs

Anise Hyssop

Cilantro

Oregano

Curly Parsley

Flatleaf Parsley

Tarragon

Thyme

Lemon Balm

Dill

Summer Savory

Sage

Basil

Rosemary

Brassicas (cole crops)

Broccoli

Brussels Sprouts

Red Cabbage & Green Cabbage

Cauliflower

Savoy Cabbage

Kohlrabi

Onion Crops

Garlic

Garlic Scape

Leek

Onion

Scallion

Roots

Beet

Carrot

Celeriac

Daikon Radish

Parsnip

Potato

New Potato

Easter Egg Radish

French Breakfast Radish

Rutabaga

Sunchoke

Sweet Potato

Turnip

For further identification assistance, including photographs, visit www.AngelicOrganics.com/vegetableguide.

Vegetable Storage Guide

Asparagus

Asparagus spears are best eaten shortly after harvest when their tips are still firm. If you must store asparagus, trim the base of the stalks and place the stalks upright in a jar filled with an inch of water. An alternative method is to wrap the cut ends of the stalks in a moist paper towel or damp tea towel, cover the bundle loosely in plastic, and put it in the refrigerator. Refrigerate asparagus for up to two weeks.

Basil . . .

See Herbs.

Beets

If your beets still have greens attached, cut them off, leaving an inch of stem. Keep these greens unwashed and refrigerated in a closed plastic bag. Store the beet roots, with the rootlets (or "tails") attached, unwashed, in a plastic bag in the crisper bin of your refrigerator. They will keep for several weeks, but their sweetness diminishes with time, so try to use them within a week.

Bell Peppers . . .

See Peppers.

Broccoli

Wrap broccoli loosely in a plastic bag and keep it in the vegetable bin of your refrigerator. Don't use an air-tight bag, because broccoli continues to respire after being harvested and needs some room to breathe. It keeps for over a week but is firmest and tastiest if used within a few days.

Brussels Sprouts

Brussels sprouts keep longest if they are left attached to the stalk, and Angelic Organics distributes them this way. If you're short on refrigerator space, snap off the sprouts and store them unwashed in a closed plastic bag in the veggie bin. Even when they are left on the stalk, Brussels sprouts should be wrapped in plastic to prevent wilting. Their flavor is sweetest right after harvest, so try to use them within a few days.

Cabbage

Cabbage is cleverly self-packaged. Just stick dry, unwashed cabbage in the refrigerator, preferably in the vegetable bin. The outer leaves may eventually get floppy or yellowish, but you can remove and discard them to reveal fresh inner leaves. Cabbage can keep for more than a month. Once it's cut, seal it in a plastic bag and continue to refrigerate it; it will keep for several weeks.

Cantaloupe . . .

See Melons.

Carrots

Remove the leafy-green tops, leaving about an inch of

stems. Refrigerate dry, unwashed carrots in a plastic bag for two weeks or longer.

Cauliflower

Wrap dry, unwashed cauliflower loosely in plastic and store it in the refrigerator. It will keep for up to a week but will taste sweetest if used within a few days.

Celeriac

Store unwashed celeriac in a plastic bag in the refrigerator, where it will keep for several weeks.

Celery

Wrap unwashed celery tightly in a plastic bag and place it in the coldest part of the refrigerator, where it will keep for up to two weeks. Or, to keep your celery extra crisp, place it upright in a container filled with an inch of water, cover with a plastic bag, and refrigerate for up to two weeks.

Celery Root . . .

See Celeriac.

Chard . . .

See Cooking Greens.

Chicories

Keep unwashed chicories in a perforated plastic bag in the refrigerator's vegetable bin for up to a week.

Chile Peppers . . .

See Peppers.

Choi

Refrigerate unwashed choi in a plastic container or loosely wrapped in a plastic bag. Choi keeps for over a week but is firmest and tastiest if used within a few days.

Collard Greens . . .

See Cooking Greens.

Cooking Greens

Cut beet and turnip greens from their roots; store roots separately. Keep dry, unwashed greens in a sealed plastic bag in your refrigerator. Thicker greens will keep up to two weeks, but tender ones like spinach and beet greens should be eaten within a week.

Corn . . .

See Sweet Corn.

Cucumbers

Most cucumbers found in supermarkets have endured a journey of hundreds of miles from where they were grown. To keep them from drying out on their long trip, their skins are usually waxed. We don't like the idea of feeding shareholders wax, so we leave our farm-fresh cucumbers in their natural, wax-free state. Because they dehydrate faster than the waxy kind, be sure to get them into the refrigerator right away. If you store unwashed cucumbers in a sealed plastic bag in the vegetable crisper bin, they'll hold for at least a week. Cucumbers store best at around 45°F, but refrigerators are usually set cooler than this. Keep cucumbers tucked far away from tomatoes, apples, and citrus—these give off ethylene gas that accelerates cucumber deterioration.

Daikon Radishes

If the greens are still attached, remove and refrigerate them in a plastic bag and use them within a week. Wrap the unwashed root in a separate plastic bag and place it in the refrigerator, where it will keep for up to two weeks.

Eggplant

Eggplant prefers to be kept at about 50 degrees, which is warmer than most refrigerators and cooler than most kitchen counters. Wrap unwashed eggplant in a towel (not in plastic) to absorb any moisture and keep it in the vegetable bin of your refrigerator. Used within a week, it should still be fresh and mild.

Endive and Escarole . . .

See Chicories.

Fennel

Cut off the stalks where they emerge from the bulb, and if you want to use the feathery foliage as an herb, place the dry stalks upright in a glass filled with two inches of water. Cover the glass loosely with a plastic bag and store it in the refrigerator for up to five days. The unwashed bulb will keep in a plastic bag in the refrigerator for at least a week.

Garlic and Garlic Scapes

Like onions, garlic can be eaten fresh or dried. Dried garlic will keep for several months in a dark, dry, well-ventilated place at a cool room temperature. Fresh green garlic must be kept in a plastic bag in the refrigerator and should be used quickly, because any accumulated moisture in the bag will cause it to spoil. Store unwashed garlic scapes in a loosely wrapped plastic bag in the refrigerator for up to two weeks.

Green Beans

Store unwashed beans in a perforated plastic bag in the vegetable bin of your refrigerator for up to two weeks.

Green Peppers . . .

See Peppers.

Herbs

Except for basil, set unwashed bunches of fresh herbs (with stems) upright into small jars filled with 1 to 2 inches of water. Then cover the herbs loosely with plastic wrap and refrigerate for up to two weeks. Roll up unwashed smaller sprigs or loose herbs in a dry towel, place the bundle in a plastic bag, and store it in the refrigerator's vegetable bin for up to a week.

Now for fresh basil. It is a warm-weather crop and is very sensitive to cold temperatures. Do not refrigerate fresh basil, as it will turn black very quickly. To keep just-harvested basil fresh for many days, strip the lower leaves off of stems and place the stems in a glass of water on the kitchen counter. Wrap the stripped leaves (or all your basil, if your fresh basil arrives without adequate stems) in a dry paper towel (damp leaves will quickly turn black) and keep in an airtight container at about 50 degrees. (Room temperature is also okay.) If you have more basil than you can use in a few days, try chopping it and adding it to butter, cream cheese, or your favorite pasta sauce. Make a batch of pesto—or simply purée extra basil with a bit of olive oil and freeze it in ice cube trays.

Honeydew . . .

See Melons.

Hot Peppers . . .

See Peppers.

Jerusalem Artichokes . . .

See Sunchokes.

Kohlrabi

If you plan to use it soon, wrap the whole unwashed kohlrabi—stem, stalks, leaves, and all—in a plastic bag and keep it in the refrigerator. Otherwise, remove the stalks and greens from the bulb and use them within a week. Store the bulb in another plastic bag in the fridge and use it within two weeks.

Kale . . .

See Cooking Greens.

Leeks

Loosely wrap unwashed leeks in a plastic bag and store them in the vegetable bin of your refrigerator. They will keep for at least a week.

Lettuce . . .

See Salad Greens.

Melons

If your muskmelon, honeydew, or butterscotch melon seems a bit short of ripe, keep it at room temperature for a few days or until there is a sweet smell coming from the stem end. Once the melon ripens, store it in the refrigerator.

Handle watermelons carefully. When harvested at their peak ripeness, they can crack or split easily if bumped or roughly handled. Refrigerate watermelons right away. (Watermelons do not ripen off the vine and do not emanate a ripe smell.)

Cut melon should be covered in plastic wrap, chunks or slices should be kept in an airtight container, and both should be refrigerated. Eat all melons within a week.

Mesclun...

See Salad Greens.

Onions and Scallions

Sweet mild onions should be kept in a plastic bag in the refrigerator, but beware the fatal moisture accumulation that causes them to spoil. Eat them within a week or two.

Red and yellow storage onions will keep in any cool, dark, dry place with adequate air circulation for several months if they have been cured. (Angelic Organics typically cures storage onions.) Uncured storage onions should be stored like sweet mild onions. (Be sure to store onions and potatoes in separate places. Moisture given off by potatoes can cause onions to spoil.)

Scallions should be stored unwashed and wrapped loosely in a plastic bag. Put them in the refrigerator where they will keep for a week. To keep scallions longer, chop off about three-quarters of the tender green tips; the end closest to the root is less perishable.

Parsnips

Refrigerate unwashed parsnips in a loosely wrapped or perforated plastic bag. Stored in the vegetable bin of your refrigerator, they can keep up to two weeks.

Peppers

Place whole, unwashed peppers in a plastic bag, seal, and refrigerate for a week or more. Beware of any excess moisture in the bag that could cause peppers to spoil. Red, orange, and yellow peppers are fully ripe and need to be eaten sooner.

Potatoes

Keep unwashed potatoes in a cool, dark, dry place—such as a loosely closed paper bag in a cupboard. They will keep for weeks at room temperature, longer if you can provide their ideal temperature of 40–50 degrees. Beware: If your refrigerator is set at the normal refrigerator temperature, somewhere in the 30s, the low temperature will convert the starch to sugars. However, new potatoes—which are young and thin-skinned—may be refrigerated if you don't plan to eat them within a few days. Do try to use new potatoes soon, because their delicate flavor wanes with time.

Moisture causes potatoes to spoil, light turns them green, and proximity to onions causes them to sprout. (You can still use a potato that has sprouted, however; simply cut off the "eyes" before use.)

Pumpkins...

See Winter Squash.

Radicchio...

See Chicories.

Radishes and Young Turnips

Remove radish or turnip leaves if they are still attached. Store the unwashed greens in a loosely wrapped plastic bag in the crisper bin of your refrigerator. Because of their high water content, turnips and radishes deteriorate quickly. Store them dry and unwashed in a plastic bag in the refrigerator. Young turnips and most radishes should keep for a week. Black radishes will keep slightly longer. (See Daikon Radishes under a separate entry.)

Rutabagas

Rutabagas store exceptionally well. Keep unwashed rutabagas in a plastic bag in the refrigerator for a month or longer.

Salad Greens

Store unwashed lettuce or mesclun in a plastic bag in the refrigerator. To store lettuce or mesclun that you have already washed and dried, roll the leaves loosely in a kitchen towel, put the towel in a plastic bag, and place the package in the vegetable crisper bin. (Wet greens will spoil quickly, so make sure they are truly dry before refrigerating them.) If you have a salad spinner, wash and spin the greens before refrigerating them. Eat mesclun mix within three or four days, and use lettuce within a week.

Spinach...

See Cooking Greens.

Squash...

See Zucchini and Summer Squash or Winter Squash.

Sugar Snap Peas

Eat sugar snap peas as fresh as possible, within four or five days of harvest. To store them, put whole, unwashed peas in a perforated plastic bag in the crisper drawer of your refrigerator.

Sunchokes

Although sunchokes can overwinter in the ground, they store poorly after they've been harvested because of their delicate skins. If you can't eat them right away, keep unwashed tubers in a perforated plastic bag in your refrigerator crisper drawer for up to two weeks. If the skin looks shriveled after you take sunchokes out of storage, rehydrate them in a bowl of cold water.

Sweet Corn

Eat it now! But if you must put off eating corn, leave the husks on and refrigerate the ears in a plastic bag for as little time as possible. After about four days most of the corn's sweetness is gone. Though it's still perfectly edible and tasty, corn at this stage is more suited for use in recipes than for eating right off the cob.

Sweet Potatoes

Keep unwashed sweet potatoes in a cool, dark place, such as a loosely closed paper bag in a cupboard or cool basement, and use them within a few months. Do not store sweet potatoes in the refrigerator; cold temperatures can darken the potatoes and will adversely affect their taste. While rugged in appearance, sweet potatoes do not keep as long as regular potatoes because their fairly thin skins make them subject to spoilage. At room temperature, sweet potatoes should be used within two months.

Tetragonia . . .

See Cooking Greens.

Tomatoes

If your tomatoes smell fragrant and yield slightly when squeezed, they are ready to use. If not, store them for a few days at room temperature until they are ripe. Putting dry tomatoes in a brown paper bag may accelerate the ripening process; a sun-free spot on your counter will also work. You can dry tomatoes for long-term storage or can or freeze them in sauces or salsas.

Tomatoes tend to lose their flavor if stored for very long in a refrigerator, but if it's hot in your kitchen and you have some very ripe tomatoes, you're better off putting them in the fridge to prevent them from spoiling too fast on your counter and attracting fruit flies. If you eat only half of a tomato, you can wrap it in plastic wrap and place in the refrigerator; just try to finish it within twenty-four hours.

Turnip Greens . . .

See Cooking Greens.

Turnips . . .

See Radishes and Young Turnips.

Watermelons . . .

See Melons.

Winter Squash

Store winter squash in a cool, dry, dark place with good ventilation. (A porch or garage can work well as long as you don't let them freeze.) They should keep for up to a month or more, depending on the variety. (Delicata, pie pumpkins, buttercup, and red kuri have a shorter storage life than acorn, sweet dumpling, and butternut squash.) You can also incorporate winter squash into a beautiful arrangement for your table. They won't keep quite as long at room temperature, but if they're already on your table, you might be inspired to eat them more quickly. Once squash has been cut, you can wrap the pieces in plastic and store them in the refrigerator for five to seven days.

Zucchini and Summer Squash

Our unwaxed farm-fresh zucchini and summer squash respire through their skins, so they need to be refrigerated as soon as possible. Store them unwashed in a perforated plastic bag in the vegetable bin, or refrigerate them in a sealed plastic container that you've lined with a kitchen towel. In the refrigerator they keep for about a week and a half.

Complementary Herbs & Spices

by Louise Frazier

Herbs and Spices: an Introduction from an Anthroposophic Perspective

Locally grown herbs create a delicate palate of flavors that go excellently with Biodynamically grown vegetables, accentuating their innate qualities and helping to balance a certain one-sidedness. In harvesting, vegetables are separated from their mother plant and often roots, and stems and leaves are removed to bring the edible portion for meal preparation. Adding complementary herbs or spices restores the whole qualities of the plant for completeness in human nutrition. Revival of this age-old wisdom brings us knowledge of the herbs and spices that best complement the various vegetables and grains coming to us from farm and garden.

Full-bodied flavor and tantalizing aroma begin the digestive process, awakening our appetites and the anticipation of our metabolic organs hungering for goodness. It is the flavorings that we savor in remembering festive foods, be our menu vegetarian or with meat. What would Thanksgiving be without parsley, sage, rosemary, marjoram, and thyme in the stuffing or exotic cinnamon, ginger, and nutmeg in all-American pumpkin pie?

According to Udo Renzenbrink in *Diet and Cancer,* herbs and spices used as seasoning aid digestion, especially when they are tasted consciously, which results in better secretion of saliva, pepsin, gall, and pancreas. Most herbs and spices bring Cosmic forces into the terrestrial-lunar nature of some vegetables. Light is prominent in the green plants, and we also can find ourselves cooled or warmed by their effects. The herbs of the *Umbelliferae* family—which include caraway, celery, dill, fennel, and parsley—carry light as well as warmth ether in their delicate, lace-like leaves and aromatic seeds. The *Labiatae,* or mint family members, retain much of the aromatic flowering processes within the realm of the leaves, leaving them aromatic and full of essential oils. This family comprises some popular herbs—basil, marjoram, mint, oregano, rosemary, sage, and thyme—widely used in Italian and Mediterranean cuisines.

Combining oregano and savory in meals during hot, humid weather lends us relief from these oppressive conditions. "Cool as a cucumber" is true, when it is balanced with mint or dill. Heavy cabbage is made more digestible with caraway seed; the watery nature of sauerkraut is aided by the fragrant fiery nature of juniper berries; chervil and caraway are good with moony cheeses. Savory accents beans, and basil and parsley complement tomatoes. Eating very hot and spicy foods can bring too much phosphorus into us, making us terrible fidgets, full of the will to do things. We must have a little phosphorus in us, however, so we can have will forces.

Herbs possess many qualities that are expressed to our senses as fragrances, pungent odors, or flavors—hot or spicy, bitter or delicate. The plant substances producing these effects are almost always small in quantity, evidencing the "dynamic" influences exerted by herbs, which make them such valuable members of our garden family. In forming essential oils, resins, and aromatic substances, herbs and spices have taken the flowering process into other parts of the plant such as the leaves, stems, roots, or seeds. Emerson tells us (in Perpetual Forces) that more servants wait on man than he'll ever notice. Certainly we are well served by complementary herbs and spices.

Louise Frazier's Complementary Herbs & Spices Chart

Vegetable	Herbs and Spices
Asparagus	Chervil, Dill, Tarragon, Curry, Mustard, White Pepper
Beets	Basil, Caraway, Fennel Seeds, Horseradish, Tarragon, Allspice, Coriander, Ginger
Broccoli	Caraway, Dill, Mint, Oregano, Curry, Ginger
Brussels Sprouts	Basil, Borage, Caraway, Dill, Parsley, Mustard, Nutmeg, Paprika
Cabbage*	Caraway, Dill, Fennel Seeds, Mint, Savory, Thyme, Coriander, Curry, Ginger
Carrots	Basil, Chervil, Fennel Green, Parsley, Thyme, Coriander, Ginger, Mace
Cauliflower	Basil, Caraway, Dill, Fennel Seeds, Thyme, Curry, Nutmeg, Paprika
Celeriac	Basil, Dill, Fennel Seeds, Marjoram, Thyme, Allspice, Coriander, Nutmeg, Paprika
Celery	Basil, Chervil, Dill, Lovage, Parsley, Curry, Paprika
Chicories*	Basil, Dill, Fennel Green, Marjoram, Thyme, Parsley, Ginger, Nutmeg
Cucumber	Basil, Borage, Dill, Mint, Parsley, Tarragon, Allspice, Coriander, Mustard
Green Beans	Basil, Chives, Dill, Lovage, Oregano, Rosemary, Savory
Eggplant	Basil, Oregano, Parsley, Rosemary, Savory, Thyme, Curry, Pepper
Fennel Bulb	Basil, Lovage, Parsley, Coriander, Nutmeg, Paprika
Kale**	Caraway, Dill, Marjoram, Tarragon, Thyme, Allspice, Coriander, Nutmeg
Kohlrabi	Basil, Chervil, Chives, Dill, Fennel Seeds, Lovage, Parsley, Allspice, Coriander, Mace
Leeks	Caraway, Dill, Lovage, Sage, Thyme, Mustard, Nutmeg, Paprika
Onions	Anise Seed, Basil, Bay Leaf, Parsley, Thyme, Clove, Curry, Paprika
Parsnips	Chives, Fennel Seeds, Parsley, Thyme, Coriander
Peas	Chervil, Chives, Dill, Mint, Parsley, Rosemary, Thyme, Curry, Nutmeg
Peppers	Basil, Lovage, Oregano, Parsley, Rosemary, Thyme, Curry, Ginger, Mustard
Potatoes	Chervil, Marjoram, Parsley, Rosemary, Sage, Thyme, Mace, Paprika, Pepper
Pumpkin	Celery Leaves, Chives, Onions, Sage, Thyme, Curry, Ginger
Radishes	Basil, Borage, Chives, Dill, Lovage, Mint, Parsley
Red Cabbage	Basil, Bay Leaf, Caraway, Onions, Thyme, Clove, Ginger, Nutmeg
Rutabaga	Basil, Borage, Caraway, Dill, Marjoram, Parsley, Rosemary, Allspice, Mustard, Pepper
Spinach	Basil, Chives, Dill, Lovage, Thyme, Allspice, Nutmeg
Squash, summer**	Basil, Chives, Dill, Marjoram, Onions, Oregano, Coriander, Pepper
Squash, winter	Celery Leaves, Marjoram, Onions, Parsley, Sage, Thyme, Allspice, Curry, Ginger
Sunchokes	Anise, Chervil, Chives, Dill, Fennel Seeds, Parsley, Sage, Coriander, Mace
Sweet Corn	Basil, Cilantro, Oregano, Parsley, Rosemary, Thyme, Chili, Mustard
Sweet Potatoes	Leek, Sage, Thyme, Allspice, Chili, Ginger
Swiss Chard	Lovage, Marjoram, Parsley, Savory, Allspice, Nutmeg, Paprika
Tomatoes	Basil, Cilantro, Dill, Oregano, Parsley, Rosemary, Curry, Paprika, Pepper
Turnips	Basil, Borage, Caraway, Dill, Marjoram, Parsley, Rosemary, Allspice, Mustard, Pepper

- Use 1 to 3 herbs or spices in a recipe to enhance, not overpower, the flavor of the vegetable.
- **Coriander** or **Curry** may be added **before** cooking; all other herbs and spices should be added **after** cooking.
- Herbs and spices may be used as a **salt substitute**—with a little lemon to enhance, and with oil or unsalted butter.
- Use **Cilantro**—the green, pungent herb of the coriander plant—fresh in salads or sauces. Cook only with **Coriander**.

- Replace **Pepper** with **Allspice** for warmth in cold weather.
- Because **lettuce** is "water-filled" and neutral, it can be mixed with any herb or spice.
- **Garlic** dominates flavors—use little with vegetables. Let it grace meat or fish dishes.

★ *Chicories include Endive, Escarole, and Radicchio. Also for Choi, Napa/Chinese Cabbage, and Salad Greens use Chicories.*
★★ *Summer Squash includes Zucchini; for Collards use Kale.*

Simple & Good Whole Grain Cookery

by Louise Frazier

Whole Grains: An Introduction from an Anthroposophic Perspective

In our history as gatherers, then cultivators, humankind and grains have long lived in partnership on the Earth. In our earliest days as nomads, we gained warmth and strength nibbling on grass-seeds, berries, and plants. Stands of wild oats, barley, millet, and other cereal grasses grew plentifully the world over, with tubers to nourish those in tropic areas. We soon learned to pound grains and soak them in water for a cereal mash. Priest-King Zarathustra is acknowledged as being the father of agriculture, with grains among the first plants grown under his tutelage over seven thousand years ago. He knew that Cosmic Forces of the Sun rayed into the grains and were able to work on within the human being, and he taught that "the Sun will rise in you when you enjoy the fruits of the field." The ancient Egyptians and Greeks cultivated fields of grain and pounded and soaked grains for their breakfast mash. However, they soon discovered that the sun baked the leftover mash patties into a cracker form they could break off and eat later in the day.

With fire, cooking began, along with stews of grains and plant roots and greens. Seafaring Phoenicians and conquering Roman legions carried their grain mills with them to provide themselves with fresh, hearty grain cereals. The Scots made crowdie, at first a soaked mash and later a cooked oat porridge. Middle Eastern tabouli has its origins as cracked wheat mash. Kept for a long time out of the sun, grain mash began to rise, becoming lighter when baked, and then we had leavened bread. Cities grew around the miller and the baker, while people in the countryside invented many more dishes that combined vegetables and herbs with whole grains, even delicious puddings, sometimes with the addition of fruit. In the Alps, rye grains were roasted and carried in deep trouser pockets for lunch.

As time passed, the monoculture of grains became more common, with the reliance on one grain bringing famine and fear when crop failure occurred. This eventually led the Europeans to introduce the cultivation of the newly discovered South American potato in the sixteenth century. At first, the populace did not take to the potato, but farmers were forced by law to grow them "to keep the bellies of the peasants full." New eating patterns were established as the potato replaced grains in the stew pot, and with this, the timeless tradition of whole grains as the staple of our diet became eroded. Whole grains were relegated more and more to their role in baked flour products.

A new art in baking came to the fore with the French chefs—Messieurs Brillat-Savarin and Cereme with their "haute cuisine"—which was still based on whole-grain flours. It is said that this cuisine underlies the high development of civilization at that time in France. And then, with the coming of the French Court and its decadence, came white flour, white asparagus, white refined food. In efforts to emulate royalty, western society sought more and more "refinement," eliminating in the process the vitality of foods in their natural state.

Today there is a growing interest in the revival of food in its more natural form. Western traditions in North America mostly go back to the era of whole grains in bread or breakfast form, save for the Native American corn recipes adapted in the New World. Westward-bound pioneers found that whole-grain flours turned rancid when held for long on a shelf or carried in wagons, and they began to prefer refined flours. In Europe, where traditions also include the older grain-pot cookery of its ethnic groups, a wide array of dishes combining whole grains, complementary herbs, and vegetables or fruit is being revived.

Louise Frazier's Whole Grain Cookery Chart

Grain (1 part)	Parts Water	Cook Time (in minutes)	After cooking, add 1 or 2 herbs or spices	Let Stand
Barley	2–3	30–45	Bay Leaf, Mint, Sage, Thyme, Allspice, Coriander, Mace	6–8 hrs
Corn	3–4	20	Oregano, Rosemary, Thyme, Chili, Mace, Nutmeg	6–8 hrs
Millet	3–4	12	Basil, Bay Leaf, Chervil, Lovage, Allspice, Coriander, Ginger	12 min
Oats	2	20	Caraway, Chervil, Fennel Seed, Oregano, Savory, Thyme, Coriander, Nutmeg	1–3 hrs
Rice & Wild Rice	2–2 $^1/_2$	20 or 40	Basil, Caraway, Oregano, Lovage, Thyme, Coriander, Curry, Paprika	20 min or none
Rye	2 $^1/_2$–3	30–40	Bay Leaf, Caraway, Marjoram, Rosemary, Tarragon, Thyme, Allspice, Mustard	6–8 hrs
Wheat/Spelt	2 $^1/_2$–3	30–40	Anise, Caraway, Marjoram, Rosemary, Sage, Thyme, Allspice, Coriander, Mustard	6–8 hrs
Buckwheat	1 $^1/_4$–1 $^1/_2$	15	Basil, Caraway, Marjoram, Oregano, Thyme, Clove, Nutmeg	15 min
Amaranth & Quinoa	3	20	Oregano, Sage, Thyme, Chili	10 min

To cook: a) measure grains, b) rinse in sieve, c) toast in cookpot, d) add water, e) cook, f) season, g) let stand, h) serve hot or cold.

- **Coriander** and **Curry** (Turmeric) may be added at the toasting (C) stage; all other seasoning should be done after cooking (E) and before "letting stand" (G).
- **Salt** toughens grains. Add only at the end of cooking or before heating to serve. $^1/_2$ tsp to 1 cup raw grain.
- **Toast** rinsed grains, either in oven at 150° F or more efficiently in cookpot over low heat. Stir until aroma rises and grains appear dry and separate.
- **Cooking** times are after bringing to boil. 1 cup raw grains = 4 servings (or 6).
- **Standing** (in a warm place, padded cloth cozy, or European grain box) allows grain to swell, absorb water, and open to fullness.
- **Seeds**—for these seasonings, use the seed state: **Anise, Caraway, Fennel,** and all of the spices.

To cook **Cracked Grains** (Pilaf): Measure cracked grains, add slightly less water than indicated above, soak 1 to 2 hours, cook 10 to 15 minutes add herbs/spices, let stand $^1/_2$ to 1 hour. (OR to save time, toast dry, add hot water to cook, let stand.)

Buckwheat is not a cereal grain, but the starchy, grain-like seed of an herbaceous plant of the rhubarb family. It requires special treatment to remove *rutin*, an allergen for some people. Stir buckwheat groats into boiling water for 1 min. or until water turns rosy, drain, toast in 2 tablespoons of oil (for 1 cup of groats), add water, cook.

Amaranth and **Quinoa** are not starchy (cereal) grains, instead, they are high protein—best accompanied by a starchy grain or a vegetable. Use one part amaranth or quinoa to four parts starch.

Wild Rice is not rice but a water grass grain with rice qualities. Prepare as rice or combine them in the pot.

Rye may contain black ergot fungus that looks like a grain. Sort rye on a light-colored surface and discard any ergot or submerse in water to float and remove ergot.

Cornmeal: use above ratio of corn to water, let soak to absorb water (10 to 15 minutes), bring to a boil, cook (stirring) over low heat for a few minutes until thick. Add seasoning and salt, cover, and let stand 15 minutes. (For still polenta use 2.5 parts or less of water.)

Notable in this regard is the nutritional research, parallel to Biodynamic farming, originating with Rudolf Steiner. Steiner suggested a rhythm of preparing a different grain for each day of the week, beginning with rice on Monday, barley on Tuesday, millet on Wednesday, rye on Thursday, oats on Friday, corn on Saturday, and wheat/spelt/kamut on Sunday. When preparing a pot of grains, it's a good idea to double the amount to have some for another meal, saving time and energy all around. Leftover cooked grains can be kept covered in the refrigerator for a few days; however, they do lose some of their qualities each day, so it is best to use them within four days. Make them into patties to bake in the oven, prepare as satisfying summer salads, or add them to soups and stir-fry dishes. Combining grains with seasonal Biodynamic vegetables and complementary herbs can bring a wealth of flavorful goodness and sunshine to our days!

The Pig Completes the Bunny

by John Peterson

Have you ever had a bunny live with you? They are so cute. But the problem with this bunny, Jasmine, is that she does not want to be handled—maybe petted a little, if it's done just so, but definitely not picked up. When I look at her, I want to pick her up and cuddle her. I find it unfulfilling that she is so cute and fuzzy and I can't pick her up. She totally freaks out when I try.

There is also a stuffed pig in the house. It is fat and pink, about the size of a football. The pig snorts, says "I love you," and squeals whenever I walk in front of it or pick it up. Something just triggers it—movement, sound, light—I'm not quite sure what.

The pig completes the bunny the way a spice completes a grain.

Yesterday, Jasmine nuzzled the pig for a while and the pig expressed his love over and over, "Snort, snort . . . I love you . . . squeal, squeal . . . snort, snort . . . I love you . . . squeal, squeal. . . ." Normally, I would hate this pig. It's just the kind of thing I don't want in my life. I would not want it anywhere I could see it, or even in storage, where I might run into it a few months from now. But I am really into this pig. Why?

In anthroposophical cooking there is the premise that grains move toward completion as they are growing, but they never complete. Certain spices and herbs complete the process, which is why well-seasoned grains sometimes can impart a deeply satisfying experience.

Well, this pig completes the bunny the way a spice completes a grain. The pig feels the way I think Jasmine would feel if I could pick her up and squeeze her.

This pig completes the bunny the way a spice completes a grain.

I am sure that if I squished and hugged Jasmine the way I would like to, because she is so cute, I would cause her great anguish. But the pig . . . the pig I can hug to my heart's content while admiring Jasmine across the room. The pig completes the bunny process.

Update: One night, the pig started saying over and over "snort, snort . . . I love you . . . squeal, squeal," no matter how many rugs and blankets I heaped on top of it. At 2 a.m. I flung the pig into the yard. When I got up in the morning, it was still yammering. Even today, after thousands of snorts, love declarations, and squeals, it still musters relentless whispers of love.

FOR MORE STORIES BY FARMER JOHN, VISIT WWW.ANGELICORGANICS.COM.

A Collection of
Anthroposophical Outtakes on Foodstuffs

We uncovered many anthroposophical gems about nutrition and general health in the course of writing this cookbook. Although the following excerpts do not apply to vegetables, they do relate to nutrition or general health, and they offer rare insights into the food we do and don't eat and into our overall well-being.

INFANTS AND SUGAR

by Rudolf Steiner

Take for instance a child who, in spite of your having given it everything which as far as you know it needs, yet when for the first time it comes to the table for a meal, cannot resist climbing on a chair and stretching across the table to pinch a lump of sugar. Now you must take this in the right way, for a child who climbs on a chair to sneak a lump of sugar has almost certainly something wrong with its liver. The fact that a child pinches sugar shows that there is something not quite in order with the liver. Only children which have something wrong with their liver—which can be cured by the sugar—only they pinch sugar. Others have no interest in sugar, they leave it alone. Of course this must not be allowed to become a bad habit, but one must understand why [he] does it.

HONEY

from Nutrition and Stimulants *by Rudolf Steiner, February 2, 1922*

We can study what honey does when we eat it. . . . Honey gives pleasure only on the tongue. The moment honey is eaten it assists the proper connection between the airy and fluid elements in man. Nothing is better for man than to add a little honey, but in the right measure, to his food. The bees, in a wonderful way, help man to learn how his soul should work on his organs. Through their honey, the bees give back to man what he needs for the work of his soul in the body. . . . When he adds honey to his food he wants to prepare his soul so that it works and breathes properly in the body. Bee-keeping, therefore, advances civilization because it makes man strong. . . .

If one thinks how greatly the bees are influenced from the starry worlds, one sees that bees are the means of ensuring that man receives what is right for him. All that lives, works together in the right way, if it is combined in the right way. When one sees a hive of bees, one should say to oneself with awe and reverence: "By way of the beehive the whole universe flows into man and makes us good, capable people." . . . Thus, knowledge of man becomes knowledge of the universe.

HONEY AND THE AGING PROCESS

from Nutrition and Stimulants *by Rudolf Steiner, November 26, 1923*

As we grow older, honey has an extremely beneficial effect on us. With children it is milk that has a similar effect. Honey helps the building of our bodies and is therefore strongly recommended for people who are growing old. It is an extremely wholesome food; only one must not eat too much of it. If one eats too much of it, using it not merely as an addition to one's food, the formative forces can become too strongly active. The form becomes too hard and brittle and one may develop all kinds of illnesses. A healthy person feels just how much he can eat. Honey is particularly good for older people because it gives the body the right firmness.

Soy and Other Legumes

from Dynamics of Nutrition *by Gerhard Schmidt*

Protein . . . stimulates the growth in life forces, as opposed to the forces of consciousness. Rudolf Steiner said, "The consumption of proteins should be held within certain limits; otherwise man will be overcome by a perceptive activity of which he should become free," namely, an activity determined by the metabolism. Steiner also said, "That is what Pythagoras meant when he taught his students: Don't eat any beans." The legumes have forces which approach animal metabolism and thus give the protein formation an animal character. We can see that the evaluation of a food such as the soybean, by a true measure of quality, will be at some variance with what is propagated today.

> *Overheard*
>
> **Customer:** Does the soup have meat in it?
>
> **Waitress:** It has beans in it. [After a thoughtful pause . . .] Beans aren't meat, are they?

Soy

from Essentials of Nutrition *by Gerhard Schmidt*

In the agricultural lectures . . . Rudolf Steiner explains that we should pay attention to the tendency of the papilionaceous flowers to "want to bear fruit before they flower." That is to say, a "kind of stunting of the actual fruit of these plants takes place," which is expressed in a shortened ability to seed. This is all an expression of the fact that "with these [leguminous] plants, much more is held to the earth which lives in nitrogen." They are not only more earthly than the other green plants, but also more animal-like. They produce a protein which tastes much like meat, as is especially evident in the case of the soybean. These plants form poisons, a fact which must be considered when we use them as food.

Peanuts

from Dynamics of Nutrition *by Gerhard Schmidt*

We thus see how this plant brings three properties to expression. First, it has a weak relation to light, which we see in its lack of directed, horizontal growth—a property which it shares with many other legumes (beans, peas, etc.). Second, it is obviously overpowered by the gravitational forces of the earth, in that it actively penetrates into the earth with its fruit-bearer. Third, once the fruits come into the earth, they ultimately behave like roots—they deny their cosmic, solar, nature and turn to earthly forces. In the darkness of the earth, the moon forces are active, as we see in the formation of mushrooms. This relationship to the fungus world is clearly shown in the susceptibility of peanuts to fungi in the soil. If the shell is damaged, fungi easily penetrate into the peanuts and there produce the highly toxic "aflatoxin."

As is known, these poisoned peanuts have caused great damage when used as animal feed. In addition, the undamaged peanut produces a substance which promotes the coagulation of the blood. This can call forth thrombophilia, which shows a heaviness of the blood and the predominance of earthly forces.

COFFEE AND TEA

from Questions of Nutrition *by Rudolf Steiner*

With nutrition, which is the thing particularly interesting us at this moment, it is really so, that one must acquire a proper understanding for the way it relates to the spirit. When people inquire in that direction, I often offer two examples. Think, gentlemen, of a journalist: how he has to think so much—and so much of it isn't even necessary. The man must think a great deal, he must think so many logical thoughts; it is almost impossible for any human being to have so many logical thoughts. And so you find that the journalist—or any other person who writes for a profession—loves coffee, quite instinctively. He sits in the coffee shop and drinks one cup after another, and gnaws at his pen so that something will come out that he can write down. Gnawing at his pen doesn't help him, but the coffee does, so that one thought comes out of another, one thought joins on to another.

And then look at the diplomats. If one thought joins on to another, if one thought comes out of another, that's bad for them! When diplomats are logical, they're boring. They must be entertaining. In society people don't like to be wearied by logical reasoning—"in the first place—secondly—thirdly"—and if the first and second were not there, the third and fourth would, of course, not have to be thought of! A journalist can't deal with anything but finance in a finance article. But if you're a diplomat you can be talking about night clubs at the same time that you're talking about the economy of country X, then you can comment on the cream-puffs of Lady So-and-So, then you can jump to the rich soil of the colonies, after that, where the best horses are being bred, and so on. With a diplomat one thought must leap over into another. So anyone who is obliged to be a charming conversationalist follows his instinct and drinks lots of tea.

Tea scatters thoughts; it lets one jump into them. Coffee brings one thought next to another. If you must leap from one thought to another, then you must drink tea. And one even calls them "diplomat teas"! While there sits the journalist in the coffee shop, drinking one cup of coffee after another. You can see what an influence a particular food or drink can have on our whole thinking process. It is so, of course, not just with those two beverages, coffee and tea; one might say, those are extreme examples. But precisely from those examples I think you can see that one must consider these things seriously. It is very important.

ALCOHOL

from Nutrition and Stimulants *by Rudolf Steiner*

You see it is extremely ingeniously arranged. These little sperm creatures are extraordinarily lively anyway and with alcohol they become really fidgety so that fertilization takes place influenced by male sperm which are abnormally mobile. The result is that the system of the nerves and senses are affected when the man drinks. So when the woman drinks the inner organs will be damaged through weight, when the man drinks the nervous system of the child will be damaged. All that takes place in the developing child will be ruined instead of taking its normal course.

So one can say: When the woman drinks, the terrestrial element is damaged. When the man drinks, it is the airy and movable elements encompassing the earth, which man also carries within him, which are damaged. So that from both sides the offspring will be damaged if both drink. Of course, the fertilization can hardly be normal, i.e. fertilization is possible, but not really the proper growth of the offspring. On the one hand the ovum wants to assert its weightiness and on the other hand everything is in fidgety movement and each contradicts the other. The male contradicts the female in such a fertilization, when both drink. So if one understands how all this hangs together then it is clear that habitual drinking is extremely damaging to the offspring. People, however, do not believe it because the influence of drink both in men and women is relatively not so very obvious. But this is only so, because the blood is well protected, being created in the marrow, and people have to do a lot if they would greatly influence their offspring. Slight influences people are not prepared to admit.

If a child is born with hydrocephalus, one does not usually ascertain whether conception took place during a night after the mother had been out to a good dinner with red wine to drink. One would find if one were to investigate that the child was born with hydrocephalus because gravity (weight) became too strong. If on the other hand a child is born with a facial, muscular twitch, one does not usually ascertain whether the man drank too much the evening before fertilization took place. The smaller things, I would say, are not taken into account, and people then think there is no influence. There always is. However, the really damaging influences are the outcome of habitual drinking. And here again we have something remarkable and rather strange.

You see when the man drinks it can happen that the nervous system of the children is weakened and they may have for instance a tendency to consumption. What is hereditary in the children, however, need not be connected with the father's drinking. For instance, they need not have a tendency to mental disturbance, it can also be consumption, or stomach upsets or suchlike. This is what is so treacherous about alcohol: the evil done by it can simply pass over into other organs.

One must notice that alcohol gradually works its way into the marrow and gradually ruins the blood. So, by damaging the offspring, the whole subsequent progeny is damaged. If a person has, let us say, three children, these children are somewhat damaged, but their offspring will be considerably damaged. And so people are ruined far into the future through alcohol. Many of the weaknesses afflicting mankind today are due to the fact that our ancestors drank too much. Now really imagine: Here is a man and a woman. The man drinks. The bodies of the offspring are weakened. Now think what this means after just one century, or even more so, after several centuries. It is no good selecting a period—say from 1870 to 1880—and saying that more people died of [contaminated] water than of alcohol. One must spread one's gaze over longer periods. And this is just what people today do not like to do.

What Should One Do?

What one can learn about alcohol can be understood by everyone. And now we come to what I always say. People come and ask: Is it better not to drink alcohol or to drink alcohol? Is it better to be a vegetarian or to eat meat? I never tell anyone whether he should give up alcohol or drink it, whether he should eat plants or meat. I say to people: Alcohol does so and so. I simply explain its effect, and then they may decide whether to drink or not. I do the same with regard to vegetarian or meat diet: Meat does this and plants do that. And the result is that they can decide for themselves.

That is what one must have above all in science—respect for human freedom. One should never have the feeling that anyone is ordered or forbidden to do something; instead one tells him the facts. What he will do when he knows how alcohol works is his own affair. What is right to do he then finds out of himself. In this way we will get somewhere. In this way free men will be able to direct themselves. This must be our aim. This is the way to real social reform.

For additional (mostly anthroposophical) insights into health and nutrition, on such topics as raw milk, fever, microwaves, and lactic acid fermentation, visit www.AngelicOrganics.com/vegetableguide, and click on Outtakes.

Rudolf Steiner (1861–1925) became a respected and well published scientific, literary, and philosophical scholar, particularly known for his work on Goethe's scientific writings. After the turn of the century he began to develop his earlier philosophical principles into an approach to methodical research of physical, psychological and spiritual phenomena. His multifaceted genius has led to innovative and holistic approaches in medicine, science, education (Waldorf schools), special education, philosophy, religion, economics, agriculture (Biodynamic method), architecture, drama, the new arts of eurythmy and speech, and other fields. In 1924 he founded the General Anthroposophical Society, which today has branches throughout the world.

—from the Anthroposophic Press

Andrew Lorand, was born on the East Coast, raised in the Midwest, and later trained in Switzerland where he first learned about Biodynamics in 1973. He holds a Zurich State Diploma in General Agriculture and Swiss Federal Certification in Farm Management (with specializations in both dairy farming/milk processing and viticulture). He also holds a Ph.D. in Agricultural Education from Penn State University's College of Agricultural Sciences. Lorand farmed full time for ten years and has been a part-time consultant since 1983. He was very much a part of the early pioneering efforts to develop and spread CSAs in the United States and in Europe. He later developed and taught a wide range of courses relating to ecological agriculture at the university level and served as a full-time agricultural consultant, making his home in northern California.

Thomas Cowan, M.D., graduated from Michigan State Medical School in 1984. He taught gardening with the Peace Corps in South Africa and is a past vice president of the Physician's Association for Anthroposophical Medicine. Thomas is now a family practitioner with special interests in nutritional and anthroposophical medicine.

Louise Frazier, author of *Louise's Leaves: Around the Calendar with Local Garden Vegetables* and a vegetable-herb and a whole-grain cookery chart (Bio-Dynamic Association of America, 1994, 1996), is well-known as a writer of numerous articles, consultant culinary specialist, and nutrition program planner. She conducts cookery workshops and lectures emphasizing delicious dishes of seasonal vegetables, complementary herbs, and daily whole grains. She operated a vegetarian restaurant in Cologne, Germany, using Biodynamic/organic foods based on an Anthroposophic approach as presented by Udo Renzenbrink, M.D. and his chefs at the Nutrition Research Institute in Bad Liebenzell. Later she helped develop Sunways CSA Farm in Massachusetts and studied nutrition with Gerhard Schmidt, M.D., in the United States and Switzerland.

In 1990 Louise traveled to Sweden on a grant from the Biodynamic Association of America to learn first-hand the art of lactic-acid (L.A.) fermentation of vegetables. Since then she has prepared articles, a booklet, menus, and recipes and given workshops about L.A. fermentation, inspiring farmers, homemakers, and new businesses to engage in this health-enhancing food process.

Contact Louise at 63 Norwood Ave., Albany NY 12208

John Peterson runs Angelic Organics, one of the largest Community Supported Agriculture (CSA) farms in the United States. More than one thousand families in the Chicago area receive a weekly delivery of vegetables and herbs from Angelic Organics. John brings the discipline of farming to his writing, with two more books scheduled for publication in 2006 (a book of short stories about farming, and his autobiography). He co-directed and co-starred in two music videos, "The Bug Song" and "The Farmer John Song," on Lesley Littlefield's debut album, *Little Songs*. John has written numerous short stories and plays. He has acted in short fiction films and has done many performances of his life on stage. Peterson is the subject of Taggart Siegel's award-winning feature documentary film *The Real Dirt on Farmer John*.

FOR MORE INFO ON ANGELIC ORGANICS BOOKS, MUSIC, AND FILM, VISIT WWW.ANGELICORGANICS.COM.